The
THIN LIGHT
of
FREEDOM

ALSO BY EDWARD L. AYERS

America's War:
Talking about the Civil War and Emancipation on Their 150th
Anniversaries (editor)

America on the Eve of the Civil War (coeditor)

The Crucible of the Civil War:
Virginia from Secession to Commemoration (coeditor)

What Caused the Civil War?
Reflections on the South and Southern History

In the Presence of Mine Enemies:
Civil War in the Heart of America, 1859–1863

The Valley of the Shadow:
Two Communities in the American Civil War—The Eve of War
(coeditor)

American Passages:
A History of the United States (coauthor)

The Oxford Book of the American South:
Testimony, Memory, and Fiction (coeditor)

All Over the Map:
Rethinking American Regions (coauthor)

The Promise of the New South:
Life After Reconstruction

The Edge of the South:
Life in Nineteenth-Century Virginia (coeditor)

Vengeance and Justice:
Crime and Punishment in the Nineteenth-Century American South

The
THIN LIGHT
of FREEDOM

THE CIVIL WAR AND
EMANCIPATION
IN THE HEART OF
AMERICA

EDWARD L. AYERS

W. W. NORTON & COMPANY
Independent Publishers Since 1923
New York | London

For information about permission to reproduce selections from this book, write to
Permissions, W. W. Norton & Company, Inc., 500 Fifth Avenue,
New York, NY 10110

For information about special discounts for bulk purchases, please contact
W. W. Norton Special Sales at specialsales@wwnorton.com or 800-233-4830

Manufacturing by Quad Graphics, Fairfield
Book design by Chris Welch
Production manager: Anna Oler

ISBN 978-0-393-29263-3

W. W. Norton & Company, Inc.
500 Fifth Avenue, New York, N.Y. 10110
www.wwnorton.com

W. W. Norton & Company Ltd.
15 Carlisle Street, London W1D 3BS

1 2 3 4 5 6 7 8 9 0

For Lance, Rachael, and Avery

The Eastern Theater of the American Civil War, June 1863–April 1865

Parkersburg

WV

Charleston

Monterey

Lewisburg

Salem

Wytheville

Saltville

Virginia and Ten

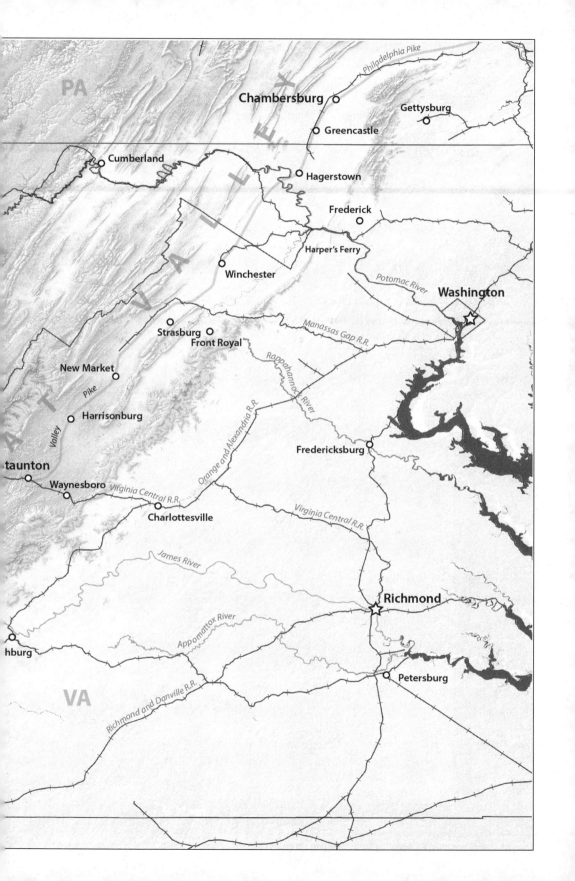

CONTENTS

List of Illustrations   xiii

List of Maps   xvii

Preface   xix

Prologue   1

PART ONE: THE SCOURGE OF WAR

July 1863 through November 1864

1. The Great Invasion
    May through July 1863   25

2. A Gigantic Forlorn Hope
    July 1863   57

3. The Great Task Remaining Before Us
    July 1863 through May 1864   97

4. The Earth Will Tremble
    April through June 1864   139

5. To Burn Something in the Enemy's Country
    June through October 1864   188

6. A Campaign of Terrible Moment
    September through November 1864   244

PART TWO: THE HARVEST OF WAR

December 1864 through 1902

7. The Colossal Suicide of World History
    December 1864 through March 1865   283

8. The Perils of Peace
    March through October 1865   323

9. Rebelism
    January through December 1866   370

10. We Must Be One People
    January 1867 through July 1869   418

11. The Past Is Not Dead
    1868 through 1902   461

Epilogue   497

Acknowledgments   499
A Note on the Documentation   503
Notes   507
Index   553

LIST OF ILLUSTRATIONS

Jedediah Hotchkiss   3
     University of Virginia

Staunton, Virginia, 1870   5
     Jedediah Hotchkiss, *Historical Atlas of Augusta County*
     (Chicago: Waterman, Watkins, And Company, 1885)

Chambersburg, Pennsylvania, c. 1857   8
     D. G. Beers, *Atlas of Franklin County, Pennsylvania*
     (Philadelphia: Pomeroy and Beers, 1868)

Samuel Cormany   18
     "Samuel Cormany" photograph from *The Cormany
     Diaries: A Northern Family in the Civil War*, James C.
     Mohr, Editor, by permission of the University of Pitts-
     burgh Press, c. 1982 by University of Pittsburgh Press.

Rachel Cormany with Cora   18
     "Rachel and Cora Cormany" photograph from *The Cor-
     many Diaries: A Northern Family in the Civil War*, James C.
     Mohr, Editor, by permission of the University of Pitts-
     burgh Press, c. 1982 by University of Pittsburgh Press.

Joseph Waddell   31
  Joseph A. Waddell, *History of Mary Baldwin Seminary,
  From 1842 to 1905 Inclusive* (Staunton: Augusta Printing
  Company, 1905)

Confederate General John D. Imboden   63
  University of Virginia

Unfinished Confederate grave   76
  Library of Congress

Alexander K. McClure   130
  Alexander K. McClure, *Recollections of Half a Century*
  (Salem, MA: Salem Press Company, 1902)

Confederate General John C. Breckinridge   151
  Library of Congress

United States General David Hunter   154
  Library of Congress

Confederate General Jubal Early   201
  Library of Congress

Confederate General John McCausland   206
  Library of Congress

Map of burned Chambersburg   211
  Benjamin Shroder Schneck, *The Burning of Chambersburg* (Philadelphia: Lindsay and Blakiston, 1865)

Photographs of burned Chambersburg   222, 224
  Library of Congress

United States General Philip Sheridan   228
  Library of Congress

Sheridan's victories in Virginia   246
  Franklin Repository

Burning of the Valley   253
  Battles and Leaders of the Civil War

John Brown Baldwin   361
    Virginia Historical Society
Alexander H. H. Stuart   361
    Library of Congress
Democratic cartoon from Pennsylvania opposing ratification
of the Fourteenth Amendment   397
    Library of Congress
Cartoon warning of the consequences of the Virginia
Constitutional Convention, 1867   422
    University of Virginia
Alexander K. McClure in later life   485
    Alexander K. McClure, *Recollections of Half a Century*
    (Salem, MA: Salem Press Company, 1902)
Willis M. Carter   489
    From the photo album of Carter's sister Jennie and reprinted
    courtesy of Carter's great grandniece, Mrs. Janis Lucas. The
    original photograph and a large collection of papers are pre-
    served at the Library of Virginia.

LIST OF MAPS

The maps for this book were created by Nathaniel Ayers and Justin Madron at the Digital Scholarship Lab at the University of Richmond. The maps emphasize the long distances troops moved, the circuitous routes they often followed, the rail networks, rivers, and mountains that defined much of the fighting, and major battles and guerrilla strongholds elsewhere that shaped the fighting in the Valley. The lines representing the troops grow darker as they approach their destinations or point of contact with the enemy. The maps were drawn digitally with a combination of geographic information systems and illustration software using United States Geological Survey data.

The Eastern Theater in the American Civil War, June 1863–
  April 1865   viii–ix
Augusta County, 1863   6
Franklin County, 1863   7
The Roads from Gettysburg, July 1863   71
Sigel's Campaign and the Battle of New Market, May 1864   150

The Battle of Piedmont, June 1864   158

Hunter's Campaign, June 1864   176

Early's Campaign and the Burning of Chambersburg, July
    and August 1864   205

Sheridan's Campaign and the Burning of the Valley, August
    through October 1864   238

The Presidential Election of 1864   267

PREFACE

Our stories of the American Civil War and Reconstruction keep changing. The generation that fought the war celebrated its sacrifices and accomplishments. By the end of World War I, leading historians considered the Civil War a waste and a delusion. Scholars who lived through World War II argued that the war against slavery had been necessary, while those who experienced the Civil Rights movement judged that Reconstruction had left the nation unredeemed.

In our own time, we can see that the Civil War and its consequences, straightforward and familiar at a distance, prove intricate and surprising when considered at closer range. The immediate, complete, and uncompensated destruction of the most powerful system of slavery in the modern world, after all, seemed impossible just a few years before it came to pass. A massive political reconstruction of the United States, based on new constitutions and fundamental rights for formerly enslaved people, went far beyond what most white Americans had thought possible, or desirable, in 1865. In recent decades scholars have found important complexities in every aspect of the conflict.

This book offers readers a close-up view of the Civil War and its aftermath that reveals those complexities, focusing on the desperate years of war from 1863 on in the Great Valley. That prosperous landscape, lying between the Blue Ridge and Appalachian mountain ranges and stretching across the boundary between the United States and the Confederacy, found itself at the center of the Civil War in these years. Without a single fixed target such as Richmond or Atlanta, the Valley was potentially one giant battlefield, with armies meeting anywhere, descending from any direction. Tens of thousands of soldiers surged through its farms and villages. Fields and towns burned while its sons and fathers died on distant battlefields. African Americans risked their lives to escape slavery, and black troops volunteered to defend the United States. Courthouses and town squares in the Valley surged with jubilant rallies and defiant speeches as Reconstruction redefined the fundamental laws of the nation.

The story told here follows a broad cast of characters from two Valley communities separated by only two hundred miles: Augusta County, Virginia, and Franklin County, Pennsylvania. Those characters include soldiers and civilians, men and women, enslaved people and freedpeople, politicians and ministers, teachers and Freedmen's Bureau agents, and Democrats and Republicans. This is history on a human scale.

The narrative draws on a digital archive called the Valley of the Shadow, which gathers and transcribes the historical record for Augusta and Franklin from the late 1850s to 1870. The archive holds the diaries and letters, newspapers and census returns, soldiers' records and Freedmen's Bureau reports, memoirs and photographs from which the story builds. The archive enables us to see connections across time, across borders, and across the lives of many kinds of people. The history in this book attempts to recapture the perspectives of these people and to show events in forward motion, as they were lived, not reassembled as a path to the present. Some sections of the narrative appear in italics, stepping out of the story for a moment to suggest what it might tell us about larger isues of the nation's history.[1]

The first book drawn from the Valley of the Shadow, *In the Presence of Mine Enemies*, traced events in Augusta and Franklin from John Brown's raid in 1859 to the eve of the Battle of Gettysburg in 1863. That account showed how Americans descended into an all-consuming war that no one sought. *The Thin Light of Freedom* begins with the confident Confederate forces of Robert E. Lee invading Pennsylvania, carries the story through the years of escalating war, and continues into the Reconstruction that followed.[2]

Those are unusual beginning and ending points. Accounts of the Civil War often conclude at Appomattox with the laying down of arms, and leave the unfolding aftershocks and consequences of the war for other books. Accounts of the Reconstruction period, on the other hand, seldom dwell on the bloodshed, burning, and political struggles of the last two years of the Civil War even though those events drove and defined the terms of the Reconstruction that followed.

The geographic and chronological focus of the story helps us see that the remarkable advances of emancipation and Reconstruction were not the inevitable victories of a modern economy, the overwhelming might of the North, or the intrinsic justice of the national cause. In fact, the full consequences of the Civil War remained in doubt far into the conflict and through its prolonged aftermath. Even though abolitionists fought for black freedom and citizenship for decades before the war, and though Republicans sought to stop the spread of slavery in the 1850s so that it would die of its own self-inflicted wounds, few people in 1860 dared imagine that slavery would be destroyed by 1865 and replaced with the rights of citizenship for formerly enslaved people by 1868.

Freedom had to be secured on every front after the war ended. Freedpeople searched for children and parents lost in slavery and war, affirmed marriages and established churches. Formerly enslaved people of all ages streamed into schools taught at first by devoted teachers from the North and then from among the freedpeople's own community. Isolated agents of the Freedmen's Bureau labored to establish economic and criminal justice. Eloquent black leaders emerged as soon as the political system opened to them. Republicans in the North worked to sustain freedom and opportunity by changing fundamental laws of the nation.

At every step, those who would advance freedom found themselves challenged and sometimes defeated. As this history shows, however, black freedom advanced faster and further than its champions had dreamed possible precisely because the opponents of freedom proved so powerful and aggressive. Without secession and the significant victories of the armies of the Confederacy, there would have been no full-scale emancipation in the 1860s. Without defiant former Confederates, an intransigent president of the United States, and Northern votes against African-American rights, there would have been no military reoccupation, Radical Reconstruction, and the most important amendments ever made to the United States Constitution. The enemies of emancipation and Reconstruction drove the revolution forward by their bitter resistance, making the collective accomplishment of black free-dom even more compelling for being won against such odds.

The opponents of black freedom remained strong after Recon-struction, retreating rather than surrendering after their defeats. The enemies of equality fought for decades to roll back the expansion of America's democracy, eventually undermining the voting and legal rights won in the late 1860s. Through violence and political manipulation, they hollowed out the democracy of their states and the nation. They won important cultural as well as political battles over the next century, as popular histories, novels, and films demonized the freedom that had been won at such great cost in the war and Reconstruction. Even during that long retrenchment, however, advocates of racial equality kept the thin light of freedom alive, determined that it would shine more brightly in a future they could not foresee.

The
THIN LIGHT
of
FREEDOM

Prologue

War had torn at the United States for two years, and yet the future of the nation and of slavery remained unsettled. By the summer of 1863 hundreds of thousands of men had died of wounds and disease in vast battles and obscure skirmishes, in lonely farmhouses and crowded hospital tents. The United States' armies and navies had conquered much of the territory claimed by the Confederacy. While slavery dissolved wherever those Federal forces established control, over three million enslaved people still labored beyond the reach of Union power.

Virginia, at the center of the fighting from the first battles of the war, remained the major stronghold of the rebellion. Even as Federal armies won crucial victories across the rest of the Confederacy, in Virginia Robert E. Lee and Stonewall Jackson rebuffed the largest army ever assembled on the North American continent in 1862. Victories in 1863 over the Federal army at Fredericksburg and Chancellorsville further elevated Lee's Army of Northern Virginia in the eyes of the Northern, Southern, and foreign press. Now, in June 1863, Lee intended to dictate the next field of battle, win a great victory, force a dispirited United States to concede that it could not defeat the South, and declare the independence of the Confederate States of America.[1]

With so much in the balance, people in both the North and the South pored over newspapers, following the armies' every movement. Anyone near those armies soon discovered, however, that the lines on the maps inscribed a false precision. Armies were not neat boxes and did not move along arcs defined by arrows and lines. Instead, armies rushed over landscapes like rank floods, leveling forests and devastating fields, stripping food and livestock, washing away in an hour the work of generations. Foreshadowed by wary scouting parties, flanked by fast-moving and restless cavalry, trailed by broken and desperate stragglers, watched by alert enslaved people and wary civilians, armies changed everything and everyone they touched.[2]

☆

TRAVELING ON HORSEBACK, the tools of his craft in a wagon driven by an enslaved man named William, Jedediah Hotchkiss translated the gentle landscape around him into a landscape of war. Hotchkiss traced the dense networks of roads crossing ridges and woods. He noted the places where rivers ran shallow and slow and where the water became deep and dangerous. He observed where railroads passed over high bridges and through narrow passes. He gauged the distances between towns and villages, measuring possible routes of attack or retreat.

Hotchkiss was an unlikely Confederate. Born in upstate New York in 1828, in the 1850s he and his wife Sara had moved to Virginia to establish a school. Hotchkiss supported the Union for as

Jedediah Hotchkiss

long as Virginia remained in the Union, but when secession and then war came in 1861 he offered his services to the rebel troops camped in the mountains to the west of his home. Self-trained as a maker of maps, a close observer of nature and of people, Hotchkiss came to serve and believe in the Confederate cause.

In 1862, General Stonewall Jackson protected the 200-mile-long valley in Virginia resting between the Blue Ridge Mountains and the Allegheny Mountains, a critical strategic location and a major supplier of food to the Confederate army. Jackson ordered Hotchkiss to make a detailed map of that valley so the Rebel army could use the topography to its advantage. For weeks, Hotchkiss covered brown sheets of paper with pencil and pen, positioning the squares on a linen backing eight feet long so that the map could be carried in the field. The young mapmaker recorded the rising and falling of the complicated landscape, the twisting course from south to north of the Shenandoah River and its tributaries, the mountains towering to the east and the west. Hotchkiss traced the route of the wide stone turnpike that stretched the length of the Valley.

Winchester, at the northern end of that turnpike, stood as the largest town in the lower Valley, where the Shenandoah River joined its tributaries with the Potomac. Winchester had been, and would remain, a battle-scarred place throughout the war, occupied in turn by the Union army and then the Confederates and then the Union again. The northern Valley of Virginia, bisected east-to-west by the Potomac River and the Baltimore and Ohio Railroad as well as the Valley Turnpike running north-to-south, stood at the crossroads of the eastern theater of the Civil War.

A hundred miles to the south, at the other end of the turnpike, stood Staunton. The pretty town of 4,000 people (pronounced "stan'tn") clustered on a range of hills, mountains hovering to the east and west. Staunton had served as the seat of Augusta County since the town's founding in 1747. The town boasted gas lights, civic and fraternal organizations, attractive hotels, and major state institutions such as an asylum for the mentally ill and an institute for the deaf, dumb, and blind. Jedediah and Sara Hotchkiss had chosen Augusta County as their home because its prosperity and refinements favored a school and raising a family.

The Virginia Central Railroad ran east from Staunton through the mountains and the wealthy Piedmont and into the thriving industrial city of Richmond. The opening of the Blue Ridge tunnel in 1858, the longest railroad tunnel in the world, dug by Irish immigrants and enslaved laborers, sped the trains to the capital of Virginia and now the capital of the Confederacy. When the war began, builders had been extending the 195-mile-long railroad to the west, planning to connect it with the distant Ohio River. They ceased their work with the arrival of the war, but the rail-

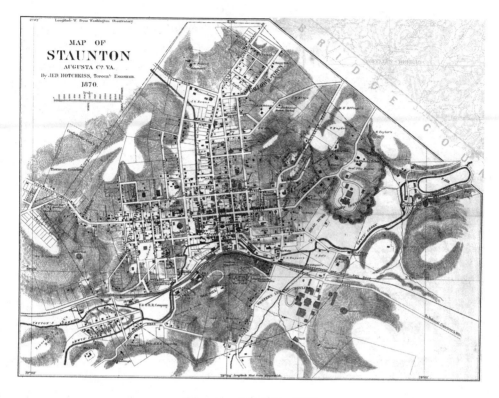

Staunton, Virginia, 1870

road had been, and would remain, a focal point of war in Virginia, a target of destruction by the Federal troops and of defense by the Confederates.

Augusta County, benefitting from its rich and well-watered soil as well as its strategic location on the railroad and turnpike, enjoyed a diverse and prosperous economy in the 1850s. With twenty-five thousand inhabitants, Augusta was the largest and richest agricultural county in the state, woven together by a network of roads converging at Staunton, harvesting over a million bushels of corn, wheat, oats, rye, and buckwheat from the surrounding farms and plantations. The wheat grown in Augusta

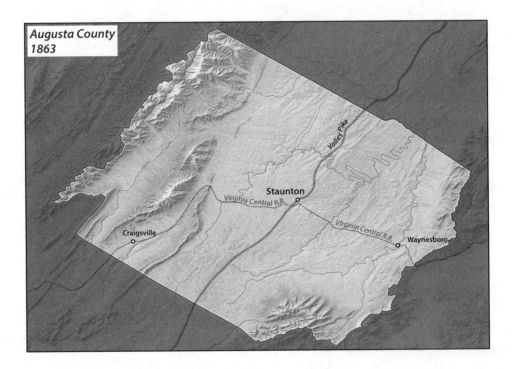

Augusta County 1863

and milled in Richmond reached markets as far away as South America. In biblical profusion, the county's farms yielded nearly half a million pounds of butter and seventeen thousand pounds of honey.

Jedediah Hotchkiss's map of the Valley stopped at Augusta's southern border. Had he extended it farther south it would have shown, seventy-five miles below Staunton and just on the eastern side of the Blue Ridge, the manufacturing center of Lynchburg. There, two railroads and a canal led to Richmond, providing a lifeline to the Confederate capital from the hinterland to the south that in the summer of 1863 had yet to be overtaken by the Union army. The rich and beautiful Valley of Virginia, from Winchester to Lynchburg, with Staunton in the center, shimmered as a precious prize to both the United States and the Confederacy.

☆

ON THE UPPER BORDER of his 1862 map Jedediah Hotchkiss's careful lines trailed off into blankness. In the summer of 1863, however, the mapmaker hurriedly sketched, on a torn and irregular sheet of paper, the terrain on the northern side of the Potomac.

The Mason-Dixon Line defined the boundary between the United States and the Confederacy at the border of Pennsylvania. On the northern side of that line stood prosperous Franklin County and its tidy towns. Chambersburg, with its eight thousand people, served as the county seat for Franklin's forty thousand people. The town prided itself on its up-to-date character, orderly streets, bustling businesses, and growing trade. Dozens of stores and shops, banks, offices, and an imposing new courthouse sur-

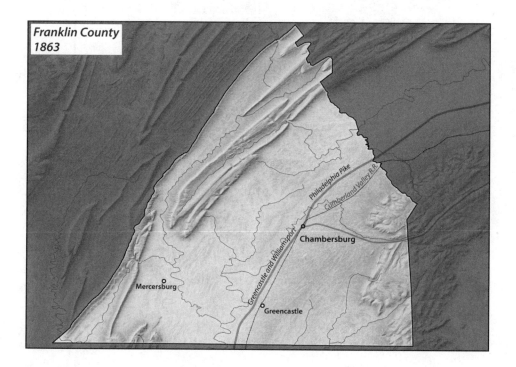

Franklin County
1863

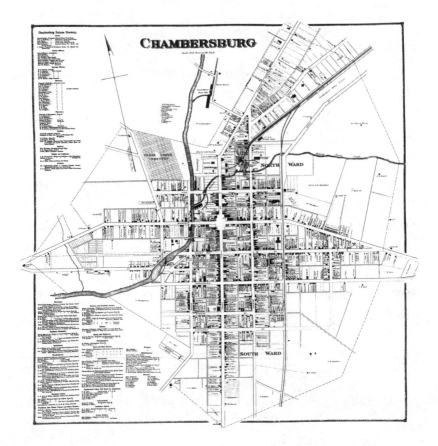

Chambersburg, Pennsylvania, c. 1857

rounded Chambersburg's town square, the Diamond. The Cumberland Valley Railroad and a turnpike from Maryland passed through Chambersburg on their way north to the state capital in Harrisburg. A road to the east cut through a pass in mountains. At the end of that road, on the edge of his paper, without enough space to write out its name in a straight line, Jedediah Hotchkiss noted the small town of Gettysburg.[3]

Chambersburg produced two weekly newspapers: the Franklin *Repository*, the Republicans' paper, and the *Valley Spirit*, the

Democrats' paper. Tied to Washington, Baltimore, Philadelphia, and the state capital by telegraph and railroads, those newspapers served as nodes on networks growing ever larger, faster, and denser. The Republicans and Democrats worked in every state in the North, in every county, town, and rural district. The party networks, like the networks of roads, rivers, and railways, had pulled the expansive United States together in the 1830s and 1840s and then had helped pull it apart in the 1850s. The newspapers carried opinion, passion, and error as well as accurate news of the world, circulating reports from the center to the periphery and back again. The newspapers both made and interpreted the history unfolding all around them.

The newspapers of America had conveyed shocking news since the 1850s. The struggle between the North and the South over the Fugitive Slave Law, which implicated all Northern communities in capturing and returning escaped enslaved people, and over the future of slavery in the western territories drove violence in Bleeding Kansas in 1854. In 1857, the Dred Scott decision of the Supreme Court of the United States, denying that the federal government possessed the authority to stop the spread of slavery in the territories, had jolted white Northerners who had previously expressed little concern over slavery. The rise of the new Republican Party in the late 1850s, dedicated to stopping the spread of the slaveholders and their power, presented a new and frightening challenge to the slave states.

The election of Abraham Lincoln in 1860 led seven Southern states to secede between November and February, before Lincoln took office in March. In the spring of 1861, Virginia struggled to stay in the Union but ultimately succumbed to the pull of other slave states and seceded when Lincoln called for troops to put down the rebellion in South Carolina. With the addition of Virginia—

the largest slave state—along with North Carolina, Tennessee, and Arkansas, the Confederate States of America claimed territory the size of continental Europe and an enslaved population of nearly four million people. Since that spring of 1861 the armies of the United States and the Confederacy had descended into a war of a scale and duration few could comprehend. Virginia, previously perched on the northern edge of the South, suddenly became the very center of the Confederacy and the war.

The center of that war lay dangerously close to Franklin County, Pennsylvania. In May 1863 the Democrats' *Valley Spirit* painted a discouraging picture of the current state of affairs in the United States. The Republican administration of Abraham Lincoln, the Chambersburg paper lamented, held out "no encouragement, gives no basis upon which to build for the future, embraces nothing but hatred and vengeance, conquest and subjugation." The editor worried that some men "sick at heart and bereft of hope, disgusted at the angry criminations and recriminations which characterize the political discussions of this day, have resolved not to mingle with either political party." In the crisis of the Union, the paper warned, such aloofness was dangerous, for no man could afford to ignore politics. A man had to "believe some things in themselves to be right, and others to be wrong" and any man who would not declare which was which simply "lacks the moral courage to avow the right and denounce the wrong."

The conflict between the Democrats and the Republicans of the North shaped every choice the people of the nation made. The Democrats thought the issues were straightforward and simple: "The administration of Abraham Lincoln has not proven true to its pledges to the people." Fixated on slavery and the people held in slavery rather than on restoring the Union, Lincoln and his party offered only an endless war and a "grand, consolidated government" in place of the old Union. The Democrats believed that "the old order of things can be restored": the Union "as it was made by our fathers, with all the equal rights and liberties of the States and the citizens under the constitution." That old Union included the right to slavery now and in the future.[4]

Republican papers would have nothing of such claims. One editor, from the small town of Waynesboro in southern Franklin County, reported a Union meeting in which the attendees pledged themselves "to an unconditional loyalty to the Government of the United States, to an unwavering support of its efforts to suppress the rebellion, and to spare no endeavor to maintain unimpaired the National unity, both in principle and territorial boundary." They resolved "to bind together all loyal men, of all trades and professions, in a common union to maintain the power, glory, and integrity of the Nation." The paper reported that some of the "copperheads," as the Democrats were called after the venomous snake, hissed the speakers at the meeting, yelled cheers for the Confederacy, and broke the windows of the hall where the meeting was being held. "The man who asserts that nobody is disloyal in the loyal states must be one of two things, a fool or full-fledged traitor."

Franklin County was the home of 1,800 African-Americans, some of whom had escaped over the Mason-Dixon Line into freedom in years past. Some white people in Franklin County sympathized with the slaveholders who lived just across the border and even captured escaped slaves for those slaveholders. On the other hand, white and black abolitionists in the county had long aided fugitives from slavery, steering them through the mountain passes to more secure freedom farther north. The abolitionist John Brown met with African-American leader Frederick Douglass in Franklin County in 1859 as Brown planned his raid at Harpers Ferry. Abraham Lincoln won Franklin in 1860 with the same proportion of votes he had received in the North over all, about 56 percent.[5]

A brief report in a Franklin Republican paper told of local "Negro Recruits." An officer from the 54th Massachusetts Infantry Regiment of the United States Colored Troops had visited Franklin County in April 1863 "and succeeded, in the short time he remained there, in enlisting twenty able-bodied Colored men for the United States service." Those recruits were on their way to join other black men from the county training in Boston. African-American soldiers had been authorized by President Lincoln in his Emancipation Proclamation of January 1863 and now, only a few months later, dozens of black men from Franklin County were already serving in defense of the United States. The Republican paper made a point of capitalizing the word "Colored" in its report, offering a sign of respect few white people offered before the war.[6]

Jacob Christy, one of the earlier recruits from Franklin, saw the new men from the county arrive in camp in Boston. Christy wrote his sister Mary Jane back home in Mercersburg that he was "very glad to see them boys coming." Jacob and his fellow soldiers did not like Boston's climate, for even in May it was "very cold out here now we heft to wear our over coats all day." The African-American soldiers knew, though, that they would soon be heading into the Confederacy and "when we go down south it will be warm enough." The United States Colored Troops from Franklin would face Confederates who saw in the black soldiers what they most hated and feared in the Yankee nation.[7]

☆

STAUNTON CONTINUED TO PUBLISH two weekly newspapers in the summer of 1863 despite the deprivations of war. The *Spectator* and the *Vindicator*, tied by the railroad and the telegraph to the Confederate capital in Richmond, told people in Augusta County about a war waged from the Atlantic to the Mississippi, from Kentucky to the Gulf of Mexico.

Three years earlier, the two newspapers of Staunton had been, like their northern counterparts, party papers. The *Spectator* had long stood as a bulwark of the Whigs, who celebrated the Union. That party and its paper believed in progress built on commerce, social improvement grounded in public-spirited citizens, moral improvement fostered by schools and churches, and Christian stewardship of the enslaved population. The *Spectator* had been one of the strongest voices in Virginia against secession, supporting delegates sent to Richmond in the winter of 1860 and 1861 to keep Virginia as part of the United States. When that effort had failed, the *Spectator* turned its devotion to the new Confederacy, shifting its loyalties overnight.

The *Vindicator* had been the paper of the Democrats. Like their compatriots in the North, the Southern Democrats believed in small government and untrammeled slavery. They had supported secession, losing at the county level in Augusta but winning at the state level when Virginia finally left the United States in April 1861. Now, the editorials and letters of the *Vindicator* differed little from those of the *Spectator*, as both set aside their party loyalties. The leaders of the Confederacy argued that partisan struggle could only weaken the new nation and the citizens of the Confederacy would not perpetuate the party bickering of their past. Let the North consume itself and its energies with fights between the Democrats and the Republicans, they urged, and let unity bind together the Confederacy.

☆

AUGUSTA AND FRANKLIN HAD SACRIFICED a great deal in the first two years of the war. Augusta had contributed 2,761 men to the Confederacy, Franklin 2,661 to the United States. Because Franklin's white population was almost twice as large as Augusta's, that meant that the Southern county had mobilized 75 percent of its men between the ages of eighteen and forty-five for the Confederacy and the Northern county had sent 40 percent to the Union army.

Augusta's men had already been involved in virtually every major battle in the eastern theater and had lost 619 men wounded and 106 men killed in action. Franklin's soldiers, fighting in fewer battles but caught in the bloody losses of Fredericksburg and Chancellorsville, had lost 143 wounded and 25 killed. Disease had taken more men from both sides than battle, with 149 from Augusta and 69 from Franklin having died over the preceding two years, with younger men more likely to die than older. Two hundred Augusta men had been captured by the enemy and 42 had been captured from Franklin's units.

Combined, Augusta County had already lost over a thousand men, about 40 percent of those who had left for the Confederate army. Franklin had lost 13 percent of the 2,500 men who had fought in the war from Tennessee to Virginia. The losses on both sides had devastated hundreds of families, leaving widows and orphans and grieving parents in every community in both counties. No one in the summer of 1863 could calculate how much more the people of Augusta and Franklin would have to give nor how or when the grinding war would end.

☆

AUGUSTA COUNTY POSSESSED the same percentage of enslaved people as the Confederacy as a whole in 1860, about a quarter of its population. About a third of slave-owning families claimed only one enslaved person, but more than two dozen slaveholders held more than twenty people each, and a few even held forty. Slave prices had risen in the 1850s and remained high during the war, driven by the demand of the booming cotton plantations to the south and a slave trade that shipped people away from Augusta and their families every year. The average adult slave cost about 1,200 dollars in 1860, the equivalent to about 24,000 dollars today, so the 5,500 enslaved people of Augusta were worth over 6 million dollars to their owners, equal to 120 million dollars today.

These enslaved people benefited their owners not only as laborers but also as a flexible form of property, lent and borrowed, rented by the task or by the year, held as collateral or escrow. Some slaves sawed lumber or tanned hides and others milled wheat or distilled whisky. Others cooked and cared for children or catered to hotel guests.

Black and white people had lived alongside each other in Augusta for more than a century by the time war descended on the Valley. About a fourth of the African-American people in Augusta County revealed some white ancestry to the eyes of the census taker, their straight hair or light skin marking them as "mulatto." About six hundred free black people made their homes in Augusta, often living with enslaved people and doing the same work.[8]

War strained slavery in Augusta. The Confederate government took, or "impressed," enslaved men from the farms and plantations of Augusta and other counties to build fortifications around Richmond. The work was brutally hard, the conditions for the workers dangerous and unhealthy even by the standards of slavery. Slave owners resented the loss of their strongest slaves and the risks to which they were put, but they protested in vain. The Confederate government announced in the spring of 1863 that "the Secretary of War has decided that no payment can be made" for "those whose slaves died while in the service of the Confederate States at labor on the fortifications." The "existing laws" did not permit such payments, so slave owners "will have to await further legislation, of which, we are sorry to say, there is no prospect of the present session of Congress." Defending slavery demanded the erosion of slave owners' prerogatives.[9]

Willis Carter, a young enslaved boy, saw his father taken to labor on the Confederate fortification. As he recalled thirty years later, "impressment began upon the poor bondsmen in the South for the purpose of getting men to throw up breastworks." As a result, "the poor slaves were seized in every section, dragged brutally to different places, and forced under the scourge to build fortifications." Even more cruelly, the fortifications the slaves erected were intended to repel Federal armies "in whose hands was the proclamation of their emancipation" and to defeat "the men who sought to save the Union from a slavish disgrace that had already with its hideous crimes shocked the world from centre to circumference."

Willis Carter's father "fell a victim to this terrible command. He was impressed in Eighteen hundred and sixty three, was taken below Richmond Virginia to help fortify it where soon afterward, he had an attack of pneumonia which proved fatal." Willis's mother would raise him and his siblings on her own in Augusta County during the years of war and its aftermath. The Civil War, even as it held out the promise of freedom, took the lives of tens of thousands of enslaved men and women.[10]

The Staunton *Spectator* criticized as "a serious evil" the policy that seized "hundreds of our stoutest and most athletic negroes from farming operations, to work on the fortifications near Richmond." Instead of impressing "our best farm hands," why could not white "deserters, and other wrong-doers" be put to work on the fortifications? "Where too, are the idlers about Richmond, and the conscripts" in the camps where drafted men were being trained? "We think this system of employing negroes ought to be stopped." Enslaved men were too valuable to use in defense of the Confederacy. Better to put useless white men to work.[11]

☆

RACHEL CORMANY, LIKE OTHER WOMEN on the Northern home front, lived far from the battlefields of the South and yet felt an intimate connection with the battles waged there. Rachel's husband was a cavalryman in the United States Army, fighting in Virginia. She kept a diary recording the dread and hope, day by day and often hour by hour, that washed over her as news arrived from the front. "Got a letter from My Samuel. it is but short. He is still safe—but were under marching orders again," she wrote in June 1863. "It has been over a week on the way—I almost feel like getting out of this to some place where the mail is uninterrupted, but then I fear, My Samuel might chance to come here & I would not see him so I shall stay."

Rachel lived with her in-laws and a young daughter in Chambersburg. She grew frustrated with the lack of control she had over her own life. Fed up with relatives—"the meanest pile of dirt I have seen for some time"—Rachel resolved "to pack up & leave in the morning. I cant bear to think of being shut up without any news another week." Rachel filled a trunk to head to Philadel-

Samuel Cormany

Rachel Cormany with Cora

phia, 160 miles to the east by train, the next day. Taking a morning walk with her young daughter, however, Rachel met Union soldiers who warned her that the Confederate army was invading Chambersburg from the south. At first, Rachel admitted, "I got so weak I could scarcely walk, but that was over in a few minutes & I could walk faster than before." She took her daughter back to the house to await, and then confront, whatever the war might bring.[12]

☆

THE CIVIL WAR, EMANCIPATION, and Reconstruction began and ended as struggles over borders, both natural and man-made. War erupted when the Republicans declared that the western boundaries of the nation would no longer accommodate a voracious slavery and Confederates decided they would not be bound by such limitations. In the war that followed, the United States' military strategy focused on dividing and destroying the rebellion within the nation's borders. Armies and navies fought to control the boundaries of the Tennessee and Mississippi rivers, the shorelines of the Atlantic and the Gulf, the mountains of Appalachia, the plains of the West, and the railroads that fed the Confederate capital at Richmond.[13]

Boundaries between the battlefield and the home front eroded as both the North and the South mobilized vast numbers of men and demanded years of sacrifice. The national governments of both the United States and the Confederacy made demands on their citizens unimagined before the war, crossing lines of local and personal autonomy that Americans had taken for granted. Political parties within the United States fought unrelenting battles over the limits of the war, the purposes of sacrifice, and the meaning of loyalty. The boundaries that defined the roles of men and women shifted within both the Union and the Confederacy, war sometimes widening and sometimes diminishing the differences between males and females. Both sides breached the boundaries between guerrilla warfare and formal warfare. Both celebrated vengeance against civilians and then worried about the cost and consequence of that vengeance.

The boundaries that defined humans as property stretched and then broke forever in these years. Enslaved people, in every way they could, pushed at the constraints that bound them. They slipped across the shifting lines between the Confederate army and the Union army. They joined with Federal troops as liberators whether those troops welcomed them or not. They sought freedom on narrow paths into mountains or on broad roads into occupied cities and contraband camps. The United States widened the war's purpose from the restoration of the Union to proclaim emancipation, enlist black men as soldiers, embrace black people as citizens, and reconstitute the government itself on a more democratic basis.

Time marked its own boundaries on the landscape of war, emancipation, and Reconstruction. Major battles became landmarks in time, points from which people repositioned themselves within history. An hour might forever alter the lives of soldiers and their families, of towns and counties. The ambitions, hatreds, and conflicts of war transgressed the boundaries between war and peace, reverberating deep into the postwar years. People revised the history through which they lived, rearranging and simplifying time so that stories flattered their purposes.

The Civil War constantly shifted borders and boundaries, on scales large and small. Everyone in Augusta and Franklin, whether black or white, male or female, soldier or civilian, had to negotiate those moving boundaries. They all knew that the men sweeping across the green landscape of Virginia and Pennsylvania in the summer of 1863 might redefine the shape of the future.

PART ONE:

THE SCOURGE OF WAR

July 1863 through November 1864

*T*he armies of the Confederacy and the United States fought on a landscape that stretched for hundreds of miles from the places they clashed in battle. The war was a vast, living web radiating from the armies and the capitals, constantly in motion, woven of railroads and rivers, muddy roads and narrow trails, marching armies and bleak hospitals.

Generals conceived of war on an enormous scale. They focused on logistics and supply lines extending far into unknown dangers. They sought new soldiers to replace those whose lives they knew would be expended. They measured political gains and losses from every movement. They calculated consequences and contingencies several moves ahead, planning for defeat as well as victory, knowing that events and accidents they could not imagine might determine a battle.

Civilians lived within that web of war as well. Every family that sent a man to the army felt the connections, knew the distances, understood how quickly death or disease could travel from a battlefield to a lonely homestead. Every mother, wife, and sister waited for letters of reassurance to reach them from some distant place, fearing letters that brought news of death, disease, or disfigurement. Every family that saw its barns and fields emptied or its taxes mount felt the voracious hunger of armies. Everyone who read a newspaper in Civil War America glimpsed the reach and constant spinning of the web, the invisible strands reaching into every corner of the continent and across oceans. Every enslaved person could feel the trembling of the web, the possibility and threat it promised.

The Great Invasion

May through July 1863

With its victory at Chancellorsville in May 1863, the Army of Northern Virginia, led by General Robert E. Lee, could finally move away from Fredericksburg and Richmond, pulling the Union army from that devastated and exhausted region. Where the Confederate army would go, however, was not obvious. Union General Joseph Hooker, eager to redeem himself after Chancellorsville, thought Lee might try to invade the North close to Washington, east of the Blue Ridge Mountains, and Hooker deployed his army's great strength to prevent that possibility. Lee, however, decided to use the Valley to the west, shielding his army behind the mountains while his troops gathered themselves for an invasion of the North.

Lee had several competing purposes to consider. From the broadest perspective, the Confederates hoped they might win support from England or France if they could land a hard blow against the United States on its own territory. More certainly, if the Confederates could win a significant victory in Pennsylvania "there will be a great change in public opinion at the North," Lee wrote his wife. "The Republicans will be destroyed & I think the friends of peace will become so strong as that the next administration will go in on that basis." A victory on Northern soil, Lee calculated, would help sustain the Confederacy for the next year until a disheartened Northern electorate would reject Abraham Lincoln and his party in 1864. The revolutionary purpose of emancipation would be replaced by a plan for peace and compromise.[1]

Lee made another kind of political calculation as well, one more immediately pressing, within the Confederacy itself. President Jefferson Davis and Secretary of War James Seddon had asked Lee about sending his troops elsewhere in the Confederacy where they were desperately needed—perhaps to Mississippi to help relieve the grinding assault on Vicksburg or to stop the Union advances in Tennessee or Kentucky. Lee wanted nothing of such plans, for his goal was to protect Virginia, the capital of the Confederacy, the threat to Washington, and the anchor of his own loyalty. To keep his men in Virginia, when they were needed elsewhere, Lee needed to take the initiative, to end a war whose continuation held out nothing good for the Confederacy.

Lee's political calculations were accompanied by a more immediate consideration: hunger. The Army of Northern Virginia, about 75,000 men, did not have enough to eat. The winter had been harrowing. Virginia had little surplus food for Lee's army, and the railroads from North Carolina and the rest of the South arrived only sporadically and carried uncertain supplies. Meat rations had to be cut back and scurvy as well as other illnesses ravaged Lee's troops. Men collected any vegetables and wild greens they could find as the weather finally turned warmer; they searched for mustard, garlic, onions, and watercress that appeared in the early spring. The soldiers asked farmers for sauerkraut, vinegar, coleslaw, and pickles to supply nutrients they needed to maintain their health.[2]

The horses and mules of Lee's army were suffering as well; some horses had starved in Virginia over the winter for lack of fodder and the Confederates had to disperse their cavalry to feed their animals. An army in the Civil War was voracious, its mode of transportation, its horses and mules, depending on food from the same farms that fed men. In the summer of 1863 the stock of Lee's army were fed only three pounds of corn a day when they required ten. The animals needed oats, hay, and fresh grass, all of which had been devoured over the winter or early spring in Virginia. They also needed shoes, for hard use had worn their hooves down to the quick. Lee's army had exhausted its supplies of horseshoes and of the materials and equipment to make more.

Hastening Lee's urgency, the United States Army, though defeated at Chancellorsville, remained in Virginia, further exhausting the devastated land it occupied. The Federal soldiers burned fences for firewood, stripped hillsides of trees, turned fields into mud, reduced barns and farmhouses to shells. If Lee could draw Hooker to Pennsylvania he could draw tens of thousands of Union soldiers off Virginia soil and away from Richmond and Washington. He could fill the mouths, stomachs, and wagons of his army while making Northerners feel what it meant to live in an occupied land. Lee hoped to disperse the United States troops and then defeat one part of them after another somewhere in Pennsylvania—anywhere but Virginia.

Lee would use the Valley as a conduit of men and materiel, moving in both directions, depending on the Valley Turnpike for all aspects of the planned invasion. Orders, supplies, and mail would flow steadily to and from Richmond on the Virginia Central Railroad, connecting with the turnpike at Staunton. Lee expected the turnpike to carry vast stores of food, livestock, and other bounty of war from the North back into Virginia. Wounded men would be sent back south along the road as well, a series of hospitals along the way treating men whose care could not wait. The turnpike would also, Lee hoped, see Union captives marched to prisons in Richmond.

The Confederates had already begun raiding the North in May and sending food and livestock back south along the turnpike. John D. Imboden of Staunton led that work. He had recently been named Brigadier General, in charge of a thousand fighters who ransacked enemy territory for supplies. A native of Augusta, college-educated, ambitious, and versatile, by the time the war began the thirty-eight-year-old Imboden had been a teacher at the Virginia Institute for the Education of the Deaf, Dumb, and Blind, an attorney, a Mason, a state legislator, a real-estate investor, a rail promoter, a commissioner of schools, a county court clerk, an officer in the militia, and an inventor. Imboden used the war as another vehicle for his ambition, throwing himself into the conflict with calculated abandon. His four brothers joined him in the Confederate army.

Beginning in the spring of 1862 the Confederacy had incorporated guerrilla-style fighting into its more formal structures by creating "partisan rangers." Partisans fought in irregular style—disconnected from larger armies and command, striking in small bands against isolated targets, living off the land—but received the same pay and were held by the same military regulations as all soldiers. Partisans differed from regular troops mainly because they were compensated for the arms and munitions they took from the enemy and delivered to the Confederacy.

Imboden quickly proved an excellent recruiter of partisans,

with a stirring vision of what awaited those who joined him. A broadside posted in Augusta County declared with reckless honesty that "my purpose is to wage the most active warfare against our brutal invaders and their domestic allies, to hang about their camps and shoot down every sentinel, picket, courier, and wagon driver we can." Partisan rangers under Imboden would "watch opportunities for attacking convoys and forage trains and thus render the country so unsafe that they will not dare to move except in large bodies." Imboden made it clear that "it is only *men* I want, men who will pull the trigger on a Yankee with as much alacrity as they would on a mad dog; men whose consciences won't be disturbed by the sight of vandal carcass." Imboden and his partisan rangers fought under Stonewall Jackson and then under Robert E. Lee in 1862 and early 1863. Now they would play an important role in the invasion of Pennsylvania.[3]

Lee began to move in late May. His first target was Winchester, in the northern part of the Valley. Winchester, caught in the borderlands between North and South, had suffered at the hands of both armies throughout the war. In the spring of 1863, Winchester was under the command of United States General Robert Milroy, notorious in the Confederacy for his hard policies against the civilian population of a northern Virginia that made no secret of its loyalty to the Confederacy. Under Milroy's orders, Union troops had burned the homes and seized the property of Rebel sympathizers, shooting some who aided the enemy. "How many pleasant homes have these barbarians desolated, strewing the gardens with fragments of glass & china, filling the air with feathers from the beds, hewing up for wood, or boxing them up to send home," an anguished Nancy Emerson of Staunton, reading of the depredations, asked her diary. "How many churches have they polluted, how many graves desecrated. How have they soaked our soil with the blood of our noblest & best & then to cap the climax of injury & insult, talk of reconstructing the union. May the righteous Lord plead our cause against an ungodly nation, as he has done already, glory to his name."[4]

On June 13, the Confederates regained Winchester in an easy victory against a surprised Milroy and drove his men from the town. In the wake of the battle, Staunton, a hundred miles to the south, became, as it had been before, "a great thoroughfare for the army." More than 4,000 captured Union soldiers passed through a few days after the battle. Joseph Waddell, a former Unionist newspaper editor whose diary recorded every public event in Staunton, refused to talk with the captured men, "feeling too much detestation of the vandals. These are the wretches who would have come to invade our homes."[5]

The news from Winchester also brought reports of Lee's movements as he crossed the Potomac into Maryland. "Gen. Lee, with another portion of our army, has disappeared somewhere, and it is not known when or where he will turn up," Waddell noted, excited and mystified by the news. "These movements are wonderful—so rapid and secret."[6] Indeed, even as the Union prisoners from Winchester came south through Staunton on their way to the prisons of Richmond, thousands of Confederate soldiers came from the other direction, "passing through to join their commands," heading north toward Pennsylvania, toward the rich farms and cities of the enemy.[7]

The powers of Europe had already shown that only events on the battlefield would tempt them to get involved in the American war. Lee wanted to demonstrate to those powers the kind of civilized people the Confederates were when they had the opportunity to occupy the North. He also expected to demonstrate the

Joseph Waddell

kind of weak people the Yankees were when their own farms, villages, and cities came under assault.

While the invasion would dramatize the character of the Confederate nation, it also offered more tangible rewards. "We shall get nearly a million dollars worth of horses, supplies of all kinds &c from this county," one Confederate officer wrote his wife back in Augusta as Lee's army marched into Pennsylvania. "The people are very submissive and comply, meekly, with the demands made on them—I think we shall be able to do a good deal towards bringing about an honorable peace."[8] "The army is in splendid condition: marches almost wholly without straggling, and is in the highest spirits," another officer assured his family back in the Valley of Virginia. "Lee is making a bold stroke for peace. Pray that it may succeed."[9]

☆

THE UNION MILITARY LEADERSHIP had fallen into disarray. President Lincoln heard that the generals reporting to Joseph Hooker had lost faith in their commander. But Lincoln, not wanting to disrupt the army any more than necessary, decided to stay with Hooker for the time being. The Army of the Potomac would soon be depleted by the completion of the terms of more than 48,000 men who had signed on for nine months or two years of service. By the spring of 1863, a thousand men a day were being mustered out of the Federal army and the largest Union force in the east would soon lose over a quarter of its men. The Union put out a call for 100,000 militia to help protect their homeland from possible invasion. The states of the North, including Pennsylvania, struggled to meet even a fraction of that number. Men who wanted to fight were already enlisted in the army.[10]

In late June, as Hooker mobilized his men to move north through Frederick, Maryland, Secretary of War Edwin M. Stanton urgently telegraphed General Darius Couch in Harrisburg, Pennsylvania, to ask about the Confederates: "What description of force is at Chambersburg; in what numbers, and under whose command? Such particulars are very necessary to be known here in determining the operations of Hooker's force. No pains should be spared to get accurate information in detail and report it here." Couch thought that fighting in the North might actually bring some benefits. "The people being friendly, there would seem that with proper diligence and system accurate and full information might be had not only of the movements being made, but who and what number is making them."[11]

People in Pennsylvania watched for signs that the war might once again turn their way. The first place any invasion from the south would hit would be Franklin County, its lower boundary the Mason-Dixon Line itself, its main corridors the extension of the Valley Turnpike. Franklin and Chambersburg stood between the Confederate army and its most likely targets: the United States Army barracks at Carlisle, the Pennsylvania capital of Harrisburg, or the major prizes of Philadelphia, Baltimore, Washington, D.C., or even New York City.

"Our town in an uproar," William Heyser of Chambersburg glumly noted the day after Milroy's defeat in Winchester. Even though the residents could not believe everything they heard, "we all feel Pennsylvania will be invaded. Many families are hiding their valuables, and preparing for the worst. . . . The stores are packing up their goods and sending them off, people are running to and fro."[12] Philip Schaff, a theologian who taught at Mercersburg Seminary in southern Franklin County, worried that the "whole veteran army of Lee, the military strength and flower of the Southern rebellion is said to be crossing the Potomac and marching into Pennsylvania. We are cut off from all mail communication and dependent on the flying and contradictory rumors of passengers, straggling soldiers, run-away negroes and spies." As a result, "all the schools and stores are closed; goods are being hid or removed to the country, valuables buried in cellars or gardens and other places of concealment."[13]

The people of Franklin knew the Civil War all too well. The county had sent men to fight from the hopeful days of 1861 to the debacle of Chancellorsville, from the western theater to the east, from the days when all soldiers were white to recent days when black men, too, fought for the United States. Franklin's citizens had already seen hundreds of their young men shattered by wounds, taken by disease, killed on the battlefield, or captured by the Rebels. They mourned sons, brothers, and fathers lying in makeshift graves in the South. Their towns and farms had been invaded by Confederate raiders just the year before, when they had witnessed enslaved people fleeing the Rebel army.

The loss and sacrifice on the battlefields intensified the political bickering that had gone on for years before the war. Alexander McClure, one of the strongest and most influential allies of Abraham Lincoln and of Pennsylvania's Republican Governor Andrew Curtin, lived in Franklin. Thaddeus Stevens, a leading Republican in Congress and the most outspoken national advocate of freedom for African-Americans, owned an iron works in the county worth over a hundred thousand dollars, or two million dollars in today's currency. Despite McClure and Stevens, however, in the election of the fall of 1862 Franklin Democrats had elected their candidates for Congress and for the state legislature, just as Democrats had won across the state.

In early 1863, as the people of Franklin County watched the battles of Virginia turn against the Union, its newspapers fought over the larger purposes of the war. The *Village Record* of Waynesboro proudly celebrated the accomplishments of Abraham Lincoln, the Republican party, and the United States Army, all portrayed as one and the same. The Emancipation Proclamation, issued on January 1, the paper claimed, had changed the course of the war and world history in "brief, eloquent, and immortal sentences," the document "the frank announcement of a brave and frank man." Anyone who expected "to read an invocation to blood and massacre and rapine will be surprised by the sincere and affectionate warning of the President to the people whose deliverance he proclaims."

The Emancipation Proclamation, the paper reassured its readers, brought "practical and immediate" gains to the Union cause.

"As a war measure, it will add strength to our armies and glory to the object of the war." It would transform enslaved people, "this silent, oppressed, and anxious race into active allies of the Union." The Proclamation "makes three million of slaves three million of able-bodied recruits, who have only to see the Union banner to follow it with their lives. It takes away the labor that sustains the power of the South, and adds to the military power of the North."[14]

A soldier from Franklin County had seen with his own eyes what freedom meant for the enslaved people who had migrated to the camps of the United States Army, people called "contra-bands." "There are about 8000 contrabands here, working on the R[ail]—R[oad]—cutting wood for the government, and raising a regiment," William Baritz wrote from North Carolina. "Schools are established for the youth, and it is surprising to see the avidity and ease with which they study and learn; how their eyes glitter with every new lesson, with what satisfaction they enter the school-room, how attentive, as if they feared they might miss something; it makes one feel humble to see the efforts these youth put forth to attain knowledge, and it is a grand omen for the amelioration of the race." Even more important, black Southern men excelled as soldiers, a role in which "they evince the same traits, attentive, active, quick to learn, ambitious, and above all courageous."[15]

Many in the North did not agree with the *Village Record*'s proud assessment of the Emancipation Proclamation or of the enslaved people of the South. The Democrats' *Valley Spirit* bitterly charged that the Proclamation was "unwise, ill-timed, outside of the Constitution and full of mischief. Its effect will be more thoroughly to unite and exasperate the whites of the South in their resistance to the National Government, and to make the war still more prolonged, bloody and bitter." The abolitionists had promised the previous year that linking the Union cause to the end of slavery would "end the war in thirty days; that it was the great remedy for the evils afflicting the country." Instead, the United States Army had lost one battle after another in the heart of slave country. The *Spirit* ended its brief commentary in smirking black dialect: "Drive on, 'Massa Linkun,' we are anxiously awaiting the result." [16]

The Democrats blamed the failures of the United States Army in Virginia and Maryland on the political meddling and incompetence of the Lincoln administration. The abolitionists cried "On to Richmond" and "their patriotism (?) was of such an intense character, that nothing would satisfy them but a direct march to Richmond by the nearest route and the capture of the rebel capital. They could brook no delays," the *Valley Spirit* charged. When McClellan failed in this effort, "his removal was demanded by ten thousand abolition voices. The clamor had its desired effect. A weak and vacillating President was made to bend before this storm of abolition fanaticism" and McClellan was replaced by the incompetent Ambrose Burnside. The result was the horror of Fredericksburg in late December 1862, a botched battle in which the patriotic devotion of Franklin boys and men had been squandered in their first engagement with the Rebels.

The Democrats charged that the Republicans, far from saving the United States, were destroying it. The president and his party had sacrificed the military salvation of the nation for the destruction of slavery, a destruction that many white Northerners did not want. The course of the entire war, the Democrats charged, could be explained by this terrible mistake: "had the war been prosecuted with the one undivided object of restoring the Union and maintaining the Constitution, we might to-day have been able at least to see 'the beginning of the end.'" Instead, the story of the last two years had been, in the Democrats' eyes, a series of despotic travesties and humiliating losses.

The Democrats' paper enumerated the ever-mounting strikes against slavery from the Republicans in Washington: "Congress rushed madly on from one wild, impracticable, revolutionary scheme to another, without regard to constitutional obligations or natural, inevitable consequences. The confiscation bill, the bill abolishing slavery in the District of Columbia, the act admitting Western Virginia, the negro enlistment bill" and other unprecedented acts, "whose only effect has been to unite the South and divide the North, were hurried through with frightful rapidity." In the judgment of the Democrats, President Lincoln had caved under pressure from the abolitionists and the radicals in his party with the Emancipation Proclamation, and, "with one stroke of his pen, drove from his support the conservatives in the Border States and northern tier of seceded States, and made them, if not friendly to the rebellion, at least luke-warm Unionists." [17]

Now, in the spring of 1863, the Democrats warned, only extreme acts could save the United States: "let the President revoke his emancipation proclamation; let negro enlistment be stopped at once, . . . let the radicals in the Cabinet be tumbled out heels over head—the people of the country are sick and tired of them and want new, reliable, competent men in their places." In short, Democrats across the North demanded that history be rolled back, that "the original purpose of the war be again declared and adhered to." [18]

Many people in the United States, whatever their party, were haunted by lost opportunities and worried about the course of the war in the east. While the Republicans in Washington navigated between due caution and clear purpose, their opponents attacked Lincoln as both too weak and too strong. The president, they charged, had shown himself too passive to stand up to the radicals who sought to make the war about slavery and too aggressive against those in the North who challenged his judgment.[19]

☆

AUGUSTA COUNTY HAD FOLLOWED the path of many counties in Virginia, turning years of proud Unionism into staunchly Confederate loyalty in a matter of weeks. Augusta had been swept up in the war from the very beginning. Many of the young men of Augusta had fought with Stonewall Jackson in the battles at Manassas, in the Valley, and around Richmond, battles that had made the Stonewall Brigade one of the most celebrated in the Confederacy. The families of Augusta had already sacrificed a thousand of their young men to death, disease, wounding, or capture.

To the former Unionists of the *Staunton Spectator*, the story of the war so far had been the story of three desperate strategies by the United States to subjugate the Confederacy. First, the United States had expected "the 'Union sentiment' of the South" to translate into support for the United States even when the federal government, as Confederates saw it, invaded its own states. Lincoln believed that secession had been forced by the Slave Power upon the men who had tried to hold the Union together through the crisis of 1860 and 1861—men, in fact, such as those who published and read the *Spectator*. But the North did not understand just how unified the white South had become when it considered itself invaded by an alien force. "They have found the Confederates true and brave and powerful."

Once the war began, the Lincoln administration had attempted a second desperate strategy, the Augusta paper charged, trying to "excite servile insurrection, and to make the poor negro do for them what they had not the courage or the power to do for themselves." Such was the Southern judgment of the confiscation acts of 1861 and 1862 that had declared that slaves laboring for the Confederates could be seized by the United States Army. And such was the white South's judgment of the Emancipation Proclamation of January 1863, which they saw as an invitation to the enslaved to rise up against their owners as outlaws or soldiers.

In the eyes of the Confederates, the United States cared little for the true welfare of the enslaved people of the South. Though white Southerners had discovered that their slaves disappeared with startling rapidity wherever the Union Army appeared, formerly trusted "servants" turning themselves into "contraband" overnight, the whites considered these desperate flights to freedom nothing more than delusion on the part of black people and duplicity on the part of the United States. The Yankees were "utterly indifferent of the fate of the negro, and anxious only to effect our ruin by whatever means."

In the Union's third strategy, the *Spectator* charged, the Federal army had thrown down "the barriers of civilized hostilities." "Read the innumerable accounts of non-combatants, old men, and women, and little children, driven from their homes without a reason in the world, and threatened with instant death if they dare to return," the paper spat. "Follow the march of the enemy's armies: Private property burnt, the implements of husbandry sought out and destroyed, the food of the people seized to the last meal, and the purpose OPENLY PROCLAIMED to prevent the cultivation of the soil or the harvesting of crops, as the means of 'starving' us into subjection." The laws of civilized warfare, the Confederates charged, gave invading armies no right "to blot out the face of nature, and reduce a country to desolation. This, however, the Yankees are attempting to do." Throughout Virginia, the signs of Northern evil were visible to everyone: "Burning homesteads, a ruined husbandry, a desolated land, and the infernal cry of 'STARVATION to the rebels!' tell us that we are now standing for our lives, against demons incarnate." [20]

Though the Confederates claimed to wage war with greater principle, one issue could not be compromised. "Let it be understood that the black flag is to wave in every battle in which the negroes are made the tools of the cowardly Abolitionists, and let there be no officer in command of a black regiment or company taken prisoner, unless it be for the purpose of giving him a more merited death by hanging." The rules of civilized warfare simply did not apply to black soldiers and their white officers, the Confederates charged. The United States had broken the compact of civilization when it armed slaves.[21]

☆

AS THE CONFEDERATES MARCHED northward from Winchester across Maryland into Pennsylvania, the destination of the invasion remained unclear. Much would depend on how the Union forces reacted. Although the Confederates had taken the initiative by invading Pennsylvania, they realized that the Union would do its best to determine the field of battle and to make the enemy pay a heavy price for coming north. Lee arrived in Chambersburg on June 27 and set up headquarters in an attractive spot not far from the town's central Diamond, on the Gettysburg road. Two-thirds of his army of 75,000 men joined him there.[22]

Lee issued orders with an eye to many audiences. He began with praise: "The commanding general has observed with marked satisfaction the conduct of the troops on the march," their conduct entitling them to "approbation and praise." There had been some "instances of forgetfulness, on the part of some," Lee admitted in a parental tone, and he reminded them that "no greater disgrace could befall the army, and through it our whole people, than the perpetration of the barbarous outrages upon the unarmed and defenseless and the wanton destruction of private property, that have marked the course of the enemy in our own country." Unlike the Federal troops in the South, the Confederates would "make war only upon armed men." The Confederate army, despite the temptation, "cannot take vengeance for the wrongs our people have suffered without lowering ourselves in the eyes of all whose abhorrence has been excited by the atrocities of our enemies." Lee therefore ordered "all officers to arrest and bring to summary punishment all who shall in any way offend against the orders on this subject."[23]

The Confederate men pouring into Franklin County had dreamed of the day they would take the war out of Virginia. Their idea of what would happen when they reached Pennsylvania did not always accord with Lee's order of restraint. As soon as they had shattered Hooker's army at Chancellorsville, some had been looking north. We will "finally make this war a war of pillaging, plundering, and destroying private citizens' property," one soldier wrote his mother. "I feel like retaliating in the strictest sense. I don't think we would do wrong to take horses; burn houses; and commit every depredation possible upon the men of the North." The Confederate soldiers had seen Virginia desecrated by the Union army and longed to move the war to enemy territory.[24]

Jedediah Hotchkiss regularly wrote his wife Sara, at home at Mossy Creek in Augusta County, providing honest if optimistic accounts of each stage of his unlikely adventure with the Confederacy. Devoutly Christian, Hotchkiss prayed that the Confederate cause would be blessed by God and the march into Pennsylvania seemed evidence of His favor. "Providence has abundantly blessed our movement, few casualties of any kind—and our success wonderful," Hotchkiss enthused. The Confederates were using the mountains as a natural shield from the Yankees, controlling the passes through those mountains so that they could threaten Baltimore, Washington, and Philadelphia to the east as well as Carlisle and Harrisburg to their north. The Rebels gathered horses, food, and everything else they might want in the Cumberland Valley and shipped it back to Staunton without fear of Union attack or disruption. [25]

Hotchkiss thought the Pennsylvanians he met were impressed with the restrained and gentlemanly Southerners. "They confidently expected us to burn every thing and lay waste the country and they thought we would be justified in so doing," Jed wrote Sara, echoing a common theme in Confederate letters home. "But when they found us doing all things decently & not disturbing them except to supply our army with every thing it needed to eat &c &c and furnish any number of big horses & wagons, all sorts of supplies, leather saddles &c all called for by a polite officer, & no pillaging, they were rejoiced to get off so well & set before our men any quantity of the good things they have so abundantly & Gen. Ewell says we will all get fat here."

"We are you may say in the very heart of Yankeedom," Benjamin Farinholt wrote his wife. "We are living very well over here and the amount of money saved to our Government every day by our subsisting on the Enemy is about $200,000." The Confederates "have burnt some larger iron works, foundries &c, and are tearing up their Rail Road by whole-sale." Chambersburg was "a very pretty town" with nice houses and good food. The local farmers "hate to see us driving their fine horses to our artillery and killing their fat beeves by hundreds." The Northerners "have known nothing of the war heretofore, and I believe unless we do bring it home to them in this manner they would be willing to carry it on indefinitely." [26]

Some of the letters home revealed envy of the enemy. James Williams wrote his father that "I just wish you could see all the crops here. Pa, I never saw such wheat & corn in my life. Every man has a little bit of a dwelling house & a magnificent barn, probably about 80 or 90 feet long." The people, Williams judged, were "the meanest looking white people I ever saw," full of abolition, but their land was unimaginably rich. The soldier could think of only one reason why the Northerners were so "submissive and badly scared." "It must be conscience. They know how their soldiers have desolated Virginia and they fear that ours will retaliate." [27]

Another Virginia soldier in Lee's army was proud to see the looks on the faces of the people of Chambersburg as they watched the seasoned Confederate troops pass through the town. "It is almost amusing to witness the anxious stare with which we are regarded as our sunburnt motley dressed regiments but moving in closed ranks with the cadenced step to the tune of Dixie and with enfield muskets glistening and the red battle flag inscribed all over with the names of our victories pass through the thoroughfare of one of the numerous towns," Thomas Pollock wrote his father back in Virginia. The North, untouched by devastation, seemed "a beautiful country overflowing with wealth & fatness."

While some of the Pennsylvanians "try to look fierce and angry and tell us confidently we will never get back," Pollock boasted of unchecked confidence in Lee's army, as did his compatriots. "The perfect reverence the soldiers feel for his orders is only equalled by their faith in him. It strikes me as a perfect picture of faith. Here they are penetrating the heart of a hostile country leaving their homes beyond broad rivers and the largest of the enemies armies while in front of them is gathering all of resistance that can be obtained by a power fruitful of every element of military power. Yet they are as happy and as secure in their feeling as if they were already won—simply because they have an almost fanatical confidence in their cause & their leader."[28]

"It is very funny to pass through these Yankee towns to see the long sour faces the people put on," Franklin Gaillard told his son. "The girls some of them wear little United States flags. Others more indecent hold their noses and make faces. Our men go on and pay no attention to them. They only laugh at them when they make themselves ridiculous." Gaillard admitted that many of his fellow soldiers "think it very hard that they should not be allowed to treat them as their soldiers treated our people. But we must not imitate the Yankees in their mean acts."[29]

The *Richmond Dispatch* urged the Confederate army to retaliate for all that the Union army had done, though the equation could not be perfectly balanced because the North did not hold slaves. The United States forces "have stolen 500,000 negroes from the South, valued at $500,000,000, at the commencement of the war. They have no negroes to steal, but they have towns and manufactories to burn, and every one of these should be reduced to ashes." The Confederate paper argued that "property is property. There is no reason why one species of it should be exempt from the laws of war more than another." Urging their soldiers to make the Valley of Pennsylvania "a sea of flame," to leave nothing "that man could eat or sleep upon, or shelter himself, or procure food with," the Southern paper judged that even if the North should be "turned into a desert" the "balance of destruction would be against us. The whole city of Philadelphia if burnt to the ground would not pay for the negroes that have carried off."[30]

The Southern soldiers agreed, as Benjamin Farinholt put it, that "we will necessarily have a big fight before we leave the state, and expect it will be somewhere north of Baltimore probably near Philadelphia or Harrisburg." The Confederates were "in fine spirit and willing to be led every where—or any where confidently expecting success under the able leadership of Genl Lee." His "Army is in excellent health, and if we keep up our present state of organization there is nothing to fear from any force they can bring against us."

☆

THE PEOPLE OF FRANKLIN COUNTY had seen the Rebels march into their county the year before, with impunity and without consequence. There was nothing to stop them from doing it again. The United States Army was far away, wounded and cautious.

The first signs of the impending Confederate invasion had arrived in Franklin County when African-Americans fled into town. "The dark clouds of contrabands commenced rushing upon us" reported a Chambersburg newspaper. "With due allowance for the excessive alarm of the slaves, it was manifest that the rebels were about to clear out the Shenandoah Valley, and, that once done, the Cumberland, with all its teeming wealth, would be at rebel mercy." The "contrabands" who rushed into Chambersburg knew that the Confederates would, even in the midst of an invasion, make a priority of capturing people they considered runaway slaves—which would be any black person. "Negroes darkened the different roads Northward for hours, loaded with house hold effects, sable babies, &c and horses and wagons and cattle crowded every avenue to places of safety."[31] African-Americans knew they were not safe within sight of the Confederates. "The colored people are flying in all directions. There is a complete state of confusion," William Heyser reported in his diary. Escaped slaves fled into town from Maryland "with the Rebels not far behind."[32]

Many African-Americans did not escape when the Confederates arrived. "Quite a number of Negroes, free and slave—men, women and children" had been captured and sent "South to be sold into bondage," the paper bleakly noted. Perhaps fifty were captured by the first Confederate units to come into Franklin. "Some of the men were bound with ropes, and the children were mounted in front or behind the rebels on their horses." Other African-Americans managed to escape, sometimes with the help of white allies. Several neighbors in Greencastle in southern Franklin captured the guard of a group of black people and "one negro effected his escape by shooting and seriously wounding his rebel guard. He forced the gun from the rebel and fired, wounding him in the head, and then skedaddled. . . . By great exertions of several citizens some of the negroes were discharged."[33]

As the Confederates continued to arrive, the people of Franklin saw heartbreaking scenes. "A terrible day," Reverend Thomas Creigh of Mercersburg wrote in his diary on June 26. "The guerillas passing and repassing, one of the saddest of sights, several of our colored persons with them, to be sold into slavery, John Philkill and Findlay Cuff. The officer with a squad of men has just passed up street making proclamation of something. I have just been to the door to inquire what it is. It is that they intend to search all houses for contrabands and fire arms and that wherever they discover either they will set fire to the house in which they may be found." The next day the guerillas left Mercersburg but took "with them about a dozen colored persons, mostly contrabands, women and children; a large flock of sheep and horses and barouche [carriages]. Sad that we can make no resistance and that the Government has sent us no help. Here we are as in a port or a prison, beleaguered on all hands and can receive no reliable intelligence in regard to the movements of our army."[34]

As the Confederates drove into Pennsylvania, Democratic newspapers, and even local Republican leader Alexander McClure, urged President Lincoln to put George McClellan back in charge of the United States Army in Virginia. Joseph Hooker had proven himself incompetent at Chancellorsville, just as the other generals put in charge since McClellan's removal had proven themselves incapable of beating Lee. William Heyser of Chambersburg thought that with McClellan's "skill and knowledge, the war could have been ended." Instead, "Washington refuses to use him, politics being behind this." Heyser traveled to the state capital at Harrisburg and found that "our state is doing nothing to defend itself against invasion. Gov. Curtain seems to be paralized and unable to act. We need decisions badly, and can't expect them from Washington." On the road back to Chambersburg, Heyser "encountered many colored people fleeing the Rebels, as not all have left the area. These poor people are completely worn out, carrying their families on their backs. Saw some twenty from Chambersburg that I recognized." His own "man," Proctor, was heading for the mountains, with Heyser's blessings. "Of Fanny, our colored girl," he knew nothing.[35]

The citizens of Chambersburg watched the arrival of the Confederates with a mixture of fear, anger, curiosity, disgust, sympathy, and dark humor. The *Valley Spirit* told the story. "First came an immense body of cavalry, steadily and quietly, every man with his hand on his carbine, and his eye glancing suspiciously at each open window and door." The paper named the generals and their corps, familiar from so many newspaper articles over the last two years. It described the Stonewall Brigade as "full fifteen thousand strong, in three divisions, each regiment bearing the 'Stars and Bars' or some regimental or State flag, and their bands, or drum corps discoursing 'the Bonnie Blue Flag,' 'Dixie,' or 'The Marsellaise.'" To the citizens' surprise, "there was but little confusion or noise, nothing but the tramp, tramp of thousands of feet, and the continual monotonous rattle of canteens and equipment. First came a brigade, then its artillery, then its ambulances, and then its baggage train."

The march continued for three full days, "until the novelty wore off, and the eye began to tire with the endless succession and the heart grew sick over the gloomy prospect before our happy valley." The editor counted "fully fifty thousand men two hundred and ten cannon, twelve, twenty-four and thirty-two pounders, and over two thousand wagons." The newspaper admitted that "the rebel army were better clad and shod than we expected to see them. Their clothes were much worn, faded and scuffed, but there were comparatively few whom you could positively call 'ragged,' and we did not see a hundred men in their bare feet."[36]

☆

RACHEL CORMANY WATCHED the Rebels' arrival in Chambersburg with condescension and defiance. Rachel was unusual in that she had been to college in Ohio and had arrived in Franklin County not long before the war broke out, but she was like many other young women throughout the North, on her own with a child while her husband fought for the Union.

Rachel watched with dismay as black people became the first victims of Lee's invasion. The Rebels "were hunting up the contrabands & driving them off by droves. O! How it grated on our hearts to have to sit quietly & look at such brutal deeds—I saw no men among the contrabands—all women & children. Some of the colored people who were raised here were taken along—I sat on the front step as they were driven by just like we would drive cattle." One mother pleaded "with her driver for her children—but all the sympathy she received from him was a rough 'March along'—at which she would quicken her pace again."

After the rush of African-Americans, "the excitement abated a little—but it was only like the calm before a great storm." Word came of fires to the south, of skirmishes, of wagon trains. Some Chambersburg people panicked. "Such a skedadling as their was among the women & children to get into the houses. All thought the Rebels had really come. The report now is that they will be here in an hour."

Rachel proclaimed herself unperturbed. While "many have packed nearly all of their packable goods—I have packed nothing. I do not think that we will be disturbed even should they come. I will trust in God even in the midst of flying shells—but of course shall seek the safest place possible in that case—which I hope will not come to us. I have just put my baby to sleep & will now sit at the front door awhile yet—then retire, knowing all will be well."[37]

☆

ROBERT E. LEE WAS A SUBJECT of great interest to the Pennsylvanians. As he rode through Chambersburg, the Northerners discovered Lee to be "a stoutly built man, apparently about fifty years of age, with gray hair and a stiff, scrubbly gray beard. He was dressed very plainly, with not a single mark of his rank about him, wearing a black slouch hat without ornament, dark blue or black military cape, and plain gray pantaloons." The Confederates with whom the editor spoke considered Lee "the greatest general the world has ever produced." In the "unbounded confidence of his men," the editor thought, "lies the great secret of his previous successes." In contrast, even educated Confederates "insisted that Lincoln was a fugitive in Boston and dare not occupy his capital," and declared that "he was habitually intoxicated and unable to attend to his official duties because of his intemperance." The Rebels expressed surprised that the President actually commanded respect and loyalty in Chambersburg.[38]

The Northerners were amused at other misconceptions the Southerners had of Pennsylvania and of the North. "Quite a number were astonished to find our people speaking English, as they supposed that the prevalent language was the German." A demand from the invaders for immense quantities of sauerkraut struck the Pennsylvanians as hilarious.[39]

The *Repository* reprinted articles from the Southern press in which the Confederacy's boasts, diatribes, and self-delusions were allowed to speak for themselves. The Richmond *Whig* called for vengeance along Lee's march. "If General Lee gets Yankeedom fairly on the rack, he should not stay his hand till every sinew in his monstrous carcass is snapped and every bone broken." The Charleston *Mercury* told Lee to forget about the opinion of the world, which had done nothing to aid Southern independence. "We hope, then, that the leaders of our armies will do away with all this sickly sentimentality, and go into the war in real dreadful earnest. Let Yankee cities burn and their fields be laid waste."[40]

☆

BY THE END OF JUNE, the Confederates had taken from Franklin County about all they could carry. During these weeks Lee's army seized between 45,000 and 50,000 head of cattle, about 35,000 sheep, and more than 20,000 horses and mules. "Every square foot of an acre of ground not occupied by a sleeping or standing soldier, was covered with choice food for the hungry," wrote one loquacious soldier about the situation near Chambersburg. "Chickens, turkeys, ducks and geese squawked, gobbled, quacked, cackled, and hissed in harmonious unison as deft and energetic hands seized them for slaughter, and scarcely waiting for them to die, sent their feathers flying in all directions; and scattered around in bewildering confusion and gratifying profusion appeared immense loaves of bread and chunks of corn beef, hams, and sides of bacon, cheeses, crocks of apple-butter, jelly, jam, pickles, and preserves, bowls of yellow butter, demijohns of buttermilk, and other eatables too numerous to mention."[41]

Gettysburg, about twenty-five miles by good road to the east from Chambersburg, promised a place to find more food and other supplies, probably guarded only by militia. Gettysburg, too, might ultimately be a sheltered place, Lee thought, to gather his forces to drive back the Yankees when they finally arrived, as they were certain to do. One Confederate battalion had already passed through Gettysburg on its way to York to burn a key bridge. The town of Gettysburg, bearing a strong resemblance to Chambersburg, offered only token resistance. The Confederates demanded bacon, sugar, salt, coffee, flour, onions, whiskey, shoes, hats, or cash. They got much less than they wanted, but took what they could find and moved on.

Lee hoped to keep his army in Pennsylvania's Cumberland Valley for the entire summer, using the mountains for protection and the turnpike to Virginia for connection with his base in the Valley and in Richmond. He was not looking for a fight so early in the occupation. Moreover, the Confederate cavalry under Jeb Stuart, which had been ranging widely across Virginia and Maryland in the aftermath of Chancellorsville, had not arrived in Pennsylvania. Without Stuart's reconnaissance, Lee had only the vaguest notion of what the Union army was doing. He was disturbed to learn from a spy that the enemy had crossed the Potomac three days before the Confederates had learned of that maneuver. Lee called together the troops that had been foraging across southern Pennsylvania. The seven divisions of Confederates in Franklin County would move east from Chambersburg while another division, near York, would come west, all converging in Gettysburg.[42]

Meanwhile, the Confederates sent three regiments ahead to Gettysburg to seize what they had heard was a large supply of shoes. As the Rebels approached, they saw Union cavalry rather than the weak militia they expected. The Confederates promptly pulled back and took word back to Lee: the Union army was closer than they had imagined.[43]

☆

THE CONFEDERATES CUT the telegraph lines and occupied the roads and towns between Chambersburg and Harrisburg, where the governor, General Couch, and, most important, the telegraph to Washington were located. Alexander McClure of Chambersburg, prominent in the state's Republican party, was part of a "most anxious party in the Governor's room at Harrisburg waiting for some information of the movement of Lee's army, and not knowing at what hour Lee would swoop upon Harrisburg and hoist the Confederate flag over the Capitol." At the end of June, the Pennsylvania leaders had received no information for three days. "There had been no sleep, except broken naps forced by exhaustion, and not one of the Governor's circle had been in bed for three nights. The whole State was simply paralyzed by the appalling situation, and one of the aggravating features of it was that no information could be obtained of Lee's movements or purposes."[44]

On the night of June 29, a young man, Stephen Pomeroy, was chosen to carry a message from Chambersburg, without date or signature, to the state's leaders in Harrisburg. A local judge prepared the message, sewed into the lining of Pomeroy's belt. Riding hard and changing horses, the messenger arrived at a telegraph station on the Pennsylvania Railroad at two or three o'clock in the morning. It was through that tenuous means that the Union leadership learned that Lee's entire army was marching from Chambersburg toward Gettysburg. The invasion was said to stretch for over a hundred miles.[45]

In the meantime, General Joseph Hooker, in one of his last acts as commander, sent cavalry to Gettysburg to assess the situation there. When General John Buford arrived in Gettysburg at eleven in the morning on June 30, he found "everybody in a terrible state of excitement on account of the enemy's advance upon this place." Unidentified Rebels had approached to within half of mile of Gettysburg when Buford and his men arrived. Buford could not get a clear sense of the situation, for the Confederate "force was terribly exaggerated by reasonable and truthful but inexperienced men."

Buford discovered evidence that Lee was indeed nearby—a pass Lee had signed in Chambersburg. But there was not much

Buford could do. "My men and horses are fagged out," he wrote to headquarters. "I have not been able to get any grain yet. It is all in the country, and the people talk instead of working. Facilities for shoeing are nothing." Even locals who tried to be helpful made things more complicated. "I have many rumors and reports of the enemy advancing upon me from toward York. I have to pay attention to some of them, which causes me to overwork my horses and men. I can get no forage nor rations; am out of both." [46]

Even as civilians and troops jostled along the roads and hills of southern Pennsylvania, Abraham Lincoln appointed George Meade as commander of the Army of the Potomac. The Union generals beneath him were happy with the choice, but the soldiers in the ranks were not sure what to think. Meade, though brave, tested, and competent, was not famous, eloquent, or physically impressive. And now he was suddenly in command on the eve of what could be a defining event in the war.

Meade worked to gain control of the situation. He knew that the Confederates occupied the road between Chambersburg and Gettysburg, but Meade admitted that he was "without definite and positive information as to the whereabouts" of other Confederate divisions. Meade's own force was "tolerably well concentrated, moving with all the speed that the trains, roads, and physique of the men will bear," but his destination would be determined by the enemy, "as circumstances and the information we receive during the day and in the marches may indicate as most prudent and most likely to lead to ultimate success." In other words, Meade had no clear idea of what the Confederates were doing or where he might confront them. He could not know that the Confederates knew even less about his whereabouts or movements. [47]

☆

═══

RACHEL CORMANY WATCHED ISOLATED riders and teams pass through Chambersburg. More Rebels came and "sawed down telegraph poles, destroyed the scotland bridge again took possession of the warehouses & were dealing out flour by the barrel & mollasses by the bucket ful—They made people take them bread—meat—&c to eat—Some dumb fools carried them jellies & the like—Not a thing went from this place." She talked with one Confederate who told her that Stonewall Jackson, recently killed at Chancellorsville, "was a christian & means it honestly & earnestly." Rachel could not imagine how a Rebel could be a sincere Christian.

Despite the ease with which the Rebels had come into the North, Rachel thought that perhaps this brazen assault on Pennsylvania might turn out to be just what the Union needed to break the Southern army. "Many think this the best thing in the world to bring the war to close—I hope our men will be strong enough to completely whip them—Now it is on our side—While down there our army was in the enemys country & citizens kept the rebels posted in our army movements—now they are in the enemys country."

Rachel, despite her disgust, could not help but feel pity for the Southern boys and young men who passed by, hour after hour. "I felt real badly to see those poor men going through as they did. likely many of them will be killed." She hoped that many would desert. On the evening of June 30, "quite a number of the young folks were in the parlor this evening singing all the patriotic & popular war songs. Quite a squad of rebels gathered outside to listen & seemed much pleased with the music—'When this cruel war is over' nearly brought tears from some. they sent in a petition to have it sung again which was done. they then thanked the girls very much & left—they acted real nicely."

Rachel Cormany, like everyone else in Chambersburg, could not know what was happening beyond the borders of their town. She could imagine, however, admitting to her diary that "I got quite weak & immagined that I could already see My Samuel falling—I feel very uneasy about him." She suspected that a battle must be underway somewhere not far away. "I almost fear to hear the result in who was killed & who wounded—still I want to know."[48]

☆

BY THE SUMMER OF 1863 many people in both the North and the South sensed that the war might be coming to a culmination. To Confederates, heartened by a string of military victories over the preceding six months, full of confidence in Robert E. Lee and his army, it seemed that a victory of any sort in the United States might break the will of the Northern people. Yet they also knew that the Confederates were virtually forced to take the war northward because Virginia and its allies could not feed and supply the very army on which its survival depended. The invasion of Pennsylvania was not the reckless gamble it seemed to many above and below the Mason-Dixon Line, but a grim reckoning with reality.

Many people of the North, recognizing their strength, actually welcomed Lee's invasion. By overextending himself, they thought, Lee might finally make himself vulnerable. It was true that the Union command seemed in disarray, and it was true that the fighting between the Democrats and the Republicans seemed to weaken Lincoln's conduct of the war. But surely the people of the North would be unified when the threat came to their very doors.

A Gigantic Forlorn Hope

July 1863

*T*he scale of the armies descending on Pennsylvania, the limitless hunger they brought with them, their capacity to devastate all they came near, could barely be comprehended. They descended like storms, relentless and unavoidable.

The Confederate and the Union forces, each swirling around a central command, were drawn toward each other. From those two moving centers spun divisions, brigades, corps, regiments, and companies, far-flung cavalry and scouts, each bound to the distant command of its army by forces of experience, expertise, and faith. African-Americans, free and enslaved, lived within the pull and turbulence around the moving armies, fleeing the Confederacy and moving toward the Federal army when circumstance created the chance.

Farmers and townspeople, anchored to their farms and homes, could only wait for the armies to arrive. The areas through which the armies moved, civilians knew, would be consumed, crops trampled, livestock and food taken. The destruction would radiate miles from the center of the fighting, feeding the surging energy of the system and pulling isolated farms and homesteads into the maelstrom.

As the battle unfolded, no one could see or comprehend all the skir-mishes, clashes, assaults, reinforcements, and retreats that would coalesce into what would become known as "Gettysburg." Even the commanders could not grasp all the carnage and struggle and heroism arrayed around them, could not gauge the effects of assaults and strategies already failed. On the ground, the battle came in fragments.[1]

The battle stretched over three full days and pitched over 160,000 men against each other. Troops fought on flanks and in the front simultane-ously, surging back and forth, turning narrow defeats into narrow victories and then to defeat once more. Horrific noise and dense smoke deafened and blinded. Trying to coordinate maneuvers with handwritten orders deliv-ered on horseback across miles of fighting led to disjointed movements and failed connections. The battle turned on hundreds of dramas, some known, remembered, and embellished, others forever lost to death and chaos.

Later, people would learn that on the first day, July 1, United States troops, met by larger Confederate forces to the west and north, fell back through the town of Gettysburg to take the high ground to the south on Cemetery Hill and Culp's Hill. On the second day, as vast numbers of infantry from both armies converged at Gettysburg, the Federal army secured a fishhook-shaped range of ridges and hills, their 90,000 sol-diers confronting 70,000 Confederate soldiers from the advantage of high ground. Lee's army attacked those Union forces, but could not displace them. On the third day, the Confederates launched a massive infantry assault of 12,000 men—Pickett's Charge—against the center of the Fed-eral line on Cemetery Ridge.

☆

JOSEPH WADDELL KEPT A CLOSE EYE on the war. He had learned not to believe much of what he read in the papers and even less of what he heard on the streets of Staunton. Through-out late June, Waddell had monitored the news for reports from

Vicksburg, Richmond, and Pennsylvania. The Virginia newspapers, like their Northern counterparts, selected articles from the enemy press that not only presented the enemy in the worst light but that also presented the enemy trying to present its own enemy in the worst light, a hall of mirrors compounding the distortion.

Waddell's diary entries bristled at the reports of the Pennsylvania papers about runaway slaves being captured by Lee's army as it came into the North. "The 'contrabands' as the Yankees call runaway or stolen negroes, won the race to Harrisburg, but arrived there with feet swollen and bleeding—They say the scene was 'enough to touch the most obdurate heart.'—it has been all right and humane, however, to drive Southern women and children from their homes!" Waddell worried about "Gen. Lee's intentions" "considering the vast odds against us in a war of invasion." Wagons of goods "purchased" in Chambersburg during the first days of the invasion rolled into Staunton on the Valley Turnpike on the evening of July 4. Other than a youth carrying word that Lee was about to move on Baltimore and that Ewell had captured Harrisburg—both untrue—the people of Staunton heard nothing from the newspapers about what was happening, or had happened, in Pennsylvania. Two Augusta-based regiments of infantry, the 5th and the 52nd, and two cavalry units, the 1st and the 14th, were with Lee, so the longing for news was great.[2]

An "extra" from Richmond the next day conveyed old, and therefore encouraging, news about the invasion of the North, what people in the North already knew to be the Battle of Gettysburg. No news appeared on the following day, a Monday. On Tuesday, July 7, the first dispatches arrived, but still carried outdated news. Finally, on July 8, "Passengers by the Richmond train this evening bring a report that Vicksburg with 19,000 men has surrendered to the Yankees!! We were totally unprepared for any such intelligence. Many persons profess to disbelieve it, while others fear that it is true." Waddell read dispatches that Lee had captured 40,000 of the enemy in Pennsylvania. "I am not prepared to believe that he took half the number stated. But what if he has? It will not compensate for the loss of Vicksburg. Better have sent a part of Lee's army to assist Johnston to raise the siege, keeping the other part to guard the line of the Rappahannock, instead of marching into Pennsylvania and capturing over 40,000 Yankees, but arousing the war spirit at the North and recruiting their ranks by means of the instinct which induces men to repel invasion."

Waddell's despair only deepened when news finally trickled in from Gettysburg. "Gen. Lee is certainly falling back, and our 40,000 prisoners seem to have come down to 4000! Thus terminated another attempt at an invasive war—impolitic from the first, as tending only to unite the Northern people and recruit their armies." The next day: "Soldiers wounded at the battle of Gettysburg give fearful accounts of the slaughter of our army. Pickett's Division annihilated. Many persons known to us killed—A disastrous affair. The news comes to us in very unintelligible forms. So far as we now see the tide is running fearfully against us." Even though wounded men began appearing in Staunton, they only added details here and there. A coherent account of events remained elusive. Whatever the full story might prove to be, Waddell could see a bold "contrast between this night and a week ago! Then everything in our affairs looked prosperous.—Now every heart is filled with anxiety. Oh that we could look to God with a proper spirit! May He deliver us!"[3]

☆

THE *FRANKLIN REPOSITORY*, days after the battle, published the account of an eyewitness correspondent. The report in the Republican paper showed admiration for the men on both sides but gloried in the Union victory. The correspondent described, among other defining moments of the battle, what became known as Pickett's Charge. The Rebels came "with war cries and a savage insolence as yet untutored by defeat. They rushed in perfect order across the open field, up to the very muzzles of the guns, which tore lanes through them as they came. But they met men, who were their equals in spirit, and their superiors in tenacity. There never was better fighting since Thermopylae than was done yesterday by our infantry and artillery." After the first wave of Confederates had fallen, "Lee's columns were collected and reformed with magical haste. Within an hour what seemed to be his whole force was again amassed directly in our front, where the contest once more opened. The assault this time was made with a fury even surpassing that of the first."

The Northern correspondent saw a metaphorical meaning in the final charge. "It would seem as if the entire rebel army had resolved itself to a gigantic forlorn hope, and bore in its collective bosom the consciousness that the effort now made was the last and only one that could be made toward retrieving the fortunes of that army, or preventing the inevitable disgrace which hovered over it." The moral for the United States was clear. "All honor to this gallant Army! Nobly and completely has it redeemed the disasters of Fredericksburg and Chancellorsville! And a terrible lesson has it taught the defiant rebel horde who flaunted their banners so insultingly in our faces, and boasted that they could march and plunder and destroy wheresoever they pleased."[4]

The Franklin paper, the next week, eagerly reprinted the "only detailed description of the Battle of Gettysburg," from the Philadelphia *Inquirer*. Paragraph after paragraph of the familiar language of warfare rushed across the page, with soldiers "dashing" from one place to another, "gallant" officers dying at the head of their troops, everyone facing the "peril of death." Men fought "nobly" and "cold steel clashed with cold steel." Units and leaders were singled out for extravagant praise, legends forming within days of battle's end. These "names of the heroes of Gettysburg will ever be handed down to posterity by the side of those who fought, bled and died at Bunker Hill, Monmouth and Lexington."

The paper reproduced in full the congratulatory order from General George Meade to his men, issued after the fighting on the fields of Gettysburg had stopped: "An enemy superior in numbers and flushed with the pride of a successful invasion attempted to overcome or destroy the army. Utterly baffled and defeated, he has now withdrawn from the contest. The privations and fatigues which the army has endured, and the heroic courage and gallantry it has displayed, will be matters of history to be ever remembered."

Meade concluded, however, with a phrase filled with meaning. "Our task is not yet accomplished, and the Commanding General looks to the army, for greater effort to drive from our soil every vestige of the presence of the invader." The Battle of Gettysburg had ended, but the invasion of Pennsylvania, and of the United States, had not. Abraham Lincoln, reading the message from the general, was exasperated. Did Meade not realize that all American soil was "our soil," the soil of the United States?[5]

☆

BRIGADIER GENERAL JOHN IMBODEN played a critical role in the Gettysburg campaign though he did not come near the Devil's Den or Cemetery Ridge. Imboden had been assigned the crucial role of protecting the route to the south, back to Virginia. After destroying stretches of the Baltimore and Ohio Railroad he and his mounted men patrolled the back roads, major high-

Confederate General John D. Imboden

ways, and railroads of southern Pennsylvania, foraging for whatever remained after tens of thousands of hungry men had passed
through. At the same time, Lee told Imboden that "it will be necessary for you to have your men well together and always on the
alert, and to pay strict attention to the safety of the trains, which
are for the present placed under your charge, and upon the safety
of which the operations of this army depend."[6]

By the time of the fighting in Gettysburg, Imboden and the
many others charged with foraging had gathered an enormous
bounty from southern Pennsylvania. When the Confederates
confronted the Union forces at Gettysburg, their wagons of seized
goods—the "trains" to which Lee referred—stretched dozens of
miles behind them.[7]

On July 3, Imboden was called from Chambersburg to Lee's
headquarters at Gettysburg. "When night closed upon the grand
scene our army was repulsed," Imboden recalled. "Silence and
gloom pervaded our camps. We knew that the day had gone
against us, but the extent of the disaster was not known except in

high quarters. The carnage of the day was reported to have been frightful, but our army was not in retreat, and we all surmised that with to-morrow's dawn would come a renewal of the struggle."

By the time Imboden traveled the crowded road from Chambersburg to Gettysburg, though, it had become clear that the Confederate dreams of the Great Invasion had died on the wheat fields and in the peach orchards of Gettysburg. No one knew how many men had been blown apart by artillery shells or sliced apart by bullet or sword, how many were bleeding to death where they lay in the rain, how many would die as gangrene and infection attacked shattered bones, ruptured intestines, and blasted faces. A Virginia officer described the horrific scenes surrounding the headquarters of the Confederate army: corpses were "swollen to twice their original size. Some of them actually burst asunder with the pressure of foul gases and vapors. . . . The odors were nauseating, and so deadly that in a short time we all sickened and we were lying with our mouths close to the ground, most of us vomiting profusely."[8]

Imboden was called to consult with Lee amid this desolation. "A flickering, solitary candle, visible through the open front of a common tent, showed where Generals Lee and Hill were seated on camp stools, with a county map spread upon their knees, and engaged in a low and earnest conversation." Lee asked Imboden to wait at headquarters and at one in the morning Lee finally "came riding alone at a slow walk and evidently wrapped in profound thought." He was exhausted. Imboden "waited for him to speak until the silence became painful and embarrassing, when to break it, and change the current of his thoughts, I remarked in a sympathetic tone, and in allusion to his great fatigue: 'General, this has been a hard day on you.' This attracted his attention. He looked up and replied mournfully: 'Yes, it has been a sad, sad day to us,' and immediately relapsed into his thoughtful mood and attitude." Reflecting on the failed final assault, "he added in a tone almost of agony: 'Too bad! Too bad!! OH! TOO BAD!!!'"[9]

☆

THE SCREAMING SHELLS OF CANNON in the battle could be heard for over a hundred miles. In Chambersburg, Rachel Cormany watched isolated squads of Rebel soldiers passing through on July 3, taking whatever remained after weeks of foraging. A friend asked her to bring her baby with her to get out of harm's way, but "I could not think of leaving now—Samuel might come this way & if I were out there I would not get to see him." The next day, the Fourth of July, "Wild rumors of a dreadful fight are numerous." But she still had no word about what had happened in Gettysburg or how Samuel may have fared.[10]

Samuel Cormany, in a Union cavalry unit, had been kept at the ready throughout the fight and so he had time to make quick notes in his diary, tracing the changing shape of the battle. "The general battle increased in energy—and occasional fierceness," he noted on July 2. The terrific cannonading "was interspersed with musketry—and Charge—yells and everything that goes to making up the indescribable battle of the best men on Earth, seemingly in the Fight to the Finish." In that fight, as Cormany watched many wounded coming in, "it seems as tho our men— The Union Army—is rather overpowered and worsted." On July 3, posted at the right of the Union center, Cormany witnessed "the heaviest canonading I ever have heard—One constant roar with rising and falling inflections." On Cemetery Ridge, he was at the center of the Confederate artillery barrage, enduring hours of incessant shelling. But the Southern artillery, unknown to the

Rebels, was having little effect, its shells often flying over their targets. As Cormany gratefully noted, "Many shells came our way—some really quite near—But it is wonderful how few really made our acquaintance."

On July 4, the Union expected Lee to continue the attack. "Our Regt layed on arms with Pickets out—on the ground where we had put in most of the day—Rather expecting attack momentarily—Rained furiously during the night." Cormany and the rest of the United States Army were ready to fight once again. "We had fed, eaten, and were standing 'to horse' when about 6 ock NEWS CAME—'The Rebs are falling back!'" Cormany went out on horseback to round up Confederates who were foraging or straggling. The rain came again that night. "Crossing the battlefield—Cemitary Hill—The Great Wheat Field Farm, Seminary ridge—and other places where dead men, horses, smashed artillery, were strewn in utter confusion, the Blue and The Grey mixed—Their bodies so bloated—distorted—discolored on account of decomposition having set in—that they were utterly unrecognizable, save by clothing, or things in their pockets—The scene simply beggars description."

Not only had Samuel survived the battle, but he was only miles from his home, his wife, and his baby. He told a corporal that he would be back in the morning and he "slipped away—and was soon making time for home." Samuel had to be careful, for town folk told him "there were still squads of rebs about town" and the "Rebel rear-guard had just left the Diamond" of Chambersburg. Samuel "was the first 'blue coat' they had seen—and the first to bring direct news of the Enemy's defeat—as communications had been cut." He made a point of avoiding the Diamond and headed straight to where Rachel and Cora lodged. "And behold They were at the door—had been watching the Reb Rear leaving town—and Oh! The surprise and delight thus to meet after the awful battle they had been listening to for passing days."

As Samuel joyfully admitted, "To attempt to describe my joy and feelings at meeting and greeting my dear little family must prove a failure." As Rachel told her diary, "little Willie Wampler came running as fast as he could to tell me a soldier had come to see me & sure enough when I got to the door Mr Cormany just rode up. I was so very glad to see him that I scarcely knew how to act. He was very dirty & sweaty so he took a bath & changed clothes before he got himself dressed." Samuel noted that "we spent the P.M and evening very sweetly and pleasantly, but only we had a few too many inquiring callers." Everyone wanted to know what history was unfolding all around them.[11]

☆

SUBSEQUENT GENERATIONS OF HISTORIANS *would eventually agree that Lee's army had been devastated because the Confederacy's poor coordination, unclear orders, and unfulfilled expectations had met with superior position, superior numbers, and superior leadership on the part of the Union army. Lee, forced into a battle in a place and time not of his choosing, had nevertheless relentlessly pressed his officers and his men beyond what they could accomplish. Though one assault after another seemed ready to break through, the Union managed to stop each offensive at a crucial moment. About 50,000 men from both sides were killed, wounded, captured, or declared missing in the three days of fighting. The Confederates lost 28,000 men to the 23,000 of the United States.*

For all the men, momentum, and reputation consumed at Gettysburg, the Confederate command knew that the wagons of food, livestock, and supplies that waited in Franklin County could help redeem the truncated and costly campaign. The bold incursion into Pennsylvania had dragged the war, at least for a few weeks, away from the ravished farms and towns of Virginia to the pristine landscape above the Mason-Dixon Line. If John Imboden and his men could lead the miles of wagons back into the Valley of Virginia at least that part of the invasion would be salvaged. The Army of Northern Virginia, for all its losses, could fight again, prolong the war into the North's election year to follow, and force the United States to continue a war that could yet bring down President Lincoln.

Long before the Battle of Gettysburg had erupted, leaders of both Union and the Confederacy had already calculated lines of supply and retreat, of provision and transport, from southern Pennsylvania. Generals and officers prepared multiple scenarios, multiple contingencies, simultaneously planning for replenishment, retrenchment, and retreat. The meaning and consequence of the battle had not been settled when the Confederate casualties had been thrown under dirt, dragged into makeshift hospitals, laid into blood-soaked wagons, or marched into prison camps. The final accounting of the Battle of Gettysburg could be recorded only when the Confederates either escaped from Pennsylvania or had been destroyed there.

☆

JOHN IMBODEN RECEIVED HIS ORDERS from Robert E. Lee: "We must return to Virginia. As many of our poor wounded as possible must be taken home. I have sent for you because your men are fresh, to guard the trains back to Virginia," Lee told Imboden. "The duty will be arduous, responsible, and dangerous, for I am afraid you will be harassed by the enemy's cavalry." The commander could offer little help despite the importance of the mission. "I can spare you as much artillery as you require, but no other troops, as I shall need all I have to return to the Potomac by a different route from yours. All the transportation and all the care of the wounded will be intrusted to you. You will recross the mountain by the Chambersburg road, and then proceed to Williamsport by any route you deem best, without halting. There rest and feed your animals, then ford the river, and make no halt till you reach Winchester, where I will again communicate with you."

Imboden knew what those words meant. He would have to lead miles of wagons, thousands of wagons, with wooden wheels rimmed by iron, pulled by mules and oxen down muddy roads, across steep mountain passes, in the middle of the night. Though Imboden would have artillery, he would be a slow-moving target, ponderous and vulnerable to fast-moving Union cavalry. "All the transportation" meant that Imboden would have to move the miles of wagons that carried the supplies the Confederates had taken in their weeks in Pennsylvania. If Imboden could not move the trains fast enough then all that the Confederates had fought for in the invasion—and maybe in the war—would be lost.[12]

One phrase in Lee's orders to Imboden was particularly chilling: "all the care of the wounded will be intrusted to you." Caring for wounded men in the Civil War was a horrible prospect even when doctors and nurses had the best hospitals, supplies, and conditions the era offered. Caring for wounded men with no resources at all, moving them when they could not stand to be moved, when they begged not to be moved, was agonizing. Everyone, including the wounded men themselves, knew it.[13]

The final phrases of Lee's order—"proceed to Williamsport by any route you deem best, without halting"—worried Imboden as well. Williamsport was in Maryland, on the Potomac River, forty-five miles to the southwest of Gettysburg. There would be no Confederate cavalry clearing the way before him or guarding places where Federal cavalry or artillery might descend on his distended lines. "Without halting" meant that the agony of the wounded could not be tended to, that the animals pulling the wagons would fall along the way from injury, hunger, or exhaustion, that men would have no chance to cook food or take rest from the desperate march. If the Potomac River was high, swollen by the summer rains, Imboden would somehow have to get thousands of wagons, many of them filled with bleeding and shattered men, to the other side.

John Imboden, untrained for military command except for his service with the militia in peacetime Staunton, did not enjoy the respect or favor of the professional soldiers who made up much of Lee's command—J. E. B. Stuart, in particular. Now, many lives of the men with the Army of Northern Virginia rested with him. Imboden, accustomed to ranging where and when he wished, now found himself with a strict mission.

A particularly important member of Imboden's team was Major John Alexander Harman, one of five brothers from Augusta who fought in the Confederate army. Before the war Harman had been a prosperous stage line owner in Augusta, owning eight enslaved men and seven enslaved women. Like Imboden, Harman had been a well-connected Democrat, an investor in local businesses, an active leader of the militia, a fervent secessionist, and an early and eager enlistee.

John Harman had served as Stonewall Jackson's chief quartermaster until the general's death a few weeks earlier and remained in that position with the corps under Richard S. Ewell. Harman "seemed to understand the management of teamsters and wagons as [Jackson] did that of soldiers," one observer noted. Harman had grown famous for riding among wagons, kicking the mules, and "pouring out a volume of oaths that would have excited the admiration of the most scientific mule-driver." Swear as the mule drivers did, their curses always fell "far below the major's

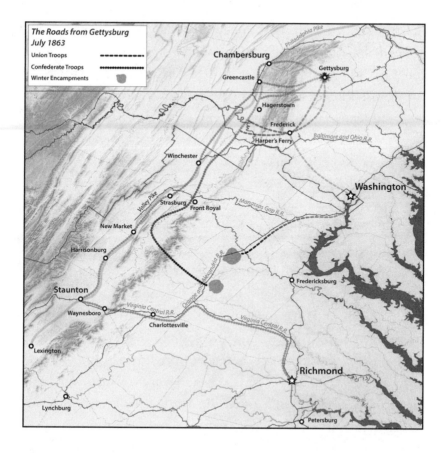

The Roads from Gettysburg
July 1863

Union Troops
Confederate Troops
Winter Encampments

standard." Harman would be responsible for driving the wagons through the mountains between Gettysburg and Williamsport, and then getting them across the Potomac.[14]

Imboden and Harman decided they would follow the shortest route through the mountains, along the accurately named Pine Stump Road. That route would take them to Greencastle in southern Franklin County and then into Maryland. Unlike the turnpike between Gettysburg and Chambersburg, the Pine Stump route was not firm and smooth. Indeed, the oldest road in Franklin and considered among its worst, the Pine Stump road, alternately filled with rocks and swampy lowlands, ascended and descended sharply through the mountains. Imboden and Harman could not know when or if or how Meade might send troops to cut them off before they reached sanctuary, to attack them from their vulnerable flanks or rear. Everything else had to be sacrificed to make it across the river before the Union could pin the Confederates on the banks of the Potomac.

As Imboden, on the Fourth of July, gathered the wagon trains and the artillery around him, "the very windows of heaven" seemed to open. Rain fell so hard that it looked as if "the whole face of the earth was covered with water," Imboden wrote. "The meadows became small lakes; raging streams ran across the road in every depression of the ground; wagons, ambulances, and artillery carriages filled the roads and fields in all directions." As the afternoon fell into night, and the seventeen-mile-long wagon train creaked west through the mountains, "the storm increased in fury every moment. Canvas was no protection against it, and the poor wounded, lying upon the hard, naked boards of the wagon-bodies, were drenched by the cold rain. Horses and mules were blinded and maddened by the storm, and became almost unmanageable. The roar of the winds and waters made it almost impossible to communicate orders."

Imboden rode up and down the road alongside the train, barely able to see in the rain and dark. What he could see, and hear, was horrifying even for a man who had witnessed so much suffering. "In the wagons were men wounded and mutilated in every conceivable way. Some had their legs shattered by a shell or Minie ball; some were shot through their bodies; others had arms torn to shreds; some had received a ball in the face, or a jagged piece of shell had lacerated their heads." In the frantic and disorganized wake of the battle at Gettysburg, "scarcely one in a hundred had received adequate surgical aid. Many had been without food for thirty-six hours. The irragged, bloody, and dirty clothes, all clotted and hardened with blood, were rasping the tender, inflamed lips of their gaping wounds."

The wagons in which these men had been loaded had not been built as ambulances. "Very few of the wagons had even straw in them, and all were without springs." The rock-filled mountain road made things worse. "The jolting was enough to have killed sound, strong men. From nearly every wagon, as the horses trotted on, such cries and shrieks as these greeted the ear:

'O God! why can't I die?'

'My God! will no one have mercy and kill me and end my misery?'

'Oh! stop one minute and take me out and leave me to die on the roadside.'

'I am dying! I am dying! My poor wife, my dear children! what will become of you?'

Some were praying; others were uttering the most fearful oaths and execrations that despair could wring from them in their agony. Occasionally a wagon would be passed from which only low, deep moans and sobs could be heard."

There was no one to help the wounded and dying men. Except for the drivers of the wagons and some guards posted every half mile along the way, "all were wounded and helpless in that vast train of misery." Imboden knew that, for the greater good, "no help could be rendered to any of the sufferers. On, on; we *must* move on." With the storm and darkness unabated throughout the night "there was no time even to fill a canteen with water for a dying man."

As long and terrible as the night was, Imboden gratefully noted, "yet in it was our safety, for no enemy would dare attack us when he could not distinguish friend from foe. We knew that when day broke upon us we would be harassed by bands of cavalry hanging on our flanks. Therefore our aim was to go as far as possible under cover of the night, and so we kept on." By daybreak on July 5, they were spread out through southern Franklin County, straggling toward the border with Maryland.[15]

☆

CONFEDERATE DEAD AND WOUNDED filled the towns and farms of Franklin County. "It is frightful how those poor wounded rebels are left to suffer," Rachel Cormany wrote in her diary. "They are taken in large 4 horse waggons—wounds undressed—nothing to eat. Some are only about 4 miles from town & those that are here are as dirty and lousy as they well can be. The condition of those poor rebels all along from Getysburg to as far as they have come yet is reported dreadful. I am told they just beg the people along the road to help them—many have died by the way."[16]

By the next day, the outlines of the situation had become clearer. On July 6, William Heyser, a sixty-seven-year-old banker, active Democrat, and leading citizen of Chambersburg, wrote in his diary that "we hear a decisive battle was fought at Gettysburg. That Lee is withdrawn towards the Potomac and that enormous amounts of supplies and prisoners have been captured. The news gave rise to the ringing of bells and general convivial in the streets. It appears the contest raged for 3 days and was the most desperate of the war."

Despite the celebration, Heyser and his neighbors recognized that the battle's consequences were still unfolding. "Reports that the Pine Stump Road is filled with broken Rebel wagons and caissons, filled with ammunition much of which is thrown in the mud with a view of destroying it. Also many dead and wounded lying by the roadside, indicating a hasty retreat." Heyser spoke with the head of the Confederate hospital rapidly assembled in Chambersburg. "He tells me most of the best men of the South were in this battle, now most of them gone." Lee had indeed lost a third of his officers. Heyser warned that "If Mead allows him to escape, it will indeed be folly."[17]

In the meantime, the suffering along the Confederate retreat horrified even their enemies. Jacob Snyder of southern Franklin County woke in the middle of the night at the sound of rumbling wagons, muffled voices, and driving rain. Lighting a lantern and going to his front porch, Snyder became like a beacon to the walking wounded alongside the trains. "In less than 15 minutes," he would recall, "the large hall of my house and the front yard were filled with wounded Confederate soldiers." The men begged for help. "Water!" they cried, "give us water!"[18]

The daylight revealed the horror of the procession. "No one with any feelings of pity," the Revered J. C. Smith of Greencastle wrote, "will ever want to see such a sight even once in a lifetime." Men injured days ago had gone untended. "Those wounded in the arms would tear away the garment and expose the wounded part. Such areas—[were] swollen to twice or thrice their natural size—red and angry." Smith had a pump in his front yard, and as the wounded men passed "one would place his wounded member under the spout while another would pump cold water on

Unfinished Confederate grave

the sore. Then he would do a like service to his comrade. Thus, the pumps were going all that day." Other Greencastle residents came out of their homes with axes and broke the wheels of several of the passing wagons. Some of the attackers were captured and taken with the trains to the south.[19]

All along, John Imboden and his troops watched for assaults from Meade, but Meade's men faced the same challenges as the Confederates. They, too, had to tend to their dead and wounded in the relentless rain. They, too, were hungry, for they had fought at Gettysburg while their supply trains were still twenty-five miles away. While Meade recognized that he needed to destroy Lee's army, and mobilized the units to do so, he was beset by harrowing problems of his own.

☆

THE CONFEDERATE TRAINS MADE it to the Potomac without serious challenge from the United States Army. At the river, though, they faced what appeared to be certain destruction: the rains had driven the river ten feet higher than men, animals, and wagons could ford. Imboden took over the small town of Williamsport, seizing every building, public and private. "Straw was obtained on the neighboring farms," while "the wounded were removed from the wagons and housed; the citizens were all put to cooking and the army surgeons to dressing wounds. The dead were selected from the train—for many had perished on the way—and were decently buried." Imboden admitted that "our situation was frightful. We had over 10,000 animals and all the wagons of General Lee's army under our charge, and all the wounded that could be brought from Gettysburg. Our supply of provisions consisted of a few wagon loads of flour and a small lot of cattle. My effective force was only about 2,100 men and twenty-odd field pieces. We did not know where our army was; the river could not be crossed; and small parties of cavalry were still hovering around."

The only hope came in the form of "two small boats and a small wire rope stretched across the river, which owing to the force of the swollen current broke several times during the day." As a Union prisoner with Imboden's caravan later put it, "My hopes rose with the river, which was a seething flood, boiling over its banks; it seemed impossible to get us across the Potomac now."[20] The Confederates would have to transport thousands of wagons, thousands of men, and thousands of livestock across the roaring Potomac, two small ferries at a time. Imboden ordered three out of every four wagon drivers to climb off their wagons, arming the teamsters with guns from men too disabled to use them, to cover the teeming crowd of men and animals. They had no earthworks or any other cover against United States troops that might assault them in their vulnerable position. Fortunately for the Confederates, they did possess artillery, which they opened against a Union force coming from the east, and Stuart's cavalry surprised that force with an attack on its flanks, driving them from the field. Later, reinforcements from Lee arrived and the weak wagon train finally had protection.

Imboden acknowledged that "a bold charge at any time before sunset would have broken our feeble lines, and we should all have fallen an easy prey to the Federals." As it was, it took sixteen hours for all the wagons to reach Williamsport and to be slowly ferried across, two wagons at a time. Livestock forced to swim across the Potomac often drowned, with thousands of sheep and seven hundred cattle swept downstream to Harpers Ferry, gathering in mountains of rotting flesh.[21]

The rest of Lee's army, which had been positioned at the western base of the South Mountain range, keeping Meade in place while Imboden's wagons escaped Pennsylvania, now snaked its way to Williamsport, foraging the whole way. The rain did not stop. Meade, realizing that Lee had decided to retreat rather than to renew the fight at Gettysburg, dispatched troops to try to cut the Confederates off at the Potomac, taking a route to the east of the mountains. But Meade's men arrived at Williamsport only to see the last squadron of Confederate cavalry as it finished crossing the river.

Lee then made it to Falling Waters by a different route before the pursuing United States troops, only to discover that a pontoon bridge he expected had been destroyed by the enemy days before. Lee rapidly built an impressive nine-mile defense line near Hagerstown while his engineers constructed a new bridge. In sixty-eight hours, the Confederates opened an 800-foot bridge supported by twenty-six pontoons. Despite attacks by the United States troops, Lee and his men made it across the Potomac without serious losses. Only "extraordinary good fortune" had "thus saved all of General Lee's trains"—and, Imboden thought, the loss of Richmond in the fall of 1863. "On such small circumstances do the affairs of nations sometimes turn."[22]

☆

A DAY OR TWO after the main armies had left Gettysburg, Abraham Essick, a Lutheran minister, visited the battlefield with a fellow parishioner to help. "When at length the welcome news came that the enemy were retreating Bro. Raby and myself went on foot to Gettysburg, taking with us such things as we could carry to assist the wounded soldiers. It was nearing night of the Sabbath when we reached the village." As the two men approached the battlefield the next morning they "saw sights which I cannot describe. Dead men and horses already far gone into decay, muskets, knapsacks, broken caissons, and cannon, etc etc. lay everywhere. During these days the entire stock of provision in the whole county for many miles, was exhausted. The railroad was broken up and bridges burned, so that we were cut off from any immediate supply." People from surrounding counties were bringing in food and other supplies for the civilians of the area. "My church was occupied for a hospital and it was several weeks before it could be used for religious services. For many weeks after the battle there was a stench filling the air, which was almost unendurable."[23]

"The brief, disastrous career of Gen. Lee on Northern soil was marked by the most reckless inhumanity to his own unfortunate warriors," bitterly charged the *Repository*. "Even when flushed with the high hope of success, those who died from disease, or skirmishes, were buried, if at all, in rude holes scarcely large enough to hide the bodies, and his sick were left in Chambersburg without medical or other supplies, and that too after he had robbed our Druggists of all medicines, and destroyed our hospital goods." After the disaster at Gettysburg, the Chambersburg paper raged, Lee "commenced his retreat without even trying to bury his dead or minister to his thousands of wounded who could not be removed. To his foe he left the lifeless forms of five thousand of his troops for sepulchre, and full ten thousand of those most seriously wounded were allowed to lie on the gory field to writhe in agonies or die, unless the humanity of strangers, whose homes they sought to desolate should in mercy care for them."[24]

☆

JEDEDIAH HOTCHKISS was in a position to see the unfolding story more clearly than most. He described the climactic charge at Gettysburg honestly but bloodlessly: there was a ridge, "crowned by a cemetery, enclosed by a substantial wall," he wrote his wife, and "their whole army was there, formidably entrenched & posted as we advanced on drove them to their works & though our men advanced boldly to the works & stormed them, some getting in to them, but the enemy repulsed us, & though we surrounded them our efforts to take the heights were unavailing & our loss was very great, both in officers & men." On July 7, Hotchkiss told Sara of the retreat through the mountains, of the close call at Williamsport, and of building the pontoon bridge so quickly.[25]

Hotchkiss assured his wife the week after the battle that "the talk of the Yankee papers about the routed & demoralized condition of our army is the purest of nonsense." And then he told a story the Confederates would tell themselves for decades afterward. "We could have remained at Gettysburg if we had seen fit—the enemy did not come out to attack us & only followed when they found we were gone—making a feeble attack upon our rear some 8 miles from Gettysburg—which our rear guard repulsed." Hotchkiss admitted that the enemy had "destroyed two or three hundred of our wagons—a third part perhaps of those we had captured from them since we started—a few pawns lost on the chess board of war."

Though the invasion of Pennsylvania, Jed admitted to Sara, had not been all that the Confederates had hoped, "today the Army of Northern Va. stands, as it has always stood, the sure defense of the heart of the Confederacy & though disaster may befall our arms elsewhere it has not as yet befallen them here & by God's blessing we hope never may." By this time news of the fall of Vicksburg had spread throughout the North and the South. Hotchkiss acknowledged the loss, but Vicksburg "is not the Confederacy & freedom does not die with her."[26]

☆

WE MIGHT IMAGINE a map of all the places entangled in the cause and consequence of the battle that erupted at Gettysburg. Such a map would stretch from Richmond to Washington to Harrisburg, where governors and presidents tried to comprehend vast processes and events beyond their sight and their control. It would stretch from the camps of the Confederacy and the Union army in Pennsylvania far to the west, where Vicksburg was finally falling on the very days battle raged in Pennsylvania. The map would stretch into the hinterlands of Pennsylvania, Maryland, and Virginia, where African-Americans fled the Confederates, only sometimes successfully. It would extend into the editors' offices of both the Republi-

cans and the Democrats as they sought to make political advantage from Meade's triumph over Lee or Meade's failure to destroy Lee's army.

The map would trace the vast areas through which both armies had passed, where their hunger had stripped the land bare. The map would trace the graves of Confederates all along the road back to the hospitals of Staunton and Richmond. It would map the homes, churches, and stores where the shattered young men of both armies suffered and died; a map coloring much of the United States and much of the Confederacy would show where they were mourned. The map would show the way the news spread, haltingly and then in a rush, across the telegraph lines and railroads of both the North and the South. The map would trace the paths of both armies as they reconstituted themselves to fight again.

Such a map would have to stretch decades into the future to record all the possibilities destroyed at Gettysburg, all the consequences of lives cut short or disabled, all the histories that might have unfolded had they not been forever stilled in those few days.

☆

STAUNTON HAD BECOME a vast hospital, a place where men came to heal or die before they were passed on to the even larger hospitals in Richmond, sent back to the army, or buried in the gravesites spreading around the town. Captured soldiers were marched through Staunton before they were loaded on the cars for Libby Prison. Newspapers from the North and the South were swapped at the railroad station next to the American Hotel.[27]

Joseph Waddell did not like what he was seeing from his vantage point in Staunton. "The report concerning Vicksburg fully confirmed," he told his diary on July 11. "I have no heart for the details which have reached us." Things were just as bad closer to home. "Great solicitude felt in regard to Gen. Lee's army.—A fearful list of casualties among the soldiers from this county. If there is the same proportion from other quarters, the army must be greatly reduced." Waddell talked with a series of wounded men from the front, getting a different story from each one of them as they had left the battlefield at different times, the story getting worse with each telling.[28]

As the days passed, the mood of Waddell and his neighbors vacillated. By the 17th, with John Imboden back in his home town with 4,000 Union prisoners, "the public mind begins to recover from the blow received by the fall of Vicksburg," but people were still wrestling with the meaning of Lee's failed invasion and "there is great diversity of opinion as to the policy of Gen. Lee's movement into Pennsylvania." Waddell had dinner with Imboden, an old friend. The general confided that he was "very sick of the war." Waddell noted dryly in his diary that Imboden had been "keen enough for it at the start."[29]

Staunton remained thronged for days with wounded men from the Army of Northern Virginia. "The condition of many of them—weary, famishing and suffering in various ways—would be heart-rending, if we were not so accustomed to the spectacle." In July alone, the hospital made from the former asylum for the deaf, dumb, and blind in Staunton treated 8,428 soldiers, casualties of the invasion that was to have ended the war.[30]

The Staunton newspapers of mid- to late-July were composed mainly of lists of casualties, like straggling columns of a retreating army: twenty-three names of the 52nd, 37 from the 10th, 68 from the 5th, and 73 from the 25th. The long gray columns listed the nature and severity of wounds, pushing aside other news. An account of the sacrifices of Pickett's men provided the only reflection on the battle at Gettysburg.

To constitute the official record, the officers of each unit recorded their role in the great battle, trying to encapsulate life and death in ritualized description and encomium. The men of the Stonewall Brigade had fought, their leader proudly claimed, with the same bravery "on any of the hard-fought fields which have been marked by their dead. Their efforts not being crowned with the usual success, they retired stubbornly from the field, manifesting a willingness to hurl themselves upon the foe again, if so ordered."[31] A third of the men who had come with Lee into Pennsylvania fell, with 24,500 casualties on the march north and on the retreat. Nearly half of the 171 regiments lost senior officers.[32]

☆

THE FRANKLIN PAPERS DEVOTED entire pages to recounting the glories of Gettysburg. Men from the county had played their part well, their officers reported. The losses from the 107th Pennsylvania Infantry were much like others: Sergeant William H. Davis was sent to the hospital in York and would later be hospitalized four more times over the coming year until he finally received a discharge on a surgeon's certificate. Jacob Gish, who had enlisted early in the war and fought at Bull Run, Antietam, and Fredericksburg, was wounded in the right leg on the first day of Gettysburg and sent to the hospital, where he would remain for the next five months. John Hughes, who had deserted twice before, once as late as April, was wounded in the face. William Shueman, a twenty-six-year-old blacksmith, never recovered from the wounds he received at Gettysburg and died in November. Jacob Horn was simply declared missing in action on July 1. These life-changing and life-ending events were rendered nearly invisible among the tens of thousands of casualties of Gettysburg. Individual sacrifice and glory were lost in the noise and blood.[33]

☆

DESPITE THE SMELL OF DEATH in the air, the people of south-central Pennsylvania began recovery. "The sudden change made by the report of Lee's defeat and the capture of Vicksburg was visible on every face, old and young," Alexander McClure recalled. "The terrible strain was ended, the invasion was repulsed, and the many thousands of people in the Cumberland Valley, scattered all through the interior and eastern part of the State, with their stock and other valuables, began a general movement homeward." In all honesty, McClure (whose fine farm was the object of pointed attack and destruction) wrote, things were not as bad as many had feared. "Many of the farmers had left their golden wheat fields ready for the reaper, but fortunately the Confederates expected to occupy the valley and harvest it, and no destruction of the grain fields was permitted." Furthermore, "in a few weeks industrial operations in the shops and valleys were very generally resumed." The army "rapidly repaired the railway and telegraph lines."[34]

"The implements of war fast disappearing by souvenir seekers," William Heyser noted only days after the battlefield in Gettysburg had been abandoned by the armies. "Soon the cultivators plow will cover it all and put an end to military glory."[35] Jacob Hoke of Chambersburg, along with "a considerable number of our citizens," visited the battlefield at Gettysburg on July 6. "Conveyances were scarce and in demand, and the majority had to walk" the twenty-five miles, but Hoke, a thirty-eight-year-old prosperous dry goods merchant, was able to secure a wagon. Along the way, he and his companions saw many exhausted Confederate troops and they picked up one who begged a ride. This North Carolinian "told us the usual story of nearly all the men we conversed with from his State that he was opposed to the war, was in favor of the Union, had been dragged away from his family, and was resolved never again to fight in the cause he detested. Of his sincerity we had not a doubt."

When Hoke and his friends approached within about five miles of Gettysburg, they saw a large gathering of tents, a Confederate hospital. "These tents and the woods around were filled with wounded men. From this place to G'burg, every house, barn and other outbuilding was improvised into a hospital. Men wounded and maimed in almost every conceivable way lay along the roadside, in yards and gardens. Some were propped against the houses, or supported against the backs of chairs with an arm or leg off, and some having lost both arms." When Hoke arrived in Gettysburg he and his companions visited the court house and there they saw that United States soldiers as well as Confederate soldiers were suffering. "Every available place in the rooms, halls, vestibule and stairway was crowded with suffering heroes. Many had lost an arm or a leg. Groans of agony were heard on every side. The churches and other public buildings were also crowded with wounded men. The amputating tables were yet standing, and arms and legs were thrown indiscriminately upon piles and covered with earth."

Early the next morning, the group visited the battlefield itself. Hoke picked up a blood-stained Bible, next to the body and dismembered leg of a Confederate soldier. He was fascinated by the Bible, which "had been cut nearly in two by some missile, the irregular edges and angles of which corresponded with both the marks upon the Bible and the soldier's leg." Hoke and his companions "divided the leaves among us, and sometimes afterwards, while in the city of New York, I gave a number of them to a friend, who placed them on sale at the great Fair held there for the benefit of the Sanitary Commission. A minister of one of the city churches, to whom my friend presented one of these leaves, took it into his pulpit and took his text from it." Other civilians gathered their own keepsakes. "Bullets could be gathered everywhere, and we saw persons engaged in collecting them by the bucketfull."[36]

☆

FOR GENERATIONS, people have argued about whether Gettysburg was a turning point in the American Civil War. Because it was the only major battle fought on Northern soil, because the Confederates had been so strong before, because the losses were so enormous, and because it coincided with the victory of the United States at Vicksburg, people at the time found great significance in the battle. Northerners and Southerners would later agree that Cemetery Ridge defined the "high-water mark" of the Confederacy.[37]

But such convenient landmarks mislead as much as they orient. Hindsight reminds us that as many months of war would be waged after the battle as before, with as many lives lost and as much at stake. At the time, the defining role of Gettysburg was even less obvious. The Army of Northern Virginia was badly wounded there, but it did not die of those wounds. The Army of the Potomac did triumph there, but many battles lay before it. Robert E. Lee resupplied his army and shifted the ground of battle, but paid an enormous cost in the death and suffering of his men. George Meade accomplished the main task before him, driving Lee out of Pennsylvania, but lost many men and failed to trap the Rebel army beyond its home base.

Though Gettysburg did not lead the Army of Northern Virginia or the white populace of the South to lose heart, and though the Confederates claimed moral and logistical triumph from the Great Invasion, everyone in the South knew they had not won an actual victory at Gettysburg. They had left the field first, and in the Civil War that constituted a defeat.

The war was, in large part, a war to win and control space, to define boundaries. Territory held great material as well as symbolic weight, for territory fed the armies, contained the enslaved population, and channeled the railroads and rivers. Lee had tried and failed to control an important part of the territory of the United States; though he always knew he would fall back at some point, he had hoped to hold part of Pennsylvania longer than he did, long enough to shake the faith of Northerners in the leadership of Abraham Lincoln, long enough to allow the farms and people of Virginia to replenish.

The United States, by contrast, had driven the Confederates from the North's homeland. The Federals had rallied their largest army from a series of defeats in Virginia over the previous six months. The Union had shown just how difficult it would be for the Confederates to invade any part of the North, much less take a major city. The Union had found new heroes and a new sense of their own resolve and abilities. And they had given Abraham Lincoln a victory that may well have been necessary for his reelection the following year.

People at the time, Union and Confederate, saw turning points day after day. This loss or that victory, they thought, might be the beginning of the end they feared or of the end they wanted. There is no difficulty in finding such sentiments and any of them might have proven to be correct in retrospect. Yet there was no denying that the Civil War remained profoundly in doubt in August 1863, when the Army of Northern Virginia and the Army of the Potomac returned to almost exactly the same places they had occupied before the Great Invasion.

☆

EVEN AS THE UNION ARMY dragged the dead into piles on the fields of Gettysburg, sorting men as best they could by the color of their coats, the relentless rain obscuring the nightmarish scenes of battle, thousands of angry men, many of them immigrants, rioted in the streets of New York City. They rioted, they said, because they had had enough of a draft that spared the rich while ripping poor men from their families. They rioted because they hated the faceless black people they blamed for the war, including the anonymous men they hanged from street lights, the blameless children burned in an orphanage. The United States rushed soldiers by rail from the bleeding fields of Pennsylvania to the lawless streets of the nation's largest city. The riots in New York City in early July 1863, killing over a hundred people, injuring thousands, and forcing black Americans to flee, testified to the divisions that threatened to undermine the Union cause even at a moment of triumph.

Both newspapers of Franklin County resolutely ignored the riots, each for its own reasons. With every column of both papers filled with thrilling stories of the great victory at Gettysburg, local Democrats did not want to call attention to the role of their party leaders and editors in the destructive riot only a few hours away. The Republicans, for their part, did not want to tarnish the Union cause by talking of the fury against the draft and against black Americans.

To the editors in Augusta County, by contrast, the New York City riots proved that the Confederate setbacks at Gettysburg and Vicksburg only delayed the collapse of the Northern cause. In papers whose other columns were filled with lists of the names of local men dead and wounded at Gettysburg and with grim news of faraway Vicksburg, the editors made the most of the news from the North: "The great event of the last week, more interesting than the result of battles, occurred among a foreign and hostile people" the Staunton *Spectator* proclaimed.

The Lincoln administration had announced a conscription act in March 1863 that mandated the registration of all males between the ages of twenty and forty-five, including aliens who planned to become citizens. Men could evade the draft by paying $300 or finding a substitute, offering ways for wealthy men to avoid fighting. Such loopholes for the rich had driven much of the outrage in the riots, the Augusta paper noted with satisfaction. "Forcible and successful resistance to Lincoln's draft has been made in the city of New York. 'The good time coming,' which we have been so long hopefully and anxiously expecting, is about to arrive. The signs which indicate the terrible social and political revolution which will soon take place in the North are now manifesting themselves." The paper quoted the details with relish: "the streets barricaded, buildings burned, stores closed, private dwellings plundered, all large manufacturing establishments closed, and every branch of business suspended."[38]

From the Army of Northern Virginia, Jedediah Hotchkiss read of the riots in Northern newspapers and reassured his wife Sara in Augusta that "you will soon see, no doubt, showing that time long predicted of opposition at home to Lincoln's domination may have already come." Two days later, Hotchkiss drew the final moral: "so you see the reputed 'victories' of the 'Union' army have not made the North a unit, and if you had seen, as we saw in Pa., the hatred of parties to one another, you would readily believe they never would become a unit."[39]

As grimly satisfying as the days of Northern riots were, though, their consequence proved disappointing to the Confederacy. The United States War Department issued an order saying that though the draft had been "interrupted" in "one or two cities," it would continue until completion.[40]

☆

WHILE PEOPLE NORTH AND SOUTH pieced together the news of Vicksburg, Gettysburg, and New York City, another event in the summer of 1863 told yet a different kind of story.

Forty-five men living in Franklin County in 1860 enlisted in the 54th Massachusetts, the most famous of all United States Colored Troops units, in April and May 1863. The 54th claimed both Lewis Douglass, the son of Frederick Douglass, and a well-connected young colonel from Boston, Robert Gould Shaw. Eleven men born in the county but living elsewhere in 1860 also enlisted with the 54th. Thirteen more Franklin men joined the 55th Massachusetts, constituted from the overflow from the 54th.[41]

David Demus, a twenty-five-year-old farm hand, had lived and worked on the farm of a white family, the Pensingers, before the war. He had recently married Mary Jane Christy, a twenty-year-old farm laborer living at home with her father and four brothers: Jacob, Samuel, Joseph, and William. Along with David's brother George, these young men from Mercersburg, just a few miles over the Mason-Dixon Line, eagerly enlisted in the United States Colored Troops. They were promised a fifty-dollar bounty, the same thirteen dollars a month white soldiers received, and eight dollars a month for their families. These young people had no property but had acquired enough literacy to write letters to one another.

Soon after their training in Boston, in the spring of 1863 the men of the 54th Massachusetts were transported to the islands and rivers of the Atlantic Coast, largely abandoned by white Southerners under military pressure by the United States. There, the soldiers, serving under white officers, burned the town of Darien, Georgia, after they had stripped it of all that was useful; they also seized food and livestock on St. Simon's Island.

In late June and early July, while Confederates were sweeping through Franklin County during their invasion, members of the Demus and Christy families were preparing for what promised to be a hard battle outside of Charleston. The Confederate installation at Fort Wagner, guarding the mouth of Charleston harbor, had come under attack by the United States Army and "the fall of Fort Wagner ends in the fall of Charleston," a paper from that city warned. The United States Army, from a beachhead on Morris Island, launched a bold assault across the narrow beaches that protected the fort, ending in desperate fighting with bayonets at the parapets.[42]

The 54th bravely held off a Confederate attack, giving white allies in another unit a chance to regroup. The largely untested black soldiers suffered for lack of water and food as they prepared to take Morris Island, the strategic position at Charleston's harbor. The island proved little more than a sandbar, erosion narrowing it so that waves washed across its entirety.

The Federal leadership decided, after the pleas of Colonel Shaw, to allow the 54th to lead the charge. The attack began at 7:45 in the evening of July 18, the 645 soldiers told to use their bayonets in hand-to-hand fighting rather than to waste fire from their guns against the walls of the fort, armored by sand and palmetto logs, surrounded by moats and rifle pits.

Lining up on the narrow beach, the soldiers of the 54th began marching the sixteen hundred feet to the parapets of Fort Wagner, with orders to move double-time the last half of the attack. The Confederate defenders opened fire with devastating canister shot that shattered the Union lines, but the soldiers pushed on to the top of the fort's walls, planted the United States flag at the parapet, and fought the Rebel soldiers for an hour before being forced to fall back. The 54th Massachusetts lost 40 percent of its men, including their colonel as well as two company commanders and 31 enlisted men. Another 11 officers and 135 enlisted men suffered wounds, while 92 were listed as missing. "The splendid 54th is cut to pieces," Sergeant Major Lewis Douglass wrote his father.

The dead of the 54th, their white colonel buried among them in a mass grave, became a symbol of the bravery of African-

American soldiers. The Confederates had not expected black men to fight, face to face, against white men, and white people in the North had wondered about that capacity as well. With news of Fort Wagner building on news of bravery by black soldiers at Port Hudson and Milliken's Bend on the Mississippi River as well— and directly following the draft riots—many white people in the North elevated their expectations of the United States Colored Troops. The change did not come overnight, and the failure of any black regiments would still be seen as the failure of black soldiers in general, but the sacrifices of the 54th advanced a cause far greater than the fate of one fort.[43]

David Demus wrote his wife Mary Jane back in Franklin County following the battle. After repeating his frequent request that she write him and send her photographic "likeness," Demus mentioned almost in passing that "i am in the hosply i Was in the battle Was sot in the head." A few days later, William Christy, more comfortable with pen and paper, wrote his sister to tell the story more fully. On the 16th of July, on St. James Island, the Confederates attacked. "We all arose and formed a lin the artilery opened fier on them and drov them bak." The 54th left the island that night and landed the next day on Morris Island where they "made a charge" on Fort Wagner. "We lost agrate meny men," he reported; the Rebels, he said, were "tow harde for us." William told Mary Jane that their brother Jacob had been wounded in the arm. Other men from Franklin County had been killed or was "ammonks the missin." William himself came close to being killed, "struck on the [breast] plate with a ball and that was all that save me." It was through "gods will that the ball struck the plate if i live to git home i will fetch the plate home me if i can."[44]

Despite his own remarkable story, William saved his strongest language for an event far from Fort Wagner: the raid of the Confederates in Franklin County while he and his comrades had been preparing for battle in South Carolina. The African-American men who enlisted in Pennsylvania to serve far away feared for the safety of their families and neighbors back home. William wrote bitterly, "My words com true juste as i sade before ilefte that the rebels wood comin and take all the Coulerd p[e]oples that they cod get and take them."

David Demus revealed his contempt for the Confederates, especially after he heard that the Rebels had created a "hard time" for their friends when they invaded Franklin County. David told his wife that he had "sean so meney rebbel[s]" that he would not get up if they walked in—a flagrant breech of racial decorum. "I se them evrey Day mor or lest and We Work everday." The Confederates "kill a man now and then," but when attacked by the black soldiers the white men "Jest git op and fly." David and his comrades "Com to fight" and were not afraid of the rebel soldiers. Demus knew that the United States Army elsewhere was "giving the rebels Hell on both sds now shuving them in it to grate god." May "the day soon Come When the Canon Bolls may thunder the Last rebel into hell."[45]

In the meantime, the soldiers of the United States Colored Troops had to worry about being paid. David mentioned in almost every letter that he had 57 dollars coming to him as soldier's pay and he was eager to send it to Mary Jane back in Mercersburg.[46] Her brother Jacob told Mary Jane that "we all like soldieren verry well but we don't like the thing of duing without money." They had yet to receive compensation for their service, a problem that wore on all the United States Colored Troops. The black soldiers' pay had been reduced to ten dollars a month and they had to pay for their own uniforms from what they did receive. Jacob Christy, like all soldiers, longed to get home. When they did, he promised his sister, "we can tell you of things that you never drem of for I have seen thing that I never drem of before."[47]

☆

A CORRESPONDENT TO THE *Franklin Repository* visited the nearby Gettysburg battlefield three weeks after its abandonment by the armies and described what people felt in the presence of such devastation. "It is not a morbid curiosity as some would claim. It is with a feeling more akin to reverence that we draw nigh to the broad and bloody altar, on which thousands of our fellow beings have so freely laid down their lives for our redemption." As the sun set and fog rose on the empty battlefield, one "could easily picture on this misty background, marshaled line and charging columns."

Even in these days so close to the battle, the events there had begun to shift and fade. It was hard "to arrive at the truth concerning the details of the fight. Each soldier claims for the point where he stood, special importance. Never was there so fierce an assault as the one repelled by his brigade." Such distorted perspectives from combatants was understandable, but a patient observer could begin to piece together the larger story from the evidence on the landscape. "The deep ruts made by the artillery wheels, the broken fragments of shell, the shrubbery cut down as with the scythe of the mower, the trampled caps and haversacks that no soldier comes to claim, and the graves, thick as if sown broad-cast on the hillside, need no interpreter."

To see the full truth of Gettysburg, the reporter quietly insisted, "one must visit the hospitals. The dead are soon covered from the sight; the scarred earth, washed by pitying rains and nursed by the sunshine, quickly recovers from its wound, but men must bleed and groan and die for long days after the shock of battle is over, and the shattered columns have swept away to other scenes." All around Gettysburg, tents for the wounded men covered acres. Local people and volunteers from elsewhere came to help, and "too much praise cannot be awarded them for their labor of love." The devotion of the volunteers who dressed wounds, washed faces, or wrote letters to the families of dying young men largely went unseen but would be remembered for lifetimes.

The suffering of the wounded Confederates who had been abandoned at Gettysburg was "indescribable. They had been left by their friends lying under trees and sheds, without any adequate medical attendance, or indeed supplies of any kind." Hunger, wounds, and rain compounded the agony. The people of the neighborhoods where they had been left gathered them in tents on the Chambersburg pike. "Indignation bursts out afresh against the wicked leaders who betrayed these misguided men to such horrible sufferings. Maimed, wounded, covered with gore and writhing in agony they lie there to mark the pathway the monster secession has trodden." The correspondent found no United States soldier who expressed regret for enlisting, fighting, and even being wounded, but he found many Confederates who wanted nothing more than the war to be over and the Union restored.[48]

3

The Great Task Remaining
Before Us

July 1863 through May 1864

T   *he months after Gettysburg, though quiet in the Eastern Theater
of the war, marked a critical juncture in the conflict. In that time,
as the armies of Robert E. Lee and George Meade recovered and rebuilt
themselves in Virginia, the United States and the Confederacy took stock.
They measured their capacities to continue waging war. They forged purposes to sustain months or years of additional sacrifice. They sifted through
their experiences, evaluating mistakes and triumphs alike.*

*The consequences of the Civil War would be defined during these
months of apparent inaction in the East. In the United States, Abraham
Lincoln and the Republicans used the commemoration at Gettysburg to
distill the Union purpose to its essence even as Northern Democrats laid the
foundations for a challenge to Lincoln in the elections of the coming year.*

*In the Confederacy, white people wrestled with the limits of their com-
mitment and of dissent. In every community and in every regiment, people
asked how much more they could, should, or would give to an imperiled*

cause. White women measured their loyalties, balancing the safety of their families against the success of the Confederacy. Soldiers, in the hard winter, struggled to sustain loyalty both to hungry wives and children back home and to their comrades in camp.

Enslaved people in the South remained, as always, watchful. Slavery grew no easier in wartime. Slaves, like their owners, had depended on the food taken by soldiers of both armies. The increasing demands of the Confederate government put enslaved men at risk of impressment while the desperation of their owners kept enslaved people at risk of sale or being rented out far from home and their families. Freedom seemed far away for most enslaved people in the Confederacy, even in Virginia, where deliverance seemed as close as the Union lines.

☆

THROUGHOUT THE FALL OF 1863, two dozen miles from Chambersburg, men labored to turn the scarred land around Gettysburg into a national cemetery. "The new Cemetery contains about ten acres of ground and is located less than half a mile south-west of the town," the Republican newspaper in Chambersburg reported. By late November, nearly five months after the battle, the memorial contained "only a portion of our dead, the work of re-interment not being yet completed. The receptacles are ditches, mostly from twenty to one hundred feet long, with proper width, and walled with stone. In every instance where the dead are known, headboards are placed properly inscribed." The men lay alongside their comrades from their home states.

The cemetery was a project of the recently reelected Pennsylvania Governor Andrew Curtin, who gave responsibility for creating the memorial to David Wills, an energetic young attorney from Gettysburg who first suggested the idea of a national cemetery. It was Wills's job to purchase the land, come up with a design satisfactory to every state, and oversee the work of exhuming the bodies and reinterring them.

The Chambersburg reporter did not need to tell his readers about the battle itself, for "our people have been made familiar with every detail in print, and many of them indeed from observation." David Wills worked throughout the fall to assemble a dedicatory exercise worthy of such a place and such a moment. His greatest accomplishment had been to recruit the man widely recognized as the greatest orator the nation had to offer: Edward Everett, the sixty-nine-year-old president of Harvard University and a confidant of President Lincoln. Everett was a powerful speaker, learned and passionate. He would give shape to the battle and its meaning as no one else could.

Wills also invited other dignitaries, all eager for a place on the platform. President Lincoln accepted the invitation to Gettysburg only a few days before the event. He would leave Washington on November 19, the day before the speech itself, so that he would be in Gettysburg with time before the ceremony. It would be the President's longest trip from Washington since he took office and he thought that he and Mrs. Lincoln might enjoy the brief respite together. Their young son, Tad, fell sick, however, and Mrs. Lincoln, having lost another son only a little more than a year before, stayed behind. The President used the trip instead to meet with politicians and citizens along the journey into Pennsylvania.

Wills had invited Lincoln to make a few "appropriate remarks," which meant several things. First, the remarks were not to be long; Everett had already been announced as the main speaker. Second, the remarks would need to focus on the work at hand as a funeral oration, honoring the men who had given their lives for their country. Third, the remarks would not be partisan; this was a speech for all Americans, not Republicans only. Lincoln recognized and accepted all these conditions. He worked on the speech for several days, first in Washington, then on the train to Pennsylvania, in a room in Gettysburg itself, and on the speakers' platform. The remarks offered a rare opportunity.[1]

The situation in mid–November 1863 called for a rededication of the nation's purpose. Events from across the war had accumulated so rapidly that success and failure lay entangled. In just the last six months, the United States had gone from the disaster of Chancellorsville in May to the glories of Vicksburg and Gettysburg in July to another disaster of Chickamauga in north Georgia in September. There, the United States had suffered a level of casualties second only to the losses at Gettysburg and had been defeated. It was the greatest Federal loss in the Western Theater of the war and another battle lay ahead.

While Lincoln's train moved through the peaceful Pennsylvania countryside, both the United States and the Confederacy were shipping every resource they could afford into the mountains and valleys of eastern Tennessee. Trainloads of men and matériel drove toward Chattanooga, where a battle that could rival the size and importance of Gettysburg loomed. The eventual outcome of the war could rest on the outcome of that struggle, hanging in the air as Lincoln arrived in Gettysburg.[2]

The political situation, too, held signs both encouraging and threatening for Lincoln. The gubernatorial elections of October 1863 had seen the Republicans win in Pennsylvania, New York, and Ohio. In Pennsylvania, though, the largest Republican stronghold, the election could easily have gone the other way if the United States had not been able to drive the Confederates from the state in July. Governor Curtin had come in for blistering criticism during the invasion but also won credit for his support for wounded veterans and their orphaned children.

The presidential election of 1864 lay almost exactly a year ahead. No one, including Lincoln himself, had any illusions that his reelection was guaranteed. Another defeat like Chickamauga might kill Republican hopes. Even the failure by Meade to destroy Lee's army in Virginia in the upcoming year might lead voters to decide that the Lincoln administration had consumed enough lives in an unwinnable war.

Lincoln would confront the hard issues of the war in his Annual Address to Congress not quite two weeks after his trip to Gettysburg. In the meantime, his remarks at the battlefield needed to rise above immediate fears and hopes. A funeral oration for more than three thousand men demanded words broader and more enduring than anything he had ever written or said.

Jacob Hoke of Chambersburg, who had visited the Gettysburg battlefield immediately after the battle, returned for the grand event with his wife Margaret. The merchant was awestruck by all that he saw. On the evening of November 18, Jacob and Margaret waited along with a crowd outside of the home of David Wills, where the President took his dinner. "After a little while the door was again opened and ABRAHAM LINCOLN stood before us. The appearance of the President was the signal for an outburst of enthusiasm that I had never heard equalled." When things quieted down Lincoln's "face relaxed its appearance of careworn sadness and anxiety, and a kind and genial smile overspread his countenance. He then said that we had doubtless expected a speech, and he would be happy to gratify us, but he dare not do it for Mr. Seward would not let him, and he could only thank us for the respect shown him and bid us all good night." The good-natured crowd then called for Seward to give a speech, which he did, "of considerable length."

On the 19th, after having somberly toured the battlefield, Lincoln joined the procession to the speaker's stand. He was "greeted with enthusiastic and long continued cheers," reported the Chambersburg paper, and "many persons gathered around the President, shaking him by the hand. He received every one in the most gracious manner." The crowd of over ten thousand "was immense, and were gathered so compactly that it was almost impossible to breathe." Several people fainted and the "value of hoops, bonnets and other articles of ladies wear destroyed in the jam would amount to no ordinary sum."

When the program began, the Chambersburg paper recounted, "America's greatest living orator, the Hon. Edward Everett, then arose and for two hours held the crowd in one of the most splendid intellectual efforts of his life." The paper promised to publish Everett's lengthy address in its entirety in the next week's paper, and it did, for the speech proved "a superb tribute to bravery and heroism; a glorious record of deeds of patriotism; a grateful remembrance of generous action; a history of glorious events for perpetual admiration and appreciation." Everett evoked powerful scenes of the struggle on the land where the audience gathered, describing the ebb and flow of the battle, helping to shape the story into the form people would remember. After Everett, a choir sang, promising that even after a "a thousand years shall pass away—a Nation still shall mourn this clay."

It was then time for President Lincoln's dedicatory remarks. Jacob and Margaret Hoke had managed to find places near the speaker's platform. "President Lincoln arose," Hoke wrote, "and amidst the thunder of artillery and the tremendous applause of the immense multitude, advanced to the front of the platform, his tall, gaunt form and sad but amiable face within the view of thousands who beheld the memorable scene." When the crowd finally grew quiet, Lincoln "proceeded in slow and measured tones to deliver his dedicatory address. His words were not heard by the larger majority of the people present, but during his address the most profound silence was observed." Hoke considered himself fortunate to hear all that was said.[3]

Five days later, Franklin's Republican newspaper reprinted the words with brackets denoting the five times applause punctuated Lincoln's eloquence. The President's 272 words flowed from the rest of the ceremony. He humbled himself and everyone there by recalling the sacrifice of the fallen soldiers. He framed the war for the survival of the United States as a struggle for all mankind, for all the earth.[4]

Lincoln reminded the nation that the victory at Gettysburg, for all its grandeur and glory, had not brought the war to an end. Indeed, his remarks dwelled on "the unfinished work" that lay before the nation. It was for the living to "be here dedicated to the great task remaining before us," to "take increased devotion" to the cause for which soldiers had died, to "highly resolve that the dead shall not have died in vain." "Shall"—a verb that lived in the future, that depended on work yet accomplished.

Jacob Hoke saw that everything in the event combined in a remarkable unity. "The Man—the President—the Government—the yet undecided peril to which it was exposed—the ground we were on—the sleeping thousands all about us, whose blood had been poured out that the Nation might live, all, all conspired to make the occasion one never to be forgotten."[5]

Lincoln's remarks took their power not only from their evocation of transcendent truths—the way that most Americans ever since have celebrated what became known as his Gettysburg Address—but also from the way they captured the uncertainty of the moment and the enormous challenge that lay before them. The speech, while not partisan, did profound political work, reminding loyal Americans what was at stake beyond the petty partisan verbiage that filled their newspapers and their speeches. Lincoln's remarks drew part of their power from their place and their moment.[6]

The context that made Lincoln's speech so powerful also helps explain why the speech did not mention slavery by name, and why Edward Everett, in his two hours, mentioned slavery only seven times and then mainly to excoriate the slaveholders for the war. The enslaved people of America stood in the background of the speeches at Gettysburg. In the summer of 1863, many white citizens understood "a new birth of freedom" to refer to the Union's reaffirmation, not the end of slavery or a transformed postwar society.

Lincoln had not forgotten slavery or the people held in slavery, nor did he flinch from addressing the issue head-on. In the months before and after the Gettysburg speech, the president wrote widely circulated public letters that addressed slavery directly. In his message to a mass meeting of Union men in his home state of Illinois three months earlier, he had confronted his critics with pointed language. "You are dissatisfied with me about the negro," he acknowledged. The difference between Lincoln and his opponents was clear: "I certainly wish that all men could be free, while I suppose you do not." His critics hated the Emancipation Proclamation, arguing that freeing the enslaved prolonged the war, but "some of the commanders of our armies in the field who have given us our important successes, believe the emancipation policy, and the use of colored troops, constitute the heaviest blow yet dealt to the rebellion." In words that recalled Lincoln's skill on the stump, he taunted his critics: "You say you will not fight to free negroes. Some of them seem willing to fight for you; but no matter."

"Like other people," Lincoln had reminded skeptics in a letter in August, black Americans "act upon motives. Why should they do any thing for us, if we will do nothing for them? If they stake their lives for us, they must be prompted by the strongest motive—even the promise of freedom. And the promise being made, must be kept." Lincoln, in language that foreshadowed his comments at Gettysburg, reminded white Americans that black soldiers have "helped mankind on to this great consummation" of freedom "with silent tongue, and clenched teeth, and steady eye, and well-poised bayonet."[7]

Lincoln, while echoing themes at Gettysburg that had defined his purpose throughout the war, introduced two innovations in that brief speech. First, he invoked a single nation devoted to a single purpose. That national purpose, a direct inheritance from the Founding Fathers, defined his second innovation at Gettysburg: the elevation of "equality" to a status with "liberty" as the twinned ideals of the nation. And if equality and liberty were to have any meaning in the newly unified nation, slavery could not stand. The new language of nationhood, wrapped in biblical imagery and cadence, consecrated by solemn mourning, managed to sound ageless from the moment Lincoln uttered it. Lincoln seamlessly melded the old and the new, the moment and the timeless.[8]

As great as the speech would reveal itself to be over time, when the words had been parsed and memorized by generations, when the war's outcome made them prescient, at the time Lincoln's remarks at Gettysburg marked no turning point or watershed in the Civil War. After November 19, as before, as Lincoln himself admitted in the speech, soldiers would decide whether the words would develop real significance. In the meantime, the actual government by and of the people remained an unruly and desperate struggle between the Republicans and the Democrats in the

North. And without victories on the battlefield and at the election box in the coming year, each reliant on the other, the eloquent words spoken at Gettysburg would remain an empty promise.[9]

☆

JUST DAYS AFTER THE CEREMONY at Gettysburg, people through-out the North received remarkable news: Union forces had broken out of Chattanooga, driving Confederate forces from the heights overlooking that town. The issue in which Franklin County's Republican newspaper reprinted Edward Everett's speech at Gettysburg shouted the story:

Glorious News!!! General Grant's Great Victory! Bragg's Army Totally Routed! Capture Of 10,000 Prisoners! Rebel Losses Very Heavy! Union Loss Comparatively Small! Series Of Impetuous Assaults! The Enemy's Position Carried By Storm! An Eventful Week's History! 60 Guns Captured! Sherman's Desperate Struggle! The Victory Complete![10]

In a war saturated by hyperbole and wishful thinking, these headlines did not exaggerate. Major railroads that connected the farms and factories of the lower South to the armies and cities of Virginia ran through the narrow valleys between the mountains at the border between Tennessee and Georgia at Chattanooga. With the loss of that artery, the Confederacy was divided north to south just as Grant's victory at Vicksburg had divided it east to west.[11]

☆

THE NEWSPAPERS OF AUGUSTA COUNTY did not mention the ceremony at Gettysburg. Even Joseph Waddell, attuned to events in the North as well as the South, ignored it in his diary. Judging from the events of the last six months of 1863, Waddell thought the war was likely to last twenty years more. Only foreign intervention could end the conflict and he saw no sign of that. He could not help but think about what could and should have happened just three years earlier. "Instead of quitting the Union on the election of Lincoln, Southern representatives ought to have held their seats in the Congress at Washington; with the aid of conservative Northern men, we would have had a majority against Lincoln, and by withholding supplies could have tied his hands completely." If war arose from such a strategy "it would have been civil, not sectional, and mainly at the North, where the people were divided in sentiment. Thus we should have had the cooperation of nearly one half of the Northern people. But as things were managed, those who were disposed to stand by us, in the Northern States, were driven off at the first step. They were left in a minority, and could not render us active assistance without incurring the perils incident to treason." [12]

That chain of events had not unfolded, of course, and the result was a war beyond anyone's control. Waddell acknowledged in private what people were not supposed to say in public: "Neither party would have entered into the contest if the present state of affairs had been anticipated. Neither can now quit." [13]

Waddell, like all white Southerners, wanted to see the North torn apart by conflict among Northerners themselves. The Confederates' only remaining chance—after hopes of foreign intervention faded, the invasion of the North failed, the defense of the Mississippi River collapsed, and the citadel of Chattanooga had fallen—was to fight long enough for those divisions within the Union to force the North to compromise. The best outcome that Southerners could imagine at the beginning of 1864 was that Northerners themselves would force their government to end the conflict.

☆

THE CONFEDERACY, for all its own internal antagonisms, had managed to remain intact enough to wage war. Through charismatic military leadership, communal demands for loyalty, and direct coercion by citizens and the government, the fragile new nation had held itself together through two years of fighting. The Confederacy had been born in war and possessed both the advantages and disadvantages of that birth. It had mobilized the white people of the South as only a warring government could, with calls to action and brute force.

The Confederacy had no identity other than as an agent of war. It had no peacetime history with which to reconcile. It tolerated no organized dissent and snuffed out what spontaneous challenge that did arise. The Confederacy's citizens aided in this enforced uniformity, shaming or imprisoning or exiling those who challenged the government and the military. With the experience of generations of vigilance against real and imagined abolitionists as well as relentless scrutiny of enslaved people, white Southerners held their new martial state together despite one setback after another.[14]

The war turned fundamental principles upside down for the Confederacy. Slavery had long been protected by the federal government and the Constitution—and would still have been protected in 1863 had the slaveholding states not gone to war against the United States. The federal government had been an ally in slavery since the nation's founding. Throughout the decades between the Revolution and secession, the slave South had dominated Congress, the Supreme Court, and the presidency, fueling fears of the Slave Power in the North and an expectation in the South that the protection and expansion of slavery would continue. The Fugitive

Slave Act of 1850 relied on the power of the federal government to protect the rights of slaveholders even in the North.

In the years immediately preceding secession, however, the slave states began to emphasize their rights to set aside any federal restrictions regarding slavery. Under the control of Republicans, they warned, the federal government could become a threat to the very existence of slavery. The Confederacy would insist on the rights of the states, especially where slavery was involved.

And yet almost as soon as the seceding states created their new Confederacy they began ceding power, authority, and resources to their new central government to a degree unimaginable, and unacceptable, before secession. Whether it was the draft of soldiers, demands for the labor of enslaved people, impressment of food and animals, heavy taxation, or control of the money supply, white Southerners watched as their new central government reached into every aspect of their lives. So long as it was understood that this sacrifice was for the armies and its men, people accepted the toll with resignation and even gratitude for the greater sacrifice offered by the men in the field. Communities in Virginia, the state in the Confederacy ravaged by the war for the longest time, gave more than most and offered less resistance than many. States farther from the fighting—and thus farther from the danger of the United States troops—aggressively resisted their new national government. Georgia and North Carolina, in particular, chafed at the demands from Richmond.[15]

The depth and speed of the Confederate government's growth was possible only because the Confederacy had been born in war and would live or die by war. People expected to sacrifice in wartime, especially when, as the Confederates saw it, they were fighting for their very survival as a people and a social order based on slavery. They directed passionate resentment against those who refused to rise to the spirit of common suffering and generosity. Speculators and shirkers made a mockery of such values, turning generosity into gullibility, eroding the public ethos of the Confederacy. The government of the Confederacy labored to hammer out policies that promised greater equity. Those policies never caught up with the real and perceived injustices evident in every neighborhood, but the new laws did keep the wheels of war turning enough to allow people to imagine a final, culminating season of fighting in the spring of 1864.

The Confederacy conducted the business of government without the machinery of political parties that had developed in the United States over the preceding quarter century, allowing Americans to govern their enormous and rapidly growing nation. The Confederate Constitution created a six-year term for the presidency, so no national election hung in the air as it did in the North. Moreover, the spirit of party competition seemed out of place in the martial Confederacy, where all energies were directed at the one great goal of driving out the armies of the United States.

The party system had been as critical to the states of the South as it had been in the Northern states before the war, but during the war Southerners rejected the legitimacy of party identity. In doing so, they also turned away from a powerful source of local expression and moderation. In the United States' brief history, parties had been constructed from the bottom up, connecting America's patchwork of localities, denominations, and ethnic groups into alliances that could win national elections. Now, in the Confederacy, those parties had been cut off at the roots.[16]

☆

RECRUITERS FOR MILITARY UNITS with Augusta ties returned to the county in the winter months for yet another scouring. Companies and regiments within the Confederacy competed with each other for able-bodied men. The Staunton Artillery needed fifty new recruits and reminded people that the unit had been fighting and winning in "desperately contested engagements" since the Battle of First Manassas in the distant early summer of 1861. A lieutenant from John Imboden's command of partisan rangers arrived in Staunton about the same time. Service in that battery held several attractions: men were mounted on horseback, the unit boasted of "excellent and accomplished officers," and it was "likely to operate near the homes of those living in the Valley." Interested men should be sure to give the lieutenant "a call before going elsewhere."[17]

The Confederacy, from the president and generals down to local officials, struggled with how best to use African-Americans to advance the cause. Enslaved men and free black men had been drafted to dig entrenchments from the first days of the war, but as hunger mounted many white people called for black men to be kept closer to home and put to work producing food. To make matters worse, Confederates knew those enslaved men went to the aid of the United States Army whenever they could and gained their freedom by doing so. "We have been informed by a gentleman who has lately returned from Winchester that the Yankees are enrolling all the able-bodied negroes in Jefferson and Berkley," a Staunton paper reported. "Poor deluded African, he leaves his kind Master and comfortable home to be placed in the front ranks of the Yankee army to save the lives of those who never had any sympathy for him and to murder those whose every thought and act was for his comfort."[18]

A county census in 1863 showed that Augusta had about 200

fewer enslaved people than it had just three years earlier, declining from about 4,700 to about 4,500. The town of Staunton had gone from 909 slaves in 1860 to 749 in 1863. Such losses mattered. As families struggled to get crops in the ground, a newspaper admitted, "the labor of the Valley is done chiefly by white persons." The slow bleeding of the institution of slavery and the more rapid bleeding of the white population demonstrated how much Augusta County, like the entire Confederacy, depended on the black people in their midst, black people who might use the first opportunity to go to the enemy and their own freedom should that enemy be allowed any closer.[19]

In the winter of 1863–1864, Confederate newspapers and the government targeted "speculation" as the great cancer eating away at their cause. Speculators bought food, horses, and other necessities and then hoarded them, forcing prices to rise and people to suffer. Greed and pride became the great sins of the Confederacy, the explanation for military setbacks and loss of heart at home.

Before the war, white Southerners had praised themselves for their lack of commercial avarice, imagining slavery as something other than mere business. In the midst of a war that demanded almost all that everyone possessed, the actions of greedy men mocked those who sacrificed. A letter from an anonymous soldier in an Augusta unit huddling on the banks of the Rapidan appeared in the Staunton *Spectator* at Christmas time in 1863. "Mr. Editor—in these 'crazy times of war' it seems like it is 'every one for himself and the devil take the hindmost.'" This soldier had been in the army for all three years of the war and knew about the effects of speculation on the people at home and in the army. While officials claimed to be doing the best they could, the soldiers of Augusta were "shivering with cold, gaunt with hunger, wasted with disease, broken spirited from oppression and tyranny of incompetent field officers and our wives and children suffering for the actual necessaries of life." The government went through the motions of helping, but "no one can attend to the wants of a family so well as the head thereof—the father and husband. I know that it is impossible for every poor soldier who has a family to go home at once," but the author of this letter proposed that Congress pass a law that allowed some men to go home on a scheduled basis. The failure of the army to honor promises of furlough had "led some of our best men to desert, who have never come back, while others have been brought back and punished in the most disgraceful manner." He had seen soldiers cry when they received letters from home, telling of the hunger of their wives and children. If something did not change, an "outburst" from the soldiers "will make citizens and everyone else quake with fear and surprise."[20]

The only hope for independence seemed to be to drag the war out for as long as possible. "We believe that if the Yankees could be thoroughly satisfied that the war would be a very long one— that we have it in our power to extend it, if necessary, through a decade or score of years, they would be willing to make peace upon our own terms," argued the *Spectator*. "From the very first their cry has been for 'a short and sharp' one, and they have endeavored to make it so. Let the prospect, then, be opened before them of an interminable war, except by their own retirement from it." The only way to wage such a long war was to *prepare* for a long war, turning the South's efforts toward the greater production of food, clothing, and everything else the Confederacy could manufacture. If the draft continued to grow, however, "if the whole population is dragged into the army, where are the supplies for the army, and bread and meat for women and children to come from?" The Confederacy already struggled to feed the soldiers it had; "how much more difficult, indeed, how impossible will it be, when the laborers are all withdrawn from their avocations— when the producers are all turned into consumers?"[21]

The Confederate government talked of extending the draft to boys sixteen years old and above and to men over forty-five. The draft of boys, many people warned, would consume the "seed corn" of the nation and the draft of older men would "furnish food for disease and death, and to crowd the hospitals and graveyards." Instead, "bring back the stragglers and the absentees, place negroes in the place of white teamsters, nurses, &c., and we shall have as large an army as the people can feed. What we need is skill and produce in the development and husbanding of our resources, rather than an increase of numbers." The blame lay with "the shameful manner in which Confederate property has been squandered and the negligence and blunders by which so many of our men have fallen into the hands of the enemy. These are the evils which must be remedied." To drag the young and the old into the army now "will be like a new inheritance to a spendthrift, who will run through it just as rapidly as his former possessions." The government should focus on deserters, "who are skulking about their homes since last summer; and harbored by their friends."[22]

The white women of Augusta County, like their counterparts across the Confederacy, had been integral to the transformation of peacetime society into a war-making society. Those women, no less than the men among whom they lived—maybe more, judging from their letters and diaries—hated Lincoln and the abolitionists, blaming them for starting the war, threatening racial insurrection, and turning it into a grinding destruction of the South. These women admired Robert E. Lee and Stonewall Jackson even as they resented the Confederate government responsible for taking the young men, food, money, and horses necessary to sustain the Confederate armies.[23]

Confederate women, as the leaders of the Confederacy proclaimed at every opportunity, sustained the cause in ways that only women could, spiritually and materially. Jefferson Davis implored his "countrywomen—the wives, mothers, sisters and daughters—of the Confederacy, to use their all-powerful influence in aid of this call, to add one crowning sacrifice to those which their patriotism has so freely and constantly offered on their country's altar." Davis pleaded with women, in his characteristically florid style, "to take care that none who owe service in the field shall be sheltered at home, from the disgrace of having deserted their duty to their families, to their country, and to their God." [24]

A public letter written from Augusta County by a correspondent identified only by his initials and his rank as captain made a specific appeal "To the Valley and Its Ladies." After effusive praise of those women, the officer urged them to act. "There are a certain class of men in Virginia, remaining at home, who look upon the progress of this war with careless indifference," he charged. Those men "have folded their arms and said, 'Let the Confederacy slide.'" The Confederate officer pleaded with the women: "Can you not reclaim them?" Women possessed a power no man did, with their "winning smiles, earnest solicitations, and patriotism." That patriotism, "so far, has no parallel in history, and we feel confident that you will not be found wanting in this instance."[25]

The flattery betrayed anxiety. The same succor the women of the Valley had offered the wounded and the hungry soldier could be turned against the cause. If the Confederacy was indeed sliding into oblivion, might not the duty of the mother, the wife, the sister, and the sweetheart be to protect the men they loved from the merciless demands of the dying Confederacy? If a woman's first duty, as men repeated endlessly, was to her family, might not the needs of that family in the hard winter, with food scarce, firewood taken by the soldiers, animals hungry or gone, and prices impossible to pay, mean that her duty was to take in a husband or son who had walked away from General Lee's army? The army was protecting the "happy homes" of the Confederacy and that protection might mean leaving the army for a while, patriotic pleas notwithstanding. Those moments of decision might confront any family at any time a man without a signed furlough—a number rapidly growing in these months—appeared at the door of his home, any time a pleading letter from home tempted a man to reconsider his loyalties.

Whatever individual struggles they might wrestle with, the white women of Augusta worked collectively and publicly to support the Confederacy. The Soldiers' Aid Society of Zion Church in Waynesboro, for example, produced "forty-four pairs of socks, ten pairs of drawers, two pairs of yarn gloves, one shirt and two barrels of provisions" for the soldiers of the 31st Virginia Regiment. Mrs. H. L. Gallaher donated fifty pairs of socks to accompany the fifty pairs of shoes her son donated to the Stonewall Brigade. Other women knitted socks for the cold and wounded men in the General Hospital at Staunton, helping men they did not know, counting on other women in other places to aid their own sons, brothers, and husbands who might lie wounded in their neighborhoods.[26] A commanding officer regretted that "those who so kindly donated these articles could not be present when they were distributed, that they might have heard the expressions of gratitude used by the thankful recipients."[27]

People accustomed to comfortable lives surprised themselves

by their ability to adapt to the unrelenting demands of war-time. Joseph Waddell confessed to his diary that "the war does not weigh as heavily as it did for many months after it began. The recollection of the security and abundance formerly enjoyed seems like a dream." Waddell permitted himself to recall "the scenes in our streets three years ago—piles of boxes before every store door, shelves and counters within filled and piled up with goods, merchants begging customers to buy; groceries running over with sugar, molasses, coffee, tea, cheese fish +c; confectioners making the most tempting display of fruits, cakes and candies; wagon loads of country produce calling at every house and farmers earnestly inquiring who wished to purchase flour, corn, potatoes, beef, pork, apples." Now, a customer was lucky to be able to purchase a needle and thread, expensive cotton cloth of dubious Southern manufacture, or clumsy dishes made of clay rather than porcelain. Cold and hungry people preyed on each other for the necessities of life. "Thefts + robberies are the common occurrences—Overcoats, cloaks and dresses are stolen from halls and chambers, meat from smokehouses, and grain from fields + barns—Such things are almost regarded as matters of course."[28]

☆

SOLDIERS IN THE FIELD suffered through the hard winter. The letters of Jesse Rolston to his wife Mary in Mt. Solon in Augusta stoically told the story. Enlisting in the 52nd Virginia in July 1861 and fighting at every major battle in Virginia and at Gettysburg, Rolston was the sort of soldier on which the Confederacy depended. The father of five, with a productive farm but no slaves, he represented many Augusta soldiers. At thirty-seven, he was more than a decade older than the average soldier. In the winter of 1863–1864, waiting in Orange County for the battles everyone knew would come, Jesse shared his hopes and worries with his wife and family.

In early December Jesse asked his sister to bring some shoes if she could. "I need them very bad. I just about Barefooted." A week later, he reported that "we have pretty good cabbins now if they will oanly let us stay in them we can keep our selves comfortabel in the way of being war[m]." Grateful for some comfort, he nevertheless admitted that "i would not injoy this way of living if i had the finest house in the state of virginia to winter in or to live in. I do not no sometimes what to think much less what to do or to rite." A month later, he told of "another unpleasant site": the shooting of a deserter, "a hard looking customer" who had deserted three times and gone into the enemy's lines. Rolston knew that desertion could not be tolerated, but he hoped that he would "never see nor hear of any more such sites."[29]

Jesse worried about the same things as other soldiers—"i could spend in one day heare what a month wages amounts to and then not get one good meals"—but he did not respect those who deserted. When he heard that two men he and Mary knew had "goan to the yankeys," he recalled that "the way they use to blow, I thought they would bin the last that would have left the Southern confederacy." Past words and deeds seemed to count for little by 1864, when "it is hard telling hoo is true and hoo haint, now a days." Jesse admitted to Mary that "i think often of the times that is past an goan and think of the times that is now. what a change of afairs in a few years. it is enough to make one shuder to think of it."[30]

The Confederate Congress wrestled with how to keep soldiers in the field and to keep people at home from suffering, adjusting policies so that prices and production of food could be controlled. The County Court of Augusta gave local attorney J. M. McCue the authority to buy 10,000 bushels of corn, at $4 per bushel, for the families of soldiers and others suffering in the harsh winter. He did all that he could, McCue reported, but "in consequence of the great demand in Virginia and North Carolina for corn, to say nothing of the wants of the army," the price "has enhanced so much in the extreme South as to render it utterly impossible to meet its wishes." The families of Augusta would have to do without in the dead of winter.[31]

Soldiers worried about their families more than anything else. A collective letter from men in the Stonewall Brigade expressed the fear of every man as well as a fury against profit-taking. A fellow member of Company E in the 5th Virginia Infantry had been killed by the enemy in late November. His "admiring and sympathizing comrades, out of their own small means, made up money enough to have the body taken from the battle field and sent to Augusta County for burial, that their gallant comrade might rest beneath the soil that he had so long defended so bravely and loved so well." But when the widow "took the twenty dollars which is allowed by the county to the wives of soldiers for their support" to a prominent cabinet maker in Greenville, he refused to make the coffin for less than forty dollars cash. Some kind neighbors made up the difference. Upon hearing the story, "many members of the company, although more accustomed to handling the musket than the pen, resolved, to try to show to their fellow citizens at home that there exists even in Old Augusta some men as mean and avaricious as even Yankee land can boast of." They did not provide the name of the greedy cabinetmaker, but they hoped "he will take warning by this exposure of his degrading and disgraceful conduct and—'go and sin no more'."[32]

James Long, a young white laborer enlisted in the 1st Virginia

Cavalry, wrote his sister Cynthia after he returned to camp following an authorized visit back home in Augusta. "I got so vext at some of thy acquaintences in the nabor hood that I did not cear about going to see eny of the nabers," James admitted. "ower Company was at home too months some of the people begrudged ower furlow they said they nowed what we war sent home far becaus they coul not feed us in the army and said we had to come and eat ofuv us." Hard-pressed neighbors were not pleased to see the arrival of soldiers who put additional demands on local households. "That did not pleas my appotite but thank god I did not pester them you may bet on that," James wrote.[33]

James McCutchan wrote his cousin Rachel with dark humor. "Gen Breckenridge is here + I think if our rations get much less, Gen Starvation will be here also or Gen. 'Skidaddle' to a quarter where there is more to eat." James admitted that "I'm getting awfully tired of this camp, I despise this inactivity. I am tired of the war - I want to fight it out, + the sooner we begin this spring the better." John Pearce, for his part, wanted to visit Lizzie Brown in Staunton. "i wish this cruel war was over so we could all come home again and enjoy ourselves once more." John knew he "could enjoy myself first rate in Staunton but there is no chance of my getting away from here a soldier is worse than a negro used to be we have to get a whole sheet of paper full of writing before we can get home." No analogy held more meaning—"worse than a negro used to be." While black people seemed to be gaining freedom in wartime, white men were losing theirs. [34]

"Im very sorry to hear of you all having to fight so much but I dont suppose peace will ever be maid without a greateal of hard fighting yet," Mollie Houser wrote her cousin James, a private in the 5th Virginia Infantry. In her late 20s, unmarried and living with her father and mother in Augusta, Mollie noted cheerfully and sarcastically that "we all are trying more to se who Can Make the nicest dresses & I think if the war lasts long we will all turn to yankeys evry one tries who Can make the nicest Cloth in Augusta & hats & Caps & most evry yhing that we used to buy." Despite her participation in the characteristic female patriotic activities of weaving, darning, and sewing, Mollie wrote what no one was supposed to admit: "I think this Confederacy is almost gone up the spout the next time you write tell me what you think about it. I dont think im wrong & the sooner the better." Mollie wrote with irreverence about the draft. "They have taken almost evry man & talk of Caling on the men from seventeen to fifty & then I suppose they will search they graveyards and sware them to the length of time they have been dead." [35]

Mollie Houser sustained few illusions. She wished she had something interesting to write to her cousin, "but I Cant interest you by writing as long as the war lasts." She knew that everyone had their own ideas of what would happen in the spring when the fighting renewed. "Perphapse it may take a notion & stop of a sudden sometime A great many persons think it will this spring but I beleave the old Prophets are all dead & the yong ones dont no any thing about it or it would have stopped long ago." Another female cousin, Kit Hanger, wrote to Mollie's sister that she had "no news but war news & I have gotten so tired of that I hate to hear of it unless their should be peace & then I would not care how much they would talk then." [36]

Letters to the Staunton newspapers offered discontented people a chance to express their anger at the inequities they saw around them. For one thing, farmers in Augusta who had corn for sale often would not accept Confederate currency, "A FARMER" complained. He said he knew "many who desire to purchase corn, and other grain, for their horses and families & cannot procure it without the gold, or silver, which few can command. Confederate money has been denounced as trash, worth nothing." The Confederate Congress, in response to such problems, adjusted the value of the currency and penalized those who would not accept the money of the struggling nation.[37]

Officers in the Confederate Army chafed at other kinds of injustice: "Why is it that Quartermasters and Commissaries with the rank and pay of Captain or Major can dress finer, ride finer and faster horses than company or field officers of the same rank and pay?," asked someone who signed himself as "JUSTICE, Co. F, 5th Va. Infantry." "Why is it that Commissaries can feed their horses on corn-meal at the rate of from two to three gallons per day, and themselves on ham, sweet potatoes, molasses and every other good thing that the country can afford, while a private or company officer does not know that there is such a thing in existence?" Unhappiness in the Confederacy did not result only from absolute suffering, but also from perceived injustice and slights accumulated over years of fighting.[38]

Despite such honest expression of what had been lost over the years of secession and war, Jesse Rolston reflected the resilience that seemed to characterize the Army of Northern Virginia as the spring of 1864 approached. "You wish to no what i think about our chance about the times of war," he wrote his wife Mary in March. "it is a hard question but i dont think that our chance looks as gloomy as it did some months a go. the soaoldiers is in pretty good sperits now to what they was some time a go." Desertion had diminished and some of the men had come back to camp. Everyone knew what was at stake. "I have not heard anything about giving up in Virginia. It may be so, but I dont believe that they are going to do it, for I think if they give up Virginia this crewell war will be over soon."[39]

A report on the "spirit of the army" in the Staunton paper argued that many soldiers agreed with Rolston. "Our armies are in fine spirits and our soldiers in all of them are re-enlisting with a spirit which reflects great credit upon their bravery, fortitude and patriotism." In heartening contrast, "the soldiers in the armies of the enemy are re-enlisting slowly and reluctantly, whereas the noble soldiers in our armies are re-enlisting with a 'perfect rush'." The United States would be forced to fight with untrained and untested men, confronting "our brave and tried veterans, whose flags have waved in triumph over so many bloody fields of battle. Whilst we will be stronger in the next campaign than ever before, the enemy will be weaker than at present." Desertion, rampant in the fall, declined rapidly in the spring as soldiers, perhaps with their crops in the ground, returned to camp.[40]

As 1864 began, the Staunton newspaper insisted that the war "will not be determined by numbers or bravery so much as by fortitude and persistent determination. We must be prepared to continue the war, and must submit to its evils with patient endurance." The South should continue to fight its defensive war, draining the North until its citizens refused to be drained any longer. In words that could not have offered comfort to even the most patriotic Confederate, the paper argued that "we intend to protract the struggle, if necessary, for years, and will transmit it, if needs be, as a woeful inheritance to our children and children's children to the third and fourth generation."[41]

People could look to the Army of Northern Virginia itself for reassurance. Company D of the 52nd held a meeting in camp "for the purpose of reiterating their determination to remain in the service of the Confederate States until the present war with the United States shall have been brought to an honorable close." Jesse Rolston was elected chairman of a committee to draft resolutions "expressive of the sentiments of the company." Though he struggled with spelling in his letters home, and though he admitted doubt in those letters, Rolston put his name after an eloquent statement from the company: "That in view of the exigencies of the crisis and the imperative duty of every patriot, to rally to the bleeding standard of his country and every Southerner to defend the battle torn and powder-stained flag of the Confederate States, do reaffirm, that we will never consent to lay down our arms, until the nationality and independence of our country shall have been achieved." [42]

As spring approached, though, soldiers alone would not be enough. John Imboden, commanding the Valley District, wrote a folksy letter to his former Augusta neighbors asking for their support. Imboden knew farmers were getting their crops in during the middle of March and he worried that "this great Valley will be subjected to plundering raids before and in corn-planting time. If the enemy comes he will seek to destroy your farming operations and resources by stealing your horses, burning your implements, and kidnapping your negroes." Imboden and his men would do their best to protect the Valley from such a calamity, but "the defence of this Valley requires a large cavalry force, and to maintain it the horses must be fed." Within sixty days, in the middle of May, there would be grass enough for animals to feed themselves. In the meantime, however, the army's horses must survive. The raids of the enemy might well come before the grass was in.

Imboden could send his quartermasters "with orders to take whatever they find." But "if this is done you will think yourselves outraged in many instances. The Quartermasters will be cursed and I shall be denounced." On the other hand, if "the Yankees ride over your country, stealing and plundering as they go, and living off the very supplies we could not get, I shall be cursed from one end of the Valley to the other for falling in my duty, and the Government will be blamed for an alleged indifference to your safety and welfare."

Imboden did not want to send his officers "to barns and corn-cribs, to your hay mows and garrets, for it is the most unpleasant task I ever have to perform." Instead, he asked that every farmer contribute what he could: "If he can't spare a ton, perhaps he can a half a ton of hay or fodder, or if that would run him too close, he would hardly miss 500 pounds." Imboden unleashed his rhetorical powers to make his case: "An acre of cabbage is of more real value to us now than would be a ship load of the richest spices of India. I would rather see a spare load of hay in one of your barns than a rosewood Chickering piano in your parlor, and would rather be invited to send for 20 shocks of corn than to attend, at one of your houses, the most sumptuous entertainment of even the halcyon days of peace."[43]

John Imboden was right to worry about the safety of the Shenandoah Valley. Since the beginning of the war, the Valley had played a critical role as a supplier of food and fodder to the Confederacy. The Valley Campaign of 1862 had been fought in part to protect that capacity and the Pennsylvania campaign of 1863 had sought to give the farms of the Valley time to replenish themselves in the summer. With the loss of Chattanooga and the cutting off of the railroads to the south, the Valley would be essential for the survival of Lee's army and the Confederate capital at Richmond.

As planting season and a renewal of war rapidly approached in the spring, with the enslaved population diminished and likely to diminish more, Augusta citizens urged the Confederate War Department to consider sending soldiers to the Valley to help get the crops in. Otherwise, "the fertile lands of the Valley will lie idle, and no crops will be raised there." The Valley had been, from the war's beginning, "the great granary" of the Confederacy and of Robert E. Lee's army. If Lee had to leave Virginia, the "withdrawal of that gallant army from Virginia by any cause whatever would depress the spirits of the people, not only in this State, but in the whole South, more than all the defeats we have suffered since the war." Despite the plea and the logic behind it, no soldiers arrived to help get in the crops; the farmers of the Valley would be on their own.[44]

The main hope for the Confederacy as 1864 began was that the coming season of fighting would be the last, that the United States would lose heart. The *Spectator* reprinted a biting attack from New York on "Lincoln's war." The New York *News*, a Democratic paper, sneered that although the United States had three times the population of the Confederacy and "a fighting population proportionately much larger—with bounties proffered, such as never tempted cupidity, in any war before—we are compelled to seduce foreigners from their homes to fight our battles for pay, and are driven to the still more degrading necessity of committing the honor of our flag and the vindication of our manhood to the hands of negroes, bond and free." The paper declared it absurd to talk of the "popularity" of a war "that can command no warmer support than this, from a brave and impulsive people."

The people of the North, the *News* declared, "do not feel any longer that the war is their war. They may support it a little while because the government is waging it and the flag is waved over it. Some of them may be willing it should continue, because it pays themselves or their friends large profits, or keeps up their influence or advances their party, or flatters their vanity or gratifies their rancor. But the great current of public feeling and opinion runs in its favor no longer." The critic challenged the administration to "tell the truth for a single month" about the true cost of the war.[45]

Such criticism was easy enough to find in any newspaper published by the Democrats of the North and hungrily reprinted throughout the Confederacy. The criticism would only grow as armies began to move when the muddy spring roads of Virginia began to dry.

☆

THE STATES STILL IN THE UNION were filled with politics during the war. The national two-party system collapsed in the 1850s and the Whigs disappeared; into that vacuum stepped the Free Soil Party, then the American or Know-Nothing Party, and then the new Republican Party. The Republicans, combining disparate fragments from the failed parties that preceded them, might have splintered in peacetime as well. Instead, the crucible of the Civil War hardened the new Republican Party. The Democrats, while surviving since the days of Andrew Jackson, had handed the presidency to the Republicans in 1860 by dividing themselves and their power. Northern Democrats and Southern Democrats had not been able to agree on a candidate for president at their convention in 1860 and so split their votes along regional lines, even though the strong pro-Southern candidate, John C. Breckinridge, had won votes across the North and the West.

Now the Northern Democrats struggled to define how an opposition party was supposed to act during wartime. Where did the line between party loyalty and national disloyalty lie? Neither Republicans nor Democrats had a clear sense of how they should behave toward each other. The crisis encouraged them to act aggressively in name-calling, speechmaking, editorial-writing, and office-taking even as they stood as a common front in their support for the soldiers. The Democrats in Congress had been abruptly weakened by the departure of Southern colleagues who had left *with secession. The Republicans held both electoral power and the power that came with leadership during a national emergency.[46]*

Even amid the intense partisan fighting, both parties agreed that the Constitution of the United States continued to define the law during wartime. The Democrats and the Republicans in the North fought over nothing as vigorously as questions of whether the Lincoln administration's strong moves to undermine slavery were constitutional. Lincoln, with the care of a skilled lawyer, strove to work within the bounds of the Constitution he revered.[47]

Political maneuvering never paused across the rising and falling of military events. The federal Constitution and its counterparts in each of the states laid out a clear schedule of elections at the local, state, and national levels. No one suggested that elections be postponed until the crisis of war had passed. Those state elections seemed to be spaced so that an election somewhere was always imminent. One political contest after another disturbed the status quo, giving the party out of power a chance to regain some power, somewhere.

Thus, while the Confederacy tolerated almost no "politics" as Americans had come to understand the word, the United States was saturated by partisan political fighting and rhetoric throughout the entire Civil War. The Republicans' success in the face of constant attacks from the Democrats disguised the profound risks Lincoln's opponents posed to the fulfillment of the president's vision of reunification and emancipation. Northerners, for good reason, often worried that the partisan fighting, and the differences in principles over which the fights raged, endangered their very cause.

☆

PENNSYLVANIA WAS CRUCIAL to the United States and to the Republicans in 1864. The state contributed more men per capita to the army than any other in the nation, rivaling New York as the largest contributor overall. Pennsylvania, moreover, was in the hands of the Republicans, unlike New York, and provided a foundation for the Lincoln administration's electoral and legislative strength. Governor Andrew Curtin was a strong ally of Lincoln and Curtin's reelection in the fall of 1863, narrow though it was, made the governor all the more valuable. That strategic importance also made him a target of the Democrats, who charged that Curtin had been fraudulently reelected. The Republicans in Pennsylvania held only a tenuous mandate and they knew it. They also knew that if they could not deliver their state in the election in November 1864 Abraham Lincoln might well lose the presidency.

The draft strained Pennsylvania. The traditionally Democratic coal-mining counties that ran through the central part of the state put forward the strongest resistance to the draft. Men in other counties across the state also challenged the provost marshals responsible for making sure Pennsylvania met its quota, a quota it struggled to fulfill with ever-growing bounties and local campaigns to raise money and men. The Democrats fed upon the resentment of the draft, and strongly Democratic counties, where officials sought to balance obligations to their party as well as to the nation, bred open resistance.

Counties to either side of Franklin—including Adams County, home to Gettysburg—had voted Democratic in the fall of 1863. But Franklin, like the state as a whole, narrowly supported the Republicans. Alexander K. McClure of Chambersburg was part of the reason. Although only in his mid-thirties, McClure had already served in the Pennsylvania house and senate and, more important, had played a critical role in the nomination of Abraham Lincoln for president in 1860. McClure worked as state chairman for the Republicans during the war and became a confidant and advisor of both Governor Curtin and President Lincoln. Thanks to McClure's stature and savvy at the county, state, and national

Alexander K. McClure

level, the editorials of his Franklin *Repository* provide a clear view
into the strategies and concerns of the Republican Party.

The weekly battle between the *Repository* and the *Valley Spirit*
showed the Republicans and the Democrats fighting on multiple
levels at the same time. They bickered over local politics in one
column and discoursed on the most important issues facing the
United States in the next. Neither paper ever forgot that it spoke
for its party.

The Democrats were not evenly matched against the Republicans in early 1864. Not only were they out of power and without capable national leadership, but every criticism they offered of
the Republicans and the armies could, and often did, sound like
disloyalty. Because Abraham Lincoln had so masterfully interwo-
ven the destruction of slavery with the saving of the Union, the
Democrats found it hard to criticize the fight against slavery without sounding as if they were undermining the war effort, or even
worse, the brave men, their neighbors, who fought for the United

States. The Democrats protested that they supported the troops and their votes for provisions for the army showed that they did. The Democrats insisted that they wanted to put the United States back together far more than the Republicans did and that they were more loyal to the Constitution.[48]

A small, lean government at all levels was a core ideological belief held by many in the Democratic Party. They saw dangerous government growth and "usurpation" in virtually every act of the Lincoln administration. The Lincoln administration and the Republicans threatened "military despotism, the worst form of tyranny."[49]

The Republicans, in turn, identified loyalty to the nation with loyalty to the Republican cause. As the war progressed, "loyal" and "Republican" came to be synonymous in the Republican lexicon. With great vehemence, the *Repository* summarized the potent Republican attack on the antiwar Democrats in a retort on the draft. "We want a conscription bill that will 'gobble up' a due share of the whining, cowardly, copperheads, who pollute the loyal atmosphere of the Free States with their denunciation of everything designed to preserve the government that protects them in their persons, their property and all their civil and religious rights."[50] The Republicans blamed the Democrats for the war in the first place, for supporting the Slave Power during all the decades between the Revolution and the Civil War. "It was by their aid" that slavery "became imperial in its demands, and proclaimed itself master of the continent."[51]

The Democrats often used a professed concern for the welfare of African-Americans as a way to attack the idea of ending slavery. "Mr. Lincoln's emancipation proclamation" had simply freed "the slaves from their masters," they charged, without providing any "remedy for the evils of slavery"—evils of poverty, ignorance, and ill health. The thousands of enslaved people who fled to the United States armies were left "in filthy camps to die of starvation and disease. Deadened as the sensibilities of the whole nation have become to scenes of suffering and distress, the tales of horror which come up to us from the camps of freed negroes along the Mississippi cannot fail to enlist our sympathies. The poor blacks, left to the tender mercies of their pretended friends, are dying daily by fifties and hundreds." The language of "pretended friends" and "tender mercies" was common in the Southern press as well, impugning the sincerity of those who called for the end of slavery, assuming an ulterior motive of financial gain or political advantage behind their pretended altruism.

The Democrats were right about the suffering in the camps. Tens of thousands of formerly enslaved people were dying in the midst of a war that had become a war to end slavery. The *Valley Spirit* reprinted paragraph after paragraph of a report from the Sanitary Commission in late 1863, detailing rampant sickness and neglect. Rather than arguing that more needed to be done to care for those in the camps, however, the Democrats betrayed themselves as far too sympathetic to the slaveholders. "This is the glorious jubilee of freedom to which Mr. Lincoln invites the slaves of the South. It is for such liberty as this he asks them to leave their master's plantations, where they were comfortably housed, clothed and fed; where they were tenderly cared for in helpless youth and feeble old age; where in sickness they received their medicines from the master's store, and gentle nursing from the members of his household." Such romanticized visions of slavery and the South left the Democrats open to legitimate charges of betraying the Union cause.[52]

And so did the nightmarish visions that often accompanied the romance. "There is another feature of this negro question which is every day becoming of vaster importance," they warned. "We are placing arms in the hands of hundreds of thousands of fierce and untutored slaves. Is it expected that when the war is over they will quietly lay down those arms? They will be acquainted with army drill and tactics, they will have learned the modes of organizing armies and conducting campaigns. Will they not strike a blow for this 'liberty and equality,' of which they have heard so much, but which they have never realized?" The Democrats, like Confederates, conjured a race war that would follow the war between North and South. The romance of a benign slavery and a contrasting nightmare of an insurrection of vengeful people held in slavery warred within Democrats' rhetoric.[53]

☆

WHILE THE DEMOCRATS and the Republicans fought at home, thousands of Franklin County men were fighting for the United States Army across an enormous expanse, from Virginia's Shenandoah Valley to the mountains of East Tennessee to the sandbars of the Atlantic Coast. The winter of 1864 offered an opportunity for one of the largest Franklin units—"what remains of the gallant 77th Pennsylvania"—to come home on furlough. The regiment, formed in Chambersburg in September 1861, had over the last two and a half years "participated in some of the hardest fights and undergone some of the severest marches in the history of the war. It was conspicuous at Shiloh; lost its commander at Stone River; and covered itself with glory at Chattanooga and Chickamauga." When the regiment had first gone into battle it claimed 1,000 men; "now it numbers scarce 250, disease and death having thus decimated its strength." Almost every man who was healthy enough to fight had reenlisted.[54]

While the 77th came home on furlough, the forty-five soldiers from Franklin in the United States Colored Troops, fighting in the famous 54th and 55th Massachusetts, were transported to central Florida. Though Florida was among the first six states to secede, it had strained to keep connection with the Confederacy. Only about 150,000 black and white people lived in Florida—about evenly divided by race—and so the state had little to contribute to the armies. The few men it did provide fought with Lee in far-off Gettysburg, participating in the charge on Cemetery Ridge, but Florida's main contributions came in the form of cattle and other food. Neither the Confederacy nor the United States exerted much energy in Florida, which remained basically undefended, encircled by the Union naval blockade.

In early 1864 the United States decided that it would launch an expedition in Florida to secure new recruits for the United States Colored Troops, destroy what remained of the railroads connecting to the Confederacy, and determine if the state might be ready to rejoin the United States. Disrupting the supply of food and men to Confederate armies in Tennessee, Georgia, South Carolina, and Virginia stood as the expedition's main goal.[55]

The marginal Union effort was poorly coordinated, as was the Confederate opposition. David Demus wrote his wife Mary Jane from South Carolina in early February that "We ar fisking to leave i Can not tell you Whear We ar going but tha think that We ar going to heav a big fite son." Three weeks later, he gave the story of the battle as he saw it. They had left Morris Island and sailed south to Florida. "We all have had a hard time cince we landed we heave bean in a fite but thank god all ar boys got out but Willam Cristy." William—the brother of Mary Jane—had been shot in the battle at Olustee. "We sow him Whean he fell but i Cant tell Whear he Was sot but We lost him in a good cos."

William, the youngest of the three Christy brothers fighting, was only eighteen. "He Was a brave boy hear feared nothing." The letter was probably the first that Mary Jane heard of her brother's death.[56]

On stationery depicting an image of the United States flag with the motto "Long may it wave!" printed underneath, Jacob Christy left his sister with a disturbing image. "The rebels gut William so I think for we haveant heard any thing of him." The Confederates were known to have murdered wounded black men where they lay, and several wrote of doing so at Olustee. Mary Jane asked her husband for more details and he told her that William had been shot in the arm "and we tolde him to go to the reayr but he Wod not go and the he Was sot in the brest and Was kill Ded." Perhaps Mary Jane preferred to believe that his death had come in the moment of battle rather than at the hands of a Confederate soldier who discovered her brother on the field after the United States Army had left.[57]

William Christy had fought with the same determination as many of his comrades in the 54th Massachusetts. The regiment had been positioned only four hundred yards from the Confederates, whose artillery fire shattered tree branches large enough to injure the Federal soldiers when they fell. The men of the 54th fought so long and hard that they consumed all their ammunition. Despite their bravery, the Union force was defeated and driven from the field.[58]

Under the title "The Black Soldiers in Florida," the Republican paper of Franklin reprinted praise from white officers at the battle. "I hear loud praises of the 54th Massachusetts, 8th United States, and 1st North Carolina (colored.) They went up at the double quick when our advance was nearly destroyed, and saved the left from being turned, in which case the whole force would have been annihilated. The conduct of the troops is represented to have been uniformly admirable." Their white colonel "told them he could not find fault with a single officer or man. And I could but admire their patience while waiting to have their wounds dressed, and to be conveyed to the hospital from the steamer." The Battle of Olustee provided another opportunity for the African-American soldiers to prove themselves to a still uncertain, and not always attentive or appreciative, nation.[59]

Within the 54th itself, their unquestioned bravery made their mistreatment by the United States even more galling. As Jacob Christy wrote home after they had once again arrived at Morris Island, "the men all says that thay will wate tell the last of this month and if thay dont pay us we will get Troublesum." In language usually reserved for the rebels, Jacob told Mary Jane that "if we cant get our rights we will die trying for them We have been fighting as brave as ever thay was any soldiers fought I know if every regiment that are out and have been out would have dun as well as we have the war would be over." Serving the United States and confronting the Confederates, Christy saw that all white people would have to be persuaded of black people's rights. "I du really think that its God will that this ware Shall not end till the Colord people get thier rights it goes verry hard for the White people to think of it But by gods will and powr thay will have thier rights."[60]

David Demus was honest with Mary Jane. He had been gone a year and it had been hard: "if i ever get home a gane safe and get out of the army Wiy i Will never live you a gane as long as i live fer i now What it is to be a soldier in a battel." David admitted that "the reasen that i Cum Was becos i thot it a big thing to be a Solder i have fond out a boute it." He had never been "as long With out money in mi life."[61]

The full meaning of the service of men like David Demus and the Christy brothers was not clear to them or to anyone else in early 1864. As Jacob Christy put it, "us that are liveing know may not live to see it I shall die a trying for our rights so that other that are born hereaffter may live and enjoy a happy life." Despite the indignities and injustices he had endured during his service Jacob Christy, somehow, refused to lose faith in the nation for which he fought.[62]

☆

THE MONTHS BETWEEN GETTYSBURG and the spring of 1864 brought a reckoning with war and emancipation. People in both the United States and the Confederacy cast their minds back over the events of the preceding years, looking for guidance for the war yet to come. People measured themselves, their neighbors, and their enemies.

In the North, the war unleashed capacities people had not known they possessed. The material and economic capabilities of their society proved even greater than they had hoped. The railroads and ships, the farms and factories, the cities and towns of the United States turned out limitless quantities of everything the soldiers of the nation required. The army and navy, growing suddenly, proved massively competent at war, mobilizing and moving and supplying millions of men at distances of thousands of miles. More millions of men awaited if the emergency demanded.

The Republicans in the United States also tapped new reservoirs of moral and ideological capacity. The white electorate had moved haltingly, often grudgingly, toward visions of freedom for the enslaved people of the South. By the fall of 1863, President Lincoln had embraced and defined that vision in new ways that many people found compelling. As the United States Colored Troops seized the opportunity to fight and to sacrifice, many white Northerners' admiration grew. As the Democrats used the turn against slavery to attack the Republicans, the Republicans in turn deepened their dedication to ending slavery as part of Union victory. Party conflict sharpened rather than dulled Republican purpose and Democratic resistance. The elections of the coming year would offer clear choices for white voters, one choice pointing toward compromise and the other pointing toward the transformation of slavery into something other than slavery.

The Confederacy, by contrast, saw its capacities weakening. While the war-born and war-fed nation sustained its fighting power, mobilizing every human and material resource it possessed, that very mobilization fractured and eroded the South. Soldiers wrestled with desertion, including their own. Slaveholders and their government wrestled with impressment and taxation. States wrestled with the central government. People of property and means wrestled with those without. Most important, slaves wrestled against the order that kept them as slaves.

The Confederate goals for the war diminished. White Southerners now fought simply to avoid being, as they put it, vanquished. Few expressed a vision of what an independent Confederacy might be, might represent to the world. As one vast territory after another fell away from the Confederacy, the Confederacy that remained fought simply for survival. Their only hope for independence and the slavery the nascent nation sustained was for the United States to capitulate. And that capitulation would only arrive if the Confederate army could defend Virginia and bleed the United States beyond its capacity for sacrifice.

The Earth Will Tremble

April through June 1864

*P*eople in both the North and the South believed that 1864 would bring the culmination of the war. The people of the United States had reason to be hopeful, for it seemed that so much of the Confederacy had been overrun that the rebel nation would be unable to sustain its armies much longer. Federal forces controlled the rivers, the ports, and the coasts; the western part of the Confederacy had been cut off from the eastern, the upper South from the lower. Black people now labored for Union benefit—and their own—from the vast Mississippi River valley to the lush lowlands of South Carolina to the rich farms of central Tennessee.

The white people of the Confederacy had their own reasons to believe that 1864 would bring the war's end, but with a different outcome. They had only to hold off the United States Army long enough for the North to lose heart, admit that the South could not be conquered, and renounce Abraham Lincoln in the presidential election of 1864. If the Confederate army could hold on through the spring and summer, many in the South felt certain, Northern voters, judging that they had sacrificed enough, would negotiate a peace.

The fate of slavery might also be determined in 1864. Slavery had been undermined wherever the United States forces had arrived with the power of the Emancipation Proclamation. Despite that progress, three million enslaved people still lived beyond the reach of the United States armies in 1864. While slavery had unraveled everywhere enslaved people had a chance to seize freedom, the institution remained intact in most of the South and still helped feed the Confederate army and civilian population. While the policies of the Lincoln administration had made slavery's end a central purpose of the war, war itself would determine how and when the nation's long history of slavery might end. In 1864, freedom for black Americans might yet be truncated, compromised, slowed, or even halted.

Everyone awaited the culminating battle between Ulysses S. Grant and Robert E. Lee. Grant, with momentous victories at Nashville, Vicksburg, and Chattanooga in 1862 and 1863, arrived in Virginia in March 1864 to take over command of all United States forces and travel with the Army of the Potomac. He would try to do what no Union general had been able to do in three years of desperate fighting: destroy the Army of Northern Virginia. Lee, for his part, welcomed the chance to confront Grant in a culminating battle while the Confederates still had a strong army.

The two armies needed, each for its own reasons, to fight as soon as possible that spring. Lee and his staff had struggled throughout the long winter to feed and arm their soldiers, had watched as desertion and demoralization eroded their ranks. By spring, however, most of the men who had left their units to visit home had returned and Lee commanded a veteran army of over 65,000 men. The Army of Northern Virginia had rarely lost over the preceding three years and both officers and soldiers had persuaded themselves that even the defeat at Gettysburg had been only a temporary setback. The Confederate command structure was stable, experienced, and confident.[1]

The United States was also ready for a final clash. It had amassed an even larger force than Lee's—120,000 men in Virginia—and could draw on virtually unlimited supplies of food and arms. Railroads brought to Grant's army the bounty of the North. Boxcars and flatcars were loaded by thousands of ships, boats, and barges freely navigating the harbors and rivers of the Virginia coast. Everyone from Abraham Lincoln to the privates in the field had confidence that Grant, given his record and resources, would soon be able to defeat Lee and the rebellion he led.[2]

Most newspapers, civilians, and political leaders in the North and the South believed that what happened in Virginia in 1864 would determine the outcome of the war. No one denied the importance of Atlanta, where William T. Sherman would confront Joseph E. Johnston for control of the deep South, but the Confederate capital had obsessed the Northern press from the first days of the war, when "On to Richmond!" blared from headlines and broadsides. The proximity of the fighting in Virginia to Washington and the leading cities of the United States gave the conflict there a powerful immediacy. Everyone understood what was at stake.[3]

☆

NO ONE DOUBTED that the struggle in Virginia would be horrible. As spring arrived, the Republican newspaper in Franklin County reprinted "a calm and soldierly article" explaining what Ulysses Grant and the Army of the Potomac were up against. The people of the North "know now by sad experience what war is and what are the obstacles to be overcome in Virginia." Experience also showed that critics would quickly turn on a failed general. "If Gen. Grant does not defeat Lee and drive the rebels out of Virginia in three months, or if he does not win in every move and every battle, he will be hooted down and disgraced."

Lee's army was positioned north of Richmond and the Virginia landscape aided the Confederates, the report admitted. Directly in front of the United States Army lay "a succession of rivers, presenting great natural obstacles to our advance, and at the same time easily defensible" by the Confederates. The slippery river banks would delay armies dragging heavy cannon and hundreds of unwieldy wagons behind horses and mules. Confederate forces could hold off attackers forced to build bridges or wade through strong currents. Between the rivers, "dense forests," often tangled masses of second or third growth, covered much of the region, making "anything like a surprise in force impracticable. A few rebel scouts may at all times easily detect and thwart such a movement." Despite a rich and powerful nation sending supplies, once Grant's Army of the Potomac launched an offensive its lifeline "is just the width of a railroad track, and that railroad furnishes really the only practicable route of communication."

Virginia bore one another feature, well known to everyone in the United States and the Confederacy, that would shape any battle between Grant and Lee: the Shenandoah Valley, a hundred miles to the west of Richmond. Bounded by "chains of mountains which enable the rebels to conceal any flanking movement they may undertake," the Valley offered "easy and uninterrupted passage to the Potomac above Washington, and one almost entirely secure from attacks in their rear." The Valley of Virginia had played a critical role in every stage of the war thus far—as battlefield, supply base, and route of invasion—and everyone knew it would soon do so again. The army that controlled the Valley would control much of Virginia and the fate of the nation.[4]

☆

THE PEOPLE OF AUGUSTA COUNTY faced the spring of 1864 with a better understanding than most of what renewed war in Virginia would bring. "In a short time the earth will be made to tremble beneath the shock of armed hosts in hostile and deadly conflict," the *Staunton Spectator* intoned in biblical cadences in April. "The armies of the South and North are now girding up their loins for a most terrible encounter. The most crimson page in the book of Time will be written in blood the ensuing Summer." The South believed the North was desperate for quick victory. "The enemy feel that, if they fail to conquer us in this campaign, the task is hopeless, and that anarchy and irretrievable ruin will be their lot."[5]

The Shenandoah Valley had seen war in various guises. Armies under strict command had fought one another in the Valley in one battle after another, but the Valley had also seen various forms of guerilla, partisan, and irregular conflict. In places near the Valley, such as East Tennessee, western North Carolina, and the new state of West Virginia, mountains prevented the easy movement or occupation of large armies. There, people fought the war among themselves on a ragged and desperate personal scale. Raiding parties, partisan rangers, and simple outlaws suddenly appeared on farmsteads and in villages, taking what they wanted. Loyalties fragmented communities and families. Crime and terror ran unchecked. Guerrilla bands destroyed railroads and bridges, stole horses and cattle, burned houses and barns.[6]

Formal warfare and guerrilla fighting exacted different kinds of costs. Armies of ten thousand men, even friendly armies, consumed the areas through which they passed, with fields, fences, livestock, and stores of food laboriously gathered over decades stripped away overnight. Except when wintering, those armies seldom stayed in a particular place for very long, though, and fortunate families might be able to hide themselves and their sustenance while the armies passed. The spasmodic presence of guerrillas, bushwhackers, and partisans, by contrast, could not be evaded. These groups survived by moving quickly, appearing and disappearing, judging for themselves whether a person or a family was loyal to the right cause, knowing who had hidden food or livestock. For good reason, the Valley trembled as the war roared into life in the spring of 1864. So sheltered a place in peace time, the Valley in war could come under assault from north and south, east and west, inside and outside.

Throughout the fall and winter of 1863 and 1864, the mountains to the west of the Valley had seen small but hard-fought struggles on narrow roads and steep slopes. The local citizens held uncertain loyalties, for they had often opposed secession and the toll of the Confederate government but also resented the incursions of Federal troops. Fugitives from the draft and deserters from Lee's army regularly fled to the mountains, where they often found sympathetic allies.

John Imboden had been returned to the Valley by Lee after leading the wagon trains of wounded men from Gettysburg in July 1863. Now, nine months later, Imboden complained that he did not have enough men, horses, or food to resist the Federal forces in the mountains. In March, he wrote Robert E. Lee to predict "a big raid some time this month." Federal Generals William Woods Averell or George Crook, both with large commands in the mountains to the west, could attack with five or six thousand men at several places at once. Imboden warned Lee that if the Union armies descended on "say Staunton, Lexington, and the Virginia and Tennessee Railroad, we shall be sorely put to meet him."[7]

Lee recognized the threat from the Federal troops in the mountains, but he hoped that Imboden would be able to drive them back on his own, for "I shall be so occupied, in all probability, that I shall be unable to aid you." Fortunately, Lee added, he did not think Grant would divert soldiers from the impending fight around Richmond to invade the Valley and he saw "no indications" of a Federal attack from the northern end of the Valley. Lee would soon prove mistaken.[8]

☆

ULYSSES GRANT DECIDED THAT he would take advantage of the numerical and logistical strength of the United States Army to launch three coordinated and simultaneous attacks in Virginia. He would send one force up the James River to threaten the Confederate capital at Richmond from the east and another force into the Shenandoah Valley from the north. The major effort, though, would be what came to be known at the Overland Campaign, driving the massive Army of the Potomac against Lee and Richmond from the north. Grant sought to force Lee to divide his forces to fend off all three threats at once or to sacrifice crucial parts of Virginia.

The movement from the north began in May at the terrible battles of the Wilderness and Spotsylvania Courthouse. Those conflicts inflicted the worst casualties in the war on both the Federal and Confederate armies. The Confederates lost 24,000 men, though ten thousand replacements would arrive from elsewhere in the South. The Union lost over a third of its men, nearly 37,000—thirteen thousand more than had been killed, wounded, or captured at Gettysburg. At the same time, thousands of Union soldiers prepared to leave for home as the terms of their enlistment expired. The departure of those men, who had signed on for three years in the spring and summer of 1861, took with them the experience and determination the Army of the Potomac most needed. As his army moved ever farther south, moreover, Grant's lines of communication and supply became ever more extended and vulnerable.[9]

People across the North read the news from the battlefields above Richmond and worried. An article in the *Valley Spirit* in Chambersburg summarized the situation. "Whilst our army has been gradually gaining ground on the enemy, its advance has been met with a stubbornness of resistance which still holds victory trembling in the balance." The latest news from Grant's army reported that "the loss in these battles, in killed, wounded and missing, has been terrific. Ours has been estimated as high as seventy thousand, and that of the enemy equal, if not greater."[10]

Those estimates would prove too high, but people in the North were willing to believe the worst. Grant was in fact making progress, paying a high price but exacting an unsustainable toll on the Confederate army, killing not only thousands of soldiers but also irreplaceable officers. Grant intended to keep pushing until he found a way to break Lee.

☆

THROUGH THESE REMORSELESS WEEKS of battle, Augusta County men fought alongside Lee near Richmond. The 5th and 52nd Virginia infantry, foundations of the famous Stonewall Brigade since the first months of the war, had served in every important battle in Virginia, Maryland, and Pennsylvania over the last three years. Augusta had sacrificed hundreds of sons, brothers, and fathers to the Confederate cause in the first three years of war, and the people of the county knew that more were being sacrificed in May 1864.

Staunton felt the suffering of the battles with terrible immediacy, for trainloads of wounded men groaned into the small and overburdened town on the Virginia Central Railroad, a hundred miles from the battlefields to the east. The hospitals, hotels, churches, and homes of Staunton, having slowly emptied of wounded soldiers from the Gettysburg campaign of the preceding summer, filled again with bleeding and dying men.

The battles outside Richmond devastated the units in which many Augusta men fought. A staccato report from the front to a Staunton paper told the chilling news: "In the Stonewall Brigade there are 926 missing. But 349 men left in this Brigade. There are 30 officers in the Brigade, killed, wounded and missing."[11]

As the fragmentary news arrived via telegraph and railroad, the people of Staunton could see for themselves the horror. "For the past few days large numbers of those wounded in the late fights have arrived at Staunton," the *Vindicator* reported. "They were met at the trains by many of the Ladies of this place." The large hospital in Staunton was "full of these gallant unfortunates, who have been wounded in defending our homes and firesides from the ruthless invader." The civilians of Staunton felt powerless, but "while we can not heal their wounds by a simple wish, we can ameliorate their condition much by sending many little things not generally needed for family use, which will be thankfully received by them." The Staunton paper called "the attention of the Country people," the people who had farms and thus perhaps food to share, to "this patriotic and humane duty. Send to the wounded anything you can spare and send at once." Women worked to provide basic medical supplies as well as any comfort they could offer.[12]

The newspapers filled columns with closely packed names of the Augusta men who had been wounded and shipped back to Staunton. From the 5th Virginia, nearly a hundred men lay in local hospitals and homes. Every part of their bodies had been damaged:

they had suffered severe facial, head, neck, and shoulder wounds, amputated arms, hands, and feet, and nearly hopeless injuries to bowels, groin, and abdomen. The list for the 52nd Virginia was devastating, too, with grave injuries to eyes, lungs, arteries, and skulls. More men arrived each day, adding to the despair.[13]

The elderly Reverend Francis McFarland of Augusta County kept a terse diary, filled mainly with notes of his physical and spiritual state. In May, that diary registered the heartbreak and uncertainty of family members across the North and the South. The Reverend McFarland had three sons fighting with Lee: James, twenty-two; Robert, twenty-five; and Francis, thirty. All farmers, all had enlisted in 1861. On May 15, their father noted during the bloodshed at Spotsylvania that "the reports continue to arrive of a terrible Battle on Thursday—it is said that the 5th Regt. Va. Infantry went in with 400 men & came out with only 150, & that the 52 also suffered severely. Oh, my Sons, my Sons! But the Lord Reigns." The next day McFarland heard in a letter that "our Son James, if alive is a prisoner, Alas. The enemy took a fortification in which he was." Two weeks later McFarland received some good news: "Thank God, a letter from James, dated Fortress Monroe, May 15. He is in good spirits & well treated-destination—Fort Delaware," a prisoner of war camp. Being captured was better than being killed.

Just two days after that reassurance from James, though, the Reverend McFarland recorded "Sad tidings. One report is that Robert was killed on Monday last. A Telegram from Francis dated the 2d inst. says 'Robert in hands of Enemy—Reported seriously wounded.' The Lord reigns & he will do what is best for him that Christ bought with his blood, I submit. A Telegram from Francis dated today, says-Robt. was shot through the heart; never spoke. Alas, alas!" This devout Christian father would never know whether his son thought of eternal life as earthly life ended.

Two days after receiving the news, McFarland "heard a telegram read that Robert was not hurt—O that it may be so." A visit with a neighboring family also brought encouragement, when a fellow soldier reported that "he saw a member of Roberts company who said R. was wounded but not badly. O, to be relieved from suspense." Finally, over a month after the first word of the battle had arrived and two weeks after hope had risen, the Reverend McFarland received a letter from a doctor saying that "he had found the body of my Dear Son Robert, covered with earth, he supposes where he fell, & had it reburied & the grave markd." McFarland and his wife received letters of sympathy. "We have been held long in suspense, now the sad reality is known." The McFarlands expressed gratitude to learn from the letters that "Glory to God, we have satisfactory evidences of his Piety."[14]

☆

AS PART OF HIS three-pronged plan to take Virginia, Grant appointed a new commander in the Valley: Major General Franz Sigel. Grant, in truth, had little faith in Sigel, who was widely considered a "political general." Sigel commanded in the field because he helped the Republicans secure the German-American vote at the ballot box. That vote had been critical for the Republicans in 1860 and would be so again in the fall elections of 1864. Grant ordered Sigel, commanding about 7,000 men, to proceed south in the Valley until he connected with the Union forces under Averell and Crook descending from the mountains of southwest Virginia. Grant expected the two armies to meet around Staunton. Facing relatively little opposition, Grant hoped, the United States would finally take control of the critical Shenandoah Valley while Lee was consumed with survival near Richmond.

The northern Valley had been bedeviled by the partisan rangers of John Singleton Mosby since early 1863. Mosby and his men, who blended in with the civilian population of Loudon County, raided Federal camps, disrupted supply lines, and captured couriers. Infiltrating the lines of the enemy, Mosby kept them off-balance and wary. Union cavalrymen repeatedly went out to capture Mosby and his men, and repeatedly failed.

John Imboden's rangers also disrupted Sigel. They attacked the B&O Railroad that served as the supply lifeline to Sigel's

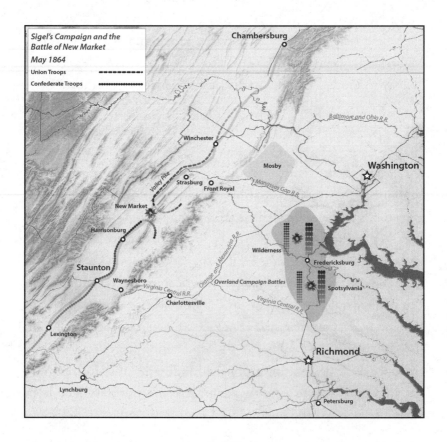

Confederate General John C. Breckinridge

troops, destroying 7 machine shops, 9 locomotives, and more than 150 loaded freight cars. Imboden's men ran 6 other locomotives into a creek and burned the railroad bridge across the Potomac. They attacked the Union's flanking cavalry wherever they could find it isolated and headed south to connect with other Confederate troops.[15]

Sigel, concerned about protecting his supply lines and wary of guerillas up and down the Valley, moved slowly. His delays allowed the Confederates to mobilize forces from farther south in the Valley to confront him before he reached Staunton. John Breckinridge, former vice-president of the United States and now a brigadier general in the Confederacy, moved north with about 2,500 troops. He ordered 229 cadets, some of them as young as 15, from the Virginia Military Institute to join him. Imboden's youngest brother, Jacob, was among the cadets.

On May 12, Breckinridge reached Staunton and gave his men a day of rest, waited for the VMI cadets, and cooked two days of rations. Once Breckinridge and Imboden connected, they possessed about 5,300 men and 18 artillery pieces to confront Sigel's much larger forces. They headed northward to stop him.

Three days later, the Staunton *Spectator* breathlessly reported that the two armies had clashed at New Market, a small town about 45 miles north of Staunton on the Valley Turnpike. To his lasting sorrow, Breckinridge sent into battle the cadets from the Virginia Military Institute who had marched north with him. Ten of the young men were killed.[16]

With sarcasm, admiration, surprise, and gratitude, the Staunton paper declared that "the strength of our force, it may not be prudent to state at this time, but it was sufficient to defeat and rout Siegel and all 'dat fites mit him'"—making fun of the German's accent and a popular dialect song in the North. The *Spectator* acknowledged that "our loss was considerable" and that "the Cadets of the Virginia Military Institute participated gallantly and efficiently in this battle." More than two hundred Union prisoners had already arrived in Staunton. The Union force retreated and burned bridges behind them, showing no signs of renewing their invasion of the Valley.[17]

Thinking the Valley safe for the time being, Breckinridge rushed to join Lee near Richmond as soon as the Battle at New Market had ended. John Imboden, with only a thousand men, would once again be left to defend the Valley on his own. Though they had turned Sigel back, the Confederates failed to take the initiative. Ulysses Grant would make the next move in the Valley.[18]

☆

DAVID HUNTER STROTHER KNEW the Valley well. A Virginian, Strother had made drawings and written stories about the region for *Harpers Weekly* in the 1850s. Now he traveled through the Valley in a different role, as an officer in the United States Army. Strother had studied art in the North and in Europe and brought a sophisticated eye—as well as an impressive Germanic beard—to the events swirling around him. Strother's military career had not been distinguished up to the spring of 1864 and he held a healthy skepticism of his own military abilities and of the men he served.[19]

Strother had served as an adjutant to Sigel and was appointed an aide to a new commander brought in to replace Sigel after the debacle of New Market. To the surprise of Strother, the new commander was Strother's cousin, Major General David Hunter.[20]

Grant recognized that Hunter, a bold, even impetuous foe of slavery, had caused turmoil wherever he had gone, but Grant wanted someone to do what no Union general had been able to do: subdue the Shenandoah Valley. Grant ordered Hunter to clear the Valley of the Confederate challenge, destroying railroads and canals along the way, wiping out the guerrillas and partisans who had bedeviled Federal soldiers. The plan called for Hunter's forces to proceed south in the Valley to Staunton, join with Union forces coming from the west, then pivot to the east and help destroy the railroads that connected the Valley to Lee's army. When Hunter combined his men with those of William Averell and George Crook, the Federal army would stand at 18,000 men, the largest the Valley had ever seen.

Hunter sent out pickets to confront the guerrillas that swarmed through the Valley and surrounding mountains, announcing that civilians who aided or harbored the guerrillas would be executed and have their houses burned. Long supply lines made an army vulnerable, diverting men to protect the wagons at the rear who could otherwise fight at the front, so Hunter would keep those

United States General David Hunter

lines of supply as short as he could. "We take with us only coffee, sugar, salt, and hard bread for some days, depending on the
country for everything else," Strother wrote in his diary. To further lessen the need for long supply trains, the men had to carry
more than twice as much ammunition as they were accustomed,
weighing them down even as they went hungry. Though he was
glad to be associated with a leader more aggressive than Sigel,
Strother admitted that Hunter's plan of rapid movement and living off the land was "a bold and almost desperate one."[21]

As the Federal troops moved south along the Valley Turnpike
in early June, two women came from their house and cheered
the troops. "That's right," they cried. "The rebels starved us and
let us go almost naked, and this serves them right."[22] But most
residents of the Valley hated the Yankee invaders and made no
secret of their hatred. Union invasion, rather than breaking the
spirit of the white people of the Valley, seemed to galvanize their
loyalty to the Confederacy. Faced with such intransigence, Union

soldiers felt justified taking whatever they wished, wherever they found it. A cycle of hatred and vengeance, years of warfare in the making, now fed on itself.[23]

Hunter ordered his men to slaughter cattle, sheep, and pigs from the farms they passed. The appropriation of local food was "necessary as the army must feed," Strother admitted in his diary, but the soldiers "are plundering dreadfully from all accounts. This is not necessary and should not be permitted, especially as there are some wounded Union soldiers here who have been well treated by the citizens." Hunter's men took their time, seeking out bushwhackers and burning their houses. They were in no hurry, Hunter assumed, because all that stood between them and Staunton was the diminished force of John Imboden.[24]

☆

LEARNING OF HUNTER'S APPOINTMENT and movements to the south in the Valley, Lee hurriedly sent William Jones to intercept Hunter before the Union army reached Staunton. Known for his discipline as well as his irascible manner (he was unaffectionately known as "Grumble"), Jones commanded troops in his native southwest Virginia, near the Tennessee line, two hundred miles south of Staunton. A graduate of West Point, Jones brought order to previously undisciplined men and had fought with audacity and success alongside John Imboden in West Virginia.[25]

In his confrontation with Hunter, Jones would be leading the largest force he had ever commanded, over 5,600 men. Jones gathered soldiers scattered along the Virginia and Tennessee Railroad. They took the train to Lynchburg, then a circuitous route on the Orange and Alexandria to Charlottesville, and then the Virginia Central Railroad through the Blue Ridge Tunnel into Staunton.

Despite the roundabout journey, the railroad allowed Jones to arrive in Staunton ahead of Hunter, who had spent several days in towns along the Valley Pike. Hunter's progress had been slowed by guerrilla attacks on his supply lines and by Hunter's furious actions against those guerrillas.

Hunter also faced dogged resistance from his front. John McCausland had been fighting in the mountains of his native western Virginia for the preceding two years, facing the much larger and better equipped forces of Crook and Averell, holding them at bay as best he could. After a series of other Confederate generals sent to command in western Virginia had failed or been killed, McCausland finally became brigadier general in May 1864, just in time to confront the combined forces under Hunter. With his 1,500 men, McCausland harassed the Federal forces at rivers, felled trees to block roads, skirmished with advance units and scouts, struck and then faded into the mountain passes, buying time for Jones to stop Hunter before the Union army could take Staunton.

Jones and Imboden joined forces in Staunton on June 4, though Imboden did not have much to offer. Desperate, he had called out the home guard of the Valley, assembling about 1,100 older men, young boys, convalescent soldiers, and government clerks from Augusta and surrounding counties. These men possessed little training or experience on the battlefield; they were armed only with the muskets and shotguns they brought with them. A broadside issued in Staunton made the situation clear: "Every man who can fire a Gun is urgently required," the text demanded. Despite the challenges of recruitment, after Jones and Imboden were joined by McCausland coming down from the mountains the Confederates would boast a larger army than Stonewall Jackson had ever commanded in the Valley.[26]

Staunton offered many inducements to an invading force, with large stores of military supplies and several small manufactories producing for the Confederate army. The town also possessed hospitals and newspapers that urged people to fight for the Confederacy. But the railroad, as always, was the major concern of both the Union and the Confederates. If Hunter seized the railhead at Staunton, the major link to the middle Shenandoah Valley would be lost to Lee's army.

Hunter could break the vital rail line by taking the Augusta town of Waynesboro between Staunton and the long Blue Ridge Tunnel to the east. From there, the Union army could move east toward Charlottesville and Richmond, destroying the railroad as it marched to join Grant. Alternatively, Hunter might decide to march south toward Lynchburg, the second largest city and industrial center in Virginia, with its own rail and canal connections to Richmond. Staunton would play a central role in either Union strategy.

The rapidly assembled Confederate force headed north to avoid the catastrophe of losing Staunton, scouts pushing ahead to determine which route in the Valley the Yankees were taking. Grumble Jones received a telegram from Robert E. Lee telling him that no reinforcements would be coming and that he must hit Hunter before Hunter converged with Averell and Crook at Staunton. Jones did not share the discouraging note with Imboden. The Confederates rushed north to find a place to try to stop Hunter's advance.

☆

GENERAL DAVID HUNTER and the Union army suddenly and unexpectedly confronted the enemy on the morning of June 5, 1864. The confrontation came at a village called Piedmont, a few

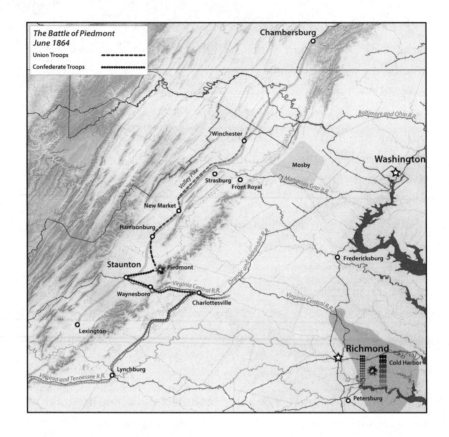

miles north of Staunton: "We were advancing over some hills and slopes, the enemy was posted on the rising ground around the village of Piedmont, concealed in the woods as usual," David Strother wrote in his diary. "Already the shells and shot began to whistle around our ears." The Confederates, in a position "strong and well chosen," commanded "an open valley between and open, gentle slopes in front." Lush spring clover and young corn covered the fields.[27]

Hunter had not heard about Grumble Jones's arrival. The Federals expected to face the diminished command of John Imboden's thousand men if they faced any opposition at all. Instead, the battle exploded into the largest the Valley had ever seen. Thousands of men from both sides poured over the rivers, bluffs, farms, and roads around Piedmont, forming constantly shifting patterns of danger and possibility. Cavalry, artillery, and infantry followed their own roles, reliant upon the other units to do their part. Officers had to read the unfamiliar landscape at a glance, comprehending in a moment which advance marked success and which left a fatal vulnerability.

In the barely controlled chaos of the instant battle, the turning point was clear to everyone: the Confederates allowed a gap, a quarter of a mile long, between two of their infantry lines facing the Union—one commanded by John Imboden and another by Brigadier General John Vaughn, who had just joined the Confederate force with a brigade of dismounted horsemen from Tennessee. Grumble Jones's orders had either been wrong, misunderstood, or not acted upon. Hunter's men drove through the gap, artillery widening the hole and infantry pouring after, attacking the Confederates from unprotected angles. The Confederates, overwhelmed, fought for about half an hour and then began to run, trying to make it across the river behind them to some kind of safety. Jones tried desperately to rally his troops, riding out in front of them, urging them to stop their retreat. Exposed, Jones was shot in the head by Union infantry and died instantly.

"The earth shook with the roar of guns and musketry, and the fresh, hearty cheers rose with the smoke and sounded like victory," David Strother wrote exultantly. "Stretcher men, ambulance drivers, wounded men, butchers, bummers, and all took up the shout and back upon the hill crests. Negroes, teamsters, and camp followers re-echoed the joyful shout." Hunter's army—the same army that had been routed at New Market only three weeks earlier—had found vindication.[28]

In the few hours of fighting the Confederates lost about 150 men killed, another 420 wounded, and over 900 captured. The Union, from a larger force, lost 166 dead, 640 wounded, and 40 captured. The Battle of Piedmont had taken more men than any battle in Stonewall Jackson's famous Valley Campaign of two years earlier. It had also seen the United States Army achieve its greatest victory in the Shenandoah Valley, its force advancing to its southernmost position in the war. Staunton, and the possibilities it held out, lay less than ten miles away.

The Confederates under Imboden and Jones retreated south toward Staunton. They used their artillery to stop the pursuit of Hunter's men and to secure a place of refuge. Vaughn sent General Lee a note: "Have been driven back. I will try to protect Staunton, but unless reinforcement's come at once I cannot do it. May have to fall back by way of Waynesborough. General W. E. Jones killed." A telegram from the commander of the military post in Staunton sent an even more direct message to General Lee: "We have been pretty badly whipped . . . . I fear Staunton will go up." What remained of the defeated Confederate force moved east to Waynesboro and the Blue Ridge Tunnel to protect the Virginia Central Railroad. Staunton sat unprotected.[29]

☆

AS THEY MARCHED INTO STAUNTON in June 1864 after the Battle of Piedmont, the Union men under the command of General David Hunter exuded confidence and pride. One soldier proclaimed himself as "happy as a big sunflower" and another noted in his diary that "Hunter is adored by his troops now. He showed the finest generalship that ever has been shown in this valley."[30]

The people along the way seemed surprisingly welcoming. "We found about one half of the families who gave evidence of sympathy and good will toward us," one soldier wrote, observing that "if proper rule was exercised over the people of this country, one half of them would be outspoken friends of the Union." As usual, David Strother, Hunter's aid and cousin, had a more cynical view. "The people along our route were either much frightened or very glad to see us," he noted with surprise. "As we neared the town a dozen or more girls in their Sunday dresses stood by the roadside in front of a cottage and presented us with bouquets. Whether this compliment was sincere and loyal or meant as a propiation of the demons I could not tell."[31] The line between welcome and self-preservation would seldom be clear in the Valley. Loyalties there, apparently so fixed for the United States before secession and apparently so solid in support of the Confederacy since, had shown themselves to be opaque and shifting.

Strother celebrated the Federal arrival in another way. "I got two bands with a large American flag to accompany the staff as we entered the town. We made a tour of the principal streets playing 'Hail Columbia' and 'Yankee Doodle' and other such airs as we thought might be useful and pleasing to the inhabitants," he bragged with his customary sarcasm. "A few skinny, sallow women peeped from between the half-closed window blinds, but generally the houses were closed and the town looked frightened."[32]

A surgeon from West Virginia marching with Hunter exulted in his diary that "the Federal army now occupies, for the first time, since the rebellion broke out, this Strong hold of Secession." He admitted that "time after time, has our army tried to reach this point for the past three years but in vain after sacrificing thousands and thousands of precious lives." But now "Genl. Hunter has been the one to plant our banner on the ramparts & Staunton, the proud city, the great base of supplies for Richmond, has fallen." An officer who "having belonged to a W. Va. Regiment that had for more than two years maintained a desire to take Staunton," asked Hunter if he could lead a charge into the town with a squadron of cavalry. Hunter gave his permission and the Union troopers swept in; the officer proudly noted that he was "the first Union soldier during the war to enter Staunton, except as a prisoner, or as a disguised scout."[33]

Officials of the town asked to meet with General Hunter, but he sent them to Strother instead. Alexander H. H. Stuart, a leading light of Unionism in Augusta and in Virginia a few years earlier as well a former member of the cabinet of United States President Millard Fillmore, led the delegation. Stuart mentioned that he had admired Strother's antebellum work as an artist and writer, and then "turned in upon the present condition of the town." Strother told them that "we were warring according to the rules of civilized nations, that all warlike stores, manufacturies, and buildings which appertained to the Confederacy would be destroyed but that private property and noncombatants would be respected." Strother assured the delegation that "schools and charitable institutions would be carefully protected," though he also warned them that "disorders might take place such as were to be expected among an ill-disciplined soldiery." Strother thought his visitors seemed reassured by the conversation."[34]

Not everything the occupying forces did furthered the "peace and order" that Strother promised. Hunter went to the Augusta County jail and "released all its inmates, thieves, spies, forgers, deserters, Irishmen, Union men, Yankee soldiers, Confederate officers, murderers, and rioters generally," as Strother described them. The next morning, perhaps not surprisingly, Strother found "everything in shocking confusion. They were burning the railroad property and public-stores and work shops. A mixed mob of Federal soldiers, Negroes, Secessionists, mulatto women, children, Jews, and camp followers and the riff raff of the town were engaged in plundering the stores and depots." Army goods, including blankets, clothes, a thousand saddles, and shoes were distributed to the Union soldiers and "plundered as freely by Negroes, Confederate bummers, and citizens."

Other Union troops knocked the heads out of "numerous barrels of apple brandy. The precious stream was running over the curbstones in cascades and rushing down the gutter with floating chips, paper, horse dung, and dead rats. This luscious mixture was greedily drunk by dozens of soldiers and vagabonds on their hands and knees and their mouths in the gutter while the more nice were setting their canteens to catch it as if flowed over the curbs." A large warehouse filled with tobacco was thrown open and the soldiers rushed in; tobacco was one commodity the United States Army did not possess in profusion. The streets of Staunton became "paved" with tobacco and the roads out of town were littered with half-chewed plugs.[35]

Amidst his gleeful boasting, Strother offered a sober accounting of what the Union army accomplished at Staunton: "We took five hundred wounded and invalid prisoners and paroled them. We destroyed one thousand stands of small arms and three guns, one thousand cavalry saddles, horse equipment and shoes and leather, several woolen factories and quantities of grey cloth and other stores, and some ammunition. The depot buildings and fifty miles of the Virginia Central railroad were destroyed."

These were significant but not debilitating costs for the Confederates, except for the railroad and its facilities. Without the railroad, Lee would not be able to send reinforcements to check the Union advance, food and other supplies Lee's army needed would be cut off, and wounded men from the massive battles being fought at Richmond could not reach the hospitals of Staunton.

The railroad could be of no benefit to the Federal troops and so they destroyed as much of it as they could.[36]

☆

MARGARET STUART, SIX YEARS old, saw Civil War Staunton from a child's perspective, in bold colors and sharp outlines, combining several visitations by Union troops and various departures of Confederates into a few deeply etched memories. The daughter of Alexander H. H. Stuart, Margaret lived in a dignified house overlooking Staunton. The family had prepared for invasion. Hearing strange sounds from the basement, the little girl descended the stairs and found her mother and sisters "stooping down over a candle, and with hatchets were pulling up the floors; and back in the cracks and corners they were poking bacon and silver and all sorts of things." Margaret crossed her heart that she would not tell, "and then made all the other children wretched by saying I knew grown-up people's secrets which even the Yankees could not find out." The Yankees did come to the house and searched it. Though they did not find the bacon and silver hidden in the floorboards, they did "steal everything that was left in the smokehouse and storeroom and all the horses except old Brutus, and he was hid in the cellar. Then they cut the spokes in papa's fifteen hundred dollar wood wagon."[37]

With the audacity of children, she and her siblings "went out and cursed the Yankees and seesawed on the back fence and sang as loud as we could:

Jeff Davis rides a white horse
　　Abe Lincoln rides a mule,
Jeff Davis is a gentleman,
　　Abe Lincoln is a fool.

At that time I was very proficient in songs and oaths, which seemed perfectly justifiable on such occasions."

As gratifying as "cursing" the Federal soldiers may have been, wartime Staunton left haunting images for the little girl. "It seemed to me the house and the town were always full of soldiers coming and going; tents on the hills one day, the next day gone in great wagon trains." A child could not escape the incessant talk of the war. "On Sundays when we went to church our minister often read out news of the battles and lists of the wounded. I recall one especial day when he told of an impending battle and asked the congregation to go home and make lint for the soldiers, how children and grown up people without waiting for dinner, turned down their plates on the table and began to scrape and ravel on them old linen napkins for the wounded."

When Confederate soldiers returned to the town, "muddy, wounded, footsore," the women Margaret knew stepped forward and even the little girl helped. "With white set faces they comforted and relieved. I stood by my mother's table with averted face, holding sponges and basin, while she dressed the bloody wounds of soldiers just in from the battle line. Five wounded men lay in our house at one time, and even the children were kept waiting on them."

Among these scenes of suffering, Hunter's raid marked a scene uniquely terrifying. "The skies were red with a great conflagration, and soldiers galloped through the streets. Along the railway tracks and in the flat below us the depots were on fire. Amidst the crackling, roaring flames fell flying stones. We heard deep intonations and explosions as great masses of the arched stone bridge were hurled into the air."

☆

WHILE IN STAUNTON on June 6, David Hunter received orders from Grant that spelled out the task before him. General Philip Sheridan was being sent from Richmond to Charlottesville, twenty-five miles to the east on the other side of the Blue Ridge, "to commence there the destruction of the Virginia Central Railroad, destroying this way as much as possible." Hunter should follow the shortest route to the Virginia Central Railroad, "destroying it completely and thoroughly until you join Gen. Sheridan." If that was not possible, or if Hunter was already on his way south, Grant told him to use his best judgment to accomplish a great purpose: cutting off Lynchburg from Lee's army. Lynchburg's railroad and canal connections, along with its manufacturing capacity, meant that it "would be of great value to us to get possession of Lynchburg for a single day," Grant wrote. He mentioned "a single day" because the city was "of so much importance to the enemy" that Grant recognized that actually taking Lynchburg would be extremely difficult.[38]

While Hunter paused in Staunton, George Crook's larger force arrived from West Virginia to join him. The generals conferred and agreed on a plan. As David Strother put it, they would continue marching south to Lynchburg and "hoped thereby to drive Lee out of Richmond by seizing and threatening all his Southern and Western communications and sources of supply." Crook asked Strother whether such a purpose could be accomplished with the men they had in their joint command. Strother was confident that "we could easily beat all the force that the enemy had in the Valley and in West Virginia combined," and they "hoped Lee would not be able to reinforce the Valley, being too closely pressed by Grant." If Lee did send reinforcements, those troops could be cut off by Sheridan.

The plan contained considerable contingencies and complexities. If Lee did manage to reinforce the Valley, the Union forces could be marching into disaster, for they would be far from reinforcement and supply. The railroad from Richmond to Lynchburg remained under the control of the Confederates and if Sheridan could not intercept them somewhere along the way nothing would stop them from arriving at Lynchburg before the Federals could march that distance. Crook, who had been fighting in the region for months, understood the difficulty. "We might take Lynchburg," he said, "but, depend upon it, Lee would not permit us to hold it long, nor could we do so for want of supplies. If we expected to take Lynchburg at all we must move upon it immediately and rapidly."[39]

In the meantime, one part of the plan was already failing. Philip Sheridan, charged by Grant with taking Charlottesville and then proceeding along the Virginia Central to connect with Hunter, was stopped on June 11 and 12. At the Battle of Trevilian Station, the largest and most costly mounted cavalry battle in the war, Confederates blocked Sheridan east of Charlottesville, exacted over a thousand casualties, and forced him back toward Richmond. Both sides claimed victory, for Sheridan had distracted the Confederates while Grant crossed the James River and assumed the position that allowed him to hold Lee in place in Petersburg.

Furthermore, Sheridan's troops destroyed a large stretch of the Virginia Central Railroad. Samuel Cormany, the young cavalryman from Chambersburg, described with considerable satisfaction a beautiful Sunday with "all hands tearing up R.R. Track." The "simple" process required a massive amount of effort. "Men stand shoulder to shoulder—say one thousand abreast along the rail—a few with fence rails, and chunks, pry the rail and ties up for 100 or more feet, underpinning the one side, for a short distance—the height of several feet." With the rail and ties in the air, "at the word of command, every man lifts harder and harder, and soon the men at the broken joint, have the ties in perpendicular position." Once this choreography began, "the R.R. track is turned upsidedown with considerable speed." The "extreme strain . . . twists and otherwise damages nearly every rail."[40]

From the viewpoint of Hunter and his allies in the Valley, this joyful labor was beside the point. Without Sheridan's arrival to join the Federal forces moving toward Lynchburg, the Confederates would have an advantage if they could get past the damaged stretch of railroad. And that was what happened: Lee dispatched General Jubal Early to Lynchburg from Richmond. Early's men had to march part of the way, but once they arrived at the railroad junction at Charlottesville they moved south far more quickly than their opponents marching on the other side of the Blue Ridge. The train could only travel twelve miles an hour on the battered railroad, but that was several times faster than Hunter's army could march.[41]

Unaware of these unfolding events across the mountains on their east but knowing that John Imboden protected the tunnel at Waynesboro, Hunter decided to move on Lynchburg rather than the Virginia Central Railroad. A combined Union force of 20,000 men set out south from Staunton to Lexington. There, David Hunter burned the Virginia Military Institute and the home of former Virginia Governor John Letcher, both for their support of the rebellion. The burning delayed the Union march, as did John McCausland. McCausland, who had bought time for Grumble Jones to join with Imboden at Staunton a few days earlier, bought time for the Confederates to reinforce Lynchburg. In one effective maneuver, McCausland burned a bridge by loading it with turpentine-soaked hay and then fired on the Union soldiers who tried to build a pontoon bridge to replace it.[42]

Hunter's army progressed slowly, for bridges were not rebuilt promptly and artillery could not cross. Strother worried about "damnable ignorance and carelessness" in the army. Hunter seemed unable to coordinate the components of his command, a "cause of great delay." Supply trains coming from the north with food and ammunition, harassed by guerrillas the length of the Valley, could not reach the Federal army. The Union soldiers, deep in enemy territory and harassed from every angle, grew hungry and furious at the rebels around them.[43]

☆

AS FEDERAL SOLDIERS HAD APPROACHED Staunton, Joseph Waddell, who worked in the Confederate Quartermaster's Office, stashed a personal trunk on the wagon carrying important documents. Waddell's trunk included "a tin box with every valuable paper I had in the world—public + private bonds, vouchers +c," including similar possessions of other people. Those valuable papers included his diary covering the first six months of 1864.

When he "heard some one say, 'Gen Jones is killed and our army routed,'" Waddell, usually stoic, admitted that "I cannot depict the horror of the feelings." He worried about his younger brother Legh, in his thirties, fighting alongside John Imboden as a member of the home guard. Waddell managed to find a mule and take a southerly road to the Blue Ridge Mountains, away from the railroad and the soldiers who would be descending from the north. Like the other men of the town, Waddell left the women in his family in their home at Staunton. "The road was full of refugees, with wagons, horses, cattle, wagons and nearly all kinds of movable property." Government officials and leading citizens of the town joined the encampment at the top of the mountains.

No one on the road knew what was happening in their town. "Every body we met was talking about the burning of property + mills in Staunton, but we could get no particulars."[44]

Waddell learned that some of the last Union soldiers to leave Staunton had visited the newspaper offices of the town. They broke the press of the *Spectator*—the same press that had extolled the Union for decades before it extolled the Confederacy—as well as the *Vindicator*, a secessionist paper long before Virginia seceded. The *Spectator* would be out of commission for months, but the editors of the *Vindicator* were able to gather type and repair their press to issue a paper. Their account of Staunton's occupation was long and bitter.

The *Vindicator* addressed any Northerner who might happen to read the paper. "To the enemies of our country, the vile Yankees, we desire, in closing to say that what they have done to us, in common with our neighbors, has not varied the tone of our feeling towards them one iota. We have always hated them and what we have seen (or felt), of them in their late raid through our valley could not possibly have lowered them in our estimation, but has served simply to prove conclusively to us that we were not wrong in the estimate we placed upon them many years ago." In response to charges from papers elsewhere that some white citizens in Augusta had aided the enemy or taken oaths of loyalty to the United States, the *Vindicator* rebutted each accusation. "No people under the sun are more loyal to their country and government than the people of Augusta. They have suffered much, but preserve the same heartfelt desire for the success of the Confederate Cause and intense hatred to the Yankee Nation and people they have ever felt."[45]

Nancy Emerson had not written in her diary for months, but the Federal occupation led her to reopen it "with the intention of telling a story about some Yankee raiders." Emerson, fifty-seven-years old in 1864, had come from Massachusetts to live with her brother Luther and his large family before the war. She was as Confederate as any native-born white Southerner could be. The first Federal troops, she wrote, "came in from the West, across the mountain. A party of 40 or 50 perhaps, came riding up, dismounted & rushed in. 'Have you got any whiskey' said they, 'got any flour? got any bacon?' with plenty of oaths." The soldiers pushed into the house. "'Come on boys,' says one, 'we'll find it all.'"

The soldiers "spread themselves nearly all over the house. Finding their way to a fine barrel of flour which a neighbor had given us, they proceeded to fill their sacks & pillow cases, scattering a large percent on the floor, till it was nearly exhausted." As much as she hated to see their food taken, Emerson saved her fury for a different kind of searching. "Some went upstairs, opened every trunk & drawer & tossed things upside down or on the floor, even my nice bonnets, pretending to be looking for arms." Emerson and the other women of the household "did not say anything to provoke them, but did not disguise our sentiments. They went peeping under the beds, looking for rebels as they said." Twelve-year-old Cate "spoke & said 'We are all rebels.' The Yankee looked up from her drawer, which he was searching just then, & said 'That's right.' Cate then said, 'I am a rebel too & I glory in it.'"

When the girl's mother asked "them why they injured innocent persons who had taken no part in the war, one of them replied, 'You need not tell me that, I know all the people along here have sons in the army.'" Catherine Emerson pointed to her young child and said "That is my only son." His oldest sister, Ellen, "then said, 'I have no brothers in the army, I wish from my heart I had.' He then said, 'Now Sis, I don't wish you had brothers in the army. I wouldn't like to kill one of your brothers.'"

Women found reassurance in a familiar convention of the time: a clear distinction between gentlemen and common men. Nancy Emerson recounted a frequent scene: "An officer rode up after the rest had gone having the appearance of a gentleman, & asked civilly if he could get some flour. Sister C. telling him how they had stripped us of nearly every thing they could find, said he could go & see what they had left, & help himself. He said no, he never had searched a house & never would, & it was a shame they should do so."

At one neighbor's house, a soldier "made up a bundle of ladies clothing to take, but his comrade shamed him out of it. They then poured out their molasses, scattered their preserves & sugar & other things about the floor, & mixed them all together & destroyed things generally. The ladies there are very amiable & genteel in their appearance which makes it the more strange." Nancy Emerson and other women expected soldiers to respect the same gradations of class they did, but such distinctions may have made things worse. Soldiers, deprived of every comfort and resentful of those who supported secession, felt justified in destroying the trappings and finery of genteel life.

Nancy Emerson tried to find patterns in the raids, but in general unpredictability ruled. "Some hid their things & had them discovered but we were more fortunate. (Some were betrayed by their servants). Some hid nothing, thinking they would not be disturbed but found themselves woefully mistaken. Others thought they might be worse dealt with if they hid anything." Emerson told of "a lady near Staunton" who "had two Yankee officers come to take tea with her. She was strong 'secesh,' but she got them a good supper. It was served up in very plain dishes. They perceived that she was wealthy, & inquired if she had not hid her plate &c. She told them she had. They asked where. She told them in the ash heap. They said 'That is not a good place. It is the first place searched.' They then very kindly & politely showed her a good place (in their opinion) She followed their advice & saved her things."

These episodes recounted in Emerson's diary occurred during the first wave of troops under Hunter and Averell on June 5 and 6. A day or two later, troops under George Crook swept into Staunton. "Several thousand of them passed our house on their way from Staunton to Lexington," Emerson wrote. "Sister C. requested one of them who was gentlemanly in his appearance, to guard us, & he did so. They were four hours in passing. None of them came in but the guard." A few soldiers, marching in the hot June sun, did go into the spring house "and helped themselves to milk, & one went off with a large panfull in each hand." The teenaged Ellen ordered him to " 'bring back those pans,' but he only laughed & went on. Another who had been taking a cool draught from a pan, came out with his chin covered & some on the end of his nose, like a cat from the cream pot." The girl "accosted him with 'Ar'nt you ashamed?' putting on as much emphasis as she well could, & adding, 'Who do you think is going to drink that milk, after you have put your nose in it!' The fellow made no reply but walked off."

The confrontations in Staunton showed that soldiers on both sides allowed women and girls to say things they would never allow men or boys to say. Women frequently took advantage of that convention to vent their fury, make political statements, and express contempt. Soldiers and officers proclaimed themselves amused by these exchanges, patronizing females and their opinions and emotions as a matter of course. On the other hand, soldiers found in female defiance a reassuring justification for looting and destruction. Though they would have looted in any case, soldiers met with contempt could think of themselves as attacking rebel households rather than defenseless civilian women.

By the summer of 1864 daily life in the war had boiled down to retribution, the chain of grievances stretching years back into the past. Excuses for many dubious actions proved all too easy to find.[46]

☆

IF DAVID HUNTER'S FORCES, having made it past Lexington, could now take Lynchburg and destroy its rail and canal connections, his strategy of destruction would be vindicated. The entire Valley would lie before the United States and Lee would be isolated in Richmond. As Hunter and his army arrayed themselves around Lynchburg, believing that they faced only the scattered forces of John C. Breckinridge, John Imboden, and the cavalry of John McCausland, he looked forward to taking the city the next day and fulfilling General Grant's wishes.

A week after they had left Staunton, the Federals could see the spires of Lynchburg's churches but the Union forces found themselves under fire and Confederates entrenching. An officer at the front told Strother that "he had heard the railroad trains coming and going all night, also cheering and military music which indicated the arrival of troops in the town. Since morning the lines were very much strengthened and were pressing him hard." The officer said he was ready to attack if ordered, "but he felt assured it would end in disaster."

As the Federal army probed to see what lay ahead, a "Rebel yell of attack sounded along our whole front," Strother wrote. Union soldiers began to flee, refusing to rally when Hunter waved his sword. The Confederate assault "was violent and sudden and it overwhelmed us like a surprise." Jubal Early and eight thousand men had arrived in Lynchburg the night before on the train from Charlottesville. The first Confederates to arrive had made as much noise as possible, playing celebratory music and marching about to create the sense that they constituted a larger force than they did.[47]

Hunter heard from prisoners that "Early's division is said to be twenty thousand strong and they have thirty days' rations and are determined to drive us out of Virginia." The Union generals conferred and agreed that "we must get out if possible." They departed silently that night, hearing that even more reinforcements for Early had arrived. Hunter ordered a retreat to the north in the Valley, the way they had come, but Confederate cavalry intercepted them. "The road was blocked with our disabled artillery," Strother wrote, "their carriages hacked to pieces, guns spiked, horses and harness gone." Rather than risk defeat or capture in the Valley, the Federal forces headed into the mountains of West Virginia. "Worn out with fatigue, without supplies in a country producing little at best and already wasted by war, the troops are beginning to show signs of demoralization," Strother admitted.[48]

The Confederates relied on deception and daring to slow Hunter's retreat. "A Rebel scout got a part of the train to take the wrong route and they had to come back to the place of starting," a soldier with Hunter admitted. "This misleading has been done several times. The Rebel scouts dress in our uniform and mix with our men and then do all the mischief they can. They are sometimes very bold and risk their lives on one bold stroke." One Confederate spy had been with Hunter's army all the way from Staunton and "was not detected until he attempted to get our train on the wrong route. Averell had him shot at once. Our scouts do the same. There are many scouts in both camps but it is dangerous business. They get big pay."[49]

Short of ammunition and food, the Union soldiers knew they could be taken if the Confederates could catch them. The Federal army struggled through the mountains for over two hundred miles, marching at night, often taking wrong turns. Passing

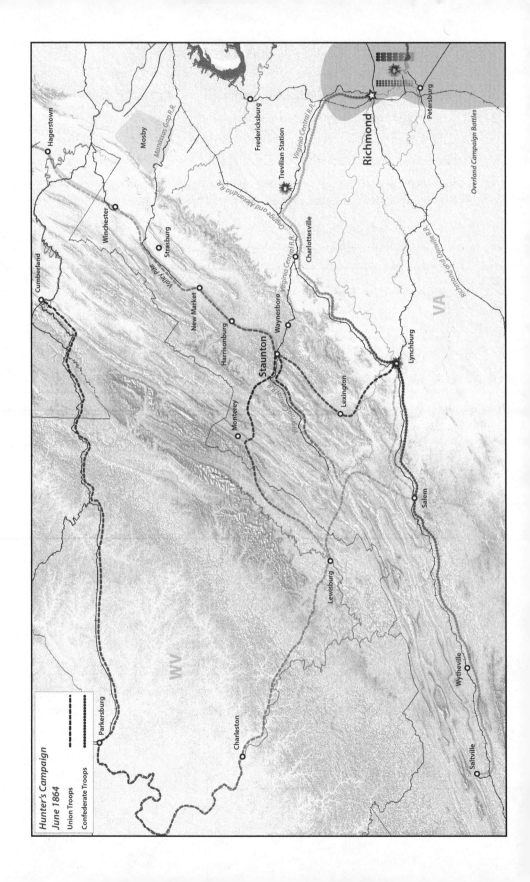

Hagerstown

Mosby
Manassas Gap R.R.

Winchester

Strasburg

Valley Pike

Cumberland

New Market

Harrisonburg

Fredericksburg

Trevilian Station

Orange and Alexandria R.R.

Virginia Central R.R.

Charlottesville

Richmond

Petersburg

Overland Campaign Battles

Waynesboro

Staunton

Virginia Central R.R.

Monterey

Lexington

Lynchburg

VA

Richmond and Danville R.R.

Parkersburg

Charleston

Lewisburg

Salem

WV

Wytheville

Saltville

burned houses and wading across rivers because bridges had been destroyed, Hunter had no news for twenty days. Finally, the hungry soldiers were met by a wagon train coming from the north carrying 70,000 rations. "We are now among our friends and in a friendly country where we may ride ahead of our escort with a sense of security I have not felt for sixty days," Strother wrote with relief. Steamboats and railroads eventually took them far away from the Shenandoah Valley.[50]

A soldier with Hunter wrote a letter to his sister proudly listing the command's accomplishments: "We have destroyed two Rail Roads, Virginia Central and Virginia & Tennessee. We destroyed the Virginia Military Institute at Lexington. We plundered the country generally. Took everything eatable on our line of march for man & beast, burned millions [of dollars worth] of Rail, relieved the Confederacy of about 2500 Contrabands, and finally tried to take Lynchburg." Though this soldier agreed that Hunter could not have seized Lynchburg, given the Confederate numbers and the Union's lack of ammunition, the retreat left him fuming. "I cannot begin to tell you any of the sufferings of this command since we began the retreat. . . . We had almost 25,000 men to feed, and almost nothing to do it on." Hunter seemed deaf to their suffering. "We have not a man . . . down to the private in the ranks who has any respect for him. We all wish that some 'bushwhacker' had killed him before he got through."[51]

The decisiveness of Robert E. Lee and the determination of Jubal Early's men to occupy Lynchburg overnight saved the city, but so did attacks on Hunter's long supply lines. Just as he had feared, the tenuous lines, stretching north the length of the Valley, doomed Hunter, for he found himself trapped without adequate ammunition deep in Virginia. Only one wagon train made it through the guerrillas of the Valley to Hunter's army in Lynchburg. The bounty of the United States meant nothing if it could not reach the men at the front. Hunter, and Sigel before him, had been right to believe that the nameless, faceless guerrillas in the Valley could cripple the powerful United States Army.

The guerrillas seemed to be everywhere in the mountains. One Union soldier told a chilling story about an event that occurred between New Market and Staunton, "an incident that put our three years discipline to a severe test. A soldier's horse had broken loose and wandered away during the night," William G. Watson wrote. "The veteran went to seek him, stopped at a farmer's house & inquired if they had seen the horse. As he turned to leave, he was struck with an axe and killed, the body was thrown into a well. Negroes came and told of it. The planter was tried and found guilty but execution was deferred till we reached Staunton. The provost guard took care of him. Many were determined to shoot him, but were assured he would be hung at Staunton."[52]

A soldier who had entered Staunton with Hunter had been dispatched with his unit to take prisoners to the nearest railroad station while Hunter's other men marched on Lexington and Lynchburg. The approach to the railroad "was the worst march of all. We had no rations for ourselves or horses, and it took us a week to cross, and by the time we got over we were nearly starved," Charles Wisewell wrote his brother. They had to shoot over three hundred mules and about two hundred horses who "gave out" and burned more than forty of their own wagons "so that they couldn't get hold of them. Above all men to be dreaded, are the Bushwackers in the mountains, which swarm full of them, and every chance they got they would pick off our men. If a man lingered behind the rear guard, he was a goner." Wisewell admitted that "I would rather be in a dozen battles than run the risk of getting bushwacked."[53]

☆

DAYS AFTER THE STAUNTON RAID, as Hunter's men stumbled through the mountains, Staunton remained "as quiet every day as Sunday," Joseph Waddell wrote. "Stores and shops closed, a few men sitting about here and there talking over the events of the last two weeks, even the little children are less noisy than usual. Every thing looks like a tornado had swept the country, and left the stillness of death in its track. Many farmers having lost their horses, are unable to work their corn." With the outcome of the battles to the south in the Valley unknown to him, Waddell could ask "And what does it all amount to? The country is further from subjugation to Yankee rule than before."[54]

Particularly concerning were stories of spies. "Many Yankee soldiers dressed in Confederate uniform, called 'Jesse Scouts,' were traversing the country, and several persons, taking them for our own soldiers, told them all about their affairs, where they had property hid +c." The "Jessie Scouts," named after the wife of Union General John C. Fremont, had begun in guerrilla-torn Missouri early in the war and remained parts of Union cavalry units elsewhere, scouting for intelligence among Confederate civilians. If caught in enemy uniform, the scouts could be summarily executed for espionage. The mountains of West Virginia, where loyalties were uncertain and shifting, provided a natural environment for Jessie Scouts.[55]

The Jessie Scouts infiltrated Augusta. "Dr. Davidson even took some of them into the woods to see a fine horse he had secluded here in charge of a negro boy—horse + boy were both taken off." The scouts also visited Waddell's brother, Legh, who was fighting with the home guard. When the scouts saw Legh's young daughter, "little Lucy," they "said to her, 'Sis, where is your father?'

She replied, 'He was at home last night, but has gone back to the army.'" Even on the day of the battle "several Yankee spies were in town" and when the Union occupied Staunton "they told Mr. Dice of the Methodist Church, that they heard him preach, on Sunday, and repeated a portion of his prayers."[56]

In such a period of confusion, Waddell tried to figure out where things stood in the war. He knew that "Grant seems to be in a position, between the James and Appomattox Rivers, from which he cannot be dislodged," but Waddell could not "learn where Breckinridge's command, including Imboden's, has gone." The war in the Valley remained as unstable and unpredictable as ever.[57]

☆

THE PRESENCE OF UNION and Confederate armies throughout the Valley tested the relationships among enslaved people and white people as no previous events had. The slavery of the Valley had been disrupted and undermined for three years now and yet without an occupying United States force enslaved people could claim no local allies. The farms and towns where enslaved people labored had been worn down, but white loss had seldom turned into black gain. The events of 1864 gave glimpses of what might lie ahead if the United States won the war, yet the unpredictable Union presence left African-American and white residents alike wondering who might control their region, town, and homestead next.[58]

In June, as Hunter's army marched into Staunton, the troops passed the Virginia State Lunatic Asylum. The superintendent warned the many hired-out enslaved people working there not to look into the "brutal eyes of the Yankees" and threatened to lock them into the cells of the institution if they became too friendly with the occupying force. One of Hunter's aides heard of the situation and advised the enslaved people that they were now free, able to do as they wished. The African-American workers' first act of freedom was showing the Union soldiers where the Confederates had hidden large numbers of uniforms and bolts of army cloth.[59]

David Strother noted what he considered self-delusion among the slaveholders of the Valley. As the Federal troops marched from Staunton, he observed, "we saw a great deal of smoke in the mountains eastward and were told it came from the camps of the refugees who were hiding from us with their Negroes and cattle." Strother was struck by the misplaced confidence of the slaveholders when they followed such strategies. "The satisfaction of these people in regard to their Negroes is surprising. They seem to believe firmly that their Negroes are so much attached to them that they will not leave them on any terms. Thus when running off their cattle, horses, and the goods into the mountains, they take their Negroes with them." Strother had seen, though, that "the Negroes take the first opportunity they find of running into our lines and giving information as to where their masters are hidden and conduct our foragers to their retreats. In this way our supply of cattle has been kept up." Beyond that, "Negroes were continually running to us with information of all kinds and they are the only persons upon whose correct truth we can rely."[60]

Joseph Waddell had admitted in his diary before the war that he worried about the justice and wisdom of slavery. His own household seemed to reflect slavery at its most benign. "Our servants were such a comfort to me—they could not have behaved better, and I really feel thankful to them," his wife Virginia wrote in a letter to Joseph immediately after Hunter's occupation. Yet Virginia Waddell's expression of gratitude and relief about her own slaves was immediately followed by another sentence, flatly conveyed: "Quite a number of negroes ran off." An enslaved man of "Aunt Sally's" named Tom "went off with the Yankees. He rode round with them here, dressed in Yankee uniform, in high glee."[61]

Joseph Waddell thought that "the poor negroes who went off are likely to suffer for it. Price says he heard a Yankee Colonel advise them to come back. An old woman of C. R. Mason's stole all the silver +c that had been hid and went to the Yankee camp. They received the stolen goods, but left her on the hill when they departed. She returned home yesterday or to-day, having no where else to go. She has but one leg!"[62]

White Southerners dwelled on stories of loyalty on the part of the enslaved people and stories of betrayal or abandonment of slaves by Federal soldiers. Some Union soldiers, after taking all the food in a household, "persuaded off their two negro men," Nancy Emerson wrote. "One of these was afterwards seen by one of our men crying to come back, but was watched so closely that he could not escape." Emerson drew out the familiar lesson: "No wonder he cried. He has been twice on the brink of the grave with pneumonia, & was nursed by his mistress as tenderly as if he had been a brother, & she was always kind to him, his master also. He will not find such treatment anywhere."

Other references to enslaved people revealed the limits of white empathy. Both sides often referred to "negroes" as simply another form of property. The Federal soldiers in Staunton, Emerson reported, "took off all the negro men & boys they could, as well as all the horses, told the women they would take them next time they came." Because people in Augusta used horses for farming, "it is an immense loss to have them & the servants swept off to such an extent, just as harvest is about to begin too." The language of white Southerners made other jumps and elisions.

Many white slave owners, Emerson observed, "sent off their ser-vants in one direction & another, some of whom were overtaken & captured & others escaped." Just what counted for capture and escape in these scenes may not have been clear to white people.[63]

White Southerners studied the Northern men they confronted to see what they really thought about black people, looking for fanaticism, hypocrisy, or conventional racism. They found what-ever they were looking for. Northern soldiers, preoccupied with staying alive themselves, noted that the enslaved people of the Valley seized opportunity even in Federal retreat. "The ever faithful colored people now began flocking to our army by the hundreds," noted one Ohio soldier, meaning "faithful" to the Union cause rather than to their masters.[64]

"The negroes have had no chance to escape until now," observed another of Hunter's men. "We have an army of them on our hands, nearly all of them carrying great bundles of cloth-ing hastily packed. Old men and women, children and babies all going for freedom." The warm and admiring words, as so often happened, were undercut by the casual language of racial stereo-type that white Americans so easily invoked. "Some of them took their masters buggys and loaded them with young nigs and rode along quite stilish."[65]

These fleeing slaves could not have ridden far in a buggy, though, for people of all stations were reduced to walking through the jagged mountains if they were to escape the Confederates pursuing them. David Strother, so disgusted with General Hunter and the debacle of the punishing retreat, took the time to record a scene that foretold many such scenes to follow: "For the last four or five days I have seen an old Negro hag about seventy-five years of age striding along on foot with wonderful endurance and zeal. She is walking for freedom I suppose."[66]

☆

PARTS OF THE CONFEDERACY *felt the war far more than others. More than two-thirds of the counties in the Confederacy never saw the Federal army. Places occupied by Union forces for longer periods of time grew relatively stable. But some areas, where neither the Confederate nor the Federal armies could establish firm dominion, experienced the harshness of war with particular force. The mountains of Appalachia and the borderlands of Missouri were notoriously chaotic.*[67]

For its part, the Valley of Virginia endured both the devastating burden of hungry armies and the prolonged torment of guerrillas, spies, and partisans. The war had escaped the boundaries of a formal military struggle from the outset. Partisan rangers, with sanction from the Confederacy, had attacked Northern and Unionist civilians and their property as early as 1862. For just as long, a series of Union commanders had punished and threatened civilians who aided the Confederate cause, especially in the northern parts of the Valley that changed hands time after time.

Throughout 1863, guerrillas and spies ranged across the western slope of the Valley and into the mountains of West Virginia. The chaos of that region periodically bled into the more secure towns and farms of the Valley's lowlands, including Staunton. Confederates such as John Imboden, William Jones, and John McCausland fought for month after month against Federal leaders such as William Averell and George Crook. Both sides employed ambush, burning, theft, and spying. Irregular and regular fighting fed each other, depended on each other.

Women became implicated in every kind of fighting. While they had proudly sewed the flags for the regular troops at the war's outset, now they fed and sheltered irregular fighters who traveled and lived among them. Women were quiet harborers and allies of deserters and shirkers as well as bold mothers, sisters, and daughters of soldiers in uniform, proclaiming their loyalty to the rebellion in the very face of occupying forces.

When outsiders such as Franz Sigel or David Hunter suddenly found themselves in charge of Union forces in the Valley they had to contend with this bitter history. The guerrillas, like their counterparts around the world, used the advantages of local collaborators, easy disguise, familiarity with the landscape, and quick movement to undermine the large but cumbersome United States force that suddenly appeared in their midst. The armies, in turn, used their own advantages of scale, armament, cavalry, and railroad connection to combat the guerrillas. Until one side or the other was defeated, the cycle would continue.

The newspapers, diaries, and letters of the time do not express outrage or surprise at the destruction of the railroads, factories, and warehouses of Staunton that supported the Confederacy. The language of anger focused instead on the Union invasion of intimate spaces, especially the home and areas of the home claimed by women. Kitchens, pantries, larders, smokehouses, and spring houses were set upon by hungry soldiers, whose frustration and resentment led to willful waste. Incursions into women's bedrooms and the wanton symbolic defilement of their possessions provoked the greatest outrage.

The occupation of Staunton in the early summer of 1864 seemed chaotic, under the control of no one. Hunter, Averell, and their officers drew uncertain lines, alternately tolerating and punishing their soldiers for acts against civilians. Without firm boundaries, many angry and hungry soldiers took or destroyed all they could. Officers, better fed and riding on horseback rather than marching, could afford to be more gentlemanly, more solicitous of women and children.

Hunter and his men expected to be in Staunton a short time, so they quickly took what they wanted and otherwise made sure the town was of little use to any Confederates who might follow them. They also took the opportunity to demonstrate their contempt for all who supported the Confederate cause. It was, they believed, people such as those of Staunton— former Unionists who abandoned their supposed loyalty to support the *rebellion—who fed the armies, sent men to the Stonewall Brigade of the Army of Northern Virginia, and made it possible for the Confederacy to sustain the war.*

The United States armies decided to supply themselves from the territory they occupied. They would travel lightly, strike quickly, and punish those who harassed them. Such a strategy kept supply trains short, exposing the armies as little as possible to guerrilla raids. This strategy of living off the land also allowed the occupying armies to justify punishment for the civilians among whom they passed. Every Southern neighborhood contained men who had helped foment secession; United States officers and soldiers felt it both appropriate and satisfying to burn the houses of such men.

Enslaved people, for their part, were like spies whose skin color allowed them passage across lines. Reports from Union soldiers and officers made it clear that the only reliable intelligence about the lay of the land and the presence of the enemy came from the black people entrusted by white people on both sides. Enslaved people could not display their loyalties openly until the safety of the Union army appeared. Then, they acted with a speed and certainty that surprised and disheartened white Southerners. Whites discovered that many "negroes" would "go off" whenever they had the chance but did not expect the "servants" they knew—and certainly not their own—to leave the security of "their homes" for the risks and dangers of the Yankees.

☆

THE FATE OF THE SHENANDOAH VALLEY and the fate of Richmond connected through the arteries and veins of the fragile and exhausted railroads of Virginia. As a result, the six weeks of fighting in the Valley in 1864 shaped the Civil War out of proportion to the size of the armies fighting there. The battles of New

Market and Piedmont have seemed, in the context of the massive fighting and suffering of the Overland Campaign, fleeting and marginal events. Yet the desperate shifts of men and generals to and from Richmond, by both Lee and Grant, up and down the Valley, across the Blue Ridge and along the Valley Pike, revealed how critical the leaders of both armies understood the Valley to be. The struggle between Grant and Lee could turn on events and men far from the burning underbrush of the Wilderness, the bloodbath at Spotsylvania, or the killing fields at Cold Harbor.

The resolution of the war, so longed for by everyone in the spring of 1864, seemed as far away as ever by the middle of the summer. Grant's campaign had led to enormous bloodshed but no defining victory or defeat. The battles in the Valley had settled nothing other than proving the challenge of controlling the Valley. The disruptions of slavery showed that enslaved people were determined to be free but would require a Federal victory to fulfill that determination.

To Burn Something in the Enemy's Country

June through October 1864

The national campaign for the Republicans had begun well in the promising days of June 1864. At their nominating convention in Baltimore, the Republican Party changed its name to the National Union Party, audacious in its claim to that title and cautious in its avoidance of the associations with the name "Republican." The delegates quickly renominated Abraham Lincoln and chose Governor Andrew Johnson of Tennessee as the vice-presidential candidate. Johnson stood as a hero to the Republicans, the only Senator from the South to remain loyal to the United States at the time of secession. Johnson was now serving as governor of Tennessee in the federally occupied state, facing great bitterness and violent threats but never backing down. A self-made man from the proudly Unionist mountains of East Tennessee, Andrew Johnson seemed the very embodiment of the hope of reuniting the nation.

The National Union Party's platform proclaimed that it would unify "every American citizen" to protect the "integrity of the Union and the paramount authority of the Constitution." These Union men would do everything in their power to crush by "force of arms the Rebellion now raging against its authority" and to punish for "their crimes the Rebels and traitors arrayed against it." Only unconditional surrender would secure that work, so there would be "no compromise with the Rebels or any terms of peace."

In a far bolder statement on slavery than the Republicans had ever made before, the National Union Party proclaimed that "as slavery was the cause, and now constitutes the strength of this Rebellion, and as it must be, always and everywhere, hostile to the principles of Republican Government, justice and the National safety demand its utter and complete extirpation from the soil of the Republic." The platform called for an amendment to the Constitution to "terminate and forever prohibit the existence of Slavery" everywhere in the United States. The Women's Loyal National League, led by abolitionists Elizabeth Cady Stanton and Susan B. Anthony, had gathered a "mammoth petition" since the spring of 1863, aiming to secure a million signatures calling for immediate abolition.[1]

The National Union Party declared its support for all that Abraham Lincoln had accomplished over the course of the war. The delegates approved, "especially, the Proclamation of Emancipation, and the employment as Union soldiers of men heretofore held in slavery." All soldiers, without distinction of color, deserved "the full protection of the laws of war." The party called for "ample and permanent provision for those of their survivors who have received disabling and honorable wounds in the service of the country." The memories of those who had fallen in the defense of the United States "shall be held in grateful and everlasting remembrance." The party also supported immigration, the railroad to the Pacific, responsible government spending, and a warning to any monarchical government that might endanger the Union, each step strengthening the Union for a glorious future.[2]

Strong and confident, forged in the crucible of the nation's great crisis, the National Union Party faced surprisingly strong opposition across the North. Despite being branded as traitors and cast out of national office for four years, the Democrats remained alarmingly robust. They sustained newspapers and local office-holders in hundreds of communities. They published tracts and pamphlets spreading the Democratic gospel of small government, hatred of black Americans, and peace with the Confederates. They funded powerful speakers in the field to rouse the faithful and appeal to voters who might waver in their faith in Lincoln and his party. The Democrats remained strong among immigrants and workers in the cities of the North as well as across the Mid-west and even in parts of New England. If they could persuade a relatively few men to change their votes in key counties and key states, the Democrats felt certain, they could stop Abraham Lin-coln and his party, whatever its name.[3]

Like their opponents, the Democrats knew that everything depended on events on the battlefield. Precisely because of those battles, the optimism of the National Republicans in June wore thin over the summer that followed their nominating convention. As the Lincoln administration and its generals failed to defeat the Confederates in Virginia and Georgia, the Democrats grew ever more emboldened. The immense bloodshed of Grant's struggle with Lee, the inability of Sherman to drive the Confederates out of Atlanta, and the failure of one general after another in the Shenandoah Valley undercut confidence in the Republican leadership that oversaw the war. As lists of dead and wounded filled the newspapers of communities across the North in July and August, the Democrats demanded compromise with the Rebels.

Alexander McClure of Chambersburg watched, concerned, as the effects of the war in the summer of 1864 wore on his party. The National Union Party put the successful conclusion of the war at the heart of everything else worth fighting for. Grant fought "with fearful sacrifice of men without attaining any material victories," McClure admitted, and Sherman struggled outside Atlanta with ever longer and more exposed lines of supply and support. McClure saw Lincoln's distress with his own eyes during a visit that summer. The president was "greatly depressed," for Lincoln was "human, as are all men."[4]

Both parties had to steer not only through the ever-shifting headlines from the battlefront but also through the ever-shifting landscape of race and slavery. The expansive platform of the National Union Party, so strong and direct in its attacks on slavery and in its call for a constitutional amendment ending slavery forever, said little about the future of African-Americans. Many white Northerners feared, and even expected, black Southerners to come north as soon as they could. Republicans, including Lincoln, continued to consider colonization of the newly freed Americans as a way to avoid fears of the "Africanization" of the North. Newspaper editorials and speakers in front of crowds steered clear of talking about black people if they could help it. With the war and the Union on which it rested so tenuous, the Republicans considered discussion of that volatile issue both premature and dangerous. Leading Republicans did not know what to say about "the Negro" and so they said as little as they could.

Such caution frustrated the abolitionists in the party. "Slavery, though wounded, dying and despised, is still able to bind the tongues of our republican orators," Frederick Douglass told an abolitionist ally. "The Negro is the deformed child, which is put out of the room when company comes." Douglass and other abolitionists urged President Lincoln to lay out a plan for black Americans after slavery ended, but without Lincoln's reelection there could be no meaningful hope for African-Americans held in slavery. Everything would have to be subordinated to victory at the polls.[5]

As a result, the summer of 1864 demonstrated one of the great paradoxes of the war. Precisely because the fate of slavery rested on the outcome of the battles and elections of the next few months, the Republicans did not discuss the fate of the people held in slavery. Precisely because the Democrats built their campaign around the threats of ending slavery, the Republicans talked instead about saving the Union. Precisely because the National Union Party put support for a constitutional amendment ending slavery throughout the nation at the center of their platform, they did not endanger support for that amendment by saying anything about what might follow its success.

The Republicans did work behind the scenes, however, to lay the foundations for black freedom. Abraham Lincoln knew that when the war ended so would the rationale for the Emancipation Proclamation as a tool of war. The Republicans wanted to assemble a majority in Congress to secure the Thirteenth Amendment, putting the end of slavery on a firmer legal grounding, but to do so they could not agitate the electorate. Lincoln continued to support incremental plans for reconstructing the Union, but he listened to other strategies that might bring the war and slavery to an end at the same time.

In this strange environment, made even stranger by the agonies of the battlefield that summer, the newspapers of the Republicans and Democrats seemed to be describing different elections. Despite Republican reticence, the Democrats did all they could to drag black Americans on center stage, feeding white fears of what black freedom would mean for white people in the North. As it became clear that slavery would not be restored, no matter how much they might wish that to be the case, the Democrats instead charged the Republicans, under their National Union disguise, with fomenting black equality after slavery's destruction.[6]

☆

THE DEMOCRATS INVENTED a new word in 1864 to capture and feed the disgust of Northern whites: "miscegenation." Two New York Democratic newspapermen wrote a pamphlet under that title—an invented pseudoscientific phrase—to make it appear that Republicans advocated the interbreeding of white and black people. The secret authors solicited endorsements from leading abolitionists, hoping to trick them into support for a "policy" the Democrats would use to tar the entire Republican party. While most of the abolitionists did not fall for the ruse, the Democrats seized upon a trace of ambiguity in a few responses to claim that Republicans championed the mixing of the races as the future of the nation.[7]

Franklin's *Valley Spirit* expressed mock concern that the new word of "miscegenation" had been invented by radical abolitionists "to soften the horrible ideas which are conjured up by the term amalgamation." Until the Republicans came to power, "we needed no word to modify the disgusting idea of white people marrying negroes, or of having negro babies without being married." But now "the worship of negroes has been introduced by the dominant party" and thus "there is ground to fear the disgusting pit which has been dug for the degradation of the white race."[8]

The Democrats, proudly racist for decades, conjured fear of black people as a central rallying cry, shoving race into every aspect of the war. When a thousand black freedpeople were allegedly brought to New York to farm, the *Valley Spirit* spat that "this is how the negroes stay in the South, as we were told they would by our

Abolition friends. This is how they are taken care of and feasted on the fat of the land while soldiers' families are suffering the pangs of want—not to mention the fact that poor white Union refugees are daily starving for food and perishing of hardships." When black soldiers acquitted themselves well on the battlefields of the South, the Democrats sputtered with contempt and racist jibes: "It is scarcely possible to take up a newspaper in the interest of Lincoln and Johnson which does not contain grandiloquent spread eagle flourishes about the black troops, and comparisons disparaging to our white veterans." The reason seemed obvious to the Democrats. The Republicans planned to extend "the right of suffrage to 'American citizens of African descent,' and that party which has been foremost in laudation of charcoal, and has gone farthest in advocacy of the 'divine commingling of races' will be most likely, it is thought, to get the votes of Caesar, Sambo and Pompey."[9]

Getting votes became the great obsession of the summer of 1864. The newspapers spent nearly as much print on the looming election as they did on the battles across the South. The Democrats of Franklin County, like their counterparts across the North, sneered at the audacious claims of the National Union Party to represent the entire North. The Democrats vilified Abraham Lincoln as "totally unfit for the position he holds. He is weak, incapable, vacillating, a time-server, without either wise comprehension of the present or sagacious forecast of the future." Lincoln's record seemed clear: "Through his mismanagement and imbecility during three years of bloody civil war, the resources of the country have been wasted, thousands of lives have been uselessly sacrificed and millions of treasure squandered, leaving the prospect of peace and a restored Union, as far as human foresight can go, as distant now as at the beginning." Far from living up to the ideals of pure patriotism, Lincoln "has lent himself to the schemes of the bold bad men around him, in whose hands he is a mere tool to carry out their wicked designs."[10]

The Democrats' key charge was that Lincoln and his party, whatever they called themselves, had "prostituted the war from the high and noble object for which it was commenced"—restoring the Union to the form created in the original Constitution—"to the basest and most ignoble partisan purposes," prolonging the fighting and bloodshed until slavery had been abolished. The Democrats saw hypocrisy and political motives behind every Republican act and word. "While our brave soldiers, the laborers and mechanics of the North, are bravely shedding their blood for the Union— Shoddy supporters of Lincoln are filling their places of labor at home with Negroes and are preparing to offer them the right of suffrage on perfect equality with and to control the votes of those same gallant white soldiers should they be spared to return home." Though there was no truth to the charges, that did not matter to the Democrats. "What will be the next step," they asked, "when Labor has been reduced to the negro standard of cheapness, and the poor whites shall be compelled to consort with the blacks as their equals? Why Miscegenation—the Shoddy hope and prayer— is what is to follow." In the face of such manufactured and hysterical charges, most Republicans chose to remain quiet about black freedom and to focus on winning the war.[11]

☆

THE DEMOCRATS RAILED against Republican failure to drive the war to a successful close. Though the maneuvers of Grant and Sherman were laying the foundations for ultimate success, throughout the summer of 1864 the Democrats emphasized the apparent failure of the largest United States armies under its most celebrated generals.

Republicans admitted the toll of military stalemate. "The tide is setting strongly against us," the chairman of the National Union Executive Committee wrote Lincoln on August 22. The party leader had heard from their best sources that Illinois, New York, and Pennsylvania were likely to go to the Democrats and that only "most strenuous efforts" would carry Indiana. One moderate Republican thought that "as things stand now, Mr. Lincoln's re-election is an impossibility." Lincoln himself said, "You think I don't know I am going to be beaten, but I do and unless some great change takes place badly beaten." The day after receiving the discouraging note from his ally, Lincoln drafted and had his cabinet sign—without reading it—a memorandum pledging to lend "all the executive power of the Government" to the new Democratic president to "try to save the country."[12]

No one—including the Democrats themselves—knew how the party would bring the war to an end. Lincoln feared, though, that the election of a Democrat would bring Union defeat. If the Democrats turned the two hundred thousand African-American soldiers out of the army, Lincoln warned, if the Union abandoned "all the posts now possessed by black men," surrendering "all these advantages to the enemy," the United States "would be compelled to abandon the war in 3 weeks."[13]

After delaying their convention to allow the discouraging failures of the Union war effort to grow heavier, the Democrats finally held their nominating convention in Chicago in late August. The delay seemed wise, for national morale had reached its lowest point for the United States in the entire war. The delegates were divided between so-called War Democrats, who supported the war for union but not for emancipation, and the Peace Democrats, who demanded a cessation of hostilities and the negotiation of a peace with slavery in place. After bitter struggle between the factions, the convention nominated George McClellan for president. Though he had been removed from command by President Lincoln, the young and appealing McClellan remained immensely popular throughout the North and within the army.

The convention's platform proclaimed that "in the future, as in the past, we will adhere with unswerving fidelity to the Union under the Constitution as the only solid foundation of our strength, security, and happiness as a people." In the Democrats' eyes, the Constitution stood "as a framework of government equally conducive to the welfare and prosperity of all the States, both Northern and Southern." While the National Republicans looked to the future, the Democrats invoked the past.

The Democrats declared "that after four years of failure to restore the Union by the experiment of war," during which the Republicans had made a mockery of the Constitution "under the pretense of a military necessity of war-power higher than the Constitution," the time had come for "immediate efforts be made for a cessation of hostilities" so that "peace may be restored on the basis of the Federal Union of the States." The Republicans had violated the Constitution by interfering in the votes of the states, by suppressing freedom of the press, and by imprisoning their opponents in a series of "revolutionary" and unconstitutional actions. They must be confronted.

The only mention in the Democrats' platform of the two million men who had fought to save the United States appeared in a tepid declaration that "the sympathy of the Democratic party is heartily and earnestly extended to the soldiery of our army and sailors of our navy." While the Democrats would bestow upon them "all the care, protection, and regard that the brave soldiers and sailors of the republic have so nobly earned," the Democrats offered no words of gratitude or admiration. The soldiers, like the nation, had been duped into fighting a misguided and unjust war.[14]

George McClellan accepted the nomination in a convoluted letter whose audience seemed to be the South as much as the North. No draft of his letter mentioned slavery, and neither did the Democrats' platform. While Abraham Lincoln had laid down two conditions for peace—reunion and the end of slavery—McClellan held out a different possibility. As soon as the Confederacy or any individual Confederate state expressed a willingness to accept reunion, the United States "should exhaust all the resources *of statesmanship . . . to secure such peace, reestablish the Union, and guarantee for the future the Constitutional rights of every state.*"[15]

☆

ULYSSES GRANT'S VAUNTED CAMPAIGN in Virginia seemed a failure on every front, the Democrats judged. The massive bloodshed of the Wilderness, Spotsylvania, and Cold Harbor had come and gone by the middle of June 1864 and the Union had lost 52,000 men compared to Lee's 33,000. While such bloody arithmetic would eventually work to the benefit of the United States, who had more soldiers to lose, the cost was nevertheless devastating to the Northern cause.

The Democrats of the *Valley Spirit* reminded the people of Franklin County how often the Republicans had predicted— virtually promised—victory. "At the beginning of our troubles they treated the matter lightly, as of very little account. They effected to despise the courage of the South, underrated her resources, told the people the war would be a mere breakfast job for the North—that the Southern people were all cowards and would run at the firing of the first gun. We well remember when it was considered treason in our own town to say that the South would fight." Once the war began, the Republicans predicted it would be over in sixty to ninety days. Now, three years into the war, the voracious war had consumed Northern men by the hundreds of thousands. If the people of the United States wanted peace, the *Spirit* declared, "They must hurl from power this imbecile, wicked and corrupt administration. They must elect Statesmen to preside over the destinies of the nation instead of buffoons."[16]

The *Repository*, the Republican paper of Franklin, disagreed on every front. "Loyal men will rejoice that the president has called for 500,000 additional troops, to serve one year," it declared. Now there could be no doubt of "the early and complete success of the war, and as such it will be accepted by a loyal people with confidence and patriotic pride. The heroic Sherman now has the rebel army of the South driven through its strongest fortifications into its last defences, and the invincible Grant closely invests the rebel capital, with its last army unable to offer battle, its communications periled, and its scanty stores well nigh exhausted. It needs but one terrible, overwhelming blow to end this causeless, unholy rebellion, and restore to us honorable Peace and enduring Union." The question was when and where and by whom that one "terrible, overwhelming blow" would be struck.[17]

☆

AS A BRUTALLY HOT SUMMER descended on the Valley in 1864 people found themselves trapped in cycles of revenge and retaliation. For three years, people on both sides of the Mason–Dixon Line had seen themselves as victims of those across the border. The armies of the Confederacy and of the United States had repeatedly swept through the farms and towns, taking what they wanted and leaving new and bitter memories. Now, in 1864, each side demanded that its armies inflict severe pain on enemy soldiers and civilians.

Throughout history, of course, armies have been a curse upon the civilians in their midst. Wars far more destructive of noncombatants than the American Civil War raged long before 1864 and still plague the twenty-first century. The particular forms of devastation—its rationale, limits, and ferocity—uniquely identify a war in its time and place. In the American struggle against Americans, armies saw themselves fighting an advanced kind of warfare, sophisticated in strategies and means, devastatingly effective on the battlefield but bounded by international law, civilized restraint, and Christian morality.

Neither the Union nor the Confederacy destroyed all that lay within their power to destroy. Neither sanctioned assaults on white women and children, and neither burned or shelled indiscriminately. But each side accused the other of doing those things and believed that their enemies did so. The war had begun through an escalation of reckless rhetoric, demonization, and miscalculation, and those forces fed the destructiveness of the war that followed. Each side believed itself justified in destroying all that it deemed necessary because newspaper reports, rumors, and witnesses told them that the enemy did so. Both sides gathered, exaggerated, and amplified evidence of the other's brutality.

The war veered into new territory in the summer of 1864. Months before Sherman's March to the Sea in Georgia, the cycle of violence in the Valley demonstrated to Americans what they could do to one another. The large-scale violence of both the United States and the Confederacy, on and beyond the battlefield, was fed by the belief that the Civil War neared its culmination. The impending presidential election in the North and the military stalemate in Virginia meant that battles had to be won now or never.

☆

AS SOON AS HUNTER had retreated into the mountains of West Virginia, Jubal Early moved rapidly. He was eager to fulfill Lee's plan to use the Valley, now free of any Union presence, to threaten the North with a large force so that Grant would have to send troops away from the campaign against Richmond. Early's troops' first stop on the way north from Lynchburg was Staunton, where the Confederates would gather themselves for an offensive strike somewhere to the north. In late June, the people of Augusta watched Early's army of more than ten thousand men pass through the county on three separate roads: the infantry

Confederate General Jubal Early

down the Valley Pike, the artillery down the road to Piedmont, and the cavalry sweeping to the west. Joseph Waddell heard that "their destination is Pennsylvania." The Confederates, "indignant at the destruction of property etc by the Yankees under Hunter, declare their purpose to take revenge on the border on the first opportunity." Waddell held reservations about such a strategy, comprehensible though the thirst for retaliation was. "Whether such a move will not do us more harm than good," Waddell worried, "by reviving the war spirit at the North and recruiting the Yankee armies, remains to be seen." He admitted that he had "no very great confidence in Early."

A forty-seven-year-old graduate of West Point, part of a prominent Virginia family, a lawyer, and a state delegate, Early had fought in both the Seminole Wars of the 1830s and the Mexican War of the 1840s. In the latter conflict Early developed rheumatism that would torment him the rest of his life; he walked and moved like a much older man. His soldiers called him "Old Jube," sometimes fondly.

Early did not embody the Christian ideals of Stonewall Jackson or Robert E. Lee. He had fathered four children that bore his name with a woman he never married. He was a profane man, a lover of whiskey and tobacco, shabby and disheveled. Early detected many failures in others and none in himself, and he never hesitated to share those judgments. He was also notoriously brave, even careless with his own well-being. Early had opposed secession, but committed himself to the Confederacy and rose quickly to brigadier general. He had fought at Manassas, the Seven Days, Antietam, Fredericksburg, and Gettysburg, where his division occupied York, Pennsylvania, and then played critical roles in the battle and the retreat. Despite his accomplishments, Early had risen to commander of a corps only a few weeks before Lynchburg, after the leadership ranks of Lee's army had been decimated. Lee believed in Early even though he recognized that Early was widely disliked and distrusted. Early would command an entire corps and two battalions of artillery, somewhere between twelve thousand and fifteen thousand infantry and two thousand cavalry. Such a large force would deplete Lee's own forces by 25 percent, leaving him vulnerable if Grant decided to move again. So important was the Valley, however, that Lee felt he had no choice.

Joseph Waddell admitted that "it is almost as great a relief to get rid of our army as of the Yankees—in some respects they have done as much injury as the latter." He listened to the music the Confederates played as they marched out of Augusta. Some of the music was "very dolorous"; one played "When This Cruel War is Over," which made Waddell "sad, sad." Despite the melancholy music, however, "the soldiers generally seemed in good spirits.

Many of those who went out this afternoon, looked really joyous. Poor fellows, I do not know how they stand such a life. As far as dress and cleanliness are concerned, they are a woebegone looking set. As usual, multitudes of them have been calling at private houses for something to eat. We thought the Yankees had left no supplies in the county, but it is hard to refuse a morsel to our men, notwithstanding the beggars are generally stragglers."

Looking upon the thousands of Confederate soldiers marching to an uncertain destination, Waddell could not help but think that "one third of them here at the right time, would have prevented all these disasters and cut off Hunter's career." The people of the Valley had seen the difference a day or two could make in the war, the difference of a railroad track, bridge, or general. Like his neighbors, Joseph Waddell forced himself to look ahead to some kind of deliverance to come, a deliverance brought by some unforeseen circumstance or good fortune.[18]

Jedediah Hotchkiss accompanied Early. Hotchkiss knew the Valley better than anyone else in either army, having mapped it since the days of Stonewall Jackson, and he busily produced one map after another as Early moved northward. As always, Hotchkiss wrote his wife Sara to describe the course of his journey and the remarkable events he witnessed. The day after the brief conflict at Lynchburg, Hotchkiss was disgusted that "the Vandals" under Hunter "ran away." The Confederates pursued them for two days, "the enemy plundering & burning as they went stripping every house of all its provisions, driving off the stock of all kinds & in many cases tearing up the clothes & plundering the trunks &c of the citizens—we could not get a chance to fight them—they moved so rapidly." Early's men grew hungry and exhausted, but "we have been getting along the best we could & the people have been very kind to us although they have suffered so terribly from the Yankees." The brief rest in Staunton replenished Early's command. As they left, Hotchkiss wrote his wife that he hoped "this campaign will end the war."[19]

☆

THE CONFEDERATE ARMY MARCHED north in the Valley in June and July, threatening Washington, D.C., defeating a Union force at the Battle of Monocacy near Frederick, Maryland, harassing Unionists, and trying to pull Union forces away from Richmond. Some of the newspapers of the North grew agitated, but the threat against the United States capital was never great. Grant did send men, but he had many men to send. What Early might accomplish remained unclear.

At the end of July, Early sent General John McCausland, practiced in irregular warfare and commanding 2,800 men, to convey a straightforward message across the border with the United States into Pennsylvania: "in retaliation of the depredations committed by Major-General Hunter, of the U.S. forces during his recent raid, it is ordered that the citizens of Chambersburg pay to the Confederate States by Gen McCausland the sum of 100,000 in gold; or in lieu thereof of 500,000 in greenbacks or national currency, otherwise the town would be lain in ashes within three hours."[20]

Early trusted McCausland, accustomed to fighting on his own in desperate circumstances time after time, to show the firmness and resourcefulness necessary for the Chambersburg raid. McCausland had extracted large sums without incident from Maryland towns in the last few weeks and now Early calculated that McCausland's reputation as a fearless partisan—as his nick-

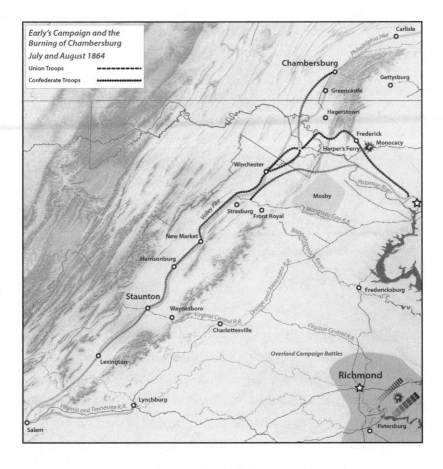

Early's Campaign and the
Burning of Chambersburg
July and August 1864

Union Troops

Confederate Troops

name of "Tiger John" conveyed—would intimidate the town fathers of Chambersburg into providing what he demanded.

The small force of Confederates fought their way for seventy-five miles into Pennsylvania, using surprise and stealth to make their way past Federal pickets, cavalry, and scouts. Gathering themselves in Mercersburg in southern Franklin County, McCausland's command then marched to Chambersburg throughout the night. When they crested the hill that overlooked the town at 5:30 the morning of July 30, one soldier with them wrote, "the city was

Confederate General John McCausland

beautifully lit up with gas," and "the order was given to charge into it." McCausland ordered a cannon shot to be fired over the town to announce the Confederates' arrival. The first troops to arrive "entered by almost every alley and by-streets," followed by several hundred others. Most of the command waited on the hills around Chambersburg, armed with cannon against any Union force that might come to the town's defense.[21]

Chambersburg's leading citizens and merchants had fled the town. McCausland tried to find someone to take charge, eventually calling together fifteen men to meet with him. He showed them Early's orders and warned that if they did not comply he would have no choice but to burn the prosperous town. The people of Chambersburg, women as well as men, openly scoffed at such threats. They simply did not believe that even the Rebels would burn a defenseless place of no military value.

The citizens' apparent lack of concern was fed by their knowledge that a cavalry division under William Averell was posted only ten miles from Chambersburg, near Greencastle in southern Franklin County. General Darius Couch, in charge of the local military district but without a force of his own adequate to stop McCausland, sent one telegram after another to Averell, pleading for his help. The last message read simply: "The enemy are just at the edge of town. Let me know what you intend doing." The townspeople stalled and McCausland knew they were stalling. Even as the two sides talked in the town's Diamond, word arrived from a captured soldier from Averell's command that he was only two or three miles away. One Confederate said that the citizens, hearing this news as well, "positively refused to raise the money, laughing at us when we threatened to burn the town."[22]

McCausland faced few options. Early's orders did not provide room for negotiation or compromise, strategies that McCausland had followed when extracting reparations from Maryland towns in preceding days. The people of Chambersburg could not compromise, either, for the bankers of the town had taken all substantial amounts of money away for safe-keeping. McCausland did not believe the citizens would allow their town to be burned and the citizens did not believe that McCausland would actually follow through when nothing could be gained. Only Averell's arrival could break the deadlock.

But Averell did not arrive. At nine on the morning of the Confederates' invasion McCausland ordered the burning to begin, starting with a government commissary building. McCausland rode through the town himself, a Union prisoner recalled, "pointing to the flames" to prove that "he intended to carry his threat into execution." Hearing that Averell was bearing down on the town, McCausland ordered the rest of the burning to commence. If Averell did arrive, McCausland needed to have his men ready to fight rather than scattered throughout the town setting blazes. The Union prisoner reported that all of the main street soon turned into "in one mass of flames."[23]

☆

EXACTLY WHAT HAPPENED IN McCausland's raid would be debated for generations. J. Kelly Bennette recorded in his diary the story from the Confederate perspective. After marching throughout the night, they arrived in Chambersburg "a little before day light. The first thing I knew of being in its vicinity was a dull 'Boom'! & a charge of grape came flying over us like a flock of pigeons." While waiting for McCausland to warn the citizens, the exhausted Bennette fell asleep. When he awoke "the town was in our hands & on fire." Even though McCausland gave "the women & children two hours to leave & remove what they could," many did nothing, still not believing there would be a fire.

Bennette admitted that "the burning of Chambersburg was generally condemned by our Regt. at first when all the sympathies were all aroused, but when reason had time to regain her seat I believe that they all thought as I thought at first; that it was Justice & Justice tempered with Mercy." Rationalization began within hours of the act. "That burning per se is wrong no one can deny; and the bare idea of turning out of doors upon the cold charities of the world unprotected women & unoffending children is sufficient to cause the feelings to rebel." That much was obvious, "but there may be circumstances under which it is not only justifiable but becomes a duty,—stern it is true but nevertheless binding."

Bennette carefully traced the logic that proved they had acted justly. First, the Confederates had been remarkably restrained in previous incursions, when "several times since the beginning of this war we have had opportunities of laying waste northern cities & private property generally. But instead of this we have pursued toward them a course uniformally conciliatory hoping by this means to set the war on a civilized footing & thus protect our defenceless ones at home." The result? Rampant burning by the United States' forces in the Confederacy. Bennette listed towns and cities across the South the Union army had devastated, where "blackened chimneys alone marking where once the farm-house stood." From the Mississippi River to Virginia, Bennette claimed, hundreds of "towns & cities have been laid in ashes & often not giving the women & children five minutes notice. Private farm houses of which there are thousands are not mentioned."

Moreover, Bennette passionately reassured himself, "We are in this war to defend the women—if we try one expedient & it fails we are recreant to our duty if we persevere in that expedient instead of changing the prescription. Now everyone knows that the conciliatory policy has failed—utterly failed." A war "to defend the women" had somehow become a war in which women and children saw their homes burned. Yet, Bennette pointed out, the Confederates had acted politely as they destroyed the civilians' homes. "Instead of snatching from the hands of the ladies what they had saved from their burning houses & throwing it back into the flames as the yankees did in K[anawha] Valley, or stealing & destroying it as they did Mrs. Anderson in the Valley of Va. our men could be seen all over the city checking the fire or carrying trunks, bundles &c. for the ladies. How beautiful the contrast!"[24]

Bennette's diary entry, written on the day of the burning of Chambersburg, captured the swings of guilt, anxiety, and rationalization that many Confederates apparently experienced. Beneath all the rationalizations lay the simple argument that the Yankees had done worse and thus deserved whatever happened to them. The war had reduced moral reasoning, even by a thought-ful man, to the thinnest of excuses.

Other Confederates present realized that a new threshold had been crossed at Chambersburg. Achilles Tynes, in McCausland's officer corps, saw the burning at close range. After providing a flat and factual account of the order and the beginning of the fire, Tynes wrote his wife that the burning was the "saddest spectacle I ever witnessed to see the women and children. This inaugurates a terrible system of retalliation, devastation and rapine."[25]

Malcolm Fleming wrote his mother about a week later, clearly disturbed by what he had seen in Chambersburg. To tell the full story, he said, would mean "consuming more time & paper than I have to spare," and no story, no matter how exaggerated, could "be fair about the burning of Chambersburg." No one who was not there "could form an approximate idea of the horrors."

Fleming, along with his comrades, entered the town—and "a beautiful place it is"—with "a stiff neck & stubborn breast." But "as much as I hate the Yankees, I could not stand it long." After the citizens "refused to pay the tribute" McCausland "at once ordered the city to be laid in ashes. The scene which followed baffles all description. Shrieking children & panic stricken men & women running in every direction, begging assistance." Fleming told his mother that "I believe somewhat in the old Mosaic law—an eye for an eye & a tooth for a tooth," but he had to admit that the scenes in Chambersburg made him "think we are going wrong."[26]

☆

WHEN THE CAVALRY of William Averell finally arrived in Chambersburg about two o'clock on the afternoon of the burning, those in the advance were stunned by what they saw. "We had no

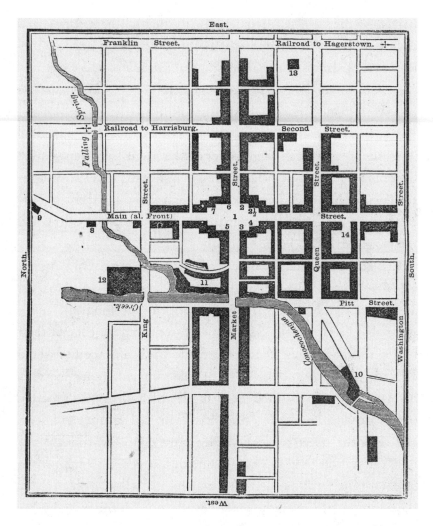

*Chambersburg, Pennsylvania. The areas in black were burned
by the Confederates in July 1863.*

knowledge of the great destruction and devastation that we should
witness," C. M. Newcomer wrote. "Houses on fire on both sides"
still raged, and "our poor horses were mad with fright." Smoke
"settled over the earth like a pall. The citizens were gathered in
groups; strong men with bowed heads, women wringing their

hands and the little children clinging to their mothers' dresses and crying." The cavalry had no difficulty determining which direction McCausland's men had left. "Merchandise of every description was strewn along the road, boots, clothing, window curtains and even infants' shoes and little slips."[27]

About five hundred buildings had burned that day, including 278 homes and stores. The center of the town had been gutted, the court house, banks, and churches destroyed. Over two thousand people had been left homeless. Miraculously, it seemed, only one person died—an elderly man, formerly enslaved, who could not escape from his home.

Benjamin Schneck, a resident of Chambersburg, wrote his sister Margaretta about the burning three days afterward. "We are all safe, though homeless and with only some clothing left." They were able to save little. Schneck had stood on the roof of their house, trying to douse the flames while women of the household carried water to him. No one else could offer aid, "for everybody had enough to do for themselves for the firing began in different parts of town at one time. Some houses in each square were fired, and then the others caught." With only one exception, "every house down on both sides for 7 Squares, is gone. So with Main Street for nearly 1/2 mile." The devastation was complete: "The Bank, all the stores, all the hotels, every shoe, clothing, and other stores (except in the outskirts some small grocery etc. shops) are all consumed. In most instances, little—in very many, nothing—was saved, not even a single change of clothing."

The few who had been spared had opened "their hearts and houses" to the rest, "But such a scene of Ruin! No imagination can conceive it." Pennsylvania Governor Curtin visited Chambersburg a few days after the burning and told Schneck that "'the reality is fearfully beyond all my conceptions.' He requested us to try + keep the people in heart, for many have left, + more do not know what to do here now." With the news of the disastrous Union attack at the Battle of the Crater in Petersburg on the same day as the burning of Chambersburg, "it looks dark for our country." Schneck admitted that "some of the rebel officers + men that were here did not expect this vandalism, + they showed a good spirit—they did + would not fire any building + even helped people to carry out things out of their houses. They denounced the whole procedure as outrageous and wicked."[28]

Emma Stouffer wrote her brother about the fire the day immediately afterward. "I suppose you hear all sorts of news. But hardly much worse than it really is." While "thanks to a kind Providence" they still had their home a bit outside of town, they had seen much suffering. "I heard of but two families who saved any thing but a few clothes." As the citizens tried to piece together how such a calamity could befall them, "some attach great blame to Gens Couch and Averel. the former some persons say should have rallied the 1500 men who went through here on Friday eve, and the latter was so drunk in GreenCastle that he could not write an answer to a dispatch sent him by Couch. It is hard to tell where the blame rests it surely is a shame that so few should come in & do so much damage."[29]

Eliza Stouffer wrote a "sister in faith" and reflected on the lessons of the fire. Since God is "ruler over all," the fire must have been His will. Perhaps the disaster was "a scourging" because the people "have perhaps grown too cold & careless and that God through mercy may have let this come upon us, to draw us nearer to him, & wean us off more from the world & the things of the world." The fire showed "how soon we may be deprived of every thing." People who owned all that they "could wish for, or make themselves comfortable, were deprived of all in one hours time."

While many of the Confederate soldiers acted brutally, Stouffer reported, others "were more merciful, & helped the women to carry out things some appeared to be very much affected that they had come to this, one in perticular I was told off, that shed tears & would not help to burn. They took him & hand cuffed him." Another soldier helped a woman with a sick child. When he asked if there was anything he could do to help, the woman bitterly told him "no, you have done me all the harm you can do, you cant do any worse, he took the child, & said This child does not feel revengeful, it has a smile on its countinance & he wept."[30]

A local Presbyterian minister described the burning itself in apocalyptic language. "The day was sultry and calm, not a breath stirring, and each column of smoke rose black, straight and single; first one, and then another, and another, and another, until the columns blended and commingled." The "vast and lurid column of smoke and flame rose perpendicular to the sky, and spread out in a vast crown, like a cloud of sackcloth hanging over the doomed city." The sounds of the burning town haunted him: "the roar and the surging, the crackling and the crash of falling timbers and walls broke upon the still air with a fearful dissonance," while "the screams and sounds of agony of burning animals, hogs and cows and horses" echoed all around.[31]

Jacob Hoke, a prominent young merchant, portrayed the human suffering. "The people were running wildly through the street, carrying clothing and other articles. Others were dragging sewing machines and articles of furniture. Children were screaming after their parents, and parents were frantic after their children. The feeble efforts of the aged and infirm to carry with them some valued article from their burning homes, were deeply distressing. The roaring and crackling of the flames, the falling walls, the blinding smoke, the intense heat intensified by the scorching sun, all united to form a picture of the terrible which no pen can describe nor painter portray. It was such a sight as no one would desire to witness but once in a lifetime."[32]

The accounts from the time, like others from years and decades to follow, differentiated among the Confederates. McCausland, of course, was the villain, and people looked for some way to explain his actions. No one knew much about him, and he had only been in Chambersburg for one morning, so people looked for clues wherever they could find or imagine them. On their way to Chambersburg, one story claimed, the Confederate officers paused at a private house. "M'Causland brought his brandy to the table, and drank freely of it while eating. When they rose from the table and were passing out of the house," an officer with McCausland "noticed a delicate child." When his companion remarked that the child looked quite pale, McCausland announced that "'Madam, in a few hours, when I get through with Chambersburg the women and children of the town will look paler than your child,' and with a fiendish chuckle of satisfaction he proceeded to execute his purpose."[33]

This melodramatic story was a caricature of the common perception of McCausland and of his men. The leaders of the raid were unprincipled, drunkards, heartless, and especially cruel to women and children. Their motives required no deep analysis.

But the people of the town made a point of telling about the doubts, fears, and even anguish of many of the Confederate soldiers they encountered. While stories of drunken men breaking through glass doors, destroying fine furniture, stealing jewelry, taking family heirlooms, and rifling through women's clothing would be repeated across the generations, so would stories of soldiers who did what they could to help. The victims looked for evidence that their suffering was so unjust that even Rebels could see that it was wrong.

Jubal Early supposedly explained his orders to burn Chambersburg by his defense of women. As he was quoted in a Philadelphia newspaper soon after the raid, Early painted a terrible picture of the Valley of Virginia in the wake of Hunter's campaign of the summer. "We found many, very many, families of helpless women and children who had been suddenly turned out of doors, and their houses and contents condemned to the flames; and in some cases where they had rescued some extra clothing, the soldiers had torn the garments into narrow strips, and strewn them upon the ground for us to witness when we arrived in pursuit." The image of torn and discarded women's clothing clearly signaled the callous and wanton behavior of troops. Such behavior demanded revenge against enemy women and their families.[34]

☆

THE ACCOUNTS OF THE BURNING of Chambersburg echoed those of the occupation of Staunton eight long weeks before. In both, a villainous general unleashes drunken soldiers on a defenseless population. Horrifying accounts of physical destruction mix with sentimental accounts of gentlemanly officers and sorrowful young soldiers forced into actions in which they did not believe. The accounts of Staunton and Chambersburg both gave a prominent role to alcohol.

The devastation of the two towns, in fact, had little in common. Staunton held crucial military resources and served as a key transportation hub and hospital base. It had been an object of fighting since the war's beginning. The United States Army was careful with Staunton, burning strategic targets while protecting homes. Soldiers had plenty of time, and considerable latitude, over two days and multiple visits, to search and plunder those homes, to demand meals and to have conversations with citizens.

In Chambersburg, by contrast, the devastation lasted only one morning, in a single strike. While some plundering soldiers certainly tried to take as much as they could, sheer limitations of time necessarily made any ransacking short and frantic. And although the stories focused on the doubts many Confederates expressed and acted upon, no soldier was punished after the fact for resisting.

The Confederates who burned Chambersburg, like the people of the town itself, would think about that July morning for the rest of their lives, trying to explain how such a thing had happened. Some would focus on personalities, on sodden and groggy generals; others would see in the burning the essence of the people Americans had become after three years of mutual hatred.

Years later, a Confederate soldier involved in the raid opened a correspondence with a resident of Chambersburg. The soldier frankly admitted that he did not hear "one dissenting voice" among the men charged with burning Chambersburg. "And why did we justify so harsh a measure? Simply because we had long come to the conclusion that it was time for us to burn something in the enemy's country." This conclusion grew from the accumulated experiences of the preceding year. In 1863, in the Gettysburg campaign, "when our whole army had passed through your richest section of the country, where the peaceful homes and fruitful fields only made the contrast" with Virginia more painful, "many a man whose home was in ruins chaffed under the orders from General Lee." But out of respect they obeyed Lee's orders and "left the homes and fields as we found them."

By the time many of those same men arrived at Chambersburg a year later, "we had so often in our eyes the reverse of this wherever your army swept through Virginia, that we were thoroughly convinced of the justice of a stern retaliation." Chambersburg simply happened to be "the nearest and most accessible place of importance for us to get to." And by the time the Confederates reached the town they had been provoked by the people of Franklin County itself. As they crossed the border, the soldiers entered a village where "the knots of men on the corners poked fun at our appearance, and jeered us, and never seemed to consider that the men upon who they expended their fun had pistols and sabres in their belts and might use them." Even stranger than this, the Confederate soldier thought, "was to see able-bodied young men out of service—a sight never seen in the South during the war. In Chambersburg itself, it seemed impossible to convince your people that we were in earnest. They treated it as a joke, or thought it was a mere threat to get the money, and showed their sense of security and incredulity in every act." The Confederates demanded to be taken seriously.[35]

☆

CHAMBERSBURG'S *FRANKLIN REPOSITORY* believed that Jubal Early fought his way to the border with the North in the summer of 1864 for reasons other than military strategy. "The great aim of Early is evidently to hover on the border of Maryland and Pennsylvania as long as he can with safety; keep both States distracted and alarmed; weary our people of war alike by atrocious robbery and applying the torch of the barbarian; disorganize us with the hope of wholly or partially defeating the coming conscription, and drive the timid and time-serving to voting the Peace ticket at the next election." Early, with Lee behind him, had calculated a political aim in the invasion.

The newspapers of Staunton, destroyed in Hunter's raid, had resumed operation in time to report on the burning of Chambersburg. The *Vindicator* announced that the burning in Pennsylvania "meets with the universal approval of the Confederate press. Just retaliation, though long delayed, has commenced at last, and will continue to be practiced until the corrupt dynasty, which rules at Washington, shall direct its minions in the field to cease their Vandalism, and return to that mode of warfare practiced by all civilized nations." The paper printed Early's explanation of Chambersburg's destruction. He supposedly said that "no man more than himself deprecated the necessity of such an act," but "he was only doing his duty to those people who had suffered by General Hunter's orders; and again, because he believed that by retaliation such barbarous practices would be sooner discontinued than in any other way." [36]

"We love to hear those cries of anguish," proclaimed the *Richmond Dispatch*, quoted in the Republican paper in Franklin County. "This howl of desolation and despair from the quarter in which it is heard comes upon our ear like 'music on the waters.' It is sweet beyond all earthly gratification. Glad are we that retribution has at last put forth its terrible arm and assumed its most terrible shape." The paper would be glad to hear, in fact, that "the whole valley of the Susquehanna was one long, unbroken, irresistible flame, not to subside as long as a house or a tree, or a blade of grass, or a stalk of corn, remains to testify that it had ever been inhabited by man." The *Richmond Enquirer* went to similar lengths. Its editor wanted Early to burn York, Lancaster, and Harrisburg, acting as a "sedative" to the "war spirit of the enemy." More burning would encourage the North to support a man for president on the peace platform. The Confederates had nothing to apologize for because the burning "would be fully justified" by "the strictest laws of war." The only way to move the North to peace was through harder war. [37]

Early engaged in theatrical warfare. He did want to loosen Ulysses Grant's stranglehold on Robert E. Lee, of course, but he could have pulled Grant's troops away without the risks of frequent raids and confrontations. He moved the United States Army, and his own, out of the Valley of the Virginia during a crucial growing season, but he could have accomplished that more quietly and cautiously. Instead, with the presidential election of the fall rapidly approaching, the Confederates aimed a clear message at the North: despite all your sacrifice, you are not safe. You are led by an incompetent administration that repeatedly chooses incompetent generals. After your untold suffering and sacrifice over three years of war, and after the brutal, costly, and ineffectual campaign of Grant in Virginia in the summer of 1864, we can still threaten your capital, cross your borders, and burn your towns at will. The Republicans have led you into devastation and despair.

The solution the Republicans offered, declared the *Repository*, was "simple, plain and within the power of all. Our armies must be reinforced!" If the Federal forces "had but 25,000 more men Early would be driven back to the capital of crime at once and the border would be speedily and forever free from thieving and destructive incursions. Had Grant 50,000 fresh men just now Richmond would be ours in thirty days; and had Sherman a like number of reinforcements the Flag of the Free would wave in triumph over Atlanta and Mobile before the frosts of Autumn reach us." The Republicans tried to persuade Northern voters to redeem years of sacrifice with more sacrifice, to use the demographic and logistical superiority of the United States to overwhelm the rebellion. "This and this only is the remedy. It is the only measure of safety to the border, to our armies, to the Republic; and it is to defeat this if possible, that the rebel chief now hovers around us."[38]

The Democrats sneered at such a response. "To the stupidity

of the War Department must we lay the destruction of Chambersburg. There is no use mincing terms about it," the *Valley Spirit* argued. "Let the blame be placed fairly and squarely where it belongs." The Democrats saw a Republican conspiracy behind the vulnerability of Chambersburg and the rest of the border. There must be answers to the obvious questions: "Why the Shenandoah and Cumberland Valleys have been left as raging grounds to the rebels? . . . Why our towns are left unprotected that they may be ransomed to enrich the rebel commissariat? Why our citizens are suffered to be carried off as prisoners—their property as plunder—and their homes burnt under their heads to benefit the rebels?"

The Democrats' vague conspiracy theories suggested that the Lincoln administration tolerated such incursions to raise the stakes of the war so that slavery would have to be completely destroyed and the Republicans kept in power. Even if the invasions of the border were not the result of intentional design, if "such management, rather mismanagement of our military affairs, is not affording 'aid and comfort to the enemy' then we know not in what direction to look for treason! 'The border shall be protected' has been the promise since the war commenced." Now, after three years of war, "burnt towns and a plundered, homeless people" showed that the promise had been broken."[39]

Jubal Early, though bereft of enduring military accomplishment, had managed to plant new doubts in the minds of Northern voters in a crucial political season. Ulysses Grant knew he would have to remove this threat to the Union cause, a threat as real as any military challenge.

☆

THE ECONOMY OF CHAMBERSBURG had been reduced to a primitive state by McCausland's raid. "Business is all conducted in little shops and shanties on the back streets, and in out of the way places," the *Valley Spirit* admitted a month after the burning. "But a small assortment of goods are kept on hand and for these the highest prices are asked. Many of our citizens have removed to other places never to return." Those who did conduct business did so in a new and unflattering spirit of hard-hearted bargaining. "One would scarcely suppose that so great a change could take

A photograph of Chambersburg's main streets taken days
after the burning of July 1863.

place in a community in so short a time. Men seem in a degree reckless, they have lost all they possessed in the world, in an hours time, through no fault of theirs, and they appear determined to make it up by hook or by crook in the shortest possible time." Credit was scarce and the phrase "trust is played out" was "posted up in stores and shops. It is cash down for everything you get and everything you sell."[40]

Such conditions would not long endure, its defenders assured themselves and the world. Chambersburg's essential nature, like that of the North more generally, was businesslike and bustling, competent and civic-minded. The small city, celebrating its centennial in 1864, had from its beginning been "the natural, healthy offspring of the great and growing wealth of the beautiful valley in which it was centered. In its business it had no rival, and can have none hereafter." Chambersburg's rise from the ashes was inevitable. "Its stores must be replaced—its shops must resound again with the sound of the anvil and chisel; its artizans must find the same demand for their handi-work, and its professions have the same duties to-day they had a month ago. Its vast water-power still courses through the heart of our ruins, and new structures must soon turn it to enterprise and profit."[41]

As inevitable as such a resurrection might be, in the meantime Chambersburg had to suffer criticism from fellow Northerners. Newspapers elsewhere, especially New York, ridiculed the Pennsylvanians for not having defended themselves against a few hundred Confederate raiders. It was true that no citizens had picked up guns to fight off the heavily armed rebels, the people of Chambersburg replied, because they were hopelessly outnumbered. Moreover, "it was very evident from the conduct of the men, from the moment they entered town, that it was a doomed place and would be destroyed under any circumstances. No attention was, there-

The columns of the Bank of Chambersburg after the burning of July 1863.

fore, paid to the demand and McCausland immediately fired the town as he would have done had every dollar of the ransom been paid down." The townspeople did "not demean themselves by any offer to compromise, or conciliate in any way the freebooters by an attempt to negotiate with them. From the moment they entered the place they gave out that they were hell-bent to burn the 'd—d town' and they were suffered to carry out their hellish inclinations without making dupes of our citizens by extorting ransom from them when ransom would not have saved the town."[42]

The defense of the character of the people of Chambersburg had more than psychological value, for the Pennsylvania state legislature was considering whether to provide relief to the town. Things began well a few weeks after the burning. "The legislature was convened in extraordinary session by the proclamation of the Governor; the members were invited to visit Chambersburg by a committee of our citizens, and the facility of an excursion train, free of charge, was tendered to them." Everyone in town assumed that "there could not possibly be any room for doubt or quibbling about the desperate condition of our people, for the legislature had been here and had witnessed the sore straits we were in with their own eyes. How could they stifle all the common sympathies of humanity, and steel their breasts against such a calamity? The thing seemed incredible to every right thinking man." But the legislature chose to supply only a fifth of the $500,000 put forward in the bill as a partial compensation. The Democrats supported the bill, the Republicans opposed it on grounds that the government was not responsible for the destruction of property by a public enemy. Efforts to gain compensation would drag on for years and in the meantime the people of Chambersburg would be largely on their own. The political consequences of the decision, and of McCausland's raid, would arrive more quickly than any relief.[43]

☆

HARPER'S WEEKLY, the leading illustrated newspaper in the United States, devoted three full pages to images based on photographs of the ruins of Chambersburg. The isolated marble columns of the Franklin County courthouse stood amid the rubble; the bleak vista down the main streets of the little city showed block after block in charred ruins. The magazine, strongly in support of

President Lincoln and the war, presented the remarkable material cost of the burning of Chambersburg—"not less than four millions of dollars," it estimated—and struck the characteristic notes that echoed in every account of burning by either side. "As if this was not enough, the rebel soldiers added insult to injury, thus interpreting their chivalry to defenseless women and helpless children. Bedridden old women even did not elicit any compassion in the breasts of these rebels. Uncoffined corpses had to be buried hastily in gardens to save them from the flames." The magazine defended General Couch, for "it is clearly impossible that he or any other General could protect Pennsylvania from being at some point infested" by an army that ignored "the amenities of civilized warfare."[44]

Supporters of the Republicans in the North reading the rest of that August 20, 1864, issue of *Harper's Weekly* would not have been heartened. The magazine included accounts and images of the failed assault at Petersburg, along with defenses of the African-American men killed in the Battle of the Crater against the "malevolent eagerness with which certain newspapers deride the colored troops for being no braver than the white troops." Advocates for President Lincoln would have been discouraged, too, by the account of the "Wade and Davis Manifesto," an attack, issued on August 5, against the president's plan for reconstructing the South. Wade and Davis were Republicans and so the manifesto's "envenomed hostility" and "ill-tempered spirit" were especially painful to read. *Harper's Weekly* warned that the Republican party could not afford such internal conflict, for "it is part of the desperate struggle of those who are hostile to the Administration to represent him as destroying all our liberties, and mismanaging the war only to secure his own re-election."[45]

Jubal Early's campaign at the border played a significant role in this disquiet. Frustration had been building in the North as large

Federal armies outside of Atlanta and Richmond failed to take the enemy. Now, without endangering Lee in Petersburg and escaping Grant's notice for weeks, Early and McCausland had struck at a vulnerable spot in the North's defenses and in the reputation of the Lincoln administration. Grant, for all the credibility he had earned, did not foresee Early's audacious surge to the north in the Valley. Critics wondered whether Grant, as commander of all Union armies, should not have been in Washington, protecting the capital and the border, rather than huddling in Virginia, fixated on Lee.

Though the valley into Pennsylvania had repeatedly provided the Confederacy a ready-made route of invasion, the command of United States forces around the border had been divided among four different military departments, an overlap that confused lines of command and communication. Units and generals came and went as they were needed elsewhere. And though the Baltimore and Ohio Railroad was essential to the survival of the United States, it continued to suffer repeated Confederate raids and attacks. Ambiguous authority and the shifting of commanders left the Federal army vulnerable to quick-hitting raids such as McCausland's. There was, in short, reason to blame the Union command for the devastation of the town.[46]

Ulysses Grant decided that such conditions could not stand. On August 7 he installed Major General Philip H. Sheridan as the commander of a new Army of the Shenandoah, consolidating previous divisions. The United States War Department rejected several other choices for the post and held deep reservations about Sheridan, for the thirty-three-year-old had never led a large army. Nevertheless, Grant trusted Sheridan and gave him a month to organize his command: 35,000 infantry and artillery and 8,000 cavalry, plus 5,000 more men at Harpers Ferry, nearly 30,000 outside of Washington, and about 9,000 in other locations. Com-

United States General Philip Sheridan

bined, the 87,000 men constituted a formidable force. Jubal Early, by comparison, commanded fewer than 9,000 total infantry and artillery and fewer than 4,000 cavalry. Sheridan's job was to drive Early out of the Valley, lay waste to the riches of the area, and cut the Virginia Central Railroad—and to do so as quickly as possible. The United States, with the most critical election in its history only three months away, needed a victory.[47]

☆

JOSEPH WADDELL ADMITTED THAT he heard the news of Chambersburg's burning with "mingled emotions." Waddell's "first feeling was one of horror and strong disapprobation." But he soon found himself "entertaining a secret feeling of gratification that the miserable Yankee nation, who have been burning and pillaging throughout our country so long, have now been made to suffer in their own homes." After this brief indulgence in feelings of revenge, however, Waddell sobered when he reminded himself that the burning of Chambersburg was, at best, "impolitic. The Yankees can burn a hundred of our towns and where we can burn one of theirs." He expected them, in fact, to burn "every place in reach of Yankee armies." Over the next two days, as he heard "much talk about the burning of Chambersburg, Pa., and diversity of opinion in regard to it," Waddell became persuaded by some of what he heard. "It may do good for the Yankees to find that some of their towns can be burnt too, and some of their women and children turned out of shelter, without beds to sleep on or clothes to wear."[48]

Soldiers who had been in Chambersburg arrived in Staunton after the burning. They told of McCausland's calm demands and of the laughter that met his stern warnings. "Our men say that the affair was extremely painful to them." A soldier from Augusta was one of the few Confederates killed in Chambersburg. He had lingered too long to steal and was surrounded by furious townsmen and beaten to death. Waddell merely noted that he "fell a victim to the rage of the populace." On that very day, Waddell carefully cut and pasted clippings from newspapers detailing the depredations of "Yankee Brigands," relating the stories of Hunter and the suffering of women and children. Waddell scribbled below: "Such is the war raged against us by the Northern people!"[49]

A former editor and still a reader of every newspaper he could get, Waddell saw that Grant assured the people of the North that victory was within reach if they would stay united. Grant told them that the Confederates "have old men and boys guarding prisoners and bridges, having robbed alike the cradle and the grave," that the "casualties of war are reducing the army at the rate of a regiment a day." Where Southerners usually scoffed at such portrayals, Waddell merely noted that they were "all very near the truth." He admitted to himself that he feared that "the

Yankees would occupy Staunton again before many weeks have passed, and perhaps winter here." He prayed for faith.[50]

In the meantime, Waddell saw signs of the moral decay the war was causing in Staunton itself. He was reading on the porch of his home in Staunton when women of the house yelled that soldiers were fighting and that "it's a black man they are beating." Running into the street, Waddell found two Confederate soldiers striking his brother's enslaved man, Stephen. "He was on the ground, his head bleeding, both of the soldiers having large stones in their hands, and one or both of them pounding him. It was the most brutal and murderous affair I ever intercepted."

Waddell, a middle-aged man wearing thick glasses, rushed up and told the soldiers to stop. "One said the negro had struck him— that he was a white man+c—All the disgusting slang indulged in by low whites to justify their maltreatment of negros." Waddell struggled with the two soldiers, both of whom were drunk and both of whom held large rocks in their hands. The larger of the men grabbed Waddell by the wrist. He admitted that "for several minutes I felt that my life was in peril," but he eventually pulled free and returned with a provost guard to have them arrested. "Stephen says they accosted him as he was going to his dinner, but observing that they were drunk he did not reply, when they caught him and pulled him about. He then no doubt defended himself, as he had a right to do."

Several days later, Waddell heard a knock on his front door. There, "a negro man" handed him a hat with a piece of paper attached. Before Waddell could ask who had sent him the gift, "the bearer moved off without replying. The hat is a very good one, such as the ladies make of wheat straw." Apparently, Waddell's bravery in hard times did not go unnoticed among his African-American neighbors.[51]

☆

JOHN C. IMBODEN, who had fought against the United States forces in the Valley since the days of Stonewall Jackson more than two years earlier, had never recovered from the typhoid fever he contracted with the army in the summer of 1864. While Imboden's star had fallen as his undisciplined cavalry came under criticism from Breckinridge, Early, and others, the former partisan's knowledge of the Valley was missed. Imboden tried to aid Early, but never regained his earlier vigor. He held on through the fall, but with his wife ill as well, Imboden requested transfer farther south and was placed in charge of prisoners of war in Georgia. In the meantime, a fragment of a song could be heard among the disheartened Confederate troops:

> Old Jimboden's gone up the spout,
> And Old Jube Early's about played out.

It seemed that the Confederacy might soon be seeing its last days in the Valley of Virginia.[52]

Jed Hotchkiss and his comrades knew they would be facing Philip H. Sheridan "who now commands the 'Yanks' here, on the track so well beaten" by a long succession of failed Union generals. Hotchkiss believed that the fight between Early and Sheridan "will go far to end the war & do not think there will be much if any fighting after this campaign."

☆

AS SHERIDAN ORGANIZED HIS FORCES and the Democrats returned home from their convention, shocking news came from Atlanta.

═══

On September 3, William T. Sherman occupied Atlanta. He sent Grant a triumphant note: "Atlanta is ours, and fairly won." The Confederates, having fought aggressively against the advancing Federal forces since May, had been forced to evacuate Atlanta after Sherman's forces cut the Confederate supply lines. As they retreated, the Confederates burned massive amounts of ammunition and other military supplies. The United States now possessed the critical rail lines of the lower Confederacy. Sherman's army could move in almost any direction.

Suddenly, the political calculus looked different. The Democrats' peace platform was much less compelling when reunion could come through victory rather than capitulation, when war rather than compromise could redeem the sacrifices made by so many in the United States.

While the great victory at Atlanta abruptly reversed the military momentum to the benefit of the Republicans, the Shenandoah Valley remained a problem throughout the months of the pending election. Guerrillas still ranged through the Valley and throughout northern Virginia, less than a day's ride from the White House. The Republicans could not claim to have won the war as long as Lee and Early remained in Virginia. Even as Northerners exulted over the news of burning Atlanta, they nervously watched their papers for news from the Shenandoah Valley.

☆

ABRAHAM LINCOLN WORRIED about the Valley. On September 12, nearly two weeks after the fall of Atlanta, Lincoln telegraphed Grant to see if he could persuade Sheridan to act. Sheridan had been ordered to pursue Jubal Early "to the death" but seemed to be making no move to do so. Grant shared Lincoln's anxiety, but did not want to undercut Sheridan. Fortunately for Lincoln and Grant, Sheridan decided on his own that he was ready to push Early out of the Valley.[53]

Sheridan, after organizing his large command, attacked Early's smaller force in Winchester on September 19, driving the Confederates south. Three days later, Jedediah Hotchkiss hurriedly described "a battle yesterday at Fisher's Hill, which resulted quite disastrously from the fact that our men broke & ran & we lost some 15 pieces of artillery & a good many small arms & some prisoners." Hotchkiss admitted that "I hope we may not have to fall back any further, but shd not be surprised if we came up to Harrisonburg or even to Staunton." Such a retreat southward in the Valley would sacrifice an enormous amount of valuable land and crops to Sheridan and his men. Not only was the Confederacy losing but it was losing in humiliating ways, through inadequate vigilance, inept cavalry, and stampedes of fleeing soldiers. The confidence, even arrogance, that had driven McCausland into Chambersburg seven weeks earlier had been shattered.[54]

A flash of black humor captured the situation as the Confederates were driven south by the enormous army of Philip Sheridan. As they retreated from Winchester, Jubal Early turned to his friend John C. Breckinridge, former vice-president of the United States and now a Confederate general serving with Early, and deadpanned, "Well, Breckinridge, what do you think of our rights in the territories now?'" Those rights to expand the boundaries of slavery, which once seemed worth war, now seemed abstract, meaningless. Everything the Confederacy had been fighting for was disappearing. Breckinridge simply laughed and kept riding, looking to make a stand somewhere to the south in the Valley.[55]

☆

PHILIP SHERIDAN BOASTED OF his quick victory at Winchester. In his report to Grant, widely published in Northern papers, the new commander in the Valley told of his overwhelming success over Early, "driving him through Winchester, and capturing about 2,500 prisoners, five pieces of artillery, nine army flags and most of their wounded. The rebel Generals Rhodes and Gordon were killed, and three other General officers wounded. Most of the enemy's wounded and all their killed fell into our hands." Even the Democrats' *Valley Spirit* had to admire "Little Phil," so-named for his stature of five feet and five inches. Wrapping grudging praise in characteristic sarcasm, the paper noted that "the President and Secretary Stanton have at length—doubtless by mistake—placed at the head of the Army of the Valley of the Shenandoah a man of talents and military skill."[56]

The Republican paper in Chambersburg shouted the lessons of Sheridan's victories in bold, and equally sarcastic, headlines.

SHERIDAN ON A 'CESSATION OF HOSTILITIES!'

HE DEMONSTRATES HOW MUCH THE WAR IS A 'FAILURE!'

HE ROUTS EARLEY AND DRIVES HIM FROM THE VALLEY!

THE BORDER NOW SAFE!

Having printed those headlines after Winchester, the Republican sheet had time to add even more enthusiastic headlines about Fisher's Hill before they sent the paper out:

LATER AND BETTER! ANOTHER VICTORIOUS BATTLE!

EARLY'S ARMY COMPLETELY ROUTED!

EARLY'S MISSION IN THE VALLEY ENDED!

These victories cleared the way for the other work before Sheridan. His orders from Grant told him to fight his way deep into the Valley and "do all damage to rail-roads and crops you can. Carry off stock of all description and negroes so as to prevent further planting. If the War is to last another year we want the Shenandoah Valley to remain a barren waste." Grant had, a few months earlier, ordered Hunter to do much the same thing. Hunter had wasted time and political capital burning the houses of prominent families and the Virginia Military Institute, to little effect. Only his destruction in Staunton had inflicted any real damage on the Confederate war effort.[57]

Sheridan, learning from Hunter's mistakes, took a different approach. Sheridan was not interested in the small theater of charred houses and scattered clothes. Instead, he would star in a much larger drama, destroying the productive capacity of a crucial part of the Confederacy. Grant's orders to Sheridan explicitly directed him to "carry off" "negroes," even if Grant mentioned enslaved people as an afterthought following "stock." The Federal army did not have an established practice regarding their dealings with the enslaved people they confronted. Some officers and enlisted men were friendly, others hostile, and many impatient with any delay or inconvenience the refugees brought. The future of the African-Americans of the Valley would be improvised, often by the enslaved people themselves.[58]

☆

WHEN NEWS OF JUBAL EARLY'S defeat at Winchester arrived in Staunton, Joseph Waddell wrote—then struck out—a phrase of despair: "to all appearance there is no help for us but in God." "A deep feeling of gloom seems to pervade the community," he admitted. "Life has no charm at present, and there is little to hope for in the future. It is like walking through the Valley of the Shadow of Death." Three days later, news of Fisher's Hill arrived.

"I thought we had reached the lowest stage of despondency yesterday," he wrote, "but there was a 'lower deep' still. Anxiety and gloom was depicted in every countenance. For myself, I confess, I feel staggered and overcome."[59]

Late September saw the Shenandoah Valley at its most fruitful. Waddell's brother told him that "he has his wheat, oats and hay on hand, his corn is ready to be gathered, while his sheep, hogs, and even milch cows are fat enough for slaughter. So it is on every farm, and the mills are full of wheat. If the Yankees come, the loss to our army will be irreparable."[60]

☆

NEWS OF WINCHESTER and Fisher's Hill echoed throughout the North. Greenbacks rose in value relative to gold and previously recalcitrant Republicans fell in line behind President Lincoln. A major in the Federal army, later to become president himself, wrote his wife that "Phil Sheridan has made a speech in the Shenandoah Valley more powerful and valuable to the Union cause than all the stumpers in the Republic can make—our prospects are everywhere brightening."[61]

Grant urged Sheridan once again—as he had urged Hunter—to take advantage of his victories in the northern Valley to destroy the Virginia Central Railroad that connected the Valley with Richmond farther south. If Sheridan could accomplish that, Grant believed, Richmond would fall within a matter of weeks. But Sheridan would not move. Despite being surrounded by the bounty of the Valley, he feared not being able to supply his men on an extended march. Sheridan was plagued by the same worries that had dragged Hunter down earlier that summer: protecting his army from guerrillas. Sheridan retaliated with hangings and shooting of the raiders they caught. He ordered punitive burnings of two dozen houses around the village of Dayton, Virginia, in response to the murder by guerrillas of one of his favorite young officers and ordered the village of Newtown and "all the houses within five miles" burned in retaliation for another guerrilla attack. Sheridan, in fact, destroyed more dwellings than Hunter had, though Sheridan's destruction of crops and barns overshadowed acts that had drawn such condemnation only a few months earlier.[62]

Faced with persistent guerrilla challenges, Sheridan thought the best strategy was to use his enormous force to accomplish another of Grant's goals, destroying the food that sustained both Lee's army and Confederate armies in the Valley. Rather than risk his army by leaving the Valley and attacking the Virginia Central Railroad, Sheridan would destroy the most important cargo carried by that railroad—food for Lee's desperate troops behind the fortifications of Petersburg. Sheridan assured Grant that "the destruction of the grain and forage from here to Staunton will be a terrible blow to them," that the "end of this campaign" would come with "the burning of the crops of the Valley."[63]

Soon, one soldier wrote in his diary, "Our cavalry are burning all the grain, every mill and every barn. The valley is all ablaze in our rear." Day after day, Sheridan's men systematically worked to "clean out the Valley." As soon as he arrived in Harrisonburg, Sheridan ordered his cavalry to begin "devastating crops and devouring cattle" the thirty miles south to Staunton.

The Federal troops moved quickly and efficiently. Unlike Hunter's leisurely burning of isolated houses or his two-day dismantling of Staunton a few months earlier, Sheridan's cavalry set out to destroy as much as they could while staying on the move. They remained close to main roads and did not push into woods where inhabitants had often driven their livestock and where

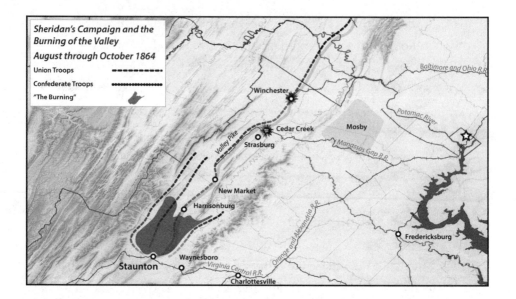

bushwhackers might be hidden. A whistle signaled to scattered units, each having burned what it could, when it was time to move on to the next farm.

Early and his tattered command, having retreated to Waynesboro in eastern Augusta to guard the Virginia Central Railroad tunnel, could only watch as the Valley, including the northern portion of Augusta County, became what Sheridan had ordered it to become: "a barren waste." A Confederate soldier wrote that "the very air is impregnated with the smell of burning property." On a plank that had survived the flames were words left by a Federal soldier: "Remember Chambersburg."[64]

☆

SIGNS OF SHERIDAN APPEARED in Augusta before his army did. An order from Richmond to Staunton commanded "all the wheat to be ground immediately, and the flour sent there as soon as possible." An enslaved man banged on Joseph Waddell's door in the middle of the night to warn that the Federal army was in Harrisonburg and that it was time for the men to again leave their homes and families. Waddell was able to catch a car on the train and made his way to Waynesboro.

As he fled through Augusta County, Waddell saw "women were wringing their hands and crying while the men were carried off as prisoners and the barns and hay stacks were burning." He could see "the whole heavens were illuminated" by the fires dozens of miles away. Waddell lamented that "the country is wasted by war; and the land mourns. Now, at this usually abundant season of the year, people heretofore accustomed to live in ease and luxury, are scuffling for the meanings of life."[65]

Daniel Schreskhise told his brother that the Union forces had "burnt both of our barns with about twenty five tun of hay in them & all of our wheat excep about twenty five bushels that we had carried out." The Federal troops had driven away all their cows and colts, though two of each returned. Daniel predicted "suffering times in the valley this winter as the yanks have burnt all of the barns from hear down & all of the mills except one occasionly." He thought "the worst of all" was that "every body paid the yanks all of their gold & silver." Schreskhise felt relatively fortunate, for others "are ruined in tirely." He told of William Pence with sympathy: "they took of both of his black men that he had bought & five head of horses & all of his cattle & sheep & burnt his barn he dident have a barrel of flour on hand. I tell you he is almost crazy." Schreskhise admitted that "I dont see how our army is to live in Va this winter the valley has bin our main support & that is nearly all destroyed."[66]

Despite the overwhelming power of the Union armies, every confrontation between their soldiers and the Confederate population was charged and dangerous. The Federal cavalry could not loiter on any particular farm but moved quickly to the next. The soldiers were not able to carry goods of any size, so they plundered in currency, in livestock that could be driven to their camp, and in food they could eat quickly.

As in raids past, Federal soldiers confronted women more than men. On one Augusta farm, a young Federal captain met a Mrs. Anderson and asked where the men of the household were. "Off fighting you all," was her steely response. The captain noticed a small cabin near the main house, tightly locked up, and asked what it was. The building was the smoke house, filled with the bacon and ham soldiers craved, but she only replied "Why don't you go see?" The cavalryman decided not to take the risk that someone with a gun might be inside.[67]

Every white Southerner had to calculate the risk from such strategies. Three stories about horses showed the range of possibilities. One farm family put all their horses in a barn and secured it with a large iron lock whose key had been "lost." The cavalrymen could hear the horses inside, neighing to their own, and could not bring themselves to burn the barn with horses inside. Another woman, using a butcher knife, slit the reins by which a prize mare was being led away by cavalrymen; impressed by her "spunk," the Federal officer laughed and told his men to let the mare run. On another farm, a Union officer ordered a fine mare bridled and led away. When the mare's colt followed its mother, the farm woman begged them not to take an animal so young that it could be of no use to an army. The officer agreed the animal was useless and simply commanded one of his men to shoot the colt. The woman wept over its body. People remembered these stories for generations.[68]

Staunton's *Vindicator* drew a moral from Sheridan's raid. When

Hunter had burned a few mills and plundered a few houses, people in the North had criticized the "detestable course" and pilloried Hunter. Only three months later, however, the United States had decided on a new course with Grant's order to Sheridan to "burn barns, wheat and hay-stacks, to drive off or kill all live stock and to carry off the negroes—in fact to make the Valley a 'barren waste.'" The people of Augusta had seen how well Sheridan had accomplished the task, yet "we hear not a word condemnatory of the vile acts of Gen. Grant through his accomplice Sheridan."

The trajectory seemed clear: "Grant, wearied and sick of fighting the veterans of Lee with no avail, has turned his arms against the women and children of our land, hoping, doubtless, that he may gain a glorious victory (!) over them." The people of the Valley would not forget. The atrocities would be "treasured up by the fathers, husbands, brothers and sons." The men would "some day have retribution. Let not the North then cry out that Southern Barbarians are let loose upon them, but remember that we can point to the campaigns in the Valley of the Shenandoah for precedents for all the acts our soldiery may commit." Some day, they would "make retribution justice."[69]

☆

AN EVENT AT THE SOUTHERN END of the Valley during the time of the burning of Augusta gave a chilling vision of the brutality the war brought to black people. Saltville, the main source of the essential preservative for the Confederacy, had been one of the original targets of the Federal army at the beginning of the long summer of 1864 and remained a site of bitter fighting as fall descended on the mountains.

A Confederate force, cobbled together by John C. Breckinridge upon his arrival after leaving Jubal Early after Fisher's Hill, combined men and boys from Tennessee, Kentucky, and southwest Virginia. The Union, for its part, hurriedly gathered 400 enslaved men in Kentucky to fight alongside white soldiers who jeered their black allies as they marched into battle. Barely trained, the African-American soldiers were thrown against heavily entrenched Confederate defenders at the salt works. The Confederates, enraged after discovering that they were fighting against black men, killed the wounded African-American soldiers left behind after the failed Union attack. The black Federal soldiers desperately tried to keep up with the Union retreat rather than surrender, riding with missing arms and bleeding lungs.

Fog covered the site of the battle the next morning. A Confederate officer was puzzled to hear gunfire: "a shot then another and another until the firing swelled to the volume of a skirmish line." Riding to the sound, he found Confederate soldiers "killing negroes." Cautiously proceeding, he saw "a squad of Tennesseans, mad and excited to the highest degree. They were shooting every wounded negro they could find. Hearing firing on other parts of the field, I knew the same awful work was going on all about me." Another Confederate noted in his diary that scouts "went all over the field and the continued sing of the rifle, sung the death knell of many a poor negro who was unfortunate enough not to be killed yesterday. Our men took no negro prisoners. Great numbers of them were killed yesterday and today."

A Union officer said that the men doing the killing "all appeared to be commanding themselves." The line between regular and irregular soldiers had been lost in appearance and in behavior. When John Breckinridge arrived at the site, "with blazing eyes and murderous tones," a Confederate observed, he "ordered that the massacre should be stopped. He rode away and—the shooting went on. The men could not be restrained." The murder continued for six more days, culminating with guerrillas forcing their way into a makeshift hospital at Emory & Henry College and shooting men, black and white, in their beds.

Word of the slaughter began to spread out of the mountains. A Richmond newspaper printed a tally that showed telling numbers: 150 black Union soldiers had been killed and only 6 wounded, while 106 white soldiers had been killed and 80 wounded. The ratios testified that dozens of wounded African-Americans had been killed, making Saltville, in October 1864, one of the bloodiest massacres in the entire Civil War. The Richmond paper celebrated the rare Confederate victory over all the "niggers" and Federal troops. Now that the black men had been driven out of Saltville, birds of "the same color, but greater respectability" have descended on the town. "They are turkey-buzzards this time, and they come in quest of Yankee carcasses."[70]

A Confederate soldier stationed in southwest Virginia wrote his cousin Mary back in Augusta County two weeks after the slaughter at Saltville. Andrew R. Barber, having played "a very active part" in the fight, took satisfaction that the Federal general was "punished very severely for bringing his mixed white & Blacks in the vicinity of Saltville where we Reserves could strike them a blow." Barber was proud that the Confederate soldiers brought into the fighting at this late point in the war could prove themselves. "Let it be said 'never more' that the silvery haired men & the beardless & down cheeked youths of old Va. will not fight." Now, after the rout of the "mixed" forces at Saltville, "the faithful Historian, & future generations will give them a high place in the annals of their country."[71]

A Campaign
of Terrible Moment

September through November 1864

*"A political campaign is before us of more terrible moment than any
military campaign," the* New York Times *declared late in the
bloody summer of 1864. If a military campaign failed, it could be redeemed
by another. But if the great campaign to reelect Abraham Lincoln failed,
the result would be "irretrievable. There will be no subsequent opportunity
to undo its effects. It would settle the war, decisively, fatally, forever."*[1]

☆

THE VICTORIES IN THE VALLEY provided the sort of overpowering triumphs the people of the United States longed for
and thought they had secured with vast numbers of men and
arms. The Valley, a place of disgrace for one Union general after
another, had suddenly become the scene of glorious victory. As
one Union soldier wrote his sister from the Valley in October,

"General Sheridan was at the head of his brave soldiers in the engagement, there is not a soldier here but would sacrifice there lives for the brave General, Sheridan's army has crowned its self with victory."[2]

Sheridan's victories in the Valley provided something else many people in the North longed for: the destruction of the bountiful landscape that had sustained Lee's army for so long. Sheridan's burning of the Valley—months before Sherman's march through Georgia—demonstrated a new resolve and a new willingness to undermine the material and spiritual resources of Confederate civilians. The Republican paper in Chambersburg published an article—"The Valley of Humiliation"—glorying in Sheridan's redemption of the Valley with his tactics of systematic burning. Sheridan's victories marked a triumph over the guerrillas who had bedeviled the Union forces in the Valley for years.[3]

And yet, as with everything else in the Civil War, the people of the North viewed Philip Sheridan's burning through a partisan lens. The Democrats blasted the policy. What were the people of the North to think of "the wanton burning of twenty-seven hundred barns, filled with wheat, and more than eighty mills for grinding wheat and corn? This was done by soldiers of 'The Union,' with the Union flag waving over them." Chambersburg's *Valley Spirit* looked past the victories of Sheridan to write harsh accounts of the burning. "Between Staunton and Strasburg, all barns containing grain, all wheat and hay stacks, all farming implements, granaries and mills, and all subsistence of whatever kind, were burned. All the horses and cattle were driven off." The paper quoted the correspondent of a New York paper: "The Valley, from mountain to mountain, was consequently the scene of a conflagration, such as has not been witnessed during the Rebellion." A correspondent from another paper described the scene in

Sheridan on a "Cessation of Hostilities!"

HE DEMONSTRATES HOW MUCH THE
WAR. IS A "FAILURE!"

HE ROUTS EARLEY AND DRIVES
HIM FROM THE VALLEY!

Rebel Loss 5,000 Killed & Wounded!

OVER 3,000 REBELS PRISONERS!

REBEL GUNS AND FLAGS CAPTURED!

THE BORDER NOW SAFE!

The Repository *celebrates*
Sheridan's victories in Virginia

evocative (and exaggerated) terms. "The Valley of the beautiful Shenandoah, from near the Natural Bridge to the gallows tree of John Brown, is a desolation."

After reprinting Sheridan's report to Grant that detailed the thousands of barns burned and stock driven off, the *Valley Spirit* expressed disbelief. "That an order so desperately wicked, so contrary to the spirit of Christianity, and so revolting to the civilization of this age, should have been issued and executed by officers commanding the armies of a free, civilized and religious nation, is, indeed, almost too incredible for human belief."

The Democrats' paper pointed out an inconsistency in the Republican defense of such actions. "If the Republican papers and speakers are to be believed, our cause was never more prosperous, and our success never more certain than now. We are told daily by them that the rebellion is in the throes of dissolution; that the rebels have robbed the cradle and the grave to fill up their depleted armies; that Sheridan has totally destroyed Early's army in the Valley of the Shenandoah; and that Grant has his hand so firmly fixed upon the throat of Lee and his army at Petersburg and Richmond, that his grip cannot be shaken off." The Republicans promised "that the war will be over before this year shall end. Now if these things, or even the one half of them, be true, why the necessity for this spoliation and destruction of the subsistence of a whole people? Why resort to arson, rapine and vandalism after the crisis of our fate has been safely passed and all danger is pronounced to be over?"

The *Valley Spirit* emphasized the dangers in Grant's orders and Sheridan's execution of them. "There is no distinction made among the citizens of the Valley; all are doomed to the same common ruin; all are marked out as victims, to gratify the savage ferocity which now characterizes the conduct of this war." The burning seemed a direct violation of the spirit that Lincoln claimed drove his and the nation's purpose. "This was to be a war, whose object should be to bring back the citizens of the seceded States to their allegiance to the Government. Mr. Lincoln declared that he intended to prosecute the war for this purpose and no other. Does any man of sane mind think that the Southern people can be conciliated and brought back into the Union, by such acts of cold blooded barbarity as Gen. Sheridan relates in his official report?"

The paper drove the question home: "Do our citizens love the vandals and cut-throats who burnt Chambersburg? Not a bit better than the citizens of the Shenandoah Valley will love the men and the Government that made their homes a waste place and a desolation." If the war continued and the Confederates returned again, the paper asked the citizens of Franklin County, "do you flatter yourselves they will not take revenge for the atrocities practiced in the Shenandoah Valley?"[4]

The Republicans' paper brushed aside such pleas with brusque sarcasm. "Sheridan is hurting our 'erring brethren' and it must be arrested," they pretended to lament. "He has destroyed their crops, and rendered it impossible for Early to winter in the Valley and send out guerrilla parties to plunder and burn towns in Pennsylvania. Such an infringement upon the constitutional rights of the South excites the liveliest indignation of the Spirit." The lesson of Sheridan in the Valley was clear, and nowhere clearer than in Chambersburg: "Rebel armies have become but hordes of vandals as our blackened walls and desolated homes testify, and we must strike boldly at their vital points and at their resources, instead of shivering like cowards over the possible 'changing fortunes of war.'" The situation was simple: "war is upon us by the act of traitors, and we must meet it like men not like trembling slaves."[5]

☆

JED HOTCHKISS AND THE REST of Jubal Early's command waited helplessly as Sheridan's cavalry burned the Valley. Hotchkiss reassured his wife Sara that if the "detail men," the men who had not been in the Confederate army before, stepped up, the South still had a chance to save the Valley. "All must put a shoulder to the wheel & roll on to the end of this campaign & I feel that the end will then come," he urged. "Our men in the field have lost none of their accustomed courage, their leaders none of their accustomed skill, but our ranks are depleted by the many bloody battles of this mighty campaign." Even as the Confederates had fewer and fewer men, their "insolent foe" has added "thousands upon thousands to his from every household in the North." The Federals might have numbers but, Hotchkiss insisted, the Confederates had "moral courage and inconquerable will."[6]

Jubal Early made a final, audacious, attempt to defeat Sheridan's army. On October 19, two weeks after the burning had seemed to bring the war in the Valley to a close, Early surprised Sheridan at Cedar Creek, near Strasburg. The Confederates drove the Union army from their encampment and threatened a major victory. The hungry Southern soldiers, however, stopped to take food and clothing from the tents of the rich Federals. The delay and confusion bought time for the Union. Philip Sheridan had been visiting with Ulysses Grant in Winchester but rushed to the battlefield and helped rally his soldiers.

The aftermath of the battle amplified its importance. Early, widely criticized for turning a bold victory into a humiliating loss, attacked his own men. "Many of you, including some commissioned officers, yielded to a disgraceful propensity for plunder," he announced to the world, "subsequently those who had remained at their post, seeing their ranks thinned by the absence of the plunderers . . . yielded to a needless panic and fled the field in confusion." Rumors flew about who such officers might be and letters appeared in Confederate newspapers refuting Early. Soldiers did not deny the looting, but they sought to shift the blame for the defeat to Early himself. Everyone involved in the ugly debate lost in the mutual recrimination.[7]

Philip Sheridan became a national hero, celebrated by everyone from Abraham Lincoln to schoolchildren. A poem, quickly composed, dramatized Sheridan's ride on his black steed. The tribute became an instant sensation. Stretching the route Sheridan rode from ten miles to twenty, the better to build the dramatic tension, the poem unleashed martial stanzas such as:

> Still sprung from those swift hoofs, thundering South,
> The dust, like smoke from the cannon's mouth;
> Or the trail of a comet, sweeping faster and faster,
> Foreboding to traitors the doom of disaster.

Sheridan received more credit than he deserved for the victory, as he cheerfully admitted, but it served the purposes of the United States well to have a young military hero in a season when the war otherwise seemed to move slowly. The Republicans gloried in Sheridan, in the poem, and in the victory that finally redeemed three years of bloodshed and loss in the Valley of Virginia. A painting of Sheridan's ride became its own sensation; later artists would make that moment in the Valley one of three most painted scenes in the entire Civil War, standing with Gettysburg and the battle of the ironclads as defining moments in the national memory and imagination.[8]

☆

THE ACCOUNTS OF THE DESTRUCTION of the Valley, detailed in boasting numbers by Philip Sheridan in his report to Grant, appeared in papers across the United States and the Confederacy. Yet the full meaning of that destruction is unclear. Sheridan took control of the Valley through three conventional military victories over Early, won through advantages of numbers and cavalry, not because Early fled the Valley out of hunger. Confederate soldiers' hunger was the result of their fighting with Sheridan, the product of relentless marching and fighting, rather than the barrenness of the landscape. Jed Hotchkiss estimated that the men with whom he had traveled that summer had marched 1,670 miles during four and a half months of fighting and seventy-five engagements. If Early's men had won a few key battles and driven Sheridan from the Valley, they could have been fed.[9]

Sheridan's burning systematically destroyed food and farms, but that burning was limited by the technologies of the time: men on horseback starting fires with torches, one building or field at a time. Compared to wars that were to follow, when bombs dropped by airplanes, rockets, or drones brought a level of devastation greater than anyone in 1864 could have imagined, the burning of that summer was archaic, using the methods of the warfare of the ancient world or of the wars between Europeans and American Indians.

Nor was the devastation of the Valley as complete as it seemed at the time, either to the destroyers or to the residents of the counties. The cavalry of Sheridan raced through their work, not taking the time to push far away from the main roads. The farmers of Rockingham County, which bordered Augusta to the north and saw more thorough burning, calculated that the Federals had destroyed a quarter of the county's productive capacity and judged their losses to be about $5 million; in Augusta, the value was estimated at about $3 million. The county, while crippled, still produced considerable amounts of food.[10]

The burning did not break the will of the people of the Valley in their support of the Confederacy. Families who saw the work of decades destroyed in a morning turned their hatred on Grant and Sheridan, the men they held responsible for the strategy that led to so much destruction. If Grant had hoped white citizens would grow disheartened enough to lessen their support for Lee, he was disappointed. In fact, the burning seemed only to deepen white Southerners' hatred for the Yankees and to make them determined to see the war through to whatever end it might bring.

The white people of the Valley surely felt more despair than they could display. With conscription of men and impressment of property imposed by the Confederate government, there was nothing a disaffected citizen could do except remain quiet and contribute as little as possible. With no party machinery and no voting, there was no public way for dissidents in Virginia to express their opposition.

The burning did not prove necessary to defeat the Confederate army in the Valley and it did not demoralize the populace enough that they ceased to support their army. But it did increase the suffering of the Confederate soldiers in the filthy, muddy, and disease-ridden trenches of Petersburg. The men of Lee's command were afflicted with night blindness for want of nutrients and some suffered from scurvy. They lived off beef from the Caribbean, delivered to Atlantic ports because the Confederate rail network could not bring cattle from the bounty in Texas.[11]

In his final accounting of what the Federal army captured and destroyed between August and November 1864, Philip Sheridan reported remarkable numbers. The 71 flour mills, 1,200 barns, 435,802 bushels of wheat, 874 barrels of flour, and 2,500 bushels of potatoes could have fed Confederate troops for weeks. Those troops' starving horses desperately needed some of the 77,176 bushels of corn, 20,000 bushels of oats, 20,397 tons of hay, or 500 tons of fodder burned by the Union army. Any of the 4,000 horses and mules taken away would have been enormously valuable to the Confederates. The woolen mills could have helped clothe some of Lee's men and the tanneries could have helped cover their freezing feet. The soldiers might have missed most

Burning of the Valley

the nearly 11,000 cattle, 12,000 sheep, and 15,000 pigs that could have given physical sustenance.[12]

By one critical measure, however, Sheridan failed. His destruction of the food of the Valley did not force Lee's army to collapse before the winter descended. Sheridan might have shortened the war by months and thousands of lives if, instead, he had destroyed the Virginia Central Railroad and the Virginia and East Tennessee Railroad; if he had forced Lee to surrender or at least to fight in the open field where Grant was certain he could defeat him. But Sheridan, beleaguered by persistent guerrilla attacks and fearful that he could not sustain his army if he left the Valley, failed to fulfill a major part of Grant's strategy.

In retrospect, knowing how the war turned out, the burning of the Valley and the burning of Chambersburg seem like wasteful mistakes. Neither accomplished military results of enduring consequence but both fostered deep and enduring resentment.

In October 1864, however, none of that was clear. What the people of the North did know was that Philip Sheridan had finally destroyed Jubal Early's army. They did know that Washington was safe and the Cumberland Valley of Pennsylvania secure at long last. They did know that Grant had finally found an aggressive ally to match his own aggressive manner of warfare. They did know that the proud farmers of the rich Shenandoah had been forced to pay the price for their disloyalty to the United States.

Sheridan's campaign told a powerful story throughout the United States and the Confederacy: no part of the Confederacy, even the Valley fabled for its military victories and fine farms, was safe from the crusading armies of the United States. Robert E. Lee could not protect the Valley a hundred miles from his trenches. Abraham Lincoln and Ulysses Grant—and now Philip Sheridan—had forged a way of making war that no amount of devotion to the Confederacy could overcome.

☆

WHILE THE DEMOCRATS did everything within their power to spin up party feeling, spirit, and devotion in the fall of 1864, the Republicans denied altogether the legitimacy of party politics during wartime. They portrayed the Democrats' partisan efforts as near-treason when so much was at stake, when the North needed unified support for the men in the field.

The Democrats raged with frustration at such a posture, pointing out that the Republicans were cynically deploying partisan machinery to great profit and advantage—thus the Democrats' preferred nickname for their foes: the "Shoddy Party," selling criminally substandard goods to the army for inflated prices. The United States Army dwarfed any previous manifestation of federal power, patronage, and communication. With over two million men enlisted in the army over the course of the war, the party in power, its opponents charged, disguised narrow political ends as the purposes of the nation. Soldiers received a steady stream of pamphlets and copies of the pro-administration *Harper's Weekly*, paid for by supporters of the party and distributed through the national post office. Victories on the battlefield and victories for the nation became victories for the party that sustained both. The Republicans boasted of their nonpartisanship even as the Democrats saw partisan purpose in every utterance of Abraham Lincoln and in every action of Congress.[13]

The leaders of the National Union party would have to focus especially upon the key states, of which Pennsylvania was foremost. Abraham Lincoln looked to Alexander McClure of Chambersburg, the young and energetic head of the Republican Party in Pennsylvania, to deliver Pennsylvania in the election of 1864. McClure had been pivotal in securing the state's support for Lincoln's nomination for president in 1860 and in sustaining support for the president through the turmoil of the draft, Confederate invasion, and divisions within the party. Now Lincoln needed Pennsylvania, the second largest state in the Union, if he was to be reelected.

At the outset of the election campaign in the spring of 1864, McClure did not expect the task of reelecting Lincoln to be all-consuming. The prospects for the party in Pennsylvania seemed excellent, for a Republican had won the governorship the preceding year. If the war went as anticipated over the summer, with Grant defeating Lee and Sherman taking Georgia, the Republicans should be able to deliver the votes for Lincoln in the fall. On the other hand, McClure had been in politics long enough to know that nothing could be taken for granted. No president of the United States had won a second term since Andrew Jackson, more than thirty years before.

In the midst of his work for the party, a new crisis seized McClure's energies: the burning of Chambersburg. The invading Confederates targeted McClure's showcase farm because of his role as the leader of the Republican Party in the state and beyond. McClure, at his wife's urging, had left town, knowing that he would be a prize catch for the Rebels. When the Confederates arrived at his farm they gave Mrs. McClure ten minutes to leave the house. She pleaded with them to reconsider, pointing out that the farm had been used as a hospital for Southern soldiers after the battle at Gettysburg the year before. She herself had helped care for the Confederate wounded and produced a letter of gratitude from one of them. Unpersuaded, the Rebels burned the house and the large barn, both of which were consumed within minutes. After the Confederates left, Alexander McClure returned to Chambersburg to help rebuild the town and his farm.[14]

Franklin County was represented by a Democrat in the state legislature and McClure, despite his other pressing responsibilities, permitted himself to be nominated for the other seat from the district in that body. He wanted to help ensure a bipartisan team that could persuade the state of Pennsylvania to compensate the property owners of Chambersburg for their losses. While he awaited the election, McClure remained in "constant communication with the leading men of the State."[15]

Pennsylvania held a referendum in early August to decide whether soldiers in the field would be allowed to vote. McClure's Republican *Repository* set the scene: "the Democratic leaders will exhaust themselves by every means short of open, manly opposition, to defeat this amendment." The Democrats opposed the extension of the suffrage to the soldiers of Pennsylvania, and so did Democrats in four other states, for they believed that soldiers would vote for Republican candidates because their officers told them to. The Democrats remained quiet on the issue on the eve of the vote, the Republicans charged, because they hoped "the election may be neglected, and that with a quiet organization they may succeed by default of its friends." If that was indeed the Democrats' plan, it failed, for voters in Pennsylvania decided that the soldiers should be able to vote. Special polling places would be set up at the headquarters of their commanding officers.[16]

The Republicans believed they had won a meaningful advantage in this decision. The sort of men likely to vote Republican— young, Protestant, and Anglo-Saxon—were heavily represented in the army. The risk and sacrifice demanded by military service bound the soldiers to one another, to their officers, and to the nation's commander-in-chief. Grant, Sherman, and Sheridan served with the support of President Lincoln and his cabinet.

The Democrats' criticism of the progress of the Union armies often sounded like criticism of the soldiers themselves, so many lifelong Democrats in the army found it better to remain quiet, restricting their opinions to sympathetic relatives in their letters. Some Democratic soldiers chose not to vote at all. Others decided they would vote for Lincoln to help drive the war to a close but remain Democrats.[17]

The elections in Pennsylvania in 1864—one in October for state offices and Congress and another in November for president— drew on all the strategies for building loyalty and fervor that had been developed over the preceding two decades. The *Valley Spirit* reported that the twenty Democratic meetings at every crossroads and village in Franklin County in the last two weeks of September had been "unprecedented in point of the numbers in attendance, and the enthusiasm of the masses in favor of 'Little Mac' and the county and district tickets." The Democrats charged that Union Party men harassed several of the Democrats' meetings, throwing stones into the crowd in Waynesboro and Greencastle, reportedly hitting a small girl in the head and seriously injuring her. "We warn these miserable creatures that if they do not entirely cease this kind of work, they will get more than they bargained for," the Democrats threatened. The Republicans, for their part, reported that "belligerent peace men" had cut the harnesses on the buggy of a prominent Republican, risking his serious injury.[18]

Politics was not a private activity, a matter of quiet deliberation of the issues, but a public stance. Everyone knew everyone else's loyalties. Long before election day, a man displayed his loyalties at meetings and rallies. A voter was known, too, by the company he kept, the family he married into, the church where he worshipped, the newspaper delivered to his home. To attack a man's political principles was to attack him personally. To change the mind of such a man was to ask him to change who he appeared to be in the world.

Watching these meetings, reading his correspondence, and poring over newspapers as well as writing his own editorials, Alexander McClure became "well convinced that there was danger of the State being close or lost in October."[19] His own Franklin County was deeply torn and the Republicans did all they could to generate enthusiasm. McClure's *Repository* told of a Union Party rally, "one of the largest political gatherings of the kind ever held in Chambersburg." The paper celebrated the many uniformed soldiers in attendance: "Probably two hundred soldiers were present, and manifested the liveliest interest in the proceedings," the Republicans boasted. "The Keystone Battery marched into the meeting in column, with a Lincoln and Johnson banner, promising 150 votes for the Union candidates. They stood in line and preserved the best of order during the whole meeting."

At that same meeting, McClure himself "was called for" to give a speech. The young party leader charged that the Democratic candidate for Congress in the district—Alexander Hamilton Coffroth—had voted "steadily against every measure designed to fill up our shattered armies so that they might give triumph to their holy cause," voted against "any measure calculated to put a single soldier in the field," and then voted "against the right of the soldiers to vote at the next election!" Coffroth, as it turned out, stood at the back of the hall, flummoxed, offering no rebuttal. The meeting ended with "cheers for the ticket, for the speakers; for the Keystone Battery, for the band, for the Union, and for the Old Flag."[20]

On the night of the October election for state officers and Congress, the offices of the *Repository* and the *Spirit* served as "the head-quarters of their respective parties, and the overly anxious rotated between the two as the news hung heavily on the wires. A few fragmentary returns from the State indicated Democratic gains, and partial returns from this county pointed to the defeat of the Union ticket on the home vote." At eleven that night, the *Repository* reported, both head-quarters heard that "the State had gone Democratic by from 20,000 to 30,000 on the home vote, and that the Union men gave up the State as heavily against them. There were dismal faces at the Repository office when the doleful news was read, and boisterous cheers were heard across the way at the Spirit office."

The *Spirit's* editorial staff immediately set their type for the next day's paper: "The election is over," their report read. "The result is not yet accurately known, but sufficient is known to exhibit the fact that the Democracy of the 'old Keystone' has won a signal triumph." All the lessons and the consequences seemed clear: "The Shoddy contractors and Government dependents are trembling for the future. They see the handwriting on the wall, and know that their doom is sealed. The immense patronage of the Administration could not save the Republican party from defeat." The Union Party had betrayed its true nature, the Democrats charged. "Money was distributed in the most prodigal manner; all manner of deception was practised—the basest falsehoods were circulated as the gravest truths—dismissal from employment was threatened as the consequence of a refusal to support the Administration ticket." Despite such tactics, "the honest masses, unawed by intimidation, uninfluenced by bribes and undeceived by lying tongues, not only annihilated the large majority of last year, but rolled up a majority of over five thousand for the Democratic ticket."[21]

All Democrats had to help ensure that the presumed victory of October became another victory in November. "Increased zeal, redoubled energy, 'one long pull, a strong pull and pull all together,' will rescue the county forever from the control of the pernicious doctrines of the Republican party." The Democrats thought that undecided or even Republican voters could still be persuaded in November. "Get every man to the polls. Reason with your neighbor. Convince him by the weighty arguments of Democratic truth that he is in the wrong and that you are in the right."[22]

The very day that plea echoed from the Democrats' paper, though, returns came in from the soldier vote and gave the election a sharply different cast. "The Union county ticket is beaten by an average majority of about 70 on the home poll, but the army vote gives not less than 130 and it may reach even 300 Union majority, thus electing the entire Union local ticket handsomely," the *Repository* exulted. With the election too close to call, the votes of two military companies from Franklin County—one in Pottsville, Pennsylvania, and the other in far-off Tennessee—gave "enough Union majority to elect the entire Union county ticket." Alexander McClure himself won a position in the state legislature by only 14 votes in his district by the home vote, but the army vote gave him a majority of over 300. The Union Party candidate for Congress won by 11 home votes but then won the army vote 171 to 32.[23]

The situation was the same on the state level: the soldier vote put the state firmly in the ranks of the Union Party. The election had concrete and immediate consequences: "Sixteen loyal, faithful members are returned to the next Congress, displacing four of the men who ever voted alike to embarrass the government and its noble armies in its fearful contest with traitors," the Republicans cheered.[24]

Behind the scenes, the Union Party was not nearly as exuberant. The morning following the October elections, in fact, President Lincoln telegraphed McClure to visit him in Washington, "as the result in the State was humiliating in the extreme." The other two states with recent elections—Ohio and Indiana—had returned large majorities for the party, but Pennsylvania had struggled, barely redeemed by the soldier vote. Lincoln asked McClure to help get "the State into position for the November election." The narrow results in Pennsylvania in October emboldened the Democratic supporters of McClellan "to believe they would give the electoral vote of Pennsylvania to the one they esteemed as Pennsylvania's great soldier." Over the next few weeks, McClure took a room in Philadelphia where he could advise Lincoln "every night by letter of any changes in the situation."[25]

With victory in Georgia and the Shenandoah Valley giving him renewed hope, President Lincoln calculated the likely votes in the Electoral College. The winner of the presidency would need 116 electoral votes to be reelected and Lincoln believed he probably had 120 and McClellan 114. One or two important states could change everything. Pennsylvania was the most competitive of the large, contested states. As Lincoln remarked, "As goes Pennsylvania, so goes the Union, they say." Lincoln telegraphed Grant about the presidential election that awaited: "Pennsylvania very close, and still in doubt on home vote—Ohio largely for us . . . Indiana largely for us. . . . Send what you may know of your army vote." The Democrats' *Valley Spirit* made exactly the same calculations about the Electoral College and concluded with a question and its answer: "Now, can General McClellan secure one hundred and sixteen votes? We think—nay, we are sure, he can and will."[26]

Alexander McClure and Abraham Lincoln knew that there was more at stake than a simple majority in the Electoral College. They knew they required a moral victory for the enormously hard work that lay ahead after the war, however the war might end. To achieve that victory, they needed New York and Pennsylvania, and both were too close to call before the election. As McClure noted, "the failure of the two greatest of the Northern States to sustain the administration" would seriously weaken Lincoln and his party.

Lincoln brought McClure to Washington once again to consult on strategy and McClure had to convey hard news: McClure told Lincoln that he saw "no reasonable prospect of carrying the State on the home vote. While the army vote would be reasonably certain to give the electoral vote of the State to Lincoln, the moral force of the victory would be seriously impaired. Lincoln was greatly distressed." The president already expected to lose New York; to win Pennsylvania only with what critics called a "bayonet vote" would tarnish the victory of the Union Party.

McClure had a solution if Lincoln was willing. If Lincoln would furlough five thousand Pennsylvania soldiers from the

Army of the Potomac outside Petersburg and five thousand Pennsylvania soldiers from Sheridan's forces in the Valley, "he would be certain to have a home majority in the State." Lincoln initiated McClure's plan that evening, working through subordinates to Meade in Virginia and writing Sheridan directly. Lincoln worried about implicating Grant in the plan, but, as for Sheridan, he reassured McClure that "Oh, Phil, he's all right." Sheridan's victories in the Valley weeks earlier were paying yet another dividend, for an active threat from Early would have prevented those men from coming home. The Republicans in Pennsylvania would have ten thousand more home votes than either party had expected even though those votes were in fact soldiers. Moreover, the presence of those soldiers in their home towns would be a visible reminder to those who hesitated to vote for the Union Party that more than sloganeering was at stake.[27]

Despite Republican advantages, Democrats had reason to hope for the soldier vote as well. Seventeen Northern states, of the twenty-two in the Union, would allow absentee ballots from their soldiers in the field in 1864 and some of those states had strong Democratic parties. Moreover, George McClellan was a soldier's soldier and exploited his networks in the army to encourage soldiers to support him.

On the other hand, many other soldiers thought it inappropriate for a general, still with rank and pay although no longer active in the field, to run against the commander he still served. McClellan's military status could both help and hurt him. The Democrats had other liabilities. The party's peace plank alienated many soldiers, who saw only capitulation in the calls for peace, and soldiers knew that many Democrats had voted to deny voting rights for soldiers.[28]

Soldiers wrote letters home to Franklin County about the opportunity to vote. "The talk is that we will all get home to the Presidential Election but that was the talk that we would get home to the State Election but it was in vain," one soldier complained. Another Franklin soldier, recovering in a hospital in Philadelphia, reported considerable confusion. "It is reported here that Pennsylvania troops are to stay here and vote. I dont know how it is." Men from other states were being furloughed home to vote and Pennsylvania men were frustrated that they would have to wait behind at the hospital. "Five sixth of the men wont vote if kept here," this soldier judged, "since men from other states were transfered. The Doctors say that they have no order for us yet and dont know if one will come for us or not."[29]

Men active at the front knew they had no chance of being furloughed. On the eve of the election, George Miller wrote home from Virginia to urge his cousin to vote to help bring the war to a close by supporting McClellan. "Our pickets are about two hundred yards apart from the rebels," Miller wrote from the James River below Richmond, "and we exchange sugar and coffee for tobacco to them and every day one or two of them desert and come over to us they say that if little Mc is elected they will come back to the union." Miller hoped his cousin and other men at home "will give him a large magority in the north for he is the only one that can settle the war. I hope you will not forget to put in a vote for little Mc and the union."[30]

From outside Petersburg, Samuel Cormany recorded the results of his regiment's election in his diary:

REGIMENT VOTED ON PICKET—398 VOTES CAST—

216 FOR LINCOLN AND

182 FOR MCCLELLAND

A LINCOLNS MAJORITY 34.

Cormany had responsibility for tallying the returns and he did not reveal his own preference, though comments elsewhere in his diary attest to the young man's admiration for Abraham Lincoln and his policies. What struck Cormany was the decorum at the voting. "I never saw an Election come off so quietly—Not even cheering. Let alone drunkenness, or quarreling."[31]

Reports from throughout the camps attested to a similar quiet elsewhere. Without the usual encouragement of rallies, speeches, parades, and drinking, enthusiasm found few channels for expression other than in voting itself. About 80 percent of eligible Union soldiers voted in the election, not far from the average of elections at the time. The numbers were relatively small—about 120,000 for Lincoln to about 34,00 for McClellan for votes that could be counted separately. About 78 percent of the soldiers voted for Abraham Lincoln.

No one, including Abraham Lincoln himself, had taken the soldier vote for granted. Men in the army, after all, had been as discouraged as had Northern civilians in August, when, one officer wrote, "almost every man has something to say against Lincoln & his *administration*. The McClellan & Peace Party are along way ahead & if no other change takes place Mr. Lincoln will move out in due time." Like the rest of the nation, though, the soldiers' spirits were lifted by the events in Georgia and in the Valley. "Since the fall of Atlanty and Early's defeat our boys have seam to have woken up from their slumber," exulted one Northern soldier. "It did look as though the men did not cair what did become of the Country in case they cood onley get out of the armey, but now they are awaik & wide awaik."[32]

☆

THE PRESIDENTIAL ELECTION in Franklin County passed off quietly as well, unlike the boisterous state election of a few weeks earlier. The *Repository* reflected on the campaign just past. "Never before have we struggled through a National contest with such a sense of responsibility, and with such mingled hopes and fears, as in the one just closed." Supporters of both candidates had worked with "sullen, earnest, tireless effort rather than the hearty shouts which have usually made the welkin ring in Presidential contests." The Democrats argued that the Lincoln administration's fraudulent handling of soldiers' votes was to blame for the Democrats' losses while the Republicans countered with their own charges of voting irregularities in Democratic districts. The election had not healed the wounded body politic; the divide between the two parties remained as wide as ever, with the election providing even more evidence of their opponents' dishonesty.[33]

Pennsylvania was the most competitive large state in the Union, with Lincoln winning by a margin of only 20,000 out of 572,000 cast. Lincoln won 28,000 more votes in Pennsylvania than he had in 1860, and 26,000 of those votes were cast by soldiers. Of the 66 counties in the state, 35 voted for George McClellan.[34]

Franklin County's experience mirrored that of the state. Franklin had voted for Lincoln in 1860 and Alexander McClure and his *Franklin Repository* had preached the Republican gospel every week for the four years that followed. In 1864, however, Franklin County, like many other places across the North, shifted toward the Democrats even as it stayed in the Republican victory column. The home voter turnout was lower in Franklin in 1864 by about 400 votes than in 1860. Lincoln received about 500 fewer votes in 1864 in Franklin than he had in 1860, even including the army vote. While Lincoln won more votes in the North than he

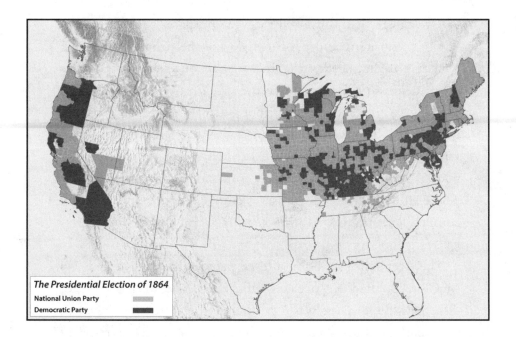

The Presidential Election of 1864
National Union Party
Democratic Party

had four years earlier, in 1864 he was running against only one competitor instead of three. His share of the Northern vote in both elections was almost exactly the same: 55 percent.

Men voted much as they had before the war began. A few dozen votes in scattered neighborhoods and regiments determined the election of 1864 in Franklin. If one or two important men could be persuaded to vote in a different way they might persuade their family members, their fellow congregants, their customers, their employees, or their neighbors to change their votes as well. In such an environment, either complacency or disenchantment could lead men to stay home on election day, passively determining the outcome of the election in the district or county or regiment. When every vote mattered, politics mattered.[35]

The Republicans charged that the Democrats, for mere partisan advantage, had subverted the very purposes of government. "Equally, earnestly and persistently were the people taught that our taxes are but needless oppression; that our debt but the fruits of remorseless tyranny, and that the calls for troops to strengthen our brave armies in the field, are but the steady strides of a grasping usurpation." The Republicans, under the banner of the National Union Party, argued that there should have been no politics at all in 1864. "Mere political differences cannot justify an open, desperate effort to defeat the measures of the government in a deadly conflict with traitors," they solemnly warned. The Democrats had verged on treason.[36]

The Republicans did not take the result for granted. As McClure pointed out decades later, with an enduring sense of disbelief, "there never was a candidate nominated for President by so enthusiastic and confident a party as that which nominated McClellan in Chicago, in 1864, who finally fell in such overwhelming and humiliating defeat."[37] A near-perfect alignment of military and political circumstances brought the Republicans victory in November 1864: Lincoln won by a 411,428 margin over McClellan—2,213,665 to 1,802,237. In the electoral vote Lincoln won by a devastating 212 to 21. McClellan carried only three states: New Jersey, Kentucky, and Delaware. The Republicans would now be in control of all but one governor's office and most of the state legislatures, giving them the power to name United States senators, tighten their control of Congress, and endorse constitutional amendments.

☆

DESPITE THE TENUOUS CONDITIONS leading to Abraham Lincoln's reelection, the American electoral system assured that he emerged from the contest immeasurably stronger than when he had entered the election. Fixed election cycles had prevented Lincoln's opponents, in and out of his party, from seizing moments of despair and crisis to launch challenges against him. The two-party system had suppressed fragmentation that would have shattered less durable coalitions. And, when the votes were in, the Electoral College created a convincing mandate from a narrower popular difference.[38]

Alongside these sources of stability in the political system, unpredictable events on the battlefield and in the parties agitated every county through a voracious party press. The wording of the Democratic platform and McClellan's awkward response, the fortuitous timing of the military victories in Georgia and Virginia in September and October, and the recent enfranchisement of soldiers in the field determined the outcome of the election. Party leaders, including Abraham Lincoln himself, recognized as much. They knew that what events had given, they could have taken away.

Abraham Lincoln's mandate was real and fairly won. But it is worth remembering the twisting path to Lincoln's reelection in the midst of the greatest crisis the nation has ever known, the number of men, including soldiers, who would not bury partisan identities in the midst of wartime, and the bitterness that followed the election. The white people of the United States did not undergo a massive conversion experience in the fall of 1864. Despite all the advantages the Republicans enjoyed, close to half of Northern white men voted against Abraham Lincoln in the most important election in the nation's history.

In retrospect, recognizing the greatness of Lincoln and his cause, it is puzzling that so few Democrats changed their minds or their loyalties. Despite the events and accomplishments of the preceding four years, the patterns of voting across the North barely shifted between 1860 and 1864. Abraham Lincoln, for all his eloquence, changed the minds of few white Americans who were not already inclined to believe him. The victory of Lincoln, his generals, his party leaders, and thousands of nameless local workers lay in mobilizing their own party, not in persuading their

Democrat neighbors. The Republicans knew they still faced a relentless opponent.[39]

American politics was deceptive. The smooth contours of the Electoral College masked the frantic hand-to-hand politics that agitated crossroads communities, tiny villages, and small towns. The Republicans' overall vote looked more overwhelming than it was because the party dominated so thoroughly in New England and in states then considered to be in the West. The broad central belt of the North, however, stretching from Connecticut to Illinois, saw the Democrats win nearly 47.8 percent of the vote in 1864, increasing their proportion from 1860 by 1.4 percent.[40]

Federal, state, and local contexts constantly interacted and shaped one another. Candidates for the state legislature had to defend a national platform they had no direct hand in shaping, while candidates for president depended on those same local party members to persuade every man to vote. State legislatures elected United States senators. State officials and officeholders navigated among all the competing constituencies and pressures, taking account of party strength, the impact of the draft or furloughs, and power struggles among ambitious men who wanted to be the next governor, congressmen, or senator. National party policy and national law were driven toward more radical ends by Republicans from strongly Republican districts, secure in their positions, who pushed the party to be more aggressive in their actions because their voters wanted them to be more aggressive against the Democrats. Moderate Republicans—like Alexander McClure of Franklin County—were moderate in part because they had to be if they were to win.

When all was said and done, two fundamental facts emerged from the election of 1864. First, neither voters nor parties converged. Despite the soldier vote, despite the power of patronage, despite the victories on the cusp of the election, the white men of the North did not unify in their fundamental political beliefs and loyalties over the course of the war. Both parties wanted "union," but they meant different things by the word.

In later years, some historians argued that the vigorous two-party system helped the North win the war, creating a democratic crucible in which white Northerners found common purpose through conflict. The election of 1864, however, suggests otherwise. The Republicans detested the Democrats who so stubbornly refused to support the war effort while the Democrats attacked Lincoln's acts as unconstitutional and despotic. The Republicans, denying the legitimacy of an opposition party in time of war, considered the Democrats disloyal at best and treasonous at worst. The Democrats, indeed, did their best to negate much that the United States had nearly accomplished in the war, placating the former Confederates and slowing and compromising slavery's end.[41]

Despite such bitter conflict and such enduring animosity, the second fact was that the Republicans won and by so doing secured a mandate to shape the nation emerging from the war. The desperate struggle against the Democrats led the Republicans to reinforce their policies and principles. Their dedication to winning the war unconditionally and to ending slavery in one blow actually grew stronger as a result of the election. The two-party system aided the nation not by unifying white voters but by legitimating the views of the winning coalition.[42]

Taking these two facts into account—that the Democrats never accepted the Republicans' plans and that the Republicans never compromised those plans—the accomplishment of Abraham Lincoln and his party becomes even greater. Their victory in the election and thus in the war came not in persuading their opponents but in unifying and mobilizing their own voters in the face of exhaustion. The military victories of Sherman and Sheridan mattered so much not because they persuaded Democrats to change their minds but because they bolstered Republicans' faith that they would indeed win the war before their irresolute neighbors abandoned the purpose.

Because the Republicans could see by the late fall of 1864 that they would win the war, because they knew they had a majority for the time being, and because they knew they might not have that majority for long after the war ended, the Republicans finally allowed themselves to talk about what would happen next. The leadership of the party had remained quiet about the future of black people over the course of the election because they knew that was the one subject that divided Republicans themselves. The next struggle among moderate and radical Republicans would be a struggle over how to secure the kind of Union that Republicans desired once the fighting had ended. They would have to decide how deeply they would try to reconstruct the defeated South and how profoundly to change the lives of the people still held in slavery.

☆

ALEXANDER MCCLURE SENT a letter from Washington to the *Franklin Repository* two weeks after the election. He, like other Republican leaders, now permitted themselves to focus on the end of slavery. McClure acknowledged that slavery's destruction had been a by-product of war but that did not diminish or distort the accomplishment. "That emancipation has sprung from the chaos of civil war to strike treason in its most vital element of power is not a perversion of the great object of the conflict."[43]

The Democrats, too, accepted that the election had decided that slavery would die. As a leading party paper admitted after the election, "unless the Democratic party is blind enough to run the hazard of disintegration, it must distinguish between questions virtually settled and questions that still remain open." The paper took a hard-headed view of the situation. The simple fact was that "there is no conceivable position on the Slavery question on which the Democratic party can plant itself and become a majority." A Republican paper offered a sarcastic comment on this true statement. Now that slavery was dead, the "great bulk" of Northern Democrats "will protest that they never believed in nor favored it—that they only stood up for the Union and Constitution." And now that the nation has "Freedom, Union and Peace" the Republicans could let their opponents say what they would about the issue of slavery; their complaints had become "wholly immaterial."[44]

The question that seized the Democrats now was "What Shall Be Done with the Negro?" The party acknowledged that "a large number of slaves have been freed as our armies have advanced into the southern country. No one pretends to believe that the former status of these negroes will be restored." What would follow slavery had yet to be determined, but one thing seemed obvious to the Democrats: "Presidential edicts, Legislative statutes and ordinances of Conventions, though they may invest the slave with the title of freedom, cannot bleach his skin, endow him with any mental or physical faculty withheld by nature, nor eradicate the inborn feeling in the white that the African is an inferior race." This Democratic newspaper, like countless others before and after, simply asserted that "it is not so much the 'prejudice of color' which makes the negro repulsive when assuming equality with the whites, as the low character given him by the Almighty."[45]

This was racism, of course, but that word does not convey the depth of conviction, the absolute certainty among Democrats that black Americans simply did not deserve, require, or even want a full acceptance of their humanity. Invoking the "Almighty" anchored ethnic difference in transcendental certainty. The article insisted, as generations of racists would, that frank acknowledgement of black inferiority "does not assume the form of hatred or hostility, for the conviction of superiority the white man experiences is generally unaccompanied with any desire to tyrannize over the negro." Ideas of racial supremacy, mercurial and shape-shifting, could instantly adapt to any social purpose, any personality, or any situation. It did not require spitting hatred and overt violence to exert its power. It could, and would, appear in limitless forms and in limitless places.

The election of 1864 immediately shifted the debate in the North from slavery to race. The transformation came with startling speed and profound consequence.

☆

JOSEPH WADDELL, normally a close observer of Northern politics and opinion, could not devote much attention to events so far away in early November 1864. Charged with supplying food for the Confederacy, Waddell struggled with the "great difficulty in procuring sustenance for Early's army" as it guarded the railroad in Waynesboro. Jubal Early's army, now under rigid discipline, was desperately hungry. One telegram arrived in Staunton saying that Early "had only a half day's rations." Waddell fretted that "nothing can be obtained from Rockingham, and Augusta is relied upon almost exclusively. It is impossible, however, for this county to feed the army, the military Hospitals here, the other public institutions, about one half of Richmond city, and our own population to boot.—Yet all this seems to be expected of her." Even after the burning of October, when about half the county was stripped of food, people far from Augusta still relied on its farms.

In the meantime, Waddell noted in early November that "tomorrow will decide who shall be President of the United States." McClellan's election would be surprising, Waddell wrote, for two reasons. "1st because I have no reason to suppose the people are tired of Lincoln and his policy, and 2nd, if they were, the party in power can carry the day by force and brand. With Lincoln re-elected I see no prospect of peace, but of long years of slaughter and bloodshed and anguish; with McClelland, we may have a change for the better. God reigns, and may He order the event in mercy."

Five days later, Waddell learned of Lincoln's reelection, though he did not know by what margin. If there was "a decided popular majority," he thought, the Confederacy faced "at least four more years of war." On the other hand, Lincoln's victory "by a small and doubtful majority would be the most favorable result for us, as likely to give rise to popular or party discontent and tumult in the North." Waddell briefly allowed himself to imagine the worst: If there were to be four more years of war, "How can we endure it!" Three days later, after Northern papers had finally gotten through the lines and the results reprinted in the Richmond papers, Waddell succumbed to the full impact of the Electoral College vote. "Thus the Northern people have declared in favor of prosecuting the war, even to our extermination."[46]

The news of Lincoln's election held a straightforward lesson for the Confederacy, an Augusta paper admitted: "We must prepare now for a longer war than many surmised, without relying upon dissentions among the people of the United States or failure of their financial system or anything else for relief except the physical force and determined will of the people of our Confederacy." The white South knew that the Republican victory would bring harder fighting before it brought the end of the war.[47]

Through the weeks of the election in the North, Jedediah Hotchkiss remained in the field with Jubal Early, warily watching for Philip Sheridan and trying to keep the fragments of the army in discipline for whatever challenges might appear, whatever service it might provide. Hotchkiss tried to be upbeat, but admitted to his wife that "I do not see that any good can come to us from this Yankee election & yet I long to know how it has gone—to know if the majority of the people have approved the course of 'Old Abe' for the last four years & desire a continuance of the same." Hotchkiss, a Northerner by birth and education, doubted that "there will be a real election, so many have been sent from the army & from government employ to use the influence, patronage & means of corruption at their disposal that they will carry the election by fraud, if no other way." When Hotchkiss finally heard the news, he made no mention of it in his diary or in his letters home.[48]

In Staunton, Joseph Waddell ended his notes for the evening of November 15 by observing that "just about four years ago I began this journal." When he had finished filling the pages of the current notebook, "I shall have no more paper—and no heart to enter upon another campaign of four years."[49]

☆

THE CONFEDERATES had always congratulated themselves on their immunity from partisan strife and on the political challenges facing Abraham Lincoln in the North. From the beginning of the war, the Confederates suppressed earlier party identities in favor of a unifying new national identity. And indeed, the Confederates were able to sustain such a government that functioned for four years of war despite inevitable squabbling. Ultimately, however, the Confederate army, not the Confederate state, provided the cohesion for the would-be nation.[50]

In the United States, by contrast, the weekly irritant of editorials, the annual turmoil of election for state or local offices in one state or another, *and the portentous election for president threatened to tear the country apart and yet did not. Lincoln had to divert scarce energy and time to deal with petty politics, to assuage egos at every level, to turn opponents into allies and to keep allies from pushing him farther or faster than he was prepared to go. He and his fellow Republicans saw few benefits from the Democratic opposition. And that opposition could indeed have wrecked the war and damaged emancipation.*

As it turned out, of course, the Democrats lost and the Republicans gained a great deal from the competition and the contest. They could claim a kind of legitimacy Jefferson Davis, with his six-year term and series of unpopular pronouncements, could not. The narrow margins of victory in Congress, in state legislatures, and in the presidential election amplified one another so that the Republicans were unified across space and time in a way they could not have been otherwise.

The elections in the fall of 1864 energized and expanded an electoral base that would prove crucial to the political challenges that lay ahead for the Union Party, and indeed, the Union itself. The election of 1864 demonstrated the ways that permanent change grew out of passing events. As obvious as it would seem to later generations that the war was going to be won by the Union in the spring following Lincoln's reelection and as obvious as it would seem that slavery would be abolished with the Thirteenth Amendment, the voters of November 1864 could not know those things. The way the war ended mattered, and so did the way slavery died. Both would be shaped by the party in power, and by the man who served as president of the United States.

PART TWO

THE HARVEST OF WAR

December 1864 through 1902

*I*n the wake of Abraham Lincoln's reelection, the president and the Republican majority that sustained him tried to reconstitute the United States without slavery. They knew they needed to act while the momentum of war and mandate of voting drove events.

Reconstruction was not the mere aftermath of the Civil War, but the culmination of the fundamental struggles of the Civil War: struggles over the nature of the Union, over the future of the people held in slavery, over the meaning of loyalty, and over the hard memories of wartime. In the South, the Republicans were up against former Confederates who bitterly fought against everything the Republicans did, using every weapon they possessed. In the North, the Republicans confronted white Democrats determined to remove them from power, to stop and even roll back the revolution of emancipation. Black Americans did all they could to seize the opportunities of the war and Reconstruction, to make a place for themselves as citizens in a new America.

The emancipatory energy released by the Civil War, to the surprise of many, grew stronger after the war ended. In 1865, 1866, and 1867, Republicans aggressively advanced civil rights, education, suffrage, and political mobilization. The party became emboldened as it met one challenge after another on the federal, state, and local levels, as it fought Andrew Johnson, former Confederate leaders, and violent resistance by white Southerners across the region.

The Colossal Suicide of World History

December 1864 through March 1865

Four weeks after his reelection, in December 1864, Abraham Lincoln delivered his annual message to Congress, talking of the twinned fates of the war and emancipation. The president reminded the people of the United States—and warned the people of the Confederacy—that "we have more men now than we had when the war began; that we are not exhausted nor in process of exhaustion; that we are gaining strength and may if need be maintain the contest indefinitely." Moreover, the Union's "material resources" for war had shown themselves to be "unexhausted, and, as we believe, inexhaustible." Lincoln's message to the Confederacy, and to the Democrats, held no room for compromise: "the war will cease on the part of the Government whenever it shall have ceased on the part of those who began it." The white citizens of the Confederacy "can at any moment have peace simply by laying down their arms and submitting to the national authority under the Constitution."[1]

Lincoln wanted to restore each of the rebellious states under a new loyal government with free constitutions, rebuilding the nation state by state, relying on loyal Southern white voters as the foundation of a new national party. The president had already demonstrated his willingness to use his powers of pardon and amnesty, and he promised similar leniency if the Confederates would reach out now. The door would not remain open forever, so people should declare their loyalty to the Union while they still had time, before the United States had defeated the Confederacy and all those who remained loyal to the rebellion along with it.

As part of the nation's renewal and reunification, Lincoln called for a constitutional amendment abolishing slavery throughout the United States. Such an amendment would put the entire country on a common basis, revise the fundamental law of the land, and prevent a court—or the next president—from rolling back the gains of wartime emancipation. Congress had debated such an amendment in June, before the presidential election took shape, but its supporters could not then secure the two-thirds votes in the House of Representatives necessary to secure it. As in the electorate as a whole, Democrats in Congress dug in against any initiative identified with the Republicans: 78 Republicans had voted for the amendment, while 58 Democrats had voted against it, with only one member of each party defying his party.

The Congress Lincoln addressed in December held exactly the same members, with exactly the same loyalties, as the body that had rejected the Thirteenth Amendment six months earlier. The Republican majority elected in November 1864 would not take office until December 1865. Lincoln, "without questioning the wisdom or patriotism of those who stood in opposition," asked the Democrats to reconsider their opposition to the amendment. He put it frankly: The result of the last election, in which the Republicans had won a sweeping majority, "shows almost certainly that the next Congress will pass the measure if this does not." That being the case, "may we not agree that the sooner the better?"[2]

The Franklin *Repository* praised Lincoln's call for ending slavery without waiting for war's end, proving there was no basis to the "flood of vituperation charging that the war is prostituted to a mere struggle for the status of the Negro race." The rebels could have peace simply by ceasing their rebellion and abandoning slavery, admitting that their Confederacy had been "the colossal suicide of world history."[3]

☆

ABRAHAM LINCOLN DECLARED in his message that the presidential election of 1864 had been a mandate on emancipation, "the voice of the people now for the first time heard upon the question." Even though the Republicans had not actively promoted emancipation in their fall campaign, their platform had indeed called for a constitutional amendment ending slavery. Therefore, Lincoln's claim was true: until his reelection, the United States had pursued the greatest transformation in its history without an opportunity for direct popular endorsement.

Though the Republican candidates elected and reelected in 1860, 1861, 1862, and 1863 had forthrightly opposed slavery and the Slave Power, they had never run on the basis of the immediate and uncompensated end of slavery. Over those years, some leading Republicans, seizing opportunities provided by secession and then war, had supported ever more aggressive means to check and then destroy slavery. Yet the main steps toward slavery's destruction—the Emancipation Proclamation and the enlistment of newly freed enslaved men as soldiers—had come from Abraham Lincoln, acting as commander-in-chief under the war powers granted to the president, without electoral mandate or even legislative provision. All Republicans, including Lincoln himself, had come to agree by 1864 that emancipation needed to be established on the permanent foundation of a constitutional amendment as soon as possible. They also agreed that emancipation should be considered a means to the central purpose of the war: the restoration of the Union.[4]

The way that slavery ended would hold profound consequences. The Democrats wanted to negotiate an end to slavery and the war at the same time, allowing slaveholders to slow or qualify the course of emancipation. Republicans, pushed by hundreds of thousands of petitioners, many of them women and African-American, knew they needed to preclude such possibilities before the war ended, when the wartime legal foundations of emancipation might be challenged. The text for the amendment, its advocates argued, could come almost word-for-word from the Northwest Ordinance, showing the consistency of the amendment with the intent of the Founders: "Neither slavery nor involuntary servitude, except as a punishment for crime whereof the party shall have been duly convicted, shall exist within the United States, or any place subject to their jurisdiction." The only other clause of the proposed amendment gave Congress "the power to enforce this article by appropriate legislation." Such an open-ended provision for future legislation reassured those who wanted deeper change.[5]

Democrats bitterly resisted the Thirteenth Amendment. They claimed that the Constitution should not be altered, that the Founding Fathers were the wisest of men and that their handiwork should not be undermined in the midst of a national crisis. More viscerally, many white Northerners expected that with the end of slavery black men would stream northward to compete for white jobs and white wives. "Miscegenation," Democrats warned, would be a much greater threat after emancipation than when slavery kept black people in their place. By resisting the Republicans on the amendment, Democrats could champion themselves as the defenders of the white North and reestablish their place as the leading party in the South, where white men might be voting again soon.[6]

The Democrats, though resolute and unified by stern party discipline, found themselves vulnerable at the beginning of 1865. The lame-duck session of Congress contained Democrats who had lost reelection in October or November but would remain in office for another year. The Republicans needed sixteen more votes from Democrats thought capable of persuasion and those Democrats found themselves the objects of great attention. Some of those Democrats used the opportunity to seek political positions; others sought to swap votes for pet projects in their districts. Some hoped for bribes and others were simply coming to accept the amendment as wise and fair.

A Democratic Congressman from Franklin County's district, Alexander Hamilton Coffroth, occupied an especially tricky position. Coffroth decided to challenge his narrow defeat in the fall 1864 election, alleging fraud. Pennsylvania's attorney general refused to accept the returns of either the Republicans or the Democrats and sent the ballots to the clerk of the United States Congress to adjudicate. The Congressman was a personal friend of President Lincoln's but had also been a loyal Democrat throughout his career. The clerk was still considering his decision when the critical vote for the Thirteenth Amendment arose in Congress on January 31, 1865.

Coffroth, his hands in his pockets and mumbling so that no one in the packed galleries could hear what he said, voted in favor of the amendment. Eleven other Democrats changed their votes as well, while two arranged to miss the session that day and three again voted no. The measure passed by that margin.[7]

The Franklin *Repository* triumphantly announced the victory with the headline "A Nation Disenthralled." The *Repository*, like other Republican papers, had not made the amendment a central part of its campaign over the preceding six months. As with all things regarding black Americans, the Republicans had said little about emancipation even though their platform championed the amendment and advocates worked hard behind the scenes to advance the cause.

The *Repository* frankly acknowledged that "the success of this measure in Congress was due to a number of Democrats who have disregarded the behests of party to preserve the life of the Republic." Among those Democrats was their own Congressman, Alexander Coffroth, who "is severely criticised by his former friends." The *Repository* admitted that "it is freely alleged that Gen. Coffroth cast the vote in question with the hope of thereby securing his seat through the judgment of the Republican clerk," but such could not be the case because no Republicans would be "a party to any such disreputable compact." Coffroth "has cast a most righteous vote, and in the absence of a palpably manifest dishonorable motive, he is entitled to full credit for it." Coffroth "will live in history as one of the men who aided in consummating the greatest moral victory achieved in the history of Nations."[8]

The Democrats' *Valley Spirit*, as Coffroth knew it would, excoriated him as a traitor. Coffroth claimed to be acting "for the good of the Democratic party" when he voted for the Thirteenth Amendment, but the *Valley Spirit*, in a typically audacious analogy, told Coffroth that he could "no more remain a Democrat and vote with the enemies of his party and his country, than a man can remain a Christian, and yet yield a willing support to the Devil whenever he may require his help." The Democrats had argued consistently that "Congress had neither the power nor the right to interfere with slavery. It was established by the local laws of States in which it existed, and was left by the framers of the Constitution to the States themselves." Alexander Hamilton Coffroth should simply acknowledge that "his political grave is open for his reception, and the sooner he gets into it the better."[9]

Unable to tolerate either the sarcastic praise of the Republicans or the outright damnation of the Democrats, Coffroth wrote a long public letter explaining his actions. The *Repository* had a good time with the document, especially because Coffroth claimed that when he cast his vote "he feared more the praise of my political foes than I did the criticism of my friends." The Republican paper mocked him: "we have not been malicious enough to speak well of him" and were not aware of any other Republican papers that have "been so ungenerous as to damn him with violent approbation." The *Repository* told Coffroth that he could and should have been proud of his vote to end American slavery forever, but he had ruined his moment in history by trying to explain away his actions.[10]

The Democrats would say no more about Alexander Coffroth; instead, they presented the recruitment of vulnerable Democrats as evidence of Republican hypocrisy. All the Republicans' "fine blather about 'universal freedom,' the 'rights of man,' the 'barbarism of slavery,' &c., is but the thin varnish over a magnificent political scheme."

The Democrats ridiculed the self-congratulation and high-flown language of the Republicans in the Pennsylvania legislature as it ratified the Thirteenth Amendment in February 1865. One young legislator, described in a sly sexual metaphor, read a long speech "in true sophomoric style." After "the herculean task" had ended, he "wiped the profuse perspiration from his brow," and looked "as well pleased with himself as a young bride during the first week of her honey-moon."[11]

Alexander McClure, a chief architect of Republican success in Pennsylvania, joined in celebrating Pennsylvania's ratification of the Amendment. The end of American slavery could and should have come earlier, he acknowledged, but gradual, compensated emancipation had been rendered impossible by "the cupidity of human nature" in both the North and the South. "Tears and blood were no obstacle to its inhuman barters. Its advantages were reciprocal. Coffers were filled at the North, where the crack of the lash and the sigh from the block were unheard; coffers were filled at the South, where both were equally unheard." The end of slavery might have come through an earlier constitutional amendment before the war had ravaged the nation, but "arrayed against the progress was every sordid and selfish interest, every besotted and brutalized instinct, every debasing and unchristian sentiment." To rationalize slavery, white people "proclaimed the African as not of human kind" or as "accursed of God."

Just "when all hope seemed to have died out," McClure grate-fully wrote, Abraham Lincoln was elected and the "revolution of slaveholders" begun. Lincoln did all he could to "win the South back," but the South spurned him. Slavery was now dying, not at the hand of abolitionists and not by executive proclamation but "by war, cruel war, provoked and made by its friend"—the Confederacy.[12]

Alexander McClure's speech, like so many delivered on the occasion of the passage and ratification of the Thirteenth Amend-ment, signalled a remarkable transformation in the mainstream Republican party. For generations, black Americans and white abolitionists had advocated for immediate emancipation and for the human rights of those held in slavery. Those abolitionists had charged the Republicans with exploiting antislavery feeling for partisan purposes, without real empathy for the enslaved people themselves. But now those same Republicans were on the cusp of military victory and were abolishing slavery just as the abolitionists had urged, without compensation to the slaveholders, without delay or intermediate steps toward freedom. With victory on the battlefield and victory against slavery within reach, Republicans such as Alexander McClure spoke against the sin of slavery with profound feeling. He and his fellow moderate Republicans acknowledged the blight bondage had been upon the proud and free United States from the nation's inception. They acknowledged that slavery had corrupted the North and the South, that greed had polluted politics and public opinion across the nation. They celebrated the end of slavery as a great event in world history.[13]

A new respect for black aspiration began to appear in Alexander McClure's *Franklin Repository* as it considered the future of the freedpeople. "Shall we keep open our stables and employ them as ostlers, use them as waiters at our dining tables, servants anywhere and everywhere? Or shall we colonize them and send them to some other part of the globe, as an inferior and useless race. No, none of these." The paper argued that "there is a higher duty required of us, and our own national salvation demands it. We must come to their help, and pour in upon them the inspiration of a higher and better life; they must be taught to read and write, under the tuition of religious teachers, and in this way, they will be elevated very rapidly and enjoy the blessings of liberty."

The entire country had an obligation to the freedmen. "They have been degraded and oppressed by our nation, and we have for years denounced the institution that bound them to the earth. We therefore owe them more than common benevolence to amend for the injury we have done them." The opportunity as well as the obligation were clear: "That they have giants among them even in their degraded condition does not admit of a doubt. In this broad land of ours, under the blessing of our Government, they can be made useful to themselves, the country and posterity. Let it the effort be fairly made." [14]

Alexander McClure, closely aligned with President Lincoln, neither a radical nor a conservative, would not have published such a document before 1865. Those bold words showed how far the mainstream of the Republican Party had moved in a matter of months. The Republicans carried humane language and concern into the daily lives of people across the North who would not have been otherwise motivated to think about, much less aid, the enslaved people of the South. The party fused the self-interest and identity of voters with high moral purpose.

The Republican party and its leadership honed those ideas in the crucible of party conflict. The new ideas were not merely the product of unfolding racial enlightenment or of the leadership of a few men, but were the result of careful cultivation, of moving voters when they could be moved. A matter of months had made a difference in the ways people saw their nation and its moral obligations. No one knew how far the Republicans would go toward securing a future for black Americans, but the party and its voters had already proceeded farther than most had imagined.

☆

THE DEMOCRATS BLAMED ABRAHAM LINCOLN for the failure of peace talks in Hampton Roads in Virginia, proceeding in early

February 1865 as the debates over the ratification of the Thirteenth Amendment raged in the states of the North. The Confederate commissioners "came prepared to enter into negotiations for a re-construction of the Union, in case they were met with just and liberal terms on the part of the Washington administration," the *Valley Spirit* charged. "But the harsh and imperious demands of Mr. Lincoln, inspired by the blood-thirsty radicals in Congress, repelled them at once." The lesson was clear: "the conference failed to produce any good result, not because an honorable peace was unattainable, but because the infernal and ruinous negro policy of this administration stands in the way of so desirable a consummation." Abraham Lincoln, "clearly responsible for the failure," needed to "beware how he trifles with the lives of his fellow men. The tears and sighs and groans of the thousands of widows and orphans in the land, made such by the unnecessary protraction of the war, will some day, sooner or later, come up in judgment against him," the Democrats bitterly warned."[15]

The Republicans brushed aside any charge that they were prolonging the war, which seemed in fact to be rushing to an overwhelming victory. "The Rebels themselves are now at war with their own rulers; the conflict is terrible and growing more so every day," the *Repository* reported. "Every newspaper brought from the South, comes filled with the reports of angry discussions, and fault finding with those in power, who are not capable of doing more than they have done to bolster up a bad cause. The whole Rebel organization, military and civil, is now groaning under internal differences of the gravest sort." The list of reasons for the dissatisfaction was long and compelling: "The lack of military success; the sad and humiliating defeats; the extreme scarcity of all the necessary munitions of war; the destitute condition of transportation; the worthless condition of their currency;

the general disaffection among their leaders themselves; the dissatisfaction of the people." Surely, such a regime could not long endure.[16]

☆

THE STAUNTON *VINDICATOR* CLAIMED not to have room to publish Abraham Lincoln's annual message in December, but little regretted the omission, "there being but little in it of interest to us." The paper sarcastically noted that "Lincoln continues to hold out the same inducements to us which he has so cheerfully offered us on previous occasions—to lay down our arms, and submit to the edicts of Lincoln." This he offers even though "he avows his determination not to deviate a hairs-breadth from his action in reference to our peculiar institution." Lincoln's firmness on slavery, in other words, meant that "no negotiation will be effective." Lincoln and the Republicans would not compromise and neither would any part of the Confederacy that remained unconquered and unoccupied by the United States Army.[17]

Joseph Waddell, studying the newspapers sporadically arriving in Staunton on the creaking train from Richmond, admitted that "every body feels that our affairs are in a very poor way." He worried that "the feeling of depression is deep and general—It seems to me impossible for us to stand out much longer." Waddell saw the suffering with his own eyes when Jubal Early's cavalry, a token force guarding the Virginia Central Railroad tunnel in Waynesboro, passed through Staunton. "Poor fellows! The weather is bitter cold, the ground covered with snow, and the roads slippery. How can men stand such hardships! No wonder that they are disheartened, as it is reported they are."[18]

The Confederate army dispersed some of its soldiers to their home communities for the winter. The Staunton Artillery arrived in Augusta right before Christmas. "Our own dear boys have returned to winter among us—battered and warworn—wanting all comforts, yet never complaining—deserving all honors, yet never claiming them—brave yet modest," a letter to the *Vindicator* sadly commented. "For nearly four years, this gallant company, composed of our sons and brothers—the choice spirits of our town and county, have bared their breasts to almost every battle throughout the glorious campaigns of the Valley, and of old Virginia." The Staunton Artillery had been "among the first to volunteer in our sacred cause"; they had accompanied John Imboden to Harpers Ferry even before Virginia had officially seceded and had fought for four years in one battle after another.

The question was, "what will their friends—their relatives—do for them now? What testimonial of gratitude and approval will be offered to the remnant of that gallant band who have periled their all for our protection? They come divested of everything but glory. They have suffered all that we might be saved." Pursuing biblical imagery, the soldiers' advocate urged that the "festivals of Christmas and New Year are at hand—let the fatted calf be killed—let a grateful people see that these, their defenders shall be warmed and fed—that having bravely periled all for us, the storms of Winter shall not consume their precious bodies that the storms of War have spared." [19]

The editor of the *Vindicator* spoke bluntly of the responsibilities of the local population. General Early had brought his troops to protect Augusta County and "their continuance in their present position will depend on the spirit which may be manifested by the people. The Army must be fed. The people have the means of doing it. If they wish protection for their families and property, they must supply their defenders with the necessaries of life." If the people of Augusta could not feed the army, "the troops must be removed, and the country left open to the incursions of the enemy. An enlightened self-interest therefore, (to say nothing of patriotism) demands that the farmers should act with liberality."[20]

Some of the people of Augusta tried to live up to the pleas. The women of Churchville's soldiers' aid society hosted a large meal for Early's brigade. A letter praising the efforts of Augusta's women reminded everyone that Confederate soldiers' "mothers sit sadly at the door where they do not come; their wives go about their domestic duties with distracted air; and their little children, when the day is done and they gather around the domestic hearth-stone, with earnest words enquire when their father will return." The women of Augusta tried, at least for one meal, to repay such sacrifice and trusted that other communities would care for the relatives of those women in turn. When the Confederacy had finally triumphed and the brave men returned home, "the patriotic kindness of the noble dames and beautiful damsels of Augusta shall not be forgotten."[21]

Augusta County, like Virginia generally, struggled to feed itself and its army in the freezing months. The Confederate government and its agents competed with local officials for food. "How our army is to subsist during the Winter, I do not know," Joseph Waddell wrote on the last day of 1864. "Forage is very scarce, and horses are dying in large numbers." The Confederate government possessed the power of impressment but local governments exercised the power of local loyalties. Prices for food were set in Richmond, but local courts in Augusta revoked those limits so that county officials could outbid state officials for food to feed indigent families in the county. The rights of the states did not seem to matter very much in this struggle for subsistence.[22]

Over the course of 1864, the official price of wheat had risen from 5 dollars a bushel to 30 dollars and the price of flour from 28 dollars to 168, about half of the increase they would have brought on the open market. Wealthier farmers and planters, the only ones who held any kind of surplus of food or animals, found themselves targeted by officials at all levels. Some planters argued that government interference impeded the normal workings of the market; left alone to charge what the market would bear, they said, they could produce more food that would benefit everyone. Their neighbors saw such logic as the mere rationalization of greed. Everyone, they said, rich and poor alike, had to accept government price-setting and impressment as the price of independence and liberty.

Augusta was relatively fortunate compared to the counties just to its north in the Valley, where in October, as the crops had come in, Sheridan's cavalry had systematically burned all the barns and mills he could reach. But now the Confederate government itself was stripping Augusta of its food to be shipped through the Blue Ridge to Richmond. People grew resentful and suspicious, with the townspeople of Staunton worried about feeding their families. Waddell recorded the strategies his family used to make the best of the situation. "For some weeks past we have been eating only two meals a day, the second one at 4 or 5 o'clock in the afternoon. Wednesdays and Fridays we have it at 5 because the weekly lecture and prayer meeting are not over before that hour." Waddell jokingly consoled himself that such deprivation was "a convenient arrangement," since "having no sugar, coffee and tea as formerly, we cannot afford supper, and do not need it after a late dinner."

Waddell devised a strategy to sustain his family of ten girls and women on the small salary from the local quartermaster's office. "The State sells salt to citizens at less price than the market affords, and I have secured all I am entitled to as the best investment for Confederate money." The loss of Saltville to the Federal army in late December spiked the value of that essential commodity. With eleven family members and 25 pounds of salt allotted per person, Waddell accumulated 275 pounds at one distribution and 220 additional pounds another. The Waddells then traded that salt to farmers unable to secure enough to cure the meat they raised.

Waddell acknowledged painfully that during the past two years his wife Virginia had "purchased only one dress. It has distressed me much that she has not been able to procure more." He thought he might be able to trade some salt for a present, but "a dress which formerly cost $10 to $15, now costs $400 to $500—that is, my pay for four or five months." Dreams of a new dress were unrealistic, he knew, when he borrowed money simply to buy "six barrels of flour, for which I am to execute my bond, amounting to $66, payable 'after the war.'" Formerly the editor of the Staunton *Spectator*, Waddell confessed that "I hardly ever look into a newspaper. Cant afford to subscribe for one, and they are filled with everything that is depressing—Their attempts to encourage the people only prove that a feeling of discouragement prevails."[23]

The *Vindicator* of Staunton, a strong secessionist paper five years earlier, "hesitated to complain" to the Confederate authorities, but argued that Augusta County had already sacrificed more than its share of food and men. Parts of Virginia to the south of Augusta "have been entirely free from the annoyances to which our Valley has been subjected" from repeated Federal invasion. Those fortunate counties "are in direct Railroad connection" with Staunton, and they could ship parts of their surplus there instead of demanding from the people of Augusta "a further draft upon their already scanty allowance."[24]

The newspaper was correct that the Confederacy as a whole

had plenty of food in the winter of 1864–1865. Vast areas had not been touched by the United States Army even after years of fighting. Texas produced prodigious numbers of beef cattle, but they could not be shipped to Lee's men in Virginia. North Carolina transported food to Lynchburg and Danville in southern Virginia, but the Confederacy struggled to get the supplies the last hundred miles to Richmond, to Lee's army in Petersburg, and to the exhausted agricultural areas of Virginia. Supplies of food sat in heaps along the rails. The choked arteries of the Confederacy could no longer sustain its would-be nation.[25]

☆

UNION GENERAL ULYSSES S. GRANT knew that the proud Army of Northern Virginia was no longer the force it had been. Lee had only the soldiers "he can rake and scrounge—clerks, Government employees, departmental men and all." Of the men that the Union had faced in the spring and summer of 1864—Lee's "old fighting stock"—the Confederate leaders now had "only about 22,000 men left." Grant believed that "these men we must kill before the country can have peace. They are old soldiers and fierce slaveholders. These men have got to be used up." Grant did his best to "use up" Lee's army by forcing the Confederacy to disperse its dwindling forces over many miles of contested terrain.[26]

Since the start of the war, almost three-fourths of the men who had served with Robert E. Lee in the Army of Northern Virginia had been killed, had died of disease, had been discharged for disease, or had been wounded or captured. About one-quarter of the officers who had served with Lee had been killed in battle and more than half of those who had survived had suffered wounds. Nearly nine in ten of all lieutenants and captains who had fought with Lee had been killed in battle, wounded, or captured by this point in the war. The discipline and order that had once characterized the army had degenerated as inexperienced or inferior officers replaced those who had fallen. After word of Lincoln's election, Sheridan's victories, and Sherman's March to the Sea reached Lee's soldiers, many of them decided that the cause had been lost and that their loyalties now lay with their families back home. Desertion spread throughout Lee's army, growing at least 50 percent higher in the winter of 1864–1865 than in any other period of the war.[27]

The civilians of Richmond relied on the Virginia Central Railroad from the Valley for their food while soldiers depended on the Southside Railroad from Lynchburg and the Richmond and Danville Railroad. The battered cars and locomotives of those two lines brought barely enough to keep the soldiers alive. Alternating between cornmeal and flour with small amounts of beef or pork, the soldiers ate about a thousand calories a day, less than half what an adult male requires. Hungry and often nearly naked, Lee's soldiers suffered from scurvy, night blindness, anemia, and chronic diarrhea.

Augusta soldiers were with Lee, as they had been throughout the war. John Dull, thirty-one years old, wrote his wife Genny, at home with their little girl Cornelia, from the freezing camps outside of Petersburg in the last days of December. "I am free to acnowlage that I do not like this country now way it can bee mixed up but if I must stay hear I will make the best of it I can, though I believe I am a little home sick," John wrote with forced cheerfulness. He hoped the war would turn out "for the best," but "if it gose hard in this world and wee should bee so hapy as to reach a better wourld heare after the change will bee the grater we will appreciate it more."[28]

A member of John's company from Augusta hoped for a furlough soon and promised to bring back "some thing to eat" from Genny. John asked for "some meet and flour some dried frute then I can have some pies made hear also some dry east to make raised bred and what ever elce you think best." Genny managed to send a barrel to her husband and he reported that he and his friends, who had received boxes of their own, were now enjoying meat on a regular basis. In fact, he reassured her that "wee are living better than meny people are at home." He listed an impressive array of food they had received, "evrey thing that house ceepers generaley have excep wimon an children."[29]

Genny told John that there had been "grate talk of pease in augusta," but John thought "it will all end in talk for this time from all that I can learn I see no sine of pease unless the South gives up the war that they will not do as long as they can ceep an army it is no use for us to build our hopes." John wished for peace as much as anyone, but "both parties seem determin to conqer the other." Like the other soldiers who stayed with Lee's army during these cold and hungry months, Dull decided "it is our duty to bear it as well as wee can, trusting to a higher pour than eney earthly for our help."[30]

Like many, John and Genny Dull found their only solace in religious faith. "The Lord can and I firmley believe will bring all things about for the best. though things seem to go hard heare it is our lot and it becomes us to endever to submit to it trusting in him for the ishue this is a fleeting world at bes." Like other Christians, too, Dull searched his own soul and admitted that "prehaps we have bin too mutch attacthed" to the world and the war "is intended to show us how transitory it is." John had enjoyed the preaching of visiting ministers but missed their own preacher from back home. With the waves of revivals in the camps, "there is more people heare to preach to than there is at home." He was "sorry to say," however, that many of the soldiers "are very careless about such things it seems as if God is not in all there thoughts."[31]

John Dull, moved along the line to breastworks closer to the enemy, was killed a few weeks after he wrote this letter. His body was brought back to Augusta and buried at Mt. Tabor Lutheran Church.

Nancy Emerson of Augusta saw such deaths through the eyes of the women at home. She took solace from the belief "that multitudes of our dying soldiers have been met by redeeming grace." For evidence, Emerson recorded the story of one of her neighbors who, herself dying, "exclaimed with delight 'O there's Jimmy & Johnny.' They had come for their departing mother. They were two of our young soldiers who had died not very long before from wounds received in battle. No one knew the state of their minds, but does not this circumstance support the hope that their pious mother's prayers had been answered for them?" Emerson celebrated this evidence of redemption and reunification because "these boys (the oldest was but just out of his teens) were excellent soldiers, went to the army at the first sound of the trumpet, & had never taken a furlough. Their bodies were brought home & buried in one grave." Women neighbors of the family "thought they deserved a monument." Emerson's sister-in-law "went around & soon collected about $500 for the purpose. It cannot be obtained however till after the war." Efforts by women to memorialize their fallen men began even before their defeat had been fully closed.[32]

D. C. Snyder, stationed in Augusta with his cavalry unit and awaiting the battles sure to come in the spring, wrote his wife Rachel about what he saw in the county. "You seem to be very despondent and think 'the South is nearly done.'" Snyder admitted "that everything is apparently dark and not very encouraging" and he shuddered "because of the suffering yet to be endured by the people, and particularly women and children." But he refused to believe that the Confederacy was dead. He thought the nation would not surrender "as long as a man can be raised to shoulder a gun," even if that fighting required "falling back from State to State until the last man is subdued." Snyder, after writing a long analysis of the political and military situation for his wife, ended with the plaintive question on the minds of many soldiers. "Do the little children miss dear little Da much and talk about him?" [33]

Snyder, despite his professed confidence in the Confederacy, was disappointed by the behavior he saw among the civilians in Augusta County. Working to gather food for his unit, Snyder discovered that "it is the greatest difficulty to get such favors of strangers. Charity seems to have played out now, and all are for taking care of no. 1." He had hoped that fellow Southerners would "put themselves to some little trouble to accommodate under such circumstances. But the people all seem to be against the army, for the reason that they think the army of government is against them, because of taking surplus Forage etc. from them. Well, let this feeling continue much longer and we are a gone up Confederacy as certain as the sun shines." This educated soldier, determined to put the best face on matters, admitted that "when I think of our nice happy home, surrounded as I was by an affectionate wife and cheerful happy children, another contrast with my situation in these dreary woods, my heart almost breaks." [34]

A cavalryman visiting Augusta in January described the scene at Jubal Early's camp at the head of the Blue Ridge Tunnel: "We marched down there in the night through a cold freezing rain over roads that were barely passable in the day time. We reached

Waynesborough about 2 oclock at night and went into camp cold, wet and hungry." The next morning, "such a wretched scene I have never before witnessed in or out of the army. Our poor horses shivering with cold and famished with hunger were neighing piteously and biting the bark from the trees to which they were tied. The men looking like graven images were crowded around the sickly fires that we could scarcely keep burning the rain came down in such torrents."[35]

At the end of February 1865, Grant ordered Sheridan to sweep south toward Staunton to connect with William T. Sherman's army moving north through the Carolinas. General George Armstrong Custer commanded a division with Sheridan and Sheridan ordered Custer to destroy what remained of Jubal Early's army. He had only about a thousand men left, for the remainder of his army had been sent to join Lee in Petersburg. Custer drove directly into Staunton, overwhelming Confederate cavalry, and then swung east to Waynesboro.

Despite Early's earthworks, Custer easily outmaneuvered and overwhelmed the Confederates on March 2. Jedediah Hotchkiss wrote with disgust that the raid on Waynesboro was "one of the most terrible panics and stampedes" he had witnessed in the entire war. "There was a perfect rout along the road up the mountain, and the enemy (all of the force being cavalry and mounted infantry) dashed rapidly forward into the swarm of flying men, wagons, etc., and pursued [them] over the mountain of Rockfish Gap, capturing over a thousand prisoners and all the artillery and trains." Hotchkiss himself barely escaped, grabbing his reports and maps from a wagon and riding on horseback into the woods before reaching the summit of the mountain. Early and fifteen of his staff also managed to escape, humiliated by their failure to even slow Custer, who proceeded along the Virginia Central into Charlottesville. After watching the Federals proceed east, Hotchkiss descended the mountain west back through the scattered remains of the debacle, through Waynesboro and Fishersville into Staunton.[36]

The brief and one-sided engagement in Waynesboro marked the end of fighting in the Valley. The glorious campaign of Stonewall Jackson, which had begun almost exactly three years earlier, now seemed like a dream. The same roads that had led Jackson's fast-moving and audacious troops through Augusta County over the Blue Ridge to help save Richmond now displayed the wreckage of the Confederate cause.

☆

THE UNION ARMY WITH GRANT enjoyed better provisions than the Confederates but still risked death, disease, and cold along the ever-lengthening lines around Petersburg. In late November 1864, Samuel Cormany was fortunate to receive a twelve-day furlough that allowed him to take a train home to Chambersburg, fulfilling every soldier's fantasy. "Met my Darling by surprise. O how sweet to meet and greet a wife, so good so true. Precious little Cora knew me. O the joy of it all—P.M. made a very few calls, but spent most of my time—as nature would suggest—to devoted man and wife, and precious little girl—talking and loving. Oh! what a happy man I am being blest with so good and devoted, and child so precious."[37]

As much as he enjoyed being back home, however, Samuel was disturbed that members of his own family in Franklin County expressed doubts about the cause he served. He and Rachel had a "fine visit" with his brother John, "but I feel sad to think how little of the true patriot my Brother possesses—He seems a little 'coppery' but I try to hope it is only in appearance and conduct, not in deep reality." Despite his hopes, Samuel discovered that not only John but their other brother expressed "such a degree of hatred towards the Administration and conduct of the war—Oh! That their eyes were opened to see properly the real situation— But Thank God! None of these things move me." Samuel was proud that he had "come away from quiet peaceful Canada, vol- untarily, and to enlist as a defender of our glorious Union and that my Darling too has the same spirit."[38]

Traveling back to the front lines near Petersburg at the end of his furlough, Samuel once again faced deprivation and death. In January, his regiment went out on a foraging expedition on which "we got lots of corn." Even such prosaic duty could lead to disaster. "Guerrillas prowl around and fire into our rear as we come away. Have quite a fight here. A rear-end engagement—At one stand we have 2 men killed, 3 men wounded, and several horses killed or disabled—and are getting away—and emptying a good many of enemy saddles." Samuel rallied his company "and we charge them furiously, driving them back and recovering our dead and wounded, and leave theirs for them to gather up later." Every trip from camp could bring death.[39]

Sylvester McElheney, a twenty-eight-year-old plasterer from Franklin, had joined the 208th Pennsylvania in September 1864, late in the war. Now, he wrote his wife Harriet, he could "set in my tent and see the steeples in Petersburg. See them very plain." Out on picket, he reported, "five rebbles comover and said that they codent stand it much longer and were laing at the breast- works. we aint in very much danger." After he was moved to another posting along the line McElheney found himself near where a relative had earlier fought and died, positioned "just there whar Joseph is bered." Sylvester planned to go "down as soon as we kin get away to fix up his grave." He asked Harriet to "Tell Pap that D. Nole said that another man come and got his son that lay with Joseph and if he comes he kin get Joseph."[40]

Sent out on a raid in December, McElheney's unit "did not capture anything but some sheep," but they "got all of them." The sheep they slaughtered on the spot was all they had to eat that day except some parched corn. Union cavalry with them "put fire to all the buildings along the road and some of them was most splendid houses but they are paying them for burning Chambersburg."[41]

Harriet McElheney had not heard from her husband for several weeks when she received a letter saying that Sylvester had been wounded. The Confederates had made a "break in through the picket line," this comrade wrote, and "Sylvester is wounded through the leg but I guess the bone is not fractered any at least he thinks so. He was in verry good spirits to day and I think it wont be sore verry long." Their unit had driven the Rebels back and the enemy "loosed a good many men."[42]

Harriet received two more letters in the weeks after that uncertain news. Those letters told the agonizing story of how Sylvester had died. He had been moved to a hospital in Philadelphia, only a safe train trip from Chambersburg, but Harriet had not received word. "How we wondered why you did not come to him," wrote a stranger, Francis Pleasants, who had befriended her husband. Pleasants hurriedly added a postscript to these painful words, noting that "it would have been but little satisfaction for you to have been here as he would not have known you, he being out of his mind for three or four days." Sylvester had imagined that he was with Harriet and their children. His new friend, comforting Sylvester, had played along with the fortunate illusion, asking "'were they all well and were they glad to see you?' 'yes, indeed' 'and were the little children glad?' he smiled & said 'I bet they were,' smiled again when I made mention of you, said the little ones had grown, it having been eight months since he saw them."

Sylvester did not acknowledge how badly wounded he was, "as he kept telling us he was better all the time. I did not think it best to tell him of his situation as we expected you every hour and wanted you to be the one, as I assure you it is a very painful thing to tell an entire stranger that he is dying." The chaplain in the hospital managed to locate a priest to offer Sylvester's last rites. Harriet's correspondent wanted her to know that the soldier nurses were "very very kind to him, uncommonly so." Francis Pleasants apologized for the haste in which the letter was written, but he had "so many letters to write at this time."[43]

The war had not ended for the soldiers fighting with Grant in the winter and early spring of 1865, or for their families. Over the preceding year, Grant's army had suffered almost 127,000 casualties from Lee's army. As miserable as Lee's soldiers were, and as doomed as the defense of Petersburg seemed in retrospect, Lee's stubborn resistance behind the earthworks and inside the trenches allowed him to protract the war in a way that fighting in the open field could not. The continued existence of Lee's army gave the Confederacy the only credibility it had with its own people and the only leverage with the United States, for whatever that might prove to be worth. The soldiers of the North and the South continued to kill each other even when the killing and dying seemed to have little meaning except to those who loved them.

☆

THE CONFEDERACY FACED a fundamental problem in the winter of 1864–1865: even though it could not get enough food to the soldiers in its ranks, it needed yet more soldiers. The embryonic nation, with only a third of the population of the United States, could draw upon fewer than a million white men between 18 and 45 years of age for military service. From that number, many had been disqualified because of infirmity or the civilian work they performed. The United States, by contrast, managed to put more than two million men into uniform and could have mobilized many more. For years, the Confederacy had countered the North's advantage of manpower by fighting on its own terrain, sustaining its armies with shorter supply chains, local support, and familiar topography. Now, those advantages had largely disappeared as the Federal army overran the Confederacy and destroyed its railroads, burned its supplies, and closed its ports. By early 1865 the Confederacy had put into the army almost every able-bodied white man between 18 and 45 within its borders. "Parents whose boys are approaching military age (17) are generally suffering great anxiety," Joseph Waddell noted sympathetically.[44]

Another potential supply of soldiers was obvious to everyone: the enslaved men who had been forced to sustain the Confederacy through their labor. If an appreciable number of those men could be converted into soldiers and induced to fight for the Confederacy, they could bolster the desperate army. General Patrick Cleburne, a wounded veteran of Shiloh and hero of Chickamauga, had reached the conclusion in late 1863 that the Confederacy should enlist enslaved men to fight and free "his whole race who side with us." When Cleburne forwarded his memorandum to Richmond in early 1864, however, Jefferson Davis and his cabinet rejected it out of hand. The president, in fact, demanded that all discussion of the inflammatory subject cease immediately and that no copies of Cleburne's document be circulated; such ideas, Davis thought, threatened morale, any international standing of the Confederacy, and the quiescence of the enslaved people. Cle-burne obeyed the order and said nothing more on the subject.[45]

After he died at the Battle of Franklin in the winter of 1864, Cleburne's ideas gathered momentum as the Confederacy became ever more hungry for men. Jefferson Davis and his cabinet were driven to the same conclusion Patrick Cleburne had reached a year earlier. The brutal arithmetic could no longer be avoided: the Confederacy was running out of white men. Davis began to prepare Confederate citizens for the possibility that enslaved men would be enlisted. In his annual address, a few days after Lincoln's reelection in November, Davis presented the idea in his charac-teristically legalistic way: "should the alternative ever be presented of subjugation or of the employment of the slave as a soldier, there seems no reason to doubt that this should be our decision."

Jed Hotchkiss forwarded his wife Sara a copy of a newspa-per containing Jefferson Davis's message. Hotchkiss admitted that "the country is much divided in regard to the proper employ-ment of the slaves—I think the soldiers are opposed to arming them—they want them used as wagoners &c but are unwilling to see arms put into their hands—the President handles the subject cautiously as though treading on uncertain ground."[46] The *Vin-dicator* reported that a newspaper in Savannah "refuses to publish communications in reference to placing negroes in the army, for the reason that it does not regard the question in detail as a proper one for newspaper discussion." The Georgia paper hoped that a "measure so disorganizing, so unnecessary, unwise and impolitic, will, we feel confident, be rejected by our people and our Con-gress. Consistency, self-respect, Southern honor and humanity demands it."[47]

People in both the United States and the Confederacy won-dered what Robert E. Lee thought about enlisting enslaved men for the Confederate army; his word carried more weight than the entire cabinet of Jefferson Davis. Lee announced in early 1865 that the question was simply whether "slavery shall be extinguished by our enemies and the slaves be used against us, or use them ourselves at the risk of effects which may be produced upon our social institutions. My own opinion is that we should employ them without delay . . . they can be made efficient soldiers." Lee supported emancipation for those men and their families who served honorably in the Confederate army, since white Southerners could not "expect slaves to fight for prospective freedom when they can secure it at once by going to the enemy."

No other Confederate leader went as far as Robert E. Lee, however, and no law ever made any such provision. Instead, the Confederate Congress narrowly passed a law in March providing that President Davis could request and accept from slave owners the service of able-bodied enslaved men for whatever purpose he thought best. The bill made no offer of, or mention of, any form of emancipation. Slavery would live even as the Confederate nation died.[48]

☆

WHILE THE CONFEDERATE LEADERSHIP struggled with the wisdom, practicality, and justice of enlisting enslaved men, slavery itself ground on within the unoccupied parts of the rebel nation. People continued to offer "Negroes for sale" in Staunton, and slave owners continued to think it worthwhile to advertise for the return of runaways. The portrayals of the runaways in the newspapers, in fact, gave glimpses of the individuality of people usually referred to by whites merely as "negroes," undifferentiated by anything more than gender, age, and monetary value.

A man named Pitman, for example, ran away in November 1864 from one of the leading men of Augusta, Hugh Sheffey, a prominent attorney, former Unionist political leader, and current representative of Augusta to the Virginia General Assembly. Sheffey described Pitman, one of the eight enslaved people Sheffey owned at the beginning of the war, as "about fifteen years old, tall and slender, a clear black color." The young man, though he could read, "has an appearance of simplicity when spoken to and often twists up his forehead when addressed." Sheffey offered four hundred dollars for his return.[49]

George Lee was also fifteen when he ran away from Joseph Hess in December. George was a mulatto boy who "walks with his toes somewhat inward." Hess would pay one hundred dollars for his capture and confinement in the Staunton or Lexington jail. Yet another fifteen-year-old male escaped from Elizabeth Marshall in January 1865, her only slave. This George was a "bright mulatto boy with straight hair" and Marshall was willing to pay five hundred dollars for his return. Finally, Harriet, also about fifteen years old, "well grown and heavy set," with "a bushy head of hair, and a small scar on her left cheek near the mouth," had run away in January from near Hebron Church. Slave owners who were willing to spend scarce money to advertise for runaways clearly did not think that slavery was going to end soon.[50]

Jed Hotchkiss took time from his duties as Confederate cartographer to purchase a slave in January 1865. Hotchkiss complained to his brother Nelson that he "went to Staunton yesterday to hire a servant, but found that I could do nothing as they were all hiring for grain or produce of some kind and I find it hard enough to get what I want to eat." Even with so much scarcity in every facet of life, the trade in renting and buying people continued to flourish. "Servants hired very high; good men for 50 bushels of wheat and 50 of corn, enough to buy a servant in the market. The supply of servants was not at all equal to the demand."

To secure the continued employment of William, who had accompanied Hotchkiss all over Virginia, Maryland, and even into Pennsylvania in the war, Hotchkiss determined that he would purchase him. Hotchkiss, who had moved to Augusta from New York in the 1850s, had owned a slave before the war and felt justified in doing so by his Christian faith. "To secure William again, who has been so faithful to me," Hotchkiss told his brother, "I bought him of his master who came up to sell him and his other servants—came in from Wisconsin, a genuine abolitionist, but like all the rest of them it must not cost him anything." Hotchkiss "paid $5,000. Managed to raise $2,000 and borrowed $3,000 which I hope to find some way to pay before it falls due." The cartographer had better luck on the hiring market a few days later when he "went to Staunton again and got a woman of Mrs. Opie—a first rate one, much better success than I expected."[51]

With potential freedom close at hand, the prospect of being sold away drove an enslaved woman in Augusta to violence against her master. Francis McFarland, a seventy-six-year-old minister, noted in his diary for December 20, 1864, that "Capt. Roberts came this evening & bought Julia of Mary Lewis for $4,000." The next morning, McFarland's wife and daughter "rushed into my room & Julia following them in an insane rage with an axe." The elderly pastor "seized the poker & ran out." Two enslaved women, Rhoda and Liz, "were holding Julia & trying to get the axe from her which she was holding up over her head & trying to get at us." Rhoda "cried to me to get out of the way, which I did & locked the door believing I could not contend with her & the axe." Rhoda and Liz "got the axe from her & took her to the kitchen." McFarland sent for two white men living nearby, who "tied her & I sent her in the Waggon to Staunton and Mr Mc Pheeters had her put in Jail." The Reverend McFarland praised "God who preserved all our lives. And I feel much indebted to the other servants whose fidelity has been instrumental in saving our lives."[52]

Slavery in Augusta County revealed obvious signs of strain in its last winter. Runaways, desperate violence, slave markets conducted with bushels of wheat, and debt calculated in nearly valueless currency spoke of an institution coming apart. And yet runaways were still caught, slaves who tried to kill their masters rather than be sold were still put in jail, and deals between sellers and purchasers of slaves were still struck. Slavery retained its cruel power until its very end.

☆

THE *VALLEY SPIRIT* of Franklin County had bitterly resisted Abraham Lincoln's decision to arm enslaved men to fight for the United States. The Democrats had argued that it was wrong to place "these poor devils in the army to be shot down like dogs, knowing that they had neither the physical nor the moral courage requisite to make good soldiers." Black soldiers' "cowardice and inefficiency" threatened to "bring defeat and disgrace upon our arms."

Despite the repeated acts of bravery demonstrated by African-American troops fighting for the United States over the preceding two years, the Democrats still refused to support the arming of black men to defend the Union. "The negro at the termination of the war will return home well skilled in the use of arms, drilled, disciplined and to the extent of his capability, a soldier," they correctly predicted. Thus experienced and emboldened, "and backed by a large political party, he will demand at least political equality with white men, and a right to participate in the selection of our rulers." The Democrats were clear: "We are opposed to negro suffrage. We desire to have a white republic and no pie-bald mixture of black and white."[53]

Black soldiers from Franklin County showed that the Democrats' fears were well-placed. They did in fact grow in their determination to be treated fairly. The letters Mary Jane Demus received from her husband David and her brothers Jacob and John traced the growing confidence of young men fighting, victoriously, for their country and for their people.

When, weeks after the burning of Chambersburg in the summer of 1864, word reached the South Carolina camp of the 55th United States Colored Troops of the Confederate raid, Jacob Christy was "verry glad to heart that the Rebels had not disturb you or none of the rest." A year earlier, the invading Confederate forces had made a point of kidnapping black residents and dragging them into slavery, so their safety was not to be taken for granted. Jacob expressed contempt for the white men back home who would let their town be destroyed without resistance. "I think that thay was pretty set of men in Chambersburg that would let two hundred rebels come and burn the place." Christy knew things would have been different if he and his comrades in the Colored Troops had been there: "I am a soldier myself and I know what fighting is." The company he belonged to "has 80 sume men in it and I know that we can Wipe the best 200 rebels that thay can fetch us to or let us get where thay are."

Jacob's company was positioned near Confederate camps in South Carolina and "we can see the rebels every days and hear them hollow" across the river. When some Confederates came with a flag of truce to exchange prisoners, they had a list of three black Union soldiers whom they had captured but would not exchange. Christy "was verry glad to hear that thay had not killed them thay been a great deal talk of them killing all the collard soldiers that thay catch." Such killing did happen, and black Union soldiers knew they were up against an enemy that would not hesitate to murder them.[54]

Mary Jane's husband David was not as outspoken as his wife's brothers, but he also embraced the army life. Wounded in the head at Fort Wagner, David Demus had been made a clerk. He enjoyed that work, in part because he had "plenty to eat and plenty to Wear and a litel money to by mi tobackto," but the responsibility suited him as well. "I am jest as big a man as eny body," he bragged to his wife.[55]

In October 1864, Mary Jane's brother John, serving in a different USCT unit, wrote her from Virginia. His regiment had marched from Petersburg to Chaffin's Bluff, only a few miles south of Richmond. The Confederates had built strong fortifications along the James River and had stopped earlier efforts by the Federal army and navy to take Richmond by water and over land. Ulysses Grant ordered attacks at the bluff to distract Lee so that the Union could cut the rail lines to the south of Petersburg. "What fun we had," John Christy wrote his sister with the jocular tone of a soldier who had survived a searing battle. "We Left front of peters burg in the evening at thre a Clock and We Marched all Night till sum of the boys give out and lay down along the rode and sum throde ther things away." When they finally stopped at four o'clock in the morning, "old Johney Reb sheled us all the time tha cut the Linbs of all rond us." Despite the artillery onslaught, the United States Colored Troops "Drove them Back five Miles that Night." The next day, "We Marched about fiftenn Miles We Drove them Back to chapens bluff and We hold that place."

The battle marked a great display of the valor and skill of the African-American soldiers of the United States. Though John thought the Confederate artillery fire "would shourley hit me," instead "We Did cut them all to peces We had a bout five or 6 Wagon Loads of them to bary thre Days after the fite." The entrenched Confederate artillery "sheled us fur fore or 6 days after the fite," but now "we Can see them every Day ther drzerting as fast as tha can." The rebel soldiers "com over by hundreds" and they arrived "Day and Night." Now "We ar With in 5 Miles of Richmond."

John Christy proudly told his family that "We gut the prais the oficers say that We fote the Best of eny new regment that ever tha sen com on the fild." In fact, the officers "could hardley get them to stop firing at the Johneys." Fourteen USCT soldiers would receive the Congressional Medal of Honor for their bravery in the furious effort at Chaffin's Bluff, a struggle that forced Lee to spend men and resources he could not afford.[56]

While Mary Jane's husband David was no longer in the midst of such fighting, he recognized the contribution that he and his comrades had made to the Union cause. On stationery emblazoned with red and blue images of the United States flag in front of a rising sun, David took enormous pride in their shared service. "Mi Dear Jest let Me say to you if it had Not a bean for the Culard trups Wiy this offel Ware Wod last fer ten years to Cum," he wrote in January, just as the Thirteenth Amendment was being debated. "It Wis plane to see that if We all had a stade at hom Wiy What Wod a becum of us Culard peapel[?]" He wondered how white people could still say that "us Culard Men Was the [cause] of this ofel Rebelon."[57]

The war was not over, however, and in March Mary Jane wrote to David to tell about her brothers. Bill Christy had been shot, though they did not know whether he was killed, wounded, or "the rabel have him." The newspapers had reported Joseph Christy was wounded in the head and Bill in the back and that someone named Demus had been killed. Mary Jane worried that it was David, though she "coud not think it wos you but wee most be thankful to god." She had been "vary much trubel."

Mary Jane wished badly that David could come home. Two other friends who had served in the United States Colored Troops had arrived in Franklin County and "look so nice" in their uniforms. Mary Jane had been expecting David for a long time. She sat up "ever nigh looking for you till ten oclock then I woud give you up and go to bed and lay and lisen." Mary Jane could not sleep, "for I was so shar you woud come." She was making 75 cents a week and she longed for him to come home so they could build their lives together. They would live in a place he and her brothers had helped make safe from those who would steal them into slavery.[58]

☆

THE GREAT CRISIS of the Confederacy arrived in the early spring of 1865. The Federal army and navy went where they pleased across the expanse of the vast territory claimed by the Confederacy. One state after another ratified the Thirteenth Amendment, ending American slavery forever. Every effort at negotiated compromise had been rebuffed. Peace could only come with surrender. Robert E. Lee's starving and isolated army in Petersburg stood as the last hope of the nation's survival.

In the midst of this defeat and despair, the citizens of Augusta County held a public meeting at the court house in Staunton in late March 1865. "Never, perhaps, was there a grander assemblage in the County of Augusta," the *Vindicator* claimed. The meeting had been spurred by a request from Robert E. Lee that "every citizen, who can, pledge himself to furnish the rations of one soldier for six months, without designating any particular soldier as the recipient of the contribution." Those who had the means could "provide the rations of 5, 10, 20 or any other number of soldiers for 6 months; while even the poor who could not afford to supply the ration of one man, by uniting their contributions" could sustain one soldier. From those at the meeting, 62 people subscribed 135 barrels of flour, 7,100 pounds of bacon and $115,000 in money and bonds. "The rush to lay their provisions and funds on the altar of their country was exciting and the scene grand, beyond description, being the offerings, not only of the man with his thousands, but also of the poor man with his mite." The *Vindicator* listed every donor and the number of barrels of flour, pounds of bacon, and number of bonds each subscribed.[59]

Presided over by men long recognized as the most prominent in the county, the meeting issued a series of defiant statements. The "Despotic Ruler of the United States" had demanded "the abject surrender of our liberty" and "deprivation of personal freedom for ourselves and children; confiscation of our property, and the destruction of every right we hold dear." The people of Augusta, like those of the entire Confederacy, would "never submit to the yoke of such a people as those with whom our brothers and sons have been engaged in deadly struggle for four years, and who have delighted in sacking and destroying our houses, devastating our lands, insulting our women and murdering our citizens."

The meeting declared that "we have a firm and certain conviction of the justice of our cause, and will maintain it at every sacrifice of blood and treasure." They announced to the world that "the watchfires of Liberty lighted in 1861 burn with undiminished brilliancy in this the 5th year of the cruel war waged against us by our unscrupulous and vindictive foe." The meeting boasted "that our subjugation cannot be effected if our people are united—and notwithstanding the vaunted superiority of our enemy in numbers, having full faith in the justice of a righteous God, in the valor of our veteran soldiers and in the patriotism of our people, we may, and do set their threats of extermination at defiance." The white people of Augusta would never go back into the Union, regarding such "reconstruction as but another name for submission to tyranny." They proclaimed that "our confidence in our Rulers, civil and military and our noble armies is unabated" and that if necessary "we are willing to open our Store Houses, and reduce our families to half rations, or even less."

The meeting in Staunton's court house ended with a resolution that would have been unthinkable only a short time before. "Whilst some of our fellow citizens oppose the arming of our negroes, we are content with the knowledge that we have the sanction of God for using all the means in our power to resist wicked oppression." If such a step "be deemed necessary and available by such men as President Davis and by Gen. Robt. E. Lee, we shall not stop to discuss abstract questions, but will cheerfully give our servants, as we have our sons to our country." [60]

These resolutions, and the contributions to the dying nation, came from men who had been outspoken and active Unionists before the war. Alexander H. H. Stuart, the most prominent man in Augusta and a former Secretary of the Interior of the United States, had pleaded with his fellow citizens not to secede. As a delegate in Richmond at the convention that decided Virginia's secession, Stuart had been an eloquent voice against leaving the Union. Once the state cast its fate with the Confederacy, however, Stuart, like other Unionists, had converted his loyalties entirely to the new nation. Now, in 1865, he chaired the committee in Staunton that screamed its defiance of the United States.[61]

Augusta County had transformed itself from one of the most proudly Unionist counties in the most proudly Unionist Southern state to a place that stood in the forefront of the war that consumed Virginia. A letter to Augusta's public meeting from former Governor Henry Wise, now a general in the trenches at Petersburg, invoked the county's wartime past. In 1861, "the men of Augusta seized the arsenal at Harper's Ferry; and as she began the struggle and set the first ball of revolution in motion in Virginia, so let her gallant and devoted people keep it rolling on until it reaches the mark of our entire, separate, and sovereign independence." In his characteristic histrionic style, Wise urged the people of Augusta to "Fight, march, suffer, struggle, starve, perish rather than take any thing short of that! Think not at all of submission or subjugation but with hot indignation and abhorrence! Be men! be free! you can be free if you will."[62]

The white people of Augusta County still responded to such pleas after four years of war and sacrifice. They did so when many other men in many other parts of the Confederacy had given up in disgust or in resignation. Augusta sacrificed once again precisely because it had suffered so much, because it had been invaded and ravaged. Like their idol, Robert E. Lee, the white leaders of Augusta County would not abandon their suffering and sacrifice until they were conquered.

☆

THE AMERICAN CIVIL WAR *did not slowly wind down as 1864 turned into 1865. Even though Abraham Lincoln and the people of the United States celebrated as Federal armies marched through Georgia and the Carolinas, Robert E. Lee and his Army of Northern Virginia still held Ulysses S. Grant at bay for month after costly month. Even though the Thirteenth Amendment was on its way to ratification, millions of people remained trapped in slavery. Even though the leadership of the Confederacy considered converting enslaved men into soldiers, they resisted that step through the desperate winter and spring. Even though the white civilians of the Confederacy could see no way forward, they still raged in defiance of the United States as another season of war threatened.*

8

The Perils of Peace

March through October 1865

"Abraham Lincoln was again inaugurated President of the United States on Saturday last, with the most imposing ceremonies, and has entered upon a Presidential term that must be fraught with the mightiest consequences for our institutions," the Franklin *Repository* solemnly reported in early March 1865. "Unlike his first inauguration, he was this time free from personal perils." The contrast was heartening, for "four years ago, he was surrounded by skulking assassins, and a population that heartily sympathized with those who sought revolution—now he is inaugurated in a National Capital made free by his own administration."

Daunting work remained, of course. Four years earlier, the newly inaugurated president "had to accept the terrible alternative of war—now he has to grapple with the question of peace," Alexander McClure's paper acknowledged. "Great as has been his responsibilities hitherto, they must still be greater hereafter." Even in the midst of the inaugural celebrations, everyone knew that "the peril to our institutions from war is past; but the perils of peace are just about to dawn upon us. The government cannot survive either a dishonorable peace or the refusal of peace on fanatical abstractions; and with these delicate and momentous issues the new administration must deal."[1]

President Lincoln's second inaugural address searched for the meaning of the preceding four years. Instead of celebrating the hard-won triumph of justice, Lincoln's brief speech implicated the North in the profits and suffering of slavery. Perhaps, he suggested, God "gives to both North and South this terrible war as the woe due to those by whom the offense came." And "if God wills that it continue until all the wealth piled up by the bondsmen in two hundred and fifty years of unrequited toil shall be sunk, and until the lash shall be paid by another drawn with the sword, as was said three thousand years ago, so still it must be said: 'The judgments of the Lord are righteous altogether.'" The North, like the South, had spent untold wealth and had endured incalculable suffering from the sword. Perhaps such were the costs of the judgment of slavery.

Lincoln concluded with words of striking generosity. "With malice toward none, with charity for all, with firmness in the right, let us strive on to finish the work we are engaged in—to bind up the nation's wounds—to care for him who shall have borne the battle, and for his widows and orphans—to do all which may achieve and cherish a just and lasting peace among ourselves and with all nations." With the war's end within sight and the Thirteenth Amendment being ratified by one state after another, Lincoln still did not speculate about what a "just and lasting peace" might demand.[2]

The reverential and modest tones of Lincoln's speech failed to earn his Democratic opponents' respect. The *Valley Spirit* reprinted the president's address even though "the people know too well how utterly his practice has been at variance with the professions he made in his first inaugural." That "variance," the Democrats disingenuously remarked, had led the American people to expect Lincoln to "make some attempt to excuse his violations of the Constitution" in his second inaugural. The president offered no such apologies, of course, and instead "has given us the mere trash to which we refer our readers as unworthy of comment. He had nothing to say, and he has said it."[3]

The Democrats assessed Lincoln's first term a complete failure. "We shall have sunk more treasure than would have purchased the freedom of every black!," they spat. Worse, the Republicans' waste of blood and wealth had doomed the very people they claimed to redeem. "Left to State action, to the action of individual benevolence, to the operation of agricultural machinery, to the influence of developed wealth and civilization, the emancipation of the negro would have been a reality. The man would have become free, and the race would have been saved." Rather than pursue this gradual but certain path of progress, however, the United States under Lincoln had descended into war that "has substituted force for reason, passion for intellect. It has turned the genius of men from inventions for production, to contrivances to mutilate and kill. It has wasted wealth and piled up debt."[4]

Any peace Abraham Lincoln hoped to oversee would confront bitterness, cynicism, and anger in the North. A parody translated the high-flown language of Lincoln's inaugural speech into plain speaking. "All pray to the same God. He don't appear to be on either side. When He makes up His mind we will have to stand it," the paper sneered. The Democrats, still calling for an immediate negotiated peace, translated Lincoln's concluding lines into what he really meant: "without malice, let us charitably and firmly continue to cut each other's throats."[5]

☆

MORE BLOOD WOULD BE SHED before any peace could come. In the spring of 1865 the two great Federal armies of Ulysses S. Grant and William T. Sherman were converging. As Grant strangled Robert E. Lee in Petersburg, Sherman drove into North Carolina and Philip Sheridan's cavalry ranged through eastern Virginia. Everyone expected a violent death struggle for the Confederacy. Some in the North thought Lee might make one final surge toward the North or Washington; others thought he might try to lead his army to the cotton South or into the mountains to his west to wage guerrilla war.

After nine months of trench warfare, Lee felt that he had no choice but to flee Petersburg. Already more than twice outnumbered, Lee knew that Sheridan would soon be joining Grant from the Valley and Sherman would be arriving from the Carolinas. The Army of Northern Virginia would try to reach supplies at Lynchburg or Danville railheads and join forces with the Confederate army from North Carolina under General Joseph Johnston. On April 2 and 3, Lee and his starving men escaped Petersburg. The Federal army determined to cut Lee off as his army straggled to the west. Fleeing Confederates, setting fire to munitions to keep them from the Union forces, saw the fire spread to consume much of Richmond.

☆

SAMUEL CORMANY'S CAVALRY UNIT seemed destined to play a prominent role in the climax of the great war. On April 3, the young officer wrote in his diary, "Petersburg fell into our hands at 5 A.M." Riding through the besieged place to "see the sights," he and his comrades found "many places throughout the City where shot and shells left their marks." Cormany enjoyed the "great day—Everything everywhere on the move—and everybody wild

with excitement over the recent victories, and the brilliant prospects before us, now that the old lines of battle are broken up—
Petersburg is taken, and we have the Rebels on the run. And we
are in good trim to keep it up." Cormany, despite his Christian
modesty, admitted there was "exileration in these events, and my
connection with and relation to them."[6]

But Lee's veteran army stood in the way of any final peace.
On April 5, Cormany's company of cavalry "made 5 or 6 charges
against vastly superior numbers, constantly becoming more solid
and formidable, and victorious." The next day there was "No time
to cook—eat—sleep or anything, but 'go in on them.'" Cormany
had been ill with pneumonia after returning from Chambersburg
and remained weak; he wished he was "fully well, & stronger, so
as to be able to fully enjoy this wild adventurous work of crushing Southern Cause Send the ragged half fed Johnies home—and
straightening things up so we could go home too to stay."[7]

Cormany's unit headed into the open country of southern Virginia in pursuit of Lee's army. Eager to help direct the marching
men who filled the road, Cormany pushed his horse to jump a
fence so he could ride alongside the columns of infantry. "Suddenly a huge ditch—or washout—8 or 10 feet wide, and 6 or 8
feet deep confronted me," Cormany wrote with wonder and relief
that night. With "a squad of rebel infantry coming out of the
brush 100 yds to my right—demanding my surrender—I gave my
horse the rein, and my two spurs and he cleared the gully—only
his hind feet did not quite go far enough, but by throwing myself
forward after a little moments awful struggle—he recovered himself and we went on." Cormany marveled at his luck. "I can't see
why those 30 or 40 rebs didn't shoot me—Guess they were too
cock sure I'd land in the gully—and be their game—or else too
startled looking at the awful venture to remember they had guns.

A minute later, they fired a volley after me, and the bullets buzzed like bees over head—but not one touched me or my horse."[8]

Two days later, Cormany's unit defended the road where Lee's main force approached from Richmond on its way to Lynchburg, where supplies waited. "Our men lying on the open ground about 4 or 5 feet apart—each one capable to shoot 13 times without re-loading—and instructed to hold his place at all hazzards—we were to hold our line by all means." Hidden by a slight elevation, the Federal troops could hear the Confederates "forming to advance." Cormany steadied the Union line and told them not to fire until so ordered. When the unsuspecting Confederates approached, "a quick Attention! Fire at will! rang out, and our line opened—with deadly aim—and volley after volley was poured into the approaching lines with terrible effect."

In what they knew was likely to be the last great effort of the war, both the Union and the Confederate soldiers lunged at each other. "In vain their Officers tried to hold their men—and keep advancing—Too many fell, and too many others wounded fell back," Cormany breathlessly related. "But they came on—in some fashion—til some were quite close—The cloud of smoke was blinding—our men knew no faltering—but with a yell, as if to Charge—many arose—using their revolvers, and now the scattering enemy broke to the rear, across the little rise of ground—leaving many dead wounded and dying." Cormany "ran along our line ordering 'Men! Load up quickly—Carbines first—Bully! Boys! you never flinched a bit. You may have to do it again, but you Can't do it better.'"

The Confederates did come again. "We hear words of Command coming across from the enemy—'Get into line there 'Right Dress' 'All at a ready' &c. &c. We can hear—while our boys are lying low, resting—waiting for orders—From the Enemys side

we can hear—dimly—Forward! and we know they are coming." And then, as deliverance, "Behind us—comes a solid line
of Colored Troops—to take our place—Fine fellows," Cormany
gratefully noted. "The transfer is made quickly—We fall back in
fine order—and they receive the rebs with a volley—followed
by some 'grape-and-canister,' and we are sure we did our part
well—and the darkies would be able to finish up the oncoming
Rebs in good shape."

Finally, as Cormany's men gathered themselves to charge with
drawn sabers against the remnants of the Confederate force, a
Federal officer furiously rode up shouting, "'For Gods sake Stop
that Charge!'—an occasional shot still goes off—The Rebels show
the white flag, and Their Bugle blows 'Cease firing' and Ours
blows the HALT! and all is quiet in an instant—

O what a lull! What a wondering Why?—Flags of Truce meet—
What's up? The News! 'Generals Grant and Lee are counselling'—
Next Comes the Cry,

   'LEE SURRENDERS!'

'Ye Gods!' What cheering comes along in waves from far off to
the right, becoming more intense as taken up by those commands
nearer to us. Now our Brigade lets loose more fully as the news
is confirmed. Hats and caps uplifted on the points of Sabers and
whirled and wave overhead—and with tearful voices—Scores
of overjoyed men exclaim 'Now I can go home to Wife Babies
Mother Sister Sweetheart, and our Country is forever safe—'"[9]

☆

THE SURRENDER AT APPOMATTOX *Court House three days later,*
on April 9, 1864, marked the symbolic and practical end of the Civil
War. The high drama and democratic ceremony of Confederate soldiers

stacking their guns and flags, of a dignified Robert E. Lee signing the surrender, and of a muddy Ulysses Grant allowing the Southern soldiers to take their horses home seemed to embody Americans at their best. The surrender offered an orderly end to a war that had lasted far longer and exacted far greater costs than either side ever expected to bear.

While Grant, Lee, and their comrades met at Appomattox, slavery was dying across the Confederacy. The institution had been mortally wounded during the war, dissolving everywhere it could dissolve, everywhere the United States Army went, everywhere the slaveholders fled.

The Confederacy's purpose died as well. Richmond fell on April 3, the city ablaze with flames the fleeing Confederates had set. Jefferson Davis had disappeared into the southern night. William T. Sherman marched northward through the Carolinas, the Confederate army scattered and powerless. Though some encouraged guerilla fighting, Lee would not support such an undisciplined tactic. He knew the war was over at Appomattox. The other Confederate generals followed his example.

But a profound difference of understanding belied the ceremony's significance. The boundary between war and peace held conflicting meanings for the North and the South. Ulysses Grant took the surrender to mean that not only the Union army but also the Union purpose had triumphed. The country would now be one nation, one in which the former Confederacy renounced not only war but the ideals and loyalties that had driven that war. Robert E. Lee, on the other hand, issued General Order Number 9 on April 10, telling his men and the South that the Confederacy had been "compelled to yield to overwhelming numbers and resources." No honor had been lost on the battlefields of the war, Lee reassured them, no principle sacrificed. His soldiers would always carry with them "the consciousness of duty faithfully performed." With surrender, Lee believed, the United States would be restored to what it had been before the trial, a nation of equal states though without slavery.[10]

At Appomattox, both sides acknowledged that boundaries bloodily con-

tested for four years would be redrawn. But the shape of the divide between enslaved and free, citizen and noncitizen, and locality and nationality would be determined at some other place, some other time.

☆

"WE HEARD LAST NIGHT from an authentic source that Gen. Lee has certainly surrendered himself with his army," Joseph Waddell wrote five days after the surrender. Lee's "address to his men states that the surrender was made in consequence of the immense superiority of force against him and the consequent use-lessness of shedding more blood." Appomattox lay seventy-five miles south of Staunton and "soldiers from the army have contin-ued to arrive." Some Confederate officers called for their men to regather and fight Grant, but Waddell presumed "that very few will respond as the cause is generally considered useless." One soldier had appeared in Staunton after walking "three days and two nights, on the retreat from Petersburg, with nothing to eat but a can of corn.—Says he saw men on the road side dying from hunger." Jimmy Tate, a nineteen-year-old private who lived with the Waddells, returned from Appomattox with "a piece of his flag, which the battalion cut up and divided among themselves."

Chaos ruled in Staunton. "For several days past the people of this town and county have been appropriating all the public property they could find—wagons, old iron picks, +c +c—distributing the assets of the Confederate States. What a termination!" Even Wad-dell succumbed to the temptation of the moment and "removed an ambulance from a late Government stable but wish now that I had not touched it. I do not like to be mixed up with the scramble for spoils. The whole affair disgusted me."[11]

Waddell admitted something few white Southerners would

THE THIN LIGHT OF FREEDOM

admit, even to themselves. "While I felt an intense indignation against the North, the Confederacy never enlisted my affections or compliance. I never ceased to deplore the disruption, and never could have loved my country and government as I loved the old United States." Though Waddell sacrificed for and even served the Confederacy for four years, he always harbored doubts. On the other hand, he felt the rebellion was justified: "our cause seemed to be the cause of state rights and involved the question whether or no the people should choose a government for themselves, or have one imposed upon them. With our fall every vestige of State rights has disappeared, and we are at the mercy of a consolidated despotism. What the conqueror will do with us we know not." [12]

Waddell noted a disheartening anniversary on April 17. "Four years ago to-day the two military companies started from Staunton to Harper's Ferry, and Virginia seceded. Now the war is virtually over, and we are —— What shall I say? A few minutes ago it made me inexpressibly sad to see Jimmy's canteen hanging up in the passage. It reminded me of the war, and our utter failure." Walking through the streets of Staunton, Waddell found himself keeping his voice low out of habit, as if he held important information that no one should hear, though he held no such information. "The people seem exhausted and hopeless; and therefore the soldiers deserted" as Lee led his army out of Petersburg. "Now almost every body looks forward to peace and reunion on any tolerable terms Lincoln may offer—To talk about re-union and contemplate it as an event about to occur, after all we have suffered, is almost intolerable, notwithstanding I never anticipated much good from the Confederacy." [13]

☆

"RICHMOND HAS FALLEN!" the Franklin *Repository* exulted. The liberation of the capital city leaves the enemy "without an army; without a government; without credit; without hope. It is the great retributive stroke which in the fullness of His time, has vindicated Humanity and Justice!" The *Valley Spirit* shared the latest news from Richmond by telegraph: "Enthusiastic Reception of our Army by the People! The City on Fire! The 'Backbone' Broken!"[14]

"The news of the capture of Richmond practically suspended business here on Monday last," the Republican paper joyously reported. "Citizens greeted each other on every hand, and the church bells rang out their loudest peals proclaiming to the world that the deathblow had been given to the rebellion. Groups were to be seen on every corner discussing the great event, and planning out Grant's pursuit of the defeated Lee." Even in the midst of the celebration, "the telegraph offices were thronged during all the afternoon by anxious men, women and children, to get the details of the news" of their loved ones. "The schools were dismissed at noon, soon after the official announcement was received, and the boys made the welkin ring with their hearty shouts for the triumphs of the brave Union army. Little girls clapped their hands and waved their handkerchiefs, and stout-hearted men who have been bereaved by the murderous work of treason, wept tears of joy." The celebration of the burning of Richmond held special meaning for a town that itself had burned nine months earlier in a rebel raid. In "desolated Chambersburg" the "very blackened walls seemed to proclaim that they have been avenged by the valor of our heroic troops."[15]

When word of Lee's surrender reached Chambersburg by telegraph about nine in the evening five days later, once again "the whole community was at once thrown into a state of wild excitement, the like of which was never before witnessed here. Every one left their beds and gathered on the streets. The bells were rung, guns, pistols and cannon fired, and bonfires blazed at every corner," the *Valley Spirit* jubilantly reported. "The excitement continued all night and increasing to a perfect panic about morning. The speech-makers were called out and mounting the store-boxes harangued the crowds in the most excited strains." Alexander McClure led off the speeches "in a blaze of glory."[16]

☆

AFTER THE SURRENDER at Appomattox on April 9, 1865, and even after Abraham Lincoln's assassination, the members of the United States Colored Troops from Franklin County continued to fight against Confederate forces that had yet to surrender. Joseph Christy wrote his sister Mary Jane from South Carolina in late April. Traveling on a steamboat from Savannah, the regiment was about to set anchor in Georgetown when "the nix thing i heard Was fall in Company J in marcing orders and the nix thing i hard Was forword March and a Way We went to hunt the Johneys and We found them too and kild a grate meney of them We fot for six days. We didin lose verry meney." The African-American troops "took all old mare meet and every thing he had to eat And burnt down thear houses We Went a but one hundred And fifty mils a bouve george town and We hard that peace Was decleard."

The pinnacle of the glorious event came when the black soldiers liberated four thousand enslaved people and brought them to Georgetown. It was "one of the grates sits that I ever seen," Joseph exulted to his sister.[17]

Mary Jane's husband David wrote from camp a few weeks later, while the 54th waited to be mustered out. He dreamed about the future. When he got home they could buy a little home for themselves, for David was not "going to spend a sent of Mi muny." He anticipated "how happy it will Be to Mi to get hom to sty with you." [18]

Three weeks later Mary Jane's brother Jacob reported that many of his comrades were being discharged. Jacob, though, "dont want no Discharge untell the Regiment is all disbanded I want to stay with the old Regiment As long as she is together." Jacob was proud that he had "come away from Massachuettes with it and I want to go back with it to march through the city of Massachuettes again." He wanted the people of Boston to see the battle-tested flag of the 54th: "our old stars and strips she is all riddle into strings just to look at it any body can tell what we have been dueing." Christy did not want the white citizens of the North to forget that "we fought hard a many A time for them."

And indeed, Jacob Christy and the surviving members of the 54th—only 589 men of the 1,007 who had enlisted—marched through the streets of Boston to disband on the Boston Common on September 1, 1865. He, his brothers, and his brother-in-law David headed back to Franklin County. [19]

White soldiers returning to Franklin received a welcome worthy of heroes, their white skin itself a theme in the celebratory words. "Let every one extend a most cordial welcome to the bronzed and battle-scarred heroes, who have just returned from their victorious fields to resume their places among us as citizens," exhorted the *Repository* in June as soldiers marched through Chambersburg. A long poem, "Welcome Home," celebrated those soldiers. The "veterans soiled and brown" were "fit to wear a crown." The women who stood "for hours, their white hands full of flowers" were heroines themselves. As they looked out "through your tears and curls, Give them welcome, happy girls!" Some girls and women mourned rather than exulted, for they remembered the "dear dead boy that lies underneath the Southern skies, far from home." Those women, "with the tender eye, weeping while the boys go by, well we know what makes you cry." As they returned to their "weary home," may "God be with you in your pain," for "you will look and look in vain, he will never come again."

All could take comfort from knowing that "Slavery's dead, and the hosts of Wrong are fled, and the right prevails instead." They could know that "limb, and tongue, and press are free, and the nation shouts to see all the glory yet to be."[20]

☆

JACOB R. HILDEBRAND and his wife Catherine saw three of their sons go into the Confederate service from Augusta County. Jacob was a Mennonite deacon; those of his faith opposed war but found themselves swept up in war nevertheless. The couple's son Benjamin enlisted in 1861 and commanded four companies under Lee at Appomattox. Benjamin's brothers Gabriel, Gideon, and Michael waited until 1864 to enlist, knowing the only other options were to be drafted, hide in the mountains, or pay a large fee they could not afford. Even their father, in his mid-forties, had to pay the fee to avoid being drafted himself.

Gideon, twenty years old when he enlisted in the 1st Virginia Cavalry, faced hard battle; two horses were shot from underneath him. The second time, the bullet passed through the horse's heart before hitting Gideon's leg. The young man came home and recovered enough to rejoin his unit for Lee's final days in Petersburg.

Gideon's father, anxiously waiting in Augusta, worried when a friend brought his son's horse home along with the news that the young soldier had accidentally been shot in the hip "by one of our own men." When Jacob and Catherine heard of Lee's surrender the deacon started for Ford's Depot "to look after my son." The minister arrived on April 20, only to learn that Gideon had died on the 2nd, and had been buried without a coffin. "I took him up & made one for him & Intered him again," Jacob stoically recorded.

Two weeks later Jacob Hildebrand again traveled to Ford's Depot to bring home "the body of my Dear Son Gideon Peter Hildebrand who died of a wound the 2nd of Aprile." Arriving back home on May 10, over a month after Gideon had been killed, his father buried him for a third time, "in the Graveyard at the Menonite Church near Hermitage augusta county Va." Jacob lamented in his diary: "Oh my son my son how I miss you. May God in his mercy grant us Grace that we may meet you in Heaven where there will be no more war & blood shed & where the wicked cease from troubling & the weary are at Rest."[21]

☆

IN THE MIDST OF THE CELEBRATION in Chambersburg, "the news of the murder of President Lincoln was received in this place on Saturday morning last, and was so astounding as to seem almost incredible. The news spread with great rapidity, causing universal gloom and sorrow," the *Valley Spirit* bleakly remarked. All business stopped in Chambersburg and bells tolled throughout the afternoon of April 15. "The several churches, on the Sabbath, were clothed in sable drapery and the services were of the most solemn and imposing character." The *Valley Spirit*, which had joined other Democratic papers in attacking, belittling, and ridiculing Abraham Lincoln for four years—as recently as his second inaugural speech weeks earlier—now judged that "all the sufferings of our citizens since the out breaking of the rebellion, are as nothing, compared with this last crushing affliction, by which the whole nation suffers." The headlines in the *Repository* spoke of "the national bereavement" and the "national calamity."[22]

For the next two weeks, on pages that would otherwise have been filled with exultation and celebration of the troops who won the war, Franklin's papers grimly chronicled the pursuit of John Wilkes Booth and the long journey of Abraham Lincoln's funeral train to Springfield, Illinois.

☆

AS SURVIVING SOLDIERS slowly returned to Franklin and Augusta, the human costs of the war became clearer. Over the last four years, news had arrived in individual, shattering pieces—in letters from strangers, in brutally brief listings in newspapers, in unwonted silence. Now, the final cost could be accounted.

In Franklin County, 3,264 men had served in the United States Army. That accounted for about 44 percent of all white men in the county between the ages of 18 and 45. Of the county's 660 African-American men of those ages, 142, or almost a quarter, had served in the two years they had been eligible to fight. Total enlistment peaked in Franklin in 1862 and 1864.

In Augusta County, 2,784 men served in the Confederate army. That accounted for about 69 percent of all white men in the county between the ages of 18 and 45. Two-thirds of that number enlisted in the first year of the war and another fifth enlisted in 1862. After that, smaller numbers of men trickled in as prior exemptions no longer protected older men, religious dissidents, or men with skills deemed essential to their communities at home.

Not only did the Virginia county commit a far larger share of its adult men to the war than its Pennsylvania counterpart, but it lost far more of those it sent into battle. While 26 percent of Augusta's men were captured, 3 percent of Franklin's became prisoners of war. While 34 percent of Augusta's men suffered wounds, 7 percent of Franklin men received battle injuries. Augusta saw a rate of battlefield fatalities more than four times that of Franklin, with 7 percent of its soldiers killed in action compared to less than 2 percent in the Northern county. Death by disease, too, hit the Confederates much harder, with 12 percent of Augusta's soldiers dying of illness while the rate for Franklin was 4 percent. Because a man might be registered as a casualty multiple times—if he was captured, released, and then wounded, for example, or became ill and recovered only to be killed in a later battle—the casualty rate for all the men who enlisted in Augusta was over 90 percent. The rate in Franklin was 26 percent. Augusta and Franklin reflected numbers and proportions typical of the South and of the North.

The greater proportion of suffering in Augusta did not, of course, diminish the suffering in Franklin. Hundreds of households in the county lost sons, brothers, and fathers. They died in far-off places, their bodies lost or destroyed, never to be brought back to the Cumberland Valley. The 87 men captured, 230 wounded, 48 killed in action, and 126 who died of disease shattered the lives of thousands of people in Franklin.

The soldiers of the North and South showed far more similarities than differences in their backgrounds. Most soldiers in Franklin and Augusta were either farmers or laborers. The difference between those two labels was probably minimal since both counties were primarily agricultural: in the Pennsylvania county, 20 percent were listed as farmers and 36 percent as laborers, while in the Virginia county, 44 percent were listed as farmers and 10 percent as laborers. Artisans, professionals, and commercial men accounted for the rest, in numbers quite similar for the two counties.

In part because the men who fought in the Civil War were, on aver-

age, in their mid-twenties, they had not acquired much property by the time they enlisted. About 40 percent of the soldiers in both Franklin and Augusta were in the bottom fifth of their population by that measure; at the other end of the scale, about 13 percent in both were among the wealthiest members of their county. In general, the soldiers of both counties reflected their county's white populations.

Both Franklin County and Augusta County mobilized themselves to a remarkable degree. These men fought because they and everyone else considered fighting their duty. Soldiers in the South did not have the luxury of calculating how they felt about slavery or states' rights; they would fight regardless. Soldiers in the North also fought for whatever purposes their nation fought for, regardless of how those purposes shifted over time. Whatever their feelings toward African-Americans, Northern men brought slavery to an end.

The soldiers who fought for the United States and the Confederacy would always bear the marks of their experience. Some had demonstrated qualities of leadership or bravery or endurance that would ennoble them the rest of their lives. Others bore the mark of weakness and failure that would follow them wherever people knew their wartime histories. Deserters and traitors would forever be branded as such.

The wounds of many men would be obvious to anyone who saw their devastated faces, their empty sleeves, their hobbled gait. The wounds of other men were hidden in their hearts and minds, evident only to themselves and those who lived with them.

By the time it ended, the American Civil War had taken the lives of more people than any other struggle over slavery in the history of the hemisphere. The cost of the American war—three times the economic value of the enslaved population in 1860—outstripped any compensation offered to any other slave owners.[23]

☆

"DON'T KNOW HOW we are to subsist—I have not a cent of money, and no prospect of getting any. Cant buy anything to eat or to wear. Confederate notes are of course, entirely worthless," Joseph Waddell lamented in April 1865. People were stealing horses, cattle, and sheep. "Such is the state of society amongst us at present. We shall be ready soon to entrust the Yankees to come in and restore order." In a swirl of rumor, Waddell could not separate truth from fantasy. Some said that the French were coming to save the Confederacy, others "that Lincoln had been assassinated in Washington city."[24]

The rumor of Lincoln's assassination slowly took form. The people of Staunton first heard that a foreign actor had shot the president from the stage in a theater in Washington. Two days later, they heard that the actor was named Booth and was an Englishman. Three days later, they heard that Andrew Johnson and Ulysses Grant had also been killed and that "Washington, Philadelphia and New York were in flames." Waddell did not know what to think of such stories, which were "not more strange than the intelligence of Lincoln's death, which we did not believe, but can it be that society is broken up, and the whole country in a state of chaos! that assassination, heretofore unknown amongst us, has become a common event! I cannot think so." There was no way to learn the truth, for "we have no mails, no newspapers, and no regular communication with the world."[25]

☆

ON APRIL 15, ANDREW JOHNSON suddenly became president. In unusual agreement, both the Democrats and the Republicans thought the nation was fortunate to have Johnson's leadership in such times. The Democrats admitted that the debates over the prosecution of the war and of the wisdom and justice of emancipation had been settled, for good and ill. Now, new issues, "fraught with important consequences to the country," immediately confronted the new president. To him would fall the "difficult and delicate work of re-constructing, re-organizing and restoring the seceded States to their position in the Union."[26]

It was good, the *Valley Spirit* thought, that "Mr. Johnson is emphatically a man of the people. Born and raised in the South, there is, perhaps, no public man who so well understands the temper and views of the people of that section, or can make better use of those influences on which reliance must be placed, to convince the larger portion of the Southern population that their true interests are adverse to those of the men who excited the rebellion." Johnson's "intellectual ability and force of character" had been "displayed in every position which he has occupied." The Democrats took heart that Johnson had been "born and raised a Democrat" and they expected to see "his native democracy cropping out and asserting itself."[27]

The Republicans laughed at the Democrats' sudden conversion into admirers of Andrew Johnson, whom the Democrats had vilified since secession as a "demagogue, boorish tailor and renegade" and as a "traitor to his section." The Republicans emphasized instead Johnson's steadfast loyalty to the Union and to the platform on which he had been elected six months before. "In view of all that President Johnson has suffered, done and is still doing, there seems little room for the Democratic party to hope to make a convert of him, and until we see more indication of it than at present, we shall rest perfectly easy."[28]

☆

ANDREW JOHNSON INTENDED to follow the path laid out by Abraham Lincoln for reconstructing the nation. But Lincoln's last speech—indeed, his last public utterance, delivered between his second inauguration and his assassination—ended with no clear direction. "In the present situation, as the phrase goes, it may be my duty to make some new announcement to the people of the South. I am considering, and shall not fail to act, when satisfied that action will be proper." Lincoln's election mandate, his popularity, his power within the Republican party, his political instincts, and his growing sense of justice for African-Americans would surely have been great gifts to the nation. The United States would have to find its way forward without those gifts.[29]

Johnson, like Lincoln, denied that the "so-called Confederate" states had ever left the Union, despite their desperate efforts to do so. Johnson believed that it was his constitutional responsibility to find loyal men within each of the Southern states who would lead the return of those states to the Union, acknowledging the end of slavery and the failure of secession. Men who aided the rebellion would have to appeal to Johnson for personal pardon, but he would dispense those pardons freely if endorsed by men he trusted. Johnson assumed that any man willing to swear an oath of loyalty to the United States was acting honestly and honorably.[30]

Johnson was glad to see slavery and the power of the slaveholders destroyed, but he had little concern for or empathy with the people who had been held in slavery. In his eyes, now that slavery had been removed, the United States could and should be unified as promptly as possible. Like Lincoln, Johnson wanted to build a party of white men of loyalty and good will who would help unify the nation.

In the meantime, the United States Army established bases in the South. Some parts of the Confederacy had been held by the Federal army since 1861, other parts had only recently been overrun by Sherman's troops, and other parts had never seen Union soldiers. In April 1865, the United States military held 120 outposts across the South; by summer,

they had a presence in more than 400 towns and would spread to 750.
They came to maintain order and to dispense justice, though never in
numbers remotely adequate to the task of controlling the vast South.

The Union soldiers also came to enforce emancipation. In many
places, such as Augusta County, slavery had survived the war. Nearly
2.8 million enslaved people lived in such places where the absence of a
consistent Federal military presence allowed slaveholders to buy, sell,
rent, and punish enslaved people even after Lee's surrender. Despite the
long and determined efforts of many enslaved people to escape slavery,
many older people, families with children, and people with nowhere to
go remained in slavery until the United States Army arrived in the late
spring of 1865.[31]

☆

STAUNTON, LIKE THE REST of the South, seemed to be living in a waking dream in the weeks after Appomattox. "It was a
curious spectacle this afternoon to see Federals and Confederates
mingling on the streets. Every body seemed to be at ease," Joseph
Waddell wrote in his diary. About five hundred Federal soldiers
were in town and the commander "is said to be very affable." But
Waddell, an affable man himself, could not bring himself to speak
to any of the soldiers. "How can we ever get along with a people
who have waged such warfare against us, and at last conquered us!
I felt greatly cast down this afternoon."[32]

People who had been held in slavery only days before had suddenly become free. "Negroes were flocking to the camp" of the
Federal soldiers. Waddell knew their names and to whom they
had belonged. "A negro woman belonging to Mrs. Sydney Crawford had gone off with her children. Some five or six." "Uncle
Lyttleton's Eliza was there too, dancing, it was said, for the enter-

tainment of her Yankee friends." Waddell's brother Legh told him that "all of his negro boys (3) had left home."

Waddell tried to discern what the Union soldiers and the freed-people thought of one another. "The officers have told everybody that they did not wish the negroes to go with them, and would furnish to them neither transportation nor rations; but they were not at liberty to send them home." The soldiers played games with the black people. Where the two sets of strangers seemed to be having fun, though, Waddell saw recklessness and disregard. The soldiers used old tents as blankets "for tossing up the colored friends. Men, women and children were thrown up into the air, at the risk of breaking skulls or breaking necks." Eliza, who had been dancing, "was tossed up several times, and finally fell on her head. At last accounts she was lying insensible." (Waddell later accused her of flirting with the Yankees, so apparently she recovered.)

Waddell thought it "provoking, ludicrous, and pitiful, all together, to see the poor negroes crowding the streets, some of them, especially the women, dressed in all their finery, rejoicing in their freedom. The poor creatures seem to imagine that to be 'free' cures all the ills of life." Waddell did not seem to think that after a lifetime of slavery people would find it quite appropriate to celebrate and to dress up for a day. Neither could he imagine that the Union soldiers actually cared about the freedpeople, many of whom "leave kind masters and good homes to suffer and die among people who have no sympathy for them, and only wish to spite us. 'Freedom' to them means respite from toil, care and trouble." The Federal soldiers were rumored to be leaving the next day, and "everybody who owns a horse has him under guard to-night, to prevent a negro from riding him off."[33]

The next day Waddell hurried to "see the negro exodus. There were negroes of all ages, and some who, I thought, had too much family pride or attachment to go off with the Yankees." Waddell recognized Peyton, who had belonged to Alexander H. H. Stuart and who "was identified with the family, and was really as free as his master, and who leaves a comfortable home and the kindest treatment for the uncertainties of freedom among Northern friends—freedom to starve and die, but hardly freedom to labor." Waddell also recognized Jim, who had been the property of Waddell's brother Legh. Legh Waddell had married into slave-holding and ever since had "been impoverished by having to maintain a troop of young negroes, and now the one most able to labor goes off, leaving his younger sisters to be maintained by others." In a professed sympathy for the freedpeople that often curdled into anger, Waddell blurted out "Miserable creatures! miserable Government! The former are lending themselves to a worthless cruelty. They must know that the poor negroes are rushing to destruction."[34]

Waddell struggled with his own emotions, swinging from one extreme to another, often in the same sentence. "It is inhuman and infamous to make such proclamations to a set of creatures who are like children in some respects, and barbarians in others," Waddell wrote after hearing of an address to the black people in a Staunton church. "As well throw around firebrands among tinder. The whole social fabrick will be destroyed, and the negroes be the chief sufferers."[35]

Waddell wondered how black people could survive their sudden freedom. "They go forth like Cain, with every man's hand against them—no friend, no protector, an inferior race, to be trampled upon and finally exterminated." He felt certain that "the next twenty years will witness scenes at which humanity will shudder, and in fifty years the negro will disappear from the continent—

Killed by the Kindness of Northern philanthropy." Waddell proclaimed that he stood "appalled at this wholesale cruelty."

Two weeks later, after talking with Selena, a woman he had
owned, "giving her information and making suggestions about
our arrangements," Waddell grew profoundly sad. "I have always
hated the institution of slavery, but I love the negro. There are
a thousand tender associations connected with family servants—
many of them have been like near relatives, and I have wept
over them when they were dying. But all this relation is rudely
destroyed."[36]

Genuine concern mingled with bitter satisfaction as Waddell
watched the first days of freedom unfolding around him. "The
negroes are beginning to find out that the Yankees are not altogether the good friends they imagined. 'Freedom' is not all that
is necessary for comfort, yet it is all the Yankees have given to
the negro."

Waddell scrutinized every gesture of the Federal soldiers and
stewed at the intruders' obliviousness to what the white people
of the town thought of them. "The Yankee gentlemen no doubt
think it strange they are not invited to partake of our hospitali-
ties. They have not sensibility enough to understand our feelings." When Waddell unexpectedly found himself "in contact
with a half dozen or more officers and soldiers" he was amazed
that "they behaved so much like other people—all of them polite,
and most even friendly—that my antipathy was overcome for the
time. It is difficult to realize that some of these men were here last
Summer, plundering and insulting our people."[37]

The modest and intelligent Waddell found himself worrying
over trivial matters of imagery and politesse. "Yesterday morning U. S. flags were hung at several street corners, so that persons
going to the Episcopal Church should have to pass under them;

and a small paper flag was suspended over the church gate." Waddell saw such expressions of national identity as mere gloating by the victors, but disapproved when "young ladies, rendered themselves ridiculous by walking in the middle of the street" to avoid walking beneath the American flag. "If U. S. officers are small enough to do such things, other people should have sense enough not to regard them."[38]

Waddell's own family became ensnared in these small dramas. On the Fourth of July, "the negroes gave the Yankee officers a dinner yesterday at their barracks. The town was full of negroes of both sexes, who celebrated the 4th by walking about. A number of drunken soldiers were also on the streets." One group sang "a Yankee war song." A number of the women in Waddell's household sat on the porch of the home of Alexander Stuart. "Not enjoying the song they went into the house and shut the door. This movement insulted the gentlemen Yankees, and they called upon one of their number to improvise a song suitable for the occasion." The song's chorus made "rude and pointed allusions to Mr. Stuart and his family. There's the magnanimity of our conquerors!"[39]

The rebellions of women in these days of testing and trial expressed contempt white men dared not show. White Southern men enjoyed and encouraged female expression of contempt at the same time they imagined themselves above such displays. Union soldiers claimed to find the female behavior amusing but revealing of the true feelings of Southern men and women alike.[40]

☆

THOUGH CRUSHING THE REBELLION proved to be "the most stupendous military achievement in the annals of history," Franklin County's Republican paper admitted that restoring the rebels "to a brotherly and harmonious sympathy with us" would be even harder. The white people of the South had suffered "the mortification of unexpected defeat in the trial of arms; the humiliation of having their territory overrun upon every acre: their forts, their ships, their arms, captured; their wealth destroyed; their unrighteous privileges rudely abrogated; their sons slain." All of those mortifications and humiliations would "prevent a ready and graceful acceptance of the offers of free and hearty fellowship we shall extend to them." To bring them back into fellowship, "no unnecessary harshness, no injudicious leniency will serve."

To accomplish true reunion, the Republicans urged, the new president and Congress would "need the support of the people now as much at least as they needed their support in waging war. It is painful to see, however, that this encouragement is not given with the unanimity that it should be." The Democrats "seem to feel that their party existence depends upon their making odious, and thwarting the administration, and are busy in impeding and deranging the efforts of the government." They "seek to make the people, North and South, believe that the Unionists are cruel and unjust; that they have the simple desire of elevating the negro and procuring him power."[41]

The Democrats took up the challenge thrown down by the Republicans. They felt certain that "a large majority" of white Southerners would support Andrew Johnson in the "the pursuit of a moderate, equitable, and genuinely concilliatory policy." Only one "fatal source of our past divisions and strifes" stood in the way: "the inevitable and eternal negro, who seems destined, whether he be slave or free, in one condition or in another, to be made, by a certain order of demagogues, a perpetual source of national contention and turmoil." All reasonable white people,

North and South, wanted a "sound, solid durable peace," a peace impossible "as long as the old ulcers of sectional jealousy and controversy are kept open and persistently irritated."[42]

Variations on these issues filled the newspapers of the North. The Republican *Repository* drew on the lessons Abraham Lincoln had offered shortly before his death: the nation owed a debt to black Americans and it must be paid. "We have committed the crime and paid the terrible penalty of their enslavement for three-quarters of a century." The debt had grown even greater when black men fought to save the United States "and sealed their devotion to free institutions with their blood. They entered the struggle in the darkest hour of the war—when treason was victorious, defiant and threatening them with pitiless butchery; and they have won from every unprejudiced mind the respect due to undaunted valor."

The Republican paper admitted that enfranchising a million men "just rescued from the cruel bondage that made it a crime to teach them the simplest rudiments of education" might seem reckless. But here, too, the fault lay with the entire nation, ruled by whites from the outset. "It is our act, our law, our social, political, and business ostracism, that has plunged and held him remorselessly in mental darkness." Thus, the nation's "first duty to the freedmen is to enlighten, encourage and strengthen them in their new state; and the problem of their citizenship will in time solve itself lawfully and justly."[43]

Both parties had an obvious self interest in deepening and refining these positions. The future of black Americans became even more of an issue for the Democrats than it had been during the war. In wartime, the Democrats could win votes by calling for peace, castigating the conduct of the war, or arguing that slavery was essential to the future of the nation. With all those causes gone, only black people themselves remained. The Democrats doubled down on race, making black people the defining difference between the parties.

The fictional Petroleum V. Nasby, a Republican humorist whose real name was David Ross Locke, ridiculed Democrats by pretending to be one of them, holding forth in a backwoods dialect to equally ignorant party members. His parodies were popular in Republican newspapers. Democratic politicians, Nasby held forth, knew that "we hev no way uv keeping our voters together. Opposin the war won't do no good, fer before the next eleckshun the heft of our voters will hev diskivered that the war is over." Faced with this challenge, the Democrats could follow simple but shrewd strategies. "Alluz assert that the nigger will never be able to take care uv himself, but will alluz be a public burden. He may, possibly, give us the lie by going to work. In sich a emergency the dooty ov every Dimecrat is plane. He must not be allowed to work." Following that policy against black people will "drive the best uv em to steelin, and the balance to the poor houses, provin wot we hev alluz claimd, that they air a idle and vishus race."[44]

Republicans, under the pressure of events and party needs, acknowledged the injustices of race and the capacities of African-Americans in ways unthinkable for a major party only months earlier. Within months of Abraham Lincoln's assassination, run-of-the-mill Republicans were making progressive arguments that Lincoln himself could not have stated so boldly.

The *Repository* of Franklin County embodied the change. The race-baiting so common among the Democrats, the paper charged, reflected "a heartless indifference to the welfare of the human race, a stupidity that would disgrace the degraded people of whom he writes, and a bigotry that could only take root in a weak intellect." Contempt for the black man might be excusable if he were "guilty of any crime or enormity," or "responsible for his present low condition," but he was not. Any "degradation is a misfortune which he could not avert." The Negro "has not intruded himself upon us voluntarily, but was brought here against his will, by overpowering force and through cunning deceit. He was here when the Republic was founded, fought for its establishment and afterwards in its defence. Though deprived of his rights he has never plotted its overthrow, but has always been true to its flag."

In the New York City draft riots of 1863, the Republicans reminded white Northerners, white men had "amused themselves by hanging innocent negros to lamp posts." Those men now voted for the Democrats, a party whose policies depended on the subjugation of innocent black people, a party that took as its main campaign strategy every opportunity to "encourage and intensify this ill feeling." Before the war, Democratic policy had taught the "unchristian doctrine that denied the black man any rights the white man was bound to respect." During the war, the Democrats became "the special champion of human slavery," teaching that the great declaration that "all men were created equal, referred only to white men." It was "humiliating" that an American political party had been sustained by "the theory that God did not 'make out of one blood all the nations of the earth.'" [45]

The Democrats did not disagree with this description of their program. The Republicans, they charged, were for the black man and would dangerously encourage any expansion of government, any exacerbation of hard feelings against former Confederates, or any retraction of white liberty to accomplish that purpose. "Consolidationists, centralizationists, negrophilists, advocates of sweeping confiscation, unlimited executions, negro suffrage and territorial or provincial pillage, are arrayed on one side," they charged, conflating every supposed sin of the Republicans. The Democrats, on the other side of the "division line," are "the friends of the Republic—the admirers of Republican institutions—the believers in the superiority of the white race."[46]

Partisan identity and political belief could not be separated in the Civil War–era North. Sometimes the parties cultivated cynical and self-serving ideas. At other times, as at the remarkable juncture when slavery died and the future of black Americans tottered among several possible futures, the Republicans generated idealistic purposes, even purposes that put their party at risk. The powerful force of partisan identity, so often a corrosive force in American life, could sometimes prove the most powerful ally of American ideals of justice and equality.

☆

THE REPUBLICANS IN CONGRESS in 1865 occupied an anomalous position. They had never been more powerful, thanks to the large majorities they had won in the election of 1864, but they were not in Washington while Andrew Johnson orchestrated reunification. Elected in the fall of 1864 and in special session in March 1865 before Abraham Lincoln's assassination, the members of Congress would not return to Washington until December 1865. During their absence, the Republicans watched warily as Johnson threatened to give away much of what had been won in the war.

The Republicans, not of one mind and not divided into clearly defined blocs, faced competing aims. Party members did not have a plan they could agree upon for accomplishing their purposes and they did not have a president who accepted the party's fundamental premises. Although everyone wanted the Federal soldiers to return home, some Republicans sought to have troops stay in the South to protect the freedpeople and prevent the rise of the recent rebels to local and state power. Major fighting in the war ended in April 1865, but some Republicans sought to delay formal reunification until the former Confederate states acknowledged that they could not restore their former leaders to power.

Most important, while some Republicans wanted to ensure black suffrage, others among them did not. White voters repeatedly rejected black suffrage in their own Northern states, but knew that the South could become even more politically powerful and dangerous if black men could be brought to vote for the Democrats.[47]

Whatever their thoughts about black suffrage in the North or in the South, Republicans agreed that black Southerners needed and deserved safety, a chance to make a living, the rudiments of education, and the opportunity to create their own churches and organizations. While the Republicans prepared to return to Washington to hammer out a plan for reconstructing the South, 450 agents of the new Freedmen's Bureau were beginning to establish offices across the former Confederacy.

The Democrats in Congress had it easier. They knew exactly what they wanted: the quickest and least disruptive reunification of the nation possible, with the smallest change in the status of black people, and with former Confederates back in power. Above all, they wanted to regain their status as a national party, a position they had occupied until they divided in 1860 and made possible the election of Abraham Lincoln. In 1865, they saw a short and direct road to renewed national power: celebration of the white race and attacks on the black across boundaries of North and South.

The ink the Democrats spent on ridiculing, trivializing, and caricaturing black people was done for the cold-blooded purpose of their own reelection. They would do everything they could to stop the Freedmen's Bureau and any other effort by the Republicans to help the formerly enslaved people.

☆

IN JULY 1865, while the nation waited to see what Andrew Johnson might do with the defeated South, General A. J. A. Torbert, commander of the Army of the Shenandoah and a veteran of Fredericksburg, Chancellorsville, Gettysburg, and Sheridan's Valley Campaign, wrote to General O. O. Howard, Chief of the Bureau of Refugees, Freedmen, and Abandoned Lands. Created in March as a component of the Department of War, the Freedmen's Bureau, as it came to be called, was to serve for one year following the end of the conflict. General Howard, a thirty-five-year-old, deeply Christian man from Maine, had lost an arm in battle in 1862 but returned to lead troops, with mixed success, for the rest of the war. Howard took charge of the Bureau in May 1865.[48]

General Torbert's letter from the Valley echoed others from across the South. Torbert requested that an agent be appointed "to look after the interests of the Freedmen. Many persons wish to get rid of the old men & women left on their places that they may hire white laborers." General Torbert admitted that he was "thus far totally ignorant of all Orders, Circulars and policy of the Bureau." Howard replied immediately and asked that Torbert "elect from the officers under your command one that is capable, reliable, and a strong friend to the Freedmen, and who will see them protected in all the rights and privileges guaranteed them by law."[49]

The Bureau organized a district office for the Valley, based in Staunton. Augusta County's connection with Richmond by railroad was reestablished by July 1865. Only twenty miles of the Virginia Central Railroad remained by the time of Appomattox, when the line possessed only a hundred dollars in gold. People along the line recognized the necessity of the railroad, however, and the company managed to raise enough money to rebuild the Virginia Central to Staunton. The town could now resume its role as a hub of the Valley.[50]

Two weeks after Torbert's letter, in the summer of 1865, Captain W. Storer How took offices in the Augusta County courthouse. Now that "mail communication by railroad" had been reestablished, How looked forward to receiving and returning necessary forms. The Freedmen's Bureau was a complex bureaucracy, ruled by clearly defined hierarchies, channels, and paperwork. Captain How wrote to a new Bureau officer elsewhere in the Valley, offering advice: "You say there are many destitute persons dependent on the government for support. See that none are supported who can take care of themselves, and that only parts of the rations are issued to such as can nearly subsist themselves." In settling disputes, "hear both sides, and decide the matter—causing each party to endorse the decision. If either refuse, refer the case to the Provost Marshall, and if possible be present at the trial."[51]

Many of the disputes, agents already knew, would be about payment for work. In those cases, How told his fellow officer, "if a freedman violates a contract he forfeits his wages, or such portion of them as are deemed just taking into consideration the damages resulting to the employer. If he cannot pay, there again his wages may be attached for the benefit of the former employer. If the employer violates a contract he must pay wages and damages." An officer of the Bureau could "reprimand but not punish or imprison for debt" or "breach of contract." In all these ways, the Freedmen's Bureau was to instill the rules of contract labor where slavery had ruled before.[52]

Former slave owners tried to keep as much control as possible over their workers. John Imboden, the former general from Staunton who had been put in charge of Confederate prisons during the last months of the war, had now returned home to reestablish himself. He wrote contracts for several of his former slaves in the first months of freedom. Israel Mosely agreed to "bind myself to serve Genl JD Imboden as a plantation hand or blacksmith as he may require until Christmas," for which Mosely would receive " 3 lbs of meat and two pecks of meal a week, and twenty five dollars in cash to be paid to me at Christmas." The contract included Mosely's family as well. "Said Imboden furnishes me a house for my wife and two children with firewood." Mosely's wife, Milly, would cook for other workers on Imboden's farm, receiving "the same rations of meat & meal I receive."

Failing to fulfill the terms of the contract with Imboden would bring harsh and immediate punishment. "If I fail or refuse to do my work faithfully, or quit him before my time is out," the contract written by Imboden in Mosely's voice read, "I am to lose my wages. If my wife neglects her duties she may be dismissed at any time and sent off with her children." Israel Mosely fell ill that fall and lost a week of work, but managed to recover and complete his contract. At the end of the year, Mosely received $15.50, Imboden having deducted the costs of a pair of shoes, credit at a local store, and a "wagon & team to move his family." While Mosely ended the year with a modest payment, other hands on Imboden's farm did not. One "went off in debt & forfeited wages by misconduct," Imboden wrote, while another left "in disgrace & in debt."[53]

As the people working for John Imboden discovered, these contracts strongly favored the employer. He could hold—and then refuse to pay—wages for months at a time. He could charge interest on money or credit he advanced. He could secure the labor of entire families, holding all responsible for the behavior of each. He could fire people and force them from the homes he rented to them. He could secure the labor of women for half of the ten dollars a month plus board that he paid men.

Not all white people in Augusta were as comfortable with contracts. The citizens of the county, a puzzled white Southerner wrote the new head of the Bureau, had held a meeting in which they resolved that hiring "the servant of another without the written permission of his master" was improper. This man's neighbors "are very much down on me" for hiring a man who had belonged to someone else, though he had done so "in good faith not intending anything wrong towards anyone." The new Bureau agent replied firmly, laying out the principles of free labor: "You are quite at liberty to hire any colored man without the consent of his former master, as he is also at liberty to engage his services without such consent." The agent also drove home the moral: the government "will see that the rights of all are respected and maintained."[54]

Bureau agents were required to submit regular reports to the headquarters in Richmond, summarizing the state of affairs they witnessed. In his first report, in August 1865, Captain How described the difficulties he faced in gaining an understanding of all that was going on in the Valley. His district stretched over two hundred miles, with "incomplete and irregular communication between the principal parts." From what he could see from Staunton, How thought that the freedmen "are generally at work and willing to work, though not treated very kindly by their former masters and others." Those white men acknowledged black freedom "in the presence of the military," but "tell the freedmen that they are not yet free as they will discover when the troops are withdrawn." This kind of warning, "together with the various misrepresentations of the 'Yankees' which are habitually made, tends to create distrust and a desire to emigrate, or to keep near the villages where they feel more secure." The lesson seemed clear: "the presence of military authority is, and for months will be indispensable for the maintenance of the rights of the freedmen in this section of our country." In the meantime, so few soldiers were available that Captain How had hired three civilians to assist him in the office.[55]

How also stationed civilians in Winchester and Lexington, at either end of the Valley, to signal "throughout this region that the freedmen are being cared for, and that they may not be ill-treated with impunity." Despite his efforts, How felt certain that "if left to themselves by the withdrawal of the military, the former masters would generally resume the old mastership, and the condition of the freedmen become worse than when they were slaves." The Union officer worried that the contracts being signed by workers and employers generally expired at the end of December. Christmas had long been a traditional holiday "when work ceases" under slavery and so ending contracts then made sense to the freedmen. Agent How, though, saw a crueler rationale for the timing of the contracts on the part of the employers. The former masters would "then be able to dispense with the services of many of them, having very little work to do in the succeeding three months." Their contractual obligations fulfilled, employers would fill "their malicious desire to throw them on their own resources in mid Winter, or compel their friends the Yankees to support them."[56]

White employers saw the situation as exactly reversed: *they* were the victims. A. J. Gilkeson described the scene as it appeared from the perspective of someone who had owned nine people a year earlier. He cared for his "negroes," but they showed no loyalty to him. "Ann & Mary are still there, but I learn indirectly that they contemplate leaving in the spring," Gilkeson wrote a relative. A slave named Henry had left Gilkeson's brother "soon after the surrender."

The moral was clear: "The negroes are very trifling, as a general thing; and none of them are willing to contract by the year, and a majority of them do not seem to be willing to contract at all for any length of time." The determination of black people to remain flexible in unpredictable times seemed justified by the other conditions Gilkeson and fellow white farmers confronted. "Business of all kinds is very flat now, and there seems to be no money in the country. It is almost impossible now to collect a few Dollars from the best men in our community." Exacerbating the difficulty, "the tax collector is here now gathering in the Land Tax. I very much fear many of our farmers will forfeit their land from their inability to pay the Tax." The tax was assessed on their land's value in 1860, before the devastation of war, and if farmers could not pay the tax on time "the government will sell the land and appropriate all the money." Gilkeson, like his white neighbors, blamed the Federal army and government for all those difficulties. "Aint the Yankees the most fiendish nation on the face of the earth?," he asked his brother. They both knew the answer.[57]

☆

VIRGINIA IN GENERAL, and Augusta County in particular, stood on shifting ground on the issue of loyalty in 1865. Virginia had resisted secession in the winter of 1860–1861 and Augusta's delegates to the statewide convention had led efforts to avoid the dissolution of the United States. John Brown Baldwin and

John Brown Baldwin   *Alexander H. H. Stuart*

Alexander H. H. Stuart had been at the forefront of compromise
efforts, trying to save the Union while still protecting slavery.
These former Whigs, both of them prominent attorneys educated
at the University of Virginia, repeatedly found themselves at the
center of events. Baldwin, eighteen years younger than Stuart,
worked as Stuart's law partner while the older man served as
Congressman in the 1840s. The two men remained close friends
and allies, becoming in-laws, each prospering and each owning
eight enslaved people in 1860.[58]

Baldwin and Stuart had been trusted by delegates on both sides
of the secession debate. When Virginia finally seceded, Baldwin
announced from the floor of the convention that "I regard this as
an exceedingly dark day in the history of this State." He could not
"see anything that can put a stop or check to the war." It would
be "a calamitous war, civil war, servile war"; it would be "a war
fraught with all conceivable and imaginable horrors for which we
have no preparation." Baldwin admitted that he could not stop

secession, but would still protest that "in view of the responsibility that I owe to God and man, I cannot concur in the act which is about to be done."

When the final vote came, still voting for Union, Baldwin announced that despite his earlier protestations "I will serve the Commonwealth in the circumstances by which I am surrounded." When Virginia committed to the Confederacy, Baldwin threw himself into the success of the new nation. "There are no Union men left in Virginia," he wrote in a public letter to a Pennsylvania attorney in May 1861. "We stand this day a united people, to make good the eternal separation which we have declared."[59]

Baldwin helped to organize Virginia's military as Inspector General, served as commanding officer of Augusta's 52nd Virginia Infantry Regiment until he contracted typhoid fever, and represented the district in the Confederate Congress throughout the war. In that body, Baldwin spoke his mind, often challenging the Davis administration's conduct of the Confederate cause. He voted against arming enslaved men to fight and tried, but failed, to organize peace negotiations with the United States, hoping to send Alexander H. H. Stuart as a delegate.

Stuart and Baldwin demonstrated their loyalty to the Confederacy to the very collapse of the regime. In late March 1865, Stuart appeared before the large public meeting organized in Staunton to raise food for Lee's starving army, personally contributing two barrels of flour, two hundred pounds of bacon, and bonds worth five thousand dollars. Baldwin, still in Richmond with the failing government, wrote a letter of support for the defiant resolutions, denouncing reconstruction "as but another name for submission to tyranny," and pledging "never to entertain even the idea of it, but to resist it in the future as we have done in the past, to the utmost extremity."[60]

Only six weeks later, in early May—after Lee's surrender—Alexander Stuart called another mass meeting in Staunton. Baldwin, having returned to his home from the ashes of Richmond, gave a speech in favor of reconstruction. The meeting unanimously resolved that the opposition to the United States was over, that the state government be reorganized to conform to the laws and Constitution of the United States, that a statewide convention would be formed to oversee Virginia's reentry to the Union, and that a committee travel to Richmond to determine whether the Federal military authorities objected to such a convention.[61]

The committee, including both Stuart and Baldwin, visited Federal commander Henry Halleck, and the new governor appointed by Andrew Johnson, Francis H. Pierpoint. Although Pierpoint, a western Virginia Unionist, welcomed the Augusta delegation—the first in the former Confederacy to propose reunification—Andrew Johnson first had to pardon John Brown Baldwin because he had been a leader in the Confederate government.[62]

Awaiting Johnson's verdict, Baldwin answered questions from a West Virginia newspaper about the "real state of things in the Valley and from there to Richmond." Baldwin told the editor that "public opinion" fully supported the United States and that voters were now looking ahead, ignoring candidates' "past positions for Secessionism or Unionism." Regarding slavery, Baldwin boldly wrote, "the people of Virginia do not believe that the government policies are just and expedient or that they serve the best interests of the slave or slave owner. They are deeply apprehensive of the future with a people who have received their freedom without 'preparation for its duties or responsibilities.'"[63]

Despite this "deep-felt concern, white people know that there is no turning back, and they will do all that is practical and necessary to carry the freeing of the slaves into full effect in a manner beneficial to all." While white Virginians held no ill will toward the former slaves, Baldwin asserted, they did think it would be "some time" before it would be "wise or safe to confer upon them additional rights and privileges," particularly the right to vote. So ready were white Virginians to govern themselves under the new order, Brown argued, there was no need for the Freedmen's Bureau or any other military presence. The former Confederates could be trusted as integral members of the Union because the inflaming issue of slavery had been removed.[64]

Voters in Augusta did not know whether President Johnson was going to pardon John Brown Baldwin or not, but in the fall of 1865 they gave him twice the votes of any other candidate to the state legislature. Those same voters also elected Alexander H. H. Stuart to the United States Congress. Baldwin and Stuart seemed prudent choices, unlikely to inflame Andrew Johnson. Voters accepted Johnson's argument that secession had never been recognized by the Federal government and that therefore Virginia had never left the Union. Thus, Virginia and its former leaders were now ready to resume their former relationships, defeated, chastened, and without slavery.

Joseph Waddell, to his surprised gratification, had been nominated by his Augusta neighbors for a seat in the state legislature. He had taken the oath of loyalty to the United States in May, and so he knew he could serve if elected. Waddell desperately needed the money from the small salary the position paid, for he had not "carried a dollar since the war ended," but was "rather forced" into being a candidate. "I have not much hope of success, nor much desire for it," he told himself, and would rather have virtually any other business "at which I could make a decent livelihood."

That said, Waddell was proud that he won more votes than every other candidate except John Baldwin, who, "of course," was chosen for the seat. Some men, to his disgust and amusement, had worked against Waddell, saying—he imagined—that he was too "bashful" to say anything if he went to the legislature and that he was "a stiff fellow anyhow, and didn't care for any body unless he was a Presbyterian." Waddell watched with satisfaction as the votes came in from across the county, expressing confidence in him. Despite losing, Waddell thought he might be chosen to serve if there were "some difficulty about Baldwin's election, as in the opinion of many persons, myself included, he was ineligible under our present Constitution."[65]

Gratified as he was by the support of his friends and voters, Waddell's defeat left him without a job and with no money. He admitted that "I have not the means of procuring the necessaries of life unless I sell some of my little property. Cant buy a blank book, and therefore must suspend my diary." And thus, unfortunately, ended the record of the candid thoughts of Joseph A. Waddell.[66]

Across the former Confederacy in the fall of 1865 voters in other places made the same calculations as those in Augusta. They elected men they knew and trusted to represent them in their state legislatures and the United States Congress that would convene in December. Voters believed that those men, whether Unionists or secessionists before 1861, had demonstrated loyalty to their communities through previous times of crisis and could be trusted to serve them in the uncertain times ahead. Most of the newly elected officials had received pardons from the president of the United States and declared themselves ready to look to the future. They accepted the Thirteenth Amendment and the end of slavery.

Republicans were livid at such arrogance or ignorance. In their eyes, any man who had supported the Confederacy—at war with the United States only months earlier—should automatically be disqualified from serving the United States. Only truly loyal men, those who had defied popular opinion and risked their lives and property to defend the Union, deserved positions of trust. The former Confederates who planned to descend on Washington would of course support Johnson and the Democrats, preventing any chance of true reunion, one based on justice and Republican leadership.

☆

PENNSYLVANIA HELD STATE ELECTIONS in the fall of 1865, along with Ohio, Indiana, and Iowa, contests just as bitter as those of the presidential election a year earlier. Huge crowds rallied, editorials challenged the integrity of opponents, and predictions of glorious success flowed. When the votes came in, the Republicans had won once again. The Democrats thought the result "a surprise to both parties," for each expected that divisions among the Republicans "on the question of reconstruction" would damage the party. The Democrats charged that Republicans had won by deceiving voters. "Instead of meeting the issue boldly and manfully like honest men they shirked it like cowards, and carefully concealed it from the masses by feigning a support of the President which they did not feel." In particular, the Republicans had disguised their true plans to institute black suffrage.

The Democrats applauded Johnson's "wise and statesman-like policy for the speedy restoration of the Southern States to their Constitutional relations to the Government" despite the "clamors of the radical crew." While the radicals thought their victory in state elections that fall gave the Republicans a fresh mandate, the president did not seem to the Democrats to be "the man to be coerced or intimidated from a wise and patriotic purpose by a set of mad zealots and fanatical revolutionists."[67]

The Republicans of Pennsylvania claimed the most outspoken leader in the House of Representatives: Thaddeus Stevens. The people of Franklin County knew Stevens well. Not only did his congressional district lay beside their own, but Stevens owned an iron foundry in Franklin, on the road between Chambersburg and Gettysburg. That foundry had been the object of Confederate marauders more than once during the war, systematically dismantled and burned in retaliation for Stevens's decades-long crusade against the slaveholding South. The congressman gave a blistering speech in Gettysburg after the fall elections of 1865, staking out the position of the men known as "radicals." Like many radicals, Stevens had been an opponent of slavery since before the war—in his case, since the 1820s. Stevens had driven the effort behind the Thirteenth Amendment and now demanded the confiscation of the leading rebels' estates to pay the national debt and the compensation of loyal men in the South for the damages they suffered. Most important, Stevens was a Republican unafraid to talk of the justice and necessity of suffrage for black men.[68]

Alexander McClure, confidant and ally of Abraham Lincoln, had supported Andrew Johnson as Lincoln's running mate. Since then, though, he had publicly worried about Johnson's actions. He called on the president at the White House at the end of October and published an account of his conversation in the *Repository*. The Executive Mansion, McClure reported, was filled with a "motley mass of men, with an anxious female face here and there," pursuing pardons from the president and often emerging with their "trophies of success." McClure thought there "are few men who could make a more favorable impression upon a stranger on first acquaintance than the President." Andrew Johnson was "about five feet ten in height, rather stoutly and symmetrically built, has long hair well silvered by the frosts of time, rather a cold grey eye that looks as if in its calmest glances there slumbers behind it quite enough to quicken it; a finely chiseled Roman face, usually sad in expression, at times relieved by a genial smile, and in manner and dress serenely plain and unaffected." He spoke in "the softest tone and in well measured sentences."

Johnson explained his position toward the South "with a frankness that left no doubt as to his purpose." He believed that the states of the South had never been out of the Union, no matter their claims at the time, and that now those states should "resume their proper place in the Union." McClure resisted, arguing that such a policy meant that traitors such as Jefferson Davis could escape punishment. Johnson said that a time for atonement would come later. Now, he argued "with emphasis," the South must reenter the Union "with all its manhood—I don't want it to come eviscerated of its manhood!" By "manhood," Johnson meant the dignity and pride that would allow Southerners to lead their communities, that would give a man command over his household and black people.

Following this vague but emphatic principle, Johnson told McClure that he would "wield all his power to effect the admission of the representatives of the rebellious States into Congress during the next session." Fearing that this very issue would "make a sad breach between the President and Congress," McClure told Johnson "that the revolted States should take no part in the government they vainly sought to destroy until all issues arising from the war, and all its logical results, should be settled by faithful men." The Republicans wanted to take advantage of their mandate, won in the fall of 1864 and reinforced by the elections of 1865, to put the nation on a firm footing before the rebels were allowed back into the councils of power. Johnson's recognition of the delegates from the unrepentant South would destroy any chance of a real reconstruction. Johnson listened but did not respond.

McClure reported Johnson's thoughts "on the future of the freedmen." McClure seemed careful not to use the words "vote" or "suffrage," but he said that Johnson, while "not eminently hopeful" of black men's "ability to win a position that will enable them to be incorporated into our system of government as citizens," feels "that it must be fairly tried with an open field for the negro." Exactly what this meant was not clear, but if plans to incorporate black people into the fabric of Southern life did not succeed, Johnson ominously asserted, colonization was the "only alternative."

McClure was careful in his final assessment of Andrew Johnson. The president did not seem inclined to compromise his determination to see the Southern states restored. "This may or may not sever him from the party that sustained and cherished him in the darkest days through which he passed," McClure warned, "and that won him the highest honors of the Nation through a flood of obloquy; but if it does, I infer that he will accept the situation." In other words, McClure saw little reason to hope that Johnson would align with the Republicans on reconstruction and on punishment of treason. McClure would "leave the future to tell the story." That future would come in a few weeks, when Congress, out of session since Johnson's inauguration, would reconvene in Washington.[69]

9

Rebelism

January through December 1866

*A*mericans tested one another in 1866. With the war and passage of the Thirteenth Amendment behind them, Northerners and Southerners, Democrats and Republicans, African-Americans and white Americans watched and listened warily. Everyone knew what they believed, what they wanted, and what they thought the nation needed. They could not know, however, how far their opponents would go to secure their own principles and desires.

The nation worried as Andrew Johnson clashed repeatedly with the Republicans. As the president vetoed one bill after another, he and the Democrats talked of returning the Southern states to the Union and returning former Confederates to power. As the Republicans overturned one presidential veto after another, they talked of redeeming the blood spilled in the war and establishing justice for the freedmen. Each side became ever less likely to compromise, ever bolder in strategy and language, ever more contemptuous of their enemies.

The intransigence of white Southerners drove Reconstruction further than many Republicans had foreseen or desired. The former Confederates *defined their surrender as narrowly as possible. They would no longer fight, they would give up slavery, and they would rejoin the Union, but they refused to admit moral guilt for secession, for fighting, or for slaveholding. They demanded all the fundamental rights of citizens who had never tried to break apart the United States. The former Confederates were surprised and outraged that the victors demanded more.*

The Republicans, for their part, were surprised and outraged that the former Confederates refused to acknowledge that they had been wrong on every front, that all of their actions had been unjust and immoral. The Republicans believed that only true repentance by the former Confederates could create a lasting reunification, a moral regeneration of the South, a redefinition of loyalty. The Republicans demanded that white Southerners acknowledge that secession had been unconstitutional, a duplicitous slaveholders' rebellion rather than a principled revolution over states' rights.

Black Southerners had to navigate this shifting and treacherous landscape. The freedpeople struggled to make a living, gather their families, and find some kind of security in an unpredictable world. Arguments and vetoes in Washington echoed in the courthouses and farmsteads of the South.

The entire nation seemed out of control. A loss, insult, or threat from one side triggered a stronger reaction from the other. The mechanisms intended to reconcile and mediate conflict—the Constitution, political parties, and local governance—instead amplified the conflict, continually raising the stakes.

☆

THE FREEDMEN'S BUREAU worked on the front lines, its agents laboring with limited power but large responsibilities. W. Storer How reported from Staunton in January 1866 that "the air is full of outrages on the Freedmen by the Whites, and will be until just laws are made and executed." While "the freedmen dare not testify through fear of yet greater violence," three incidents in three different neighborhoods of Augusta County left visible evidence of the violence. Sam Crawford, a sixty-year-old black man, had been scarred in an attack by a white co-worker who assaulted him with a knife. Jane Walker, twenty years old, told how her white employer "beat her with his fist, and kicked her, and that his mother threatened to beat her with a shovel." Mary Ann Jackson, about thirty-five years old, testified that her employer beat her children and "rode a horse over her boy of 12 yrs. who now bears the marks of the horses hoofs on his head." The white man had "threatened to shoot her if she went away and came back." Staunton had been on the verge of a riot on Christmas Day 1865, when "bad men who were but lately 'masters',", after the "free use of liquors" shouted that they "would now override any civil laws not in accordance with their notions of a White man's privilege."[1]

When How learned that the Federal troops would be removed from Staunton in January 1866, he warned that the Bureau could not survive "without the presence and support of a military force." He requested that twenty men be posted in Staunton, "instructed to respond to the requests of any duly authorized agents of this Bureau." The Freedmen's Bureau assistant superintendent, Frederick Tukey, pleaded that "a very small number, for the purpose of making arrests, when necessary" would allow the Bureau to function there. He had faced several cases when "men refuse to appear here when summoned, that they refuse to come, and treat the summons with contempt." Sometimes, too, "persons refuse to comply" with the decisions of the Freedmen's court, and "in such cases as these I am completely powerless without any troops." The Bureau's office in Richmond sent no troops; the Staunton office would be on its own.[2]

The agents of the Staunton Freedmen's Bureau, because of

their role as judges and adjudicators, saw the black and white people of the county mainly in moments of conflict. Hundreds of complaints came before the agents, sometimes more than a dozen on a single day. Most of the complaints developed when white employers refused to pay black workers what they were owed. Given how little the freedpeople earned, the amounts were small, often a few dollars, but such amounts could mean the difference between feeding a family or not. White people, for their part, read any resistance or resentment about work and payment as signals of disrespect. Blows, threats, and hard words erupted repeatedly. Among the black people themselves, many conflicts grew out of arguments over pieces of clothing or small amounts of food. Other clashes came when women became pregnant from relations with men who had promised to stay with them as husbands. Some black men and women came to the courts for divorce or to determine with whom a man or wife belonged when one returned to Augusta after having been sold away years earlier.[3]

In scenes repeated across the South, black people turned to the Freedmen's Bureau to help find or return family members lost in slavery and war. Federal troops, a letter from one agent to another explained, had taken James Stuart forcibly "from his home and family to act as guide to our forces upon the Lynchburg raid of 1864, he having lived in the county and being familiar with the locality." Stuart did "good service as a guide for six weeks" without remuneration, but was now "afraid to return to Va. as it was known in Staunton he acted as a guide." He was now living in Ohio and requested the Bureau's aid in reuniting him with his wife. He "has money to defray her expenses to Ohio if the Bureau will aid her in her arrangements and journey."[4]

The freedpeople counted on the Bureau for its networks of information as well as transport. Patience Spencer sought her children, James and Melissa Ann, fifteen years old and eleven years old respectively, who were taken from her by "John Mitchell, a slave trader who then lived at Lynchburg and who sold them at Richmond, Va. in July 1861." The mother could not learn "who bought them or where they were taken," but she thought the slave trader himself might know. "The poor woman it appears hid herself in the woods with her children to escape the sale but hunger compelled her to let her children return to the house for food, when they were seized and carried off." The agent in Staunton worried that "her information is I fear too indefinite for discovery but she is so earnestly desirous of regaining them that I respectfully forward her request in the hope some clue may be obtained" from the former traders.[5]

Augusta County, a mature slaveholding county with no booming cash crop, had seen many enslaved people sold away in the half century before secession. A letter to Memphis from Staunton held out the prospect for reunion. Jane Bethell begged her sister to "return to this place, whence you was sold some 10 years ago. Your relatives are well and able to help you much if you could reach here, but like nearly all, have not money to send you to pay your expenses hither." The letter encouraged the woman to "call upon the officer in charge of the Bureau at Memphis and ask him to procure transportation for you."[6]

Abraham Doke of Naked Creek in Augusta had heard that his fourteen-year-old daughter Estaline might be in Richmond. She had been sold to Richmond in 1862 by James E. Carson, a slave trader. Her father "has heard indirectly she is still in Richmond and he is anxious to find her and have her come to his home where he can take good care of her." The agent in Staunton wrote his counterpart in Richmond to suggest that "perhaps enquiry through the schools may lead to her discovery." Despite adver-

tisements in the African-American schools and churches of Richmond, Estaline could not be located.[7]

Just as agents and freedpeople hoped that former slave traders
would help reconstitute families they had broken apart, so did
they count on former masters. Ann Wallace longed to find her
parents, Isaac and Hester Wallace, in Maryland. The Staunton
agent wrote to their former owner, for Ann had "been sold by
you" to an owner in Augusta. She was "a good industrious girl
and I hope you can give the requested information or if her parents live near you may see them and ask what arrangements they
can make for their daughter to reach Baltimore."[8]

Parents desperately used whatever scraps of information they
had to find their children. Isabella Burton brought a statement to
the Freedmen's Bureau in Staunton. "Horace Bucker sold my two
sons (seven & five years age) Benjamin & Horace, sold to Larke &
Wright in Maddison County Va. Johnny Gilgarnett & Jeremiah
Gilgarnett were playmates." Burton hoped those details might
help locate her young sons, "for I am living in Staunton Now a
widow & alone, would like very much to see them." The census
two years later showed that she still lived alone.[9]

Slavery had taken people unimaginably far from their families.
Letters to and from the Staunton office connected with Washington, D.C., New Orleans, Mobile, and Nashville as well as Ches-
ter Courthouse, South Carolina; Parkersburg and Shepardstown,
West Virginia; Tuscaloosa, Alabama; Morehead City and Golds-
boro, North Carolina; Galveston, Texas; Chillicothe and Cincin-
nati, Ohio; and Jacksonville, Florida. Family members looked for
one another in all corners of Virginia. Without information about
their whereabouts, they might as well be in Texas or Florida.

In a few instances, the efforts worked. Benjamin Kiner had
moved to Ohio and wrote his wife Frances back in Augusta in

1866, through the connections of the Freedmen's Bureau. "I would like to have you come out here and I hope you will make up your mind and come with the children," he urged. "I should like to have all the children with me as they can go to school." If Frances was staying in Virginia because of her mother, Benjamin told his wife to bring her, too, because "the sooner we get together the better it will be for all of us."[10]

☆

FRANKLIN COUNTY, its southern border the Mason-Dixon Line, had long been a haven for those fleeing slavery. Before the war, a large African-American population called the county home, especially communities near the border such as Greencastle and Mercersburg. That large population permitted Franklin to contribute many men to the United States Colored Troops, but the proximity to the border proved a great danger during the war, when Confederate raiders seized black people and dragged them into Virginia and into slavery.

The Freedmen's Bureau in the Valley of Virginia dealt with several families who had been victimized by the Confederates in Franklin. "A man named MacRichardson is charged with having forcibly taken a freedwoman & (3) three children from near Greencastle Pa. in July 1864," Storer How wrote from Winchester in November 1865. MacRichardson then took the four freedpeople "to one Madison Leary, living near this place, who is said to have sold them" as his own slaves. How heard that MacRichardson had moved near Lynchburg and he wrote the agent there to investigate whether MacRichardson had indeed taken Eliza Alesouth and her three children "and what was done with them." The next month, a telegram arrived from the war department ordering prompt attention to the "three colored children" taken from Thaddeus Stevens's "place in Pennsylvania" by the "Rebel army" when Stevens's iron furnace had been raided and burned by the Confederates.[11]

Mrs. Priscilla Marshall of Franklin County wrote a letter asking for help finding her children "carried off by some rebel soldiers." She accompanied her letter with a statement, signed by six neighbors, testifying that "an armed Rebel force claiming to be under the command of Gen'l Jenkins of the Rebel army in the year 1863 did by force take three of said Marshall's children named respectively Rosa, Sallie, and Jack." Marshall and her petitioners had heard that two of the children were in the care of the Freedmen's Bureau and asked for their return to Greencastle. The mother wrote that she could "furnish any amount of testimony to losing the children and they being taken by the Rebels."[12]

More than two years after the end of the war, a man in Franklin County relied on the Freedmen's Bureau to reunite with his wife in Augusta County. Anthony Marston sent ten dollars to Agent Thomas P. Jackson in Staunton to help convey his wife Mary Ann to Chambersburg "without delay." Marston could meet her there "almost anytime as I only live sixteen miles from there." The husband urged the agent to write "ameadeately on receipt of this." He wanted to be sure "when to be there to meet her." Anthony Marston ended his urgent and hopeful letter with "thanks for your kind favors."[13]

The Freedmen's Bureau used its unique national network to accomplish things no other organization in the nation could. Had it done nothing else but rejoin families that had been ripped apart by slavery and war, the Bureau would have been essential.

☆

BLACK CHILDREN IN AUGUSTA became subjects of contention, tangled in connections among family members as well as former masters and other white people. Richard Monroe, "a first class hand and entirely able to make a judicious and sufficient provision for his family," claimed that a boy named James was the much younger brother of his wife. G. L. Peyton, who owned a hotel in Staunton, had James with him. The white man testified that the boy did not want to go with Monroe, who was not his brother in any case. Peyton had owned James's mother, but she had died at James's birth and Peyton had raised the boy. Peyton charged James was "just getting large enough to do a little something—which is the reason for Monroe's interest." The hotel owner claimed that he could provide better care for the boy than the freedman could and that "I will not give him up until compelled to."[14]

Another white man, charged with keeping Mary Gordon from her African-American father, replied that "I will just say to you that the girl Mary Gordon that was her mothers name was free born and on her way to the poor house when about 14 months old my wife took charge of her and when about two years of age the County Court bound her to us." The white man saw a selfish purpose behind the request. "She is now eleven years old past and just getting so she can pay for her raisen. The Bureau has nothing more to do with her than they would have with a bound white girl. Her grandmother was a white woman." There was no legal record of the girl being declared in the charge of the white couple, however, and the agent encouraged her father to "call at the office first opportunity" to see if his daughter could be recovered.[15]

A freedwoman in Augusta, Mary Harris, claimed that a white man, Reuben Moore, was holding her daughter against her will. Moore wrote that "I told Martha that she was free to go and she could go if she chose to do so. She said, she did not want to go." In fact, Moore only let her stay "because I had raised her and her

anxiety to stay with me. She now says she will not go. I am willing for any of her family to take her away at any time and never
did persuade her to stay, much less force her."[16]

A key responsibility for agents in Staunton, as across the South,
was to compile a register of "colored persons . . . cohabiting
together as man and wife." Only weeks after Appomattox, the
Bureau began registering men and women who knew themselves
to be married even though Virginia law recognized no marriages
between enslaved people. The Bureau's registration accelerated
after the Virginia General Assembly, as part of its recasting of
its laws after slavery, declared in February 1866 that formerly
enslaved men and women could now legally marry. Most of the
couples registered in the spring and summer of 1866, especially in
June, and the files were largely complete by August. The Bureau
made copies of the records for state officials and put the originals
in the Augusta County courthouse. The register recorded 896
couples and their children by name and age.

The register of marriages brought a gift impossible under slavery. Though they might have been joined by a white minister
before white witnesses, marriages between slaves had no legal
standing. Though a woman and a man might have demonstrated
their devotion to one another for decades, slave owners could and
did regularly separate husband and wife, parent and child, with
no legal consequence. Marriages in which family members lived
on different farms, or in town and in the country, were especially
vulnerable.

The files compiled by Storer How and Frederick Tukey traced
the tortuous paths the enslaved people of Augusta had followed to
their moment of freedom. Of the 896 couples listed, in only 276
cases had both husband and wife been born in Augusta County.
While 389 of the men had been born in Augusta, the other 500
men listed in the register had been born in 80 different locations,

ranging from Pennsylvania to Tennessee, from North Carolina to Missouri, from Kentucky to Florida. Most had been born in other counties of Virginia and West Virginia, from the Tidewater region to the mountains. The women in these couples were more likely to have been born in Augusta—423 of the 896—but the remainder had come from locations as scattered as those of their husbands, from Maryland to Alabama.

Slavery in Augusta County, with about as many enslaved people being taken out of the county as being born or brought in, demonstrated the profound wrenching of the institution. Marriage records showed that men and women in enslaved couples had often found one another after having been shipped or marched a thousand miles to the Valley. The couples who came to the courthouse in Staunton to make sure their names and the names of their children were recorded in the columns of the register knew what freedom had brought and how fragile it could be.

The work those men and women did revealed a range of capacities among black people that neither white Southerners or Northerners acknowledged and that the census did not record. The men in Augusta recorded 46 different occupations, from farm laborer to silversmith, from barkeeper to brick molder, from hotel servant to lime burner. They made carriages, chairs, shoes, leather, and wagons. They worked in bars, hotels, and stables; they cut hair, cooked, and waited tables; they knew how to forge iron and feed furnaces and lay stone; they built houses and made barrels; they could butcher meat and cultivate gardens; they worked on railroads and at sawmills. The register recorded no occupations for the women, but they too—as the advertisements for their sale had long testified—possessed the essential skills of the household, the farm, and the town.

Many of these couples had been together for years, as the ages of their children attested. About a quarter of those who came before the Freedmen's Bureau in Staunton had sons and daughters. Of the 228 families with children, almost a quarter had one child and more than half had up to three. Some of the children were over twenty years old, and many had been sold or taken out of Augusta County in the decades of slavery. Of the husbands, about a quarter were in their twenties, about a quarter in their thirties, about a quarter in their forties, and a quarter over fifty. The wives tended to be younger, most of them in their twenties and thirties. About a quarter of those registered lived in Staunton in 1865 and 1866; the remainder traveled in from dozens of remote farms and villages across the very large county of Augusta to make sure their names were inscribed in the marriage book.

Part of the process of marking freedom was claiming a common last name. Although whites for the most part did not recognize surnames among enslaved people, many in the register had long claimed their names and had been known to some by that name. The register recorded different last names for the husband and wife under slavery, with more women than men recording no last name. Following Virginia law, the women in the newly recognized marriages took the names of their husbands. The Freedmen's Bureau and the government of Virginia agreed that a proper family would be overseen by a male and that whatever autonomy a woman had exercised under slavery would now be subordinated to her husband.

In this way and in others, the Freedmen's Bureau both enabled and enforced structures of marriage and gender relations dominant at the time. Women who had been responsible for themselves and their children as much as possible under slavery were now expected to assume a subordinate position as wives. If they did not, they would be considered less worthy of support by the

Bureau. While everyone in the African-American community understood that many women with children would never be able to locate the fathers of those children because of the dislocations of slavery and war, leaders of churches expected men and women with children to marry. Some black women benefited from the new expectations of marriage and others lost autonomy when they married, but influential people of both races saw marriage as a valuable new right and responsibility for formerly enslaved people. White people and black people, Northerners and Southerners, would be held to the same standards.[17]

Many of the couples took common American names such as Brown, Carter, Green, Hall, Hill, Jackson, Johnson, Jones, Miller, Moore, Smith, White, or Williams. A few chose Franklin, Jefferson, Monroe, Madison, or Washington. Their first names, too, were largely indistinguishable from their white neighbors.

Whatever rationale motivated newly freed men to choose names, flattering the richest men in the county apparently was not part of the calculation. The newly married couples seldom adopted the names of the prominent families who had owned them. The 69 men in Augusta who owned at least fifteen slaves in 1860, for example, collectively possessed power over 1,371 people. When families registered their names with the Freedmen's Bureau, only 114 registered names that overlapped with those large slaveholders—and 45 of those names were "Johnson" and "Smith." Of the 69 largest slaveholders, 31 saw no former slaves adopt their name.

A report from the Staunton office of the Freedmen's Bureau observed that "the Record of Marriages is carefully preserved in this office, in good order for reference, and is frequently consulted." While formerly enslaved couples continued to come forward in 1867, the Bureau agent now directed them to the County

Court to secure a marriage license.[18] A profound and enduring change in African–American life had taken place in a single year, with widely accepted conventions of women's place in marriage providing a ready-made blueprint for family life after slavery.

☆

THE UNITED STATES SENATE passed a bill in February 1866 enlarging the powers of the Freedmen's Bureau. The Democrats were incensed when they saw that the agents in each county were to receive a salary of $1,500 per year; those thousand men would cost the government over a million dollars a year and the Freedmen's Bureau would dispense large sums. "Naturally lazy, the Southern negro would at once avail himself of this offer of Government care and support," snarled the Democrats' paper in Franklin County. The consequence of this expansion would be "to maintain an army of greedy office-holders, and a million or more of lazy negroes in idleness"; it would "override" the white citizens of the South "and paralyze the industry of the South, and retard the sorely needed development of its resources." The Republicans acted out of spite; they knew the extension of the Freedmen's Bureau contradicted the wishes of President Johnson and would "embarrass his policy of Restoration."[19]

Andrew Johnson vetoed the bill extending the Freedmen's Bureau in February. This veto, the first in what would prove to be a long series of vetoes, proved that Johnson's "complete apostasy was predetermined and but a question of time," the Republicans' *Repository* observed with exasperation. Johnson offered the usual Democratic reasons for the veto, turning on states' rights and government economy, but the Republicans argued that he vetoed the Freedmen's Bureau because "the Traitors demanded it.

This is the simple, unvarnished truth, and the whole truth, and the Nation must look it in the face."[20]

Congress failed to override Johnson's veto but in April the Republicans, faced with the passage of discriminatory laws throughout the South, physical abuse of the freedmen, and the unwillingness of Southern whites to abide by contracts, passed the Civil Rights Bill over Johnson's veto. They then wrote a new Freedmen's Bureau Act, extending its work until July 1868. Johnson vetoed this act as well, but this time Congress overrode him.

While Johnson and Congress jostled in the spring of 1866, a report "on the Condition of the Freedmen's Bureau in the Southern States" offered a discouraging assessment of the agency's situation and progress. Written by two United States generals, the report found in Virginia, as elsewhere, that "everything depends upon the agents." Where "men of sound judgment and discretion" presided, "there has been no conflict between agents of the Bureau and the citizens"; where lesser men presided, the result was "bitterness and antagonism between the whites and the freedmen." The report judged that "at the close of the war, in the chaotic condition in which society was left in the entire absence of all civil authority, the judicious and sensible officers of the Bureau, supported by the military, exercised a good influence, and did much to preserve order and assist in the organization of free labor." But now that civil order had been restored a year later, the freedpeople were secure—"as evidenced by the changes made by the Legislature in the laws of Virginia—giving them the right to hold property, to sue and be sued, and to testify in the courts in all cases in which they may be interested, (a gratifying proof of the growing feeling of kindness toward them on the part of the whites)—render the freedmen, in our opinion, perfectly secure, if left to the care of the law and the protection of the troops."

The generals who issued the report thought it better that "the services of the Bureau in Virginia be dispensed with and their duties be performed by the officers commanding the troops in the department." The Democratic press eagerly reprinted the report and crowed about its critiques. The Republicans took from the report a different lesson: the military presence of the United States Army, as well as the Freedmen's Bureau, was essential. Despite their own reservations about costs and sustaining a large army in peace time, the Republicans posted about 54,000 soldiers in the South and the West, three times the number the United States maintained overall in 1860 and yet still small relative to the needs of the freedpeople. Although they recognized the military necessity of this presence, the Republicans never reconciled themselves to the political and economic costs of that presence. They began looking for ways to limit the commitment as quickly as they could.[21]

☆

CONGRESS CREATED A JOINT COMMITTEE of nine representatives and six senators to conduct hearings "into the condition of the States which formed the so-called Confederate States of America, and report whether they, or any of them, are entitled to be represented in either house of Congress." The committee, created in late 1865 by a resolution sponsored by Thaddeus Stevens, conveyed the Republican position on the status of former Confederates: "By withdrawing their representatives in Congress, by renouncing the privilege of representation, by organizing a separate government, and by levying a war against the United States, they destroyed their State constitutions." The Confederate government these rebels created was "usurped and illegal. They chose the tribunal of arms" to determine the legality of that government "and they were defeated."

The Republicans held that President Johnson had no right "to decide upon the nature and effect" of the form of government those defeated states might now assume. That power was "lodged by the Constitution in the Congress of the United States." The elections of the fall of 1865, under the provisional governments established by Johnson, "resulted, almost universally, in the defeat of candidates who had been true to the Union, and in the election of notorious and unpardoned rebels, men who could not take the prescribed oath of office, and who made no secret of their hostility to the government and the people of the United States." In the wake of that election, the new joint committee would "investigate carefully and thoroughly the state of feeling and opinion existing among the people of these States; to ascertain how far their pretended loyalty could be relied upon, and thence to infer whether it would be safe to admit them at once to a full participation in the government they had fought for four years to destroy."[22]

The committee told those testifying before its subcommittees, each one covering a different part of the South, what it was seeking. The "burden of proof rests upon the late insurgents who are seeking restoration to the rights and privileges which they willingly abandoned." Those insurgents must prove that they are "extending to all classes of citizens equal rights and privileges, and conforming to the republican idea of liberty and equality." The former Confederates also had to "exhibit in their acts something more than an unwilling submission to an unavoidable necessity—a feeling, if not cheerful, certainly not offensive and defiant."[23]

The committee made no pretense of impartiality. They held the power to inform Congress whether the white South had truly repented, whether the former rebels were, in their hearts, prepared for reunion. And the committee members were deeply skeptical whether either of those conditions had been met. The subcommittee responsible for Virginia interviewed thirty-eight Republicans, nine conservatives, and two moderates, ranging from the head of the United States military in the state to Robert E. Lee, then a college president.

The subcommittee consisted of Senator Jacob M. Howard of Michigan, Representative Roscoe Conkling of New York, and Representative Henry T. Blow of Missouri. Howard had worked closely with Abraham Lincoln on the Thirteenth Amendment, Conkling was known as a leading Radical, and Blow had been a staunch Unionist throughout the Civil War. The three men knew what they were looking for, what they called "rebelism": a defiant spirit that acknowledged military defeat without accepting moral defeat.

Two men from Augusta County testified before the committee in Washington, painting sharply contrasting portraits of the past, present, and future of the South. John Brown Baldwin, a life-long resident of Staunton, now served as Speaker of the House of Representatives in Virginia. Asked on February 10 if he had been "an original Union man," Baldwin declared himself "the most thorough-going I ever knew." He had argued against secession in the state convention to the very moment of disunion, pleading with his fellow delegates to stay in the United States, and meeting with President Lincoln in April 1861 immediately before Fort Sumter in a failed attempt to avert war. When war came, though, Baldwin had become a loyal Confederate, serving in the national government and rallying people to fight until the very end.

With the war over, the committee asked, was there any longer a "combination" in Virginia aimed to overthrow the government? Baldwin assured them he did not know of one, even if his language was not reassuring: "I have been in intercourse with the most bitter, determined, obstinate, and violent of all the men in Virginia" and he would have known if any such combination existed. Everyone accepted that secession had been defeated and that the government of the United States was once again the government of Virginia.

Asked about Republican plans to reunify the nation, Baldwin warned that a fourteenth amendment to the Constitution, discussed by some in Washington, would "plant a root of bitterness such as has not been known even in the bitterness of war." Should Congress "place the negro on the ground of political equality," Baldwin warned, that action would not only open the door to "advocates of suffrage of women, of minors, and foreigners, and negroes, in every shade of combination and confusion," but would also serve as the "entering wedge of more mischief, more trouble, more ill will, more dissatisfaction and disloyalty to the government of the United States, than all other causes that have ever combined together." Baldwin had "no doubt at all that if that constitutional amendment were adopted, all the expedients which ingenuity and chicane could suggest would be resorted to to get around it and evade it in every possible way; and I do consider that one of, by no means the least of, the objections to it." A corrupt constitutional amendment would lead to corrupt attempts to evade its provisions, demoralizing the spirit of the people.

Baldwin reassured the committee that the Virginia General Assembly, in which he played a leading role, had been systematically reviewing the laws of the state, striking out "the peculiar distinctive features separating the black and white races before the law." That was true: Virginia's legislature, seeing the Northern outcry against the openly racist "black codes" of Mississippi and South Carolina, had carefully tailored its statutes to avoid controversy but still control the freedpeople. While apparently nondis-criminatory, Virginia's laws gave wide discretion to local judges and juries, allowing them to hand down sentences of widely vary-ing length and severity for crimes such as petty theft or vagrancy. Such relatively minor crimes could result in long sentences in prison or on a chain gang for black people convicted of them.[24]

The Virginia General Assembly had acted in good faith, Bald-win assured the committee, but he lectured the national legisla-tors about the challenges and dangers of such profound revision: "You, gentlemen of the north, who have not a mass of 300,000 or 400,000 suddenly emancipated negroes in your midst, can hardly appreciate the caution which we feel to be necessary in dealing with any of these problems" of maintaining order. "However much we may be determined to do them justice, there are ques-tions of safety and expediency which must be considered by pru-dent and discreet men." Baldwin and his colleagues wanted "to place the blacks on an equal footing of equality before the law. That is my judgment and the temper of the legislature—to allow them all the civil rights, the same as white men."

Baldwin's bold statement contradicted the actions of state legis-latures across the South, including Virginia, as they compromised the most basic freedoms of the former slaves. Baldwin, patroniz-ing both the committee and his fellow white Virginians, argued that, despite his own enlightened feelings, "we must let the public feeling of the white people mature. Our local government must conform to the judgment and opinion of our own people, and they must have time to make up their mind to this thing. If you attempt to force the matter, you will see that it will bring about an enmity between the races."

In a kind of circular logic and self-fulfilling prophecy, Baldwin explained that white Southerners had "no unkind feeling toward the negro in a position where he is not asserting an equality; but the best friend the negro ever had in the world, the kindest friend he ever had, a young boy or girl raised by a negro mammy, and devotedly attached to her, would become ferociously indignant if the old mammy were to claim equality for a moment." If the Republicans would allow black rights to emerge gradually, the white people "will come to it without any shock to their feelings. I think I can say with perfect confidence that our people will deal with the negro in all respects as kindly, and extend privileges to him as rapidly, as if he had been manumitted by the judgment of our own people, without any foreign influence at all."

If white Southerners were forced into equality too abruptly and clumsily, by contrast, chaos and hatred would follow. Baldwin admitted that "I do not like the negro as well free as I did as a slave, for the reason that there is now between us an antagonism of interest to some extent, while, before, his interest and mine were identical." When Baldwin owned a man, "I was always thinking of how I could fix him comfortably. Now, I find myself driving a hard bargain with him for wages." Asked if the black man "loves money as well as the white man," Baldwin said the black man did love money, but "knows nothing about taking care of it. My negroes, when they draw their month's wages now, give a blow-out and have a dance in my kitchen." Asked if that was because they had been slaves, Baldwin blandly asserted that such behavior was "the intrinsic character of the animal." In "reading, and writing, and spelling, negroes learn almost as quickly as whites," but that was about "the highest position they can get." Baldwin believed that black people lacked "the persistence of purpose, or the energy, or the intellectual vigor to rise to anything like intellectual equality with the white race." He did think "they will get along very well in the ordinary domestic relations, as servants and inferiors."

Baldwin did not worry about "armed collision between the two races." Because they were "so intermingled in the business of life," black people were "under the influence of the white." In fact, "they like the white people better than they do their own," he assured the committee. Black Southerners were "the best and kindest people I know of," and only some "aggressive movement from without" could lead to violence.

John Brown Baldwin's confident and contradictory racial ideas were those of the men who ran Augusta County, and Virginia, and the South. Such men, often former Whigs and reluctant Confederates, were respected in their communities as the most reasonable and responsible leaders among them. Such men believed they knew black people inside and out, now and in the future. And their presumed racial certainty underpinned political certainties, their articles of faith, what they called their "principles." They deserved to control black people, they must, and they would.[25]

The second witness from Augusta, speaking to the committee four days later, differed from John Brown Baldwin in almost every way. He was William J. Dewes, an itinerant professor of music. Born near Richmond and "uniformly" a Union man before, during, and after the war, Dewes had left the Confederate capital for the new state of West Virginia in 1864 and moved to Staunton after the war. There, Dewes had served on the Freedmen's Bureau court, advocating for the area's black residents.

The committee's questions to William Dewes were direct and so were the answers, with half-hearted qualifiers tacked on:

QUESTION: What is the feeling among the ex-rebels there towards the government of the United States?

ANSWER: As a general thing, the feeling is one of opposition, as far as my knowledge extends.

QUESTION: How are they in the habit of speaking of the government?

ANSWER: Disrespectfully. Of course there are exceptions.

QUESTION: Are they understood as speaking against the present administration, or against the government as a government?

ANSWER: I understand that it is against the United States government.

QUESTION: How do they feel in regard to the emancipation of their slaves?

ANSWER: Generally speaking, they do not recognize it, only just so far as they are compelled. Some few do.

QUESTION: How do the ex-rebels treat Union men?

ANSWER: As a general thing, they look upon them with contempt.

QUESTION: Do they exhibit in their intercourse bitterness and hostility toward the Union men?

ANSWER: They do.

Asked whether a Union man could get justice, Dewes thought not. In fact, Union men in Augusta—led by Dewes himself, it subsequently turned out—had prepared "a petition to Congress to have all their lawsuits, of every description, referred to a military court or some other tribunal." Dewes estimated that "two hundred and fifty persons in the county have already signed the petition." Two weeks before Dewes's February testimony, in fact, the papers of Staunton had picked up news of the petition from a Washington paper. The document asked for protection of the

Union men of Augusta against the "usurpations and proscriptions of the dominant majority." Even before Dewes testified, the *Spectator* had demanded to know what the petition said. "Are these men petitioning for 'protection'?—If so, protection against whom? Have any threats been made against one? Do they desire troops to be sent here? If so, for what purpose? Are not the citizens peaceable, quiet, harmless?"[26]

The last thing Staunton needed, the *Spectator* declared, was the return of Federal troops, for since their departure in January 1866 "there has not been half the disorder that there was before." The paper felt certain that "the citizens do not want any soldiers here—the head of the Freedmen's Bureau does not want them, and the Freedmen themselves do not want them." The *Spectator* sneered that the protection the soldiers offered the freedpeople had been "of the kind which the vulture gives to the dove, and the wolf to the lamb." The sort of men who would send such a petition to the Federal government "are not, in truth, true Union men, but trifling characters who have gotten into some positions which they do not deserve to fill where they can exercise a 'little brief authority.'"[27]

Dewes, before his testimony before the committee, had responded to the *Spectator* with relish. The editor had "'made bold' to hurl his thunderbolts (Jove like) at my devoted and unprotected self." Dewes pronounced "all assertions relating to myself false" except that he did originate the petition. Dewes embellished his response with poetry and ornate language, alternately goading his attacker and backing away. The editor of the *Spectator* believed that Dewes was spoiling for a fight so that "he may occupy the position of a persecuted Union man, that he may gain that kind of notoriety which would enable him to get some more desirable position."

The bold petition enhanced Dewes's credibility before the committee and may in fact have accounted for his being called to testify in the first place. Asked how the white people of the area felt about the freedmen, Dewes responded with a potent analogy: "to use their own terms, they regard the Union man about as they do the nigger." Asked if those white people would "willingly contribute for the education of all classes, blacks and whites?" Dewes thought not. "The papers discountenance it, and make fun of the negro schools and school teachers and Freedmen's Bureau."[28]

The two witnesses from Augusta County provided, in different ways, just what the committee was looking for. John Brown Baldwin embodied the white South's intransigence and arrogance, lecturing the senator and congressmen on their limited understanding of both the black people and the white people of the South. William J. Dewes embodied the beleaguered Union man in the South, engaged in a dangerous, lonely, and principled resistance against a white majority determined to negate all that the war and emancipation had so recently won at such a great cost.

☆

THE REPORT OF THE Joint Committee on Reconstruction, its hundreds of interviews transcribed and published in May 1866, triggered the partisan responses everyone knew it would. In Franklin County, the Democrats' *Valley Spirit* proclaimed the report "so universally condemned by the loyal and patriotic Unionists of the country that the disunion Committee feel that they have made a grave mistake." The Republicans' *Repository* admitted that men in the party differed over various parts and emphases of the report, but concluded that "what the loyal men of the nation most desire is to have some definite policy, not wholly dictated by traitors, that can be made the fixed and settled policy of the Government."[29]

That "definite policy" called for a Fourteenth Amendment to the Constitution. The amendment bore the marks of its moment of creation. It was in part a response to the black codes of unrepentant Southern legislatures and to Andrew Johnson's two vetoes of the Civil Rights Bill, which finally passed with a two-thirds majority in April 1866. The proposed amendment defined citizenship to include everyone born in the United States, including those born into slavery. It prohibited state and local governments from depriving persons of life, liberty, or property without due process of law and it required each state to provide equal protection under the law to all people under its jurisdiction. The amendment apportioned votes for federal offices according to the number of authorized voters in a state, diminishing representation for states that disfranchised voters. In clauses even more obviously the product of the time, the amendment prevented anyone from holding office who had "engaged in insurrection or rebellion" and prevented either the nation or any state from paying debts incurred in rebellion. The final clause gave Congress the power to enforce those provisions through "appropriate legislation."

Although the Fourteenth Amendment divided Republicans, with some thinking it went too far and others that it did not go far enough, the intransigence of Andrew Johnson and the white South unified the party behind the necessity for the action. The amendment passed both houses of Congress in June 1866 and went before the states for ratification.

"A more nefarious and reckless scheme for party aggrandizement and power never disgraced the history of any country or age," spat Staunton's *Vindicator* in response to the provisions of the proposed amendment. The clause proclaiming former Confederates ineligible for office holding "would deprive us of the services of the ablest statesmen among us, in a Federal capacity, and force us to elect a set of incapacitated upstarts, who could be manipulated at will by the vile tricksters who now disgrace our National Legislature." The verdict before the voters of Virginia was clear: "Better to be unrepresented forever." Even if white Virginians found themselves currently powerless to prevent the imposition of such provisions, "we can at least have the proud satisfaction of knowing that we had no hand in riveting on ourselves this diabolical scheme."[30]

Alexander H. H. Stuart warned that "should the radicals succeed in the coming elections, I can see nothing but disaster to the country. The Southern States will be continued in their present anomalous condition—neither in nor out of the Union—taxed without being represented, and governed by laws, in which they have no voice." Stuart declared that it was up to the people of the North and West to decide "whether they prefer angry passions, anarchy, and disunion, and probably bloodshed on the one hand, or tranquility, fraternity and a restored nation on the other."[31]

The newspapers of Franklin County, like those across the North, explicated and analyzed each step in the drama between Andrew Johnson and his congressional opponents in the spring and summer of 1866. Everyone agreed on one point: the Democrats and the Republicans were growing ever further apart. Johnson vetoed one bill after another and the Republicans overrode those vetoes. The editorials of the Democrats across the North were indistinguishable from editorials in the South, denouncing the Freedmen's Bureau, black voting, the Federal military presence, and any step toward equality of rights for African-Americans. The editorials of the Republicans expressed ever greater disgust with

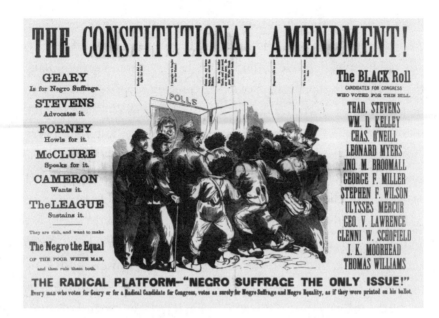

*Democratic cartoon from Pennsylvania opposing ratification of
the Fourteenth Amendment*

Johnson, his allies in the South, and the Democrats of the North who sought to stop the necessary transformation of the South.

☆

WHILE POLITICAL LEADERS and ordinary people struggled over the unfolding consequences of the Civil War, others sought to enshrine the war in people's memories. In February 1866, the *Spectator* reminded the white citizens of Staunton of "a brigade of noble souls and gallant soldiers," about two thousand men who had "sacrificed their lives in defense of the South" who remained half-buried outside Staunton. In March 1866, the *Valley Virginian*, in an article titled "Our Unhonored Dead," reminded people of their responsibility to those fallen soldiers. "Nothing has been done to enclose their graves or mark their last resting place." Such a condition "is a shame and disgrace to our people, and if there is any public spirit left, we call upon the ladies of Staunton" to make things right. In April, the *Spectator* expressed surprise that no one had stepped forward to take up this work but took solace in "the tender hearts" of local women. A committee "representing every congregation in town" had organized to raise money to bury those soldiers and those who fell at the Battle of Piedmont in the summer of 1864. "We hope the men will co-operate with this committee of ladies and give them the benefit of practical council." [32]

In these admonitions the papers of Staunton echoed calls from across Virginia and the South. Editors filled columns with long poems celebrating the Confederacy, its soldiers, its cause, and its leaders, especially the martyred Stonewall Jackson. In the same way that poetry seemed to translate such unrepentant "rebelism" into more acceptable form, so did the leadership of women. Men, at the same time they took oaths of loyalty and testified of their eagerness to return to the United States, urged white women to commemorate and consecrate the fallen soldiers of the Confederacy. [33]

In April, Staunton's women formed a Cemetery Association that proposed to "gather together all the Augusta dead, as well as all Confederates buried in the county, and bury them in the Soldier's Cemetery. Soldiers from every state in the South are now buried here, and their friends should aid in this patriotic work." Staunton would not be alone, for "nearly every town in Virginia is raising funds to enclose and ornament the Soldiers' Cemeteries." The *Valley Virginian* urged all citizens to "pay a merited tribute to those who died heroes," for such a tribute "is all that is left us." [34]

The *Vindicator* applauded the idea of creating a day, all across the South, "on which the ladies of the South might unite, annually, in an ovation to our departed heroes, by strewing flowers on their graves planting evergreens &c., and otherwise showing their regard for those who fell in the late war in defence of our cause." The paper supported the suggestion of "the 10th day of May, the anniversary of the death of our beloved 'Stonewall Jackson'," when "the Christian, the Soldier and the greatest military genius of the age, passed from earth to Heaven," as that day of commemoration.[35]

Although preparations for the commemoration had been made in just a few weeks, the paper felt confident that the people of Augusta would demonstrate their devotion to the Confederacy. Virginia, where so many men from so many places had fallen, held a special responsibility. "Brave hearts and true, they lost all, even life, for us, and it will gladden the hearts of many widows and orphans in the far distant South, to know that the remains of their loved ones are not neglected by the fair women of the Valley." The stores of Staunton closed for the day and "it is hoped that all will unite to pay that respect due those who gave all for their country and their principle."[36]

The next day, "at an early hour in the morning crowds could be seen pouring in to town on every road, until perhaps, a larger number of our people assembled in Staunton, than were ever congregated here on any previous occasion." A quiet parade passed through the town, with Jedediah Hotchkiss (now a "captain," though he had never held military rank) one of the two main assistants. The order of procession embodied the entire white community:

THE 'STONEWALL' BAND.

CLERGY AND PRESS.

SPEAKERS AND SINGERS.

SURVIVING MEMBERS OF 'STONEWALL' BRIGADE.

SURVIVING SOLDIERS OF THE LATE C. S. ARMY.

LADIES BEARING FLOWERS.

SABBATH SCHOOLS BEARING FLOWERS.

SCHOOLS BEARING FLOWERS.

PUPILS OF THE DEAF DUMB & BLIND INSTITUTE.

CITIZENS GENERALLY.

Songs, alternating between Christian and Confederate, were sung between the five addresses, creating a "pathos which stirred to their depths the feelings of the vast auditory."

The procession to Thornrose Cemetery was the longest ever seen in Staunton, "being nearly a mile in length and supposed to number 2500 persons." Reaching the cemetery, children spread flowers across the two thousand gravesites. After the harsh divisions that had torn at Augusta County for the preceding five years, with elections, war, and privation setting people against one another, the unity among white people was cathartic. "Tottering age and tender youth united in a harmonious and heartfelt offering to our dead kindred and friends, and not forgetting the stranger, who battled shoulder to shoulder, with our loved and fallen ones, and now takes his last sleep by their side." Credit for this inaugural Confederate memorial day went "to our noble ladies, who are ever first in every good work." The next week a public letter called for a monument to Augusta's Confederate dead in the court house square.[37]

Memorialization, however, demanded more than parades, speeches, and flowers. Hard physical work had to be performed. In June, at the request of the ladies of the Cemetery Committee, the businesses of Staunton closed once again. This time, the citizens "repaired to the Cemetery with picks, hoes, spades and shovels to dig graves to receive the remains of the soldiers buried on the battlefield of Piedmont and of such others as were buried at Stribling Springs and other places in the county." Those who could not work themselves hired others to labor in their stead. "Some colored persons volunteered to assist, and many were hired." By the end of the day, the black and white men had dug enough graves to receive the remains, including one large square for the "unknown dead." "The next labor will be to disinter and have the remains of the soldiers . . . brought to the Cemetery and properly buried." Challenging and disturbing as such work must necessarily be, "the Cemetery Committee will not cease their labors till this be accomplished."[38]

The white people of Staunton took pride not only in the work they had accomplished but in the presence of black people. "The colored people did their share and worked most faithfully," the *Valley Virginian* remarked. "Prominent in the procession were the colored workmen, and if a 'radical' could have seen them, he would have changed his ideas about how the people get along together here."[39]

☆

WHILE THE PEOPLE OF Augusta County celebrated the Confederate dead, the North debated whether the people of the South had truly repented. Events in Memphis in May 1866 suggested otherwise. A letter from "a highly respectable citizen" describing those events was reprinted in the Franklin *Repository*. "The diabolical spirit which has been manifested by the rebel, negro-hating party is enough to make one ashamed of his race." The Irish police and the black men of the city had been caught in a violent spiral. When some United States Colored Troops got into a fight with police, the officers used the opportunity to launch "an indiscriminate slaughter of the blacks, especially the soldiers, wherever found. From all that I can learn, twenty-five or thirty blacks have been killed, nearly all of them without the least provocation." Women as well as men were slaughtered. "The hellish spirit manifested by many of the old rebels has been shocking in the last degree. They are only too glad to get a chance to kill a nigger. They were out on the street with revolvers in their hands, ready to kill at once."[40]

Democratic and white Southern papers portrayed the story differently. "The origins of the riots seems destined to be buried in oblivion," claimed one, "for it seems impossible, even four days after the occurrences, to trace the real cause of the disturbance." The one thing "all agree on" is that "those who engaged in the riot were persons of irresponsible character, and it will be unfair to charge these untoward disturbances to the good, law-abiding citizens of the city of Memphis." White Southerners could not be held responsible for violence in the city they governed.[41]

A congressional investigation of the so-called riot, which was actually a massacre, blamed not only the Irish policemen and their allies but also the "Rebel" press that fed their resentment and justified their violence, along with the city government of Memphis that did nothing to stop the killing. The investigation found that 46 black people (including 14 former Federal soldiers) had been killed, 75 injured, 5 raped, and 100 robbed, in addition to the 4 black churches, 12 schools, and 91 dwellings that had been destroyed. Only three white people died, none at the hands of black people.

White Northerners willing to tolerate the celebrations of the Confederate dead and reports of personal violence between former slaves and former slave owners could not so easily look past a massacre in which dozens of black people had been killed. The white South seemed incapable of, and uninterested in, instituting anything like order or justice. The Memphis bloodshed helped mobilize support for Republicans who argued that only a reassertion of military power and the complete removal of the old leadership of the South could bring about a real change in the former Confederacy.[42]

Two months later, in July 1866, another conflict broke out, this time in New Orleans. There, hundreds of white men raged in the streets after learning of a political meeting of radical whites and blacks. The death toll in New Orleans was lower than in Memphis—several dozen, including some whites—but the explicitly political nature of the riot and its brazen echo of Memphis fed the fires of Northern anger. The headlines in the Franklin *Repository* testified to the riots' meaning for the Republicans: "Rebel Massacre in New Orleans!—Most Horrible and Wanton Butchery! Over 200 Killed And Wounded! The Rebel Authorities Sustaining The Murderers! President Johnson Approves The Acts Of The Rebel Fiends!"[43]

Andrew Johnson refused to be chastened by the riots and the reaction in the North. Rather than reconsidering his tolerance of Southern white control, he decided to campaign actively for Democratic candidates in the fall state elections. In a series of rabid harangues delivered during a trip through the North, Johnson alienated many voters who might otherwise have shared his distaste for the actions and goals of the Republicans. Johnson's speaking tour, like the riots in the major cities of the South, advanced Reconstruction in ways the Radicals themselves never could.

Across the South, moreover, white people refused to support the Fourteenth Amendment and spoke defiantly against it. In Augusta, a public meeting in July proclaimed its gratitude that God had given the presidency to Andrew Johnson, who possessed "the wisdom to discern" and "the moral courage to act upon" principles of liberty and the Constitution. The people in the meeting recognized their duty to obey the laws, but could never authorize their delegates to vote for the proposed amendment. "Without passion or excitement, and with no view to disturb the order or harmony of the country," they declared it their "fixed purpose" to "decline even to consider any proposed amendments to the Constitution" until their senators and representatives had been readmitted to Congress. Reading such pronouncements, voters across the North, weary though they were of the South and its problems, voted for the Republicans.[44]

By September, it had become clear that the Republicans would carry the congressional delegation of almost every state in the North and that Reconstruction would be strengthened rather than abandoned. John B. Baldwin wrote a public letter assessing the situation. "The progress of the political canvass now going on at the North renders the complete success of the Radicals a result by no means improbable. In such an event the people of the South will have need of all the calm courage and patient endurance that can be opposed to a dominant and overwhelming majority of number and of wealth, bent upon our humiliation and destruction." The white South, absent the protection of Andrew Johnson's vetoes, "must expect and be prepared for every outrage upon our rights and feelings that greed and hate can suggest." The only hope was to remain united, for the Fourteenth Amendment could not be ratified without the support of two-thirds of the states. And that would require the South's support.[45]

The editor of the *Valley Virginian* wrote more boldly. "Suppose the negroes are, by force, endowed with all the privileges of freeborn white men; suppose the Radicals carry the day." What then? "If forced to meet the issue of practical negro suffrage, we can meet it and control it, as we have always controlled the negro element among us. And, while utterly and forever refusing to accept the principles, or endorse in any way, shape, or form, the proposed amendment, let us prepare for the worst and look the future steadily and calmly in the face."[46]

In the elections of early October the Republicans won by 200 votes in Franklin—a large margin in the closely contested county—and all across the North. The Democrats admitted that the gist "of the whole story is that for the next three years the Radicals will have complete control of the legislation in the House of Representatives, and of that in the Senate for a longer period." The Democrats hoped that the Republicans "will manifest more regard for the real interests of the country, irrespective of their party, than they have done in the past. But we fear that this hope will prove vain."[47]

The Republicans proclaimed their sweeping victory "the solemn, deliberate decree of the PEOPLE, asserting their supreme power in opposition to perfidy in the highest places within their gift. By an aggregate popular majority of nearly HALF A MILLION have the loyal States declared against the policy of Andrew Johnson, and in favor of the policy of Congress as defined in the proposed amendments to the constitution."[48]

The provisions of the Fourteenth Amendment, the *Repository* pointed out, were "designed to restore the Union with the least possible inconvenience to the people of the South and with the fewest possible restraints consistent with the peace and security of the Government. They were dictated by considerations of mercy as well as expediency." If the white South would not "consent to the disfranchisement of her leading, active Rebels," then "the nation will require of her the complete disenthrallment of the millions of loyal black men scattered throughout her borders and their elevation to all the rights and privileges of citizenship." The change in Republican policy would not offer less magnanimity but more—to the freed people rather than to the former rebels. "The effect will be to raise all men up rather than drag any down." The message, and the possibility, were clear: "If the South shall longer persist in her refusal to accept the terms offered, let us take advantage of her refusal, and rebuild the nation's walls on the sure foundation of equal rights." And south-central Pennsylvania's Thaddeus Stevens stood as "the one man who towered over all in marshaling the forces of Freedom and maintaining its holy citadel inviolate."[49]

The Democrats of the North called the upcoming session the "Congress of Madmen." The white South steeled itself for what the Republicans might do. "The brutal course of the radicals has made the South a unit in the belief—that we were right, and that is a great point gained," proclaimed an Augusta paper. "The foolish hopes of representation, encouraged by the over sanguine, have faded away—and a united and harmonious people have gone bravely to work, with a settled determination to build up their shattered fortunes, and in spite of everything, be the people a just God intended them to be." As in secession, the white people of Augusta submitted to a history that seemed to be overwhelming them, taking solace in unity as they anticipated defeat, believing themselves more righteous as a result of their loss.[50]

☆

THE BLACK RESIDENTS of Augusta and the Freedmen's Bureau worked to create schools from the first days of freedom in the summer of 1865. The American Missionary Association of Albany, New York, recruited teachers to come south to teach the freedpeople, and the women and men they sent taught with energy and devotion. To black people for whom literacy had been illegal only months before, the coming of schools seemed among the greatest gifts of freedom.

Some of the most heartening scenes of the early days of freedom played out in the schools. "I have a House all ready to receive your Teachers + should be glad if you could forward two besides Mrs Dunn or Miss McLeune as there is plenty of work for them to do and I will strive hard to see that neither the Educational or Missionary interest of your Teachers suffer in Staunton," Frederick Tukey wrote from the Freedmen's Bureau office in October 1865. He requested readers, spellers, geographies, pencils, pens, outline maps, and song books.[51]

Tukey later requested a male teacher as well, and John Scott arrived. A devoted white New England man in his twenties, Scott threw himself into the work. "It is Saturday night and I am very weary," he wrote in November 1865. "Our school commenced night before last and we had two rooms full. The first 3 days of the week we spent in hunting for rooms in which to teach, the people being bound to keep us out." By "the people," Scott meant the white people of Staunton. While the town prided itself on its excellent private academies for white boys and girls, it, like the rest of Virginia, had not supported public schools before the Civil War. The idea of a government agency and a Northern philanthropy teaching black students seemed both a reproach and a threat to local whites. Despite such obstacles, Scott reported, "Last night we had three rooms open and full. To day I have been at work fiting up the fourth room ready for Monday. The four will hold at least 200."

Scott told his Northern friends that "we get frequent sneers, but good treatment to the face." He was frustrated that the white members of a church "have shut the colored People out of a church which they helped to build and own 1/2 of it," though he hoped they would "allow them to occupy their own church if they will have a white leader." Despite such problems, Scott reassured his supporters that "I love my work. The books have come that you sent." On his way to "a colored Prayer Meeting here this eve," and needing to hurry, Scott ended his letter with "God Bless you."[52]

Miss C. E. Dewey, a teacher sent to Staunton to work alongside Scott, had been told by parents that "we hear of very many who intend to send after Christmas, whose children are hired out till then. We have new scholars every day." Though the school had been in session only a few weeks, "I can see an astonishing progress in the acquirements of the children." At the outset, the children were just learning their letters and now several were already reading. "The children are generally orderly, quiet and obedient." She had worried about one boy, "who is a constant subject of ridicule to the school, but by placing him by himself + trusting him while I reprove the school for laughing at his particularities, he has proved one of my best children."

The night schools conducted by the teachers "seem even more important than our day schools. The majority are under twenty years of age," kept out of day school by the "necessity of labor." The rooms "are crowded every night, many standing or sitting on the floor all evening rather than lose the instruction of one evening." Dewey found some local white allies, two women and a man, plus a soldier, who "have offered their assistance in the night school." Though "not trained to the business" of teaching, they "have commenced teaching with pretty good success."[53]

Although the American Missionary Association attempted to supply the teachers and the materials they needed, the organization found itself overwhelmed by the demand. They were grateful for the support of Frederick Tukey of the Freedmen's Bureau, who supplied the teachers with room and board at his own expense. An association official, in fact, wrote that Tukey "has done and is doing more for the schools than any Bureau Supt I know of." The search for decent facilities and equipment preoccupied both the superintendent and the teachers.

Everyday items mattered a great deal. Meeting in the basement of an African-American church, the classes desperately needed lamps. When lamps did arrive, they were the wrong kind and the students had to write by candles. Scott made jokes about "a brighter day coming" and "we must have light!," but despaired of trying to teach dozens of students in a dark, cold basement. Frustrated, he rather boldly challenged his supervisor to "extinguish the gas in your office at night, or in your parlor, and there for the next week do your business, or engage in social employment at these places by the dim light of a tallow candle and that without a sconse, or holder, and call upon your friends to do the same, and then think of me and 200 others who can sympathise with you." Scott begged for books of religious instruction for Sunday school: he dreaded having to "stand before 100 children next Sunday and watch their disappointment, and see them waste sacred time especially precious to them by mere reading a school book."[54]

Scott judged that by the end of 1865 "the whites here have little faith about ever making anything of a 'nigger' but they are growing more and more used to us and our schools and I think are generally in favor of trying to educate them." As the Federal soldiers left, though, Scott was not sorry to see them leave. "I am glad this drunken set are going," for their "influence is bad."[55]

The young teacher waited anxiously for a box of donated

clothes for the freedmen. "Even 2 or 3 barrels of clothing would be of great use." They most needed clothes for their children, especially shoes. Although Scott believed it was "better for the freedmen to help themselves where they can," he was troubled by cases "of extreme destitution, mostly among children many of whom have lost one or both parents. I know of some 30 children who are shoeless and otherwise very thinly clad." Scott and his fellow teachers had "tried to fix up some of these children with a few remnants," but "it amounts to very little."[56]

As the teachers settled in, they saw progress. Miss Dewey reported that she had arrived at class several mornings to "find my children all in their seats, either studying or with folded hands + as quiet + orderly as if I had been present. I asked them one day who had told them to get in order thinking Mr Scott might have been up stairs, but they replied quite proudly 'Nobody! We's got ourselves in order.'" Dewey admitted that her job was easier because "my scholars as you will see number among them very few boys + of course are much easier to govern than Miss Williams department which is entirely without the civilizing influence of the gentler sex." One freedwoman walked six miles to school and back every day, and was never late. "She is much interested in her book and told me she would be willing to walk twice as far for the privilege of learning." Though "the novelty has worn off," the students "are improving very fast and do not seem to lose their interest in school." For herself, Dewey wrote, with some surprise, "that I love my work, as well as my people, far better than I did when we began."

Dewey and her fellow teachers did not forget their missionary motivations. "I think I can detect signs of special religious interest here. I have had conversations of a personal character with several and found their hearts very tender and some really in earnest in seeking the Saviour." Dewey judged that "the morals of these people, like the colored race everywhere, are much worse than their religion and whenever I have an opportunity I give advice on this subject." The teacher was relieved to report that "though we are without military protection we have had no trouble and I think the feeling toward 'Nigger Teachers,' the little which we have the honor to receive, grows less bitter every day." Some white ladies had been solicitous and "have even taken the trouble to write excuses when they were obliged to keep their hired people out of school."[57]

John Scott despaired when a trusted supervisor had been removed from the Valley because the schools there "were not as promising in other places." Scott could see important progress in Augusta County. "Children are being brought within range of school influence as fast as they can be." Parents paid others to board their children or moved their families to places with schools. Staunton belied the judgment of the central office about the schools in the Valley. "I have been connected with schools at the north for about 10 years, and have seen as many schools as most men my age, and studied them as carefully; and a more promising school than this I never saw, and do not believe such could exist in the nature of circumstances." Scott tried to convey the inspiration of what he saw. About a third of the 434 students in Staunton were young adult men and women. "When warm weather comes many a barefoot will step out of the cabin and in to the school room to enjoy the same blessing that the older brother and sister have during the cold weather."

Scott could see the positive effects of the schools far beyond the schools themselves. "Behold 400 colored persons passing quietly through the streets, treating whites with civility, performing school requirements with military exactness." Many of them attended Sunday School, all dressed as well as they could. "Compare this state of things with what it was 4 months ago when there was no school. Could a more noisy set of rowdies be found than these boys They were idle ignorant and vile." Those boys were "often insulting the white citizens with taunts, feeling the Yankee bayonets would protect them." They knew nothing about the sacred meaning of Sunday "and many of the children looked as much like young monkeys from the rill swamp of Bengal as like human beings." What had these children learned since? Not only to write but also that the world turns around and the location of countries. Some could now begin to add, subtract, and even multiply. "Has heaven blessed another field under your race more or even as much?"[58]

Despite his impassioned defense of the Valley and of the deportment of his students, in April 1866 John Scott suddenly found himself at the center of public controversy in Staunton. "Sunday morning our citizens were shocked and disgusted by an exhibition one John Scott, from Waterbury, Conn., a teacher in the Freedmen's School, made of himself, by escorting a negro girl down New Street," the *Valley Virginian* sputtered in an article titled "Miscegenation in Staunton." "On coming down the street white persons 'hissed' this creature, Scott; soon afterwards, the girl came back by herself, and the coloured people, collected on Crawford's corner, 'hissed' her. She had evidently disgraced herself in their eyes, by associating with this fellow, and we agree with them."

The paper called on the superintendent of the Freedmen's Bureau in Staunton to take action. He "owes it to himself; to the ladies who teach in the School, as well as to this community, to discharge this disciple of Miscegenation at once." As for John Scott, "If he wants to marry the negro, let him do so, if he is willing; and speedily emigrate to Liberia or some congenial clime, where, to his heart's content, he can dwell in the sweet embrace of the 'negro de l' Afrique.' He don't suit this country."[59]

The Staunton *Vindicator* quickly trumped the ugly language of its competitor. "A man calling himself Scott and hailing from the land of wooden nutmegs and white oak hams, who 'teaches the young African idea how to shoot' in these parts, undertook on Sunday morning last, to give the young men of Staunton a lesson in gallantry." The *Vindicator* described the exact offense: "With a brazen effrontery he played the gay gallant to his sable companion, at the crossings giving her the inside of the pavement, while the negress seemed ashamed of herself, and, at one or two stages of their walk, hesitated to proceed." The paper ended its account with the same allusions to interracial sex as the other account. "We do not care how much Mr. Scott fraternizes with negro wenches, if his taste runs in that line, but we advise him that such violations of public decency and decorum, as was exhibited by him on Sunday last, shall not go unscathed in this community, as long as we are permitted the free use of our pen."[60]

The young Yankee teacher wrote a polite public response, referring to himself in the plural. "At the close of Sabbath School, a pupil, wishing to obtain a hymn book, was told, that those for sale were at our house." Scott set out to get a book and she set out beside him. "We thought of asking her to walk behind, lest we might be misrepresented. But the thought that she was, as we supposed, known to be a pupil, and that we were going nowhere else than from School home, and that it was known that our business brings us necessarily into contact with these people, more than it does citizens, would, we thought, save us from being misunderstood in our motives." Scott, after his formal language, sarcastically noted that "as to 'Miscegenation in Staunton' we will not deny so plain a fact; but do most emphatically deny being a 'Disciple' ourselves, as no man can be more opposed to the doctrine than we are, and have ever been." Scott suggested, in other words, what abolitionists had long pointed out: the mixing of the races was far more the result of the behavior of white Southern men than Northern ones.[61]

Frederick Tukey came to Scott's defense. The *Vindicator* did not feel obligated to publish Tukey's letter, but since he "has shown a disposition to act with fairness to our people" they deigned to print it. Tukey's case rested on the assertion that "a large number of the intelligent, reflecting portion of the community" would have behaved as Scott did. Tukey even suggested that "had the Editor himself been placed in the same circumstances, he would have done precisely as the Teacher did; that is, allow a colored woman who had called on him on business, to walk with him to his office." The *Vindicator* editor denied that he would have done as Scott did, which would have cost "an utter abnegation of self and self-respect, and a total disregard of the feelings and sentiments of the community at large."[62]

Out of such issues of politesse and etiquette, with threats of violence and sexual innuendo, did the white South draw the boundaries of the new order. With the omnipresent and all-inclusive boundaries of slavery erased, white Southerners slid into crude, vicious, and contemptuous language to justify their actions.

☆

AS FORMER SLAVE OWNERS and Confederates jostled with Freedmen's Bureau agents and white Northern teachers over the future of black people, the black residents of Augusta County did not have many opportunities to speak for themselves. White people imagined, and wished, thoughts and words for the African-Americans among whom they lived. Those white people generally told themselves what they wanted to believe.

A lacerating letter in October 1866 from an African-American man to General John M. Schofield showed the limits of white understanding, whether by native Southerners or the Northern people at work among them. "Living within your military department, I am forced to appeal to you in my own behalf. My case and cause are those of thousands and just as I am effected they will be effected also. There is a deep laid organization here that governs and controls every thing by might in defiance of truth and justice." Irwin charged that on "even the least pretense a black man is taken up and imprisoned. His color is his condemnation, and every lawless act committed he is accused of. At present my brethren are living in a reign of terror and many of them are locked up in Staunton Gaol."

Irwin described a recent event in Augusta, in which a "theft has been committed here by one or two black men and lo! four are taken up and all of us are accused. Some of us had to fly, who were and are as innocent of the crime as you are." The body that was to protect them was useless, for "the Freedmen's bureau is ineffective, laughed at and despised." A trial for these men would be held in a few weeks, and "we cannot expect justice unless the strong arm of military protection is reached out to us."

The moral was clear and painful. "We gave to the rich white man our best years, our strength, our youth, our sweat, and now that we are free, we get in return meaness, tyranny and injustice." Some of the black men of Augusta live "in a state of perpetual terror. If you turn your back on us, who can we appeal to." They were content to be "judged impartially by the laws, but let us not be condemned without a cause. From this depth of degradation we look to you, and in the name of suffering humanity, I trust I do not write in vain."[63]

To the credit of the United States Army and the Freedmen's Bureau, officers looked into the matter promptly. The men had been tried before a magistrate in Augusta, with Frederick Tukey representing the Freedmen's Bureau and Alexander H. H. Stuart representing the accused. According to the inquiry, most of the evidence against the men came from other freedpeople. They had been committed to jail and awaited the Circuit Court. The author of the report thought that the guilt of the men was "quite evident" and he did not think they should be cleared of the charge. The officer also thought, however, that though the "reign of terror" charge might be "overdrawn," it was clear that "there is more foundation for the assertion than there should be. A black man, to live peaceably must be very careful." The danger came because "the whites seem very jealous of them, and any show of impertinence or independence, in so many instances leads to blows on the parts of the whites." Those white people of Augusta "say a Colored man must keep his place, and not be setting himself up as a rival to the white." As a result, "the Colored people generally submit quietly, as resistance, they are well aware, is perfectly useless."[64]

Nelson Irwin did not appear in any newspaper account of the Circuit Court's proceedings in the coming months. Two black men were convicted of housebreaking and perhaps that was the crime to which he referred. Perhaps Alexander H. H. Stuart, one of the most successful lawyers in the county, was able to get Irwin released. In any case, the black man's eloquence testified to the profound injustice that filled the apparently peaceful Valley. White people were enforcing their newly drawn boundaries with law, intimidation, and violence.

The twenty months since Appomattox had witnessed the

beginning of the deepest transformation in American history. Black and white people in the South had to learn new ways to live together, even as the legal and political atmosphere changed almost weekly. Nearly two years after the end of slavery, the shape of freedom had not yet been defined. That definition would come with startling speed over the next eighteen months.

We Must Be One People

January 1867 through July 1869

*T*he United States remained in turmoil in April 1867, two years after Appomattox. The healing everyone hoped for had instead festered, the wounds of loss infected with accusations of betrayal. Northern Republicans attacked white Southerners for refusing to admit sin as well as defeat, while Northern Democrats attacked Republicans for refusing to accept the end of the war as victory enough over the Confederacy. White Southerners raged at Northern Republicans for supposedly reneging on the terms of reunion that Ulysses S. Grant had offered at Appomattox. Former masters alternately lectured, patronized, bargained with, threatened, and assaulted the formerly enslaved people among whom they lived. Black Southerners were hopeful and yet wary of all white people, for they had seen loyalties and priorities shift many times over the years since 1860.

The Repository, the Republican paper of Franklin County, admitted at the beginning of 1867 "that after two years of earnest effort, no common platform for the restoration of the rebellious States has been harmoniously devised." Proposals came forward from fellow Pennsylvanian Thaddeus Stevens, but "one portion of the House resisted it because it was too radi-

cal, others opposed it with equal earnestness" because it was too generous to the former Confederates and so the proposals for a coherent reconstruction failed. The Republicans admitted that "the longer this question is delayed, the more difficult will be its solution." If another year passed, "the struggle will be protracted beyond another Presidential election, with treason steadily growing more and more defiant and the breach between the two sections still widening." The Republicans had to find a way to enact a plan and Southern whites felt they had to find a way to stop it.[1]

Staunton's Vindicator *warned that the long delays by the Republicans had "driven the nation further and further from the prospect of quick reconciliation." With no plan for reconstruction, every action of the Republican-dominated Congress "has tended, if it was not designed to, widen the breach between the North and South, and render final re-construction more hopeless—to foment sectional discord, and especially to intensify the already embittered feelings of the Northern people, against the crushed and desolated South." A tremendous opportunity had been lost. "The readiness and unanimity with which the South surrendered the great cause of our quarrel—African slavery—the great efforts she has made in her extreme poverty, to pay the heavy federal taxes—her ready submission to everything that has been required of her, short of degradation, proves the sincerity of her desire for re-construction." If Congress had only followed the example of Andrew Johnson, who in turn was following the example of Abraham Lincoln, "what a glorious nation this then would have been!"*

That moment having passed, now white Southerners begged the "honest and virtuous masses of the North to come to our aid, and arrest the wild career of partisan passion and hatred, which seems to bear away in Washington." The South appealed to white Northerners' "ancient affections—to the kindred blood that flows in their veins, and the many bonds of common interest that should bind us together. We appeal to their magnanimity, as brave conquerors dealing with a brave and but prostrate foe. We appeal to their self-interest. We must be one people."[2]

In March 1867, just as its congressional session was running out of time, the Republicans passed the first of what would be four Military Reconstruction Acts and overrode, on the same day it was issued, Andrew Johnson's veto. The act divided the ten states of the former Confederacy (Tennessee had already been readmitted) into five districts under military control until they held elections for delegates to conventions to write new constitutions that ratified the Fourteenth Amendment and provided for black male voting. African-American men would be allowed to vote for those delegates and to serve as delegates; former Confederate leaders would not. When those conventions had created new constitutions, the states could apply to Congress for readmission under their own civil governments.

☆

AUGUSTA COUNTY MIGHT HAVE expected to follow a relatively smooth path through Reconstruction. The county had been steadfastly Unionist before the war, its former Whig leadership desperately trying to hold the nation together to the very edge of secession. Those same officials had then become leaders within the Confederacy, giving them credibility with white voters, unlike the tiny minority of men who sided with the United States throughout the war. Those former Whigs and former Confederates could counsel reconciliation and people might listen.

The white people of Augusta also expected to be able to control the black population of the county. Without the strength that came from large numbers, African-Americans in Augusta might, whites hoped, listen to messages that mixed sentimentality with threat. Instead, like their counterparts across the South, black people in Augusta followed their own minds and their own leaders.

As before and during the Civil War, Augusta showed that the experience of slavery cut across the contours of geography, demography, and cash crop. Enslaved people in Augusta shared the same threats and challenges as areas that were majority black or that grew cotton on large plantations. White people displayed the same fears and determination. Proximity to the Mason-Dixon Line did not dilute the power of slavery or its many legacies.

The *Valley Virginian* denounced the Military Reconstruction Act but did so, it knew, fruitlessly. "Never did the Southern people need all their native manhood; all their pride of character so much as now. And their course is simple. We must endure the evils inflicted on us by a base and cowardly foe, and work out of our troubles." The only bright spot for Virginia was that the First Military District would be commanded by General John C. Schofield, whose orders conveyed the sense "that he is performing a disagreeable though obligatory duty." Schofield, only thirty-six years old and from upstate New York, had graduated from West Point and had risen steadily in responsibility. The first impression he created as commander of Virginia proved to be accurate: Schofield had doubts about the reconstruction process he oversaw and would conciliate the white South as much as possible.[3]

Word arrived in Augusta almost immediately after the passage of the first act in March that the Loyal Political Society, "an association of negroes," was mobilizing to "send lecturers throughout the State to inform the negroes in regard to their newly acquired privileges and for whom they should vote." White Southerners knew what to expect: "these lecturers will endeavor to poison the minds of the negroes against their only friends, the whites of the South." The sole antidote to the poison was for the white people "in every community, who have the greatest influence with the colored class, to call them together and explain carefully and truthfully the situation in which they are placed." Those local white leaders should instruct the new black voters on "the

Cartoon warning of the consequences of the
Virginia Constitutional Convention, 1867

course they should pursue, which leads to no conflict with, but will retain the friendship of their white friends of the South, with whom their lot is inevitably cast, and upon whom they are certainly dependent."[4]

The meaning of the new Reconstruction Act immediately became clear in Staunton. Two weeks after its passage, four hundred freedmen and two hundred white men filled the Augusta County Court House for a meeting on a Saturday evening in April. "For the first time since the war our people fully realized the immense political revolution that has been forced upon the country," editor W. H. Lynn of the *Vindicator*—elected secretary of the meeting—noted in his detailed and surprisingly supportive transcription of the proceedings. The editors of the other two Staunton papers were in attendance as well. "All classes were represented, and the best order prevailed during the meeting." A freedman, Philip Roselle, "was unanimously elected chairman and took the Judge's seat, where he presided with a dignity and decorum that seemed, almost, to make the portrait of Chief Justice Marshall, just above him, smile with satisfaction!"

The freedmen had invited General John Echols to speak with them. A Staunton native and Harvard graduate who had fought with Stonewall Jackson and then throughout the rest of the war, Echols by 1867 led a successful law practice in town. An imposing physical figure, Echols did not flatter his black listeners. He had been disenfranchised for his role with the Confederacy and wanted no office from his audience, so he would tell them the truth. "The history of the world gives us no record of a change so monstrous and so sudden—a few years ago 4,000,000 colored people had no political rights—now the position is changed, the result of a long, bloody and disastrous war has changed you from slave to freemen," Echols marveled before the silent audience. "You stand under the law as free, personally and politically, as the white man of every condition of society!" Echols explained the provisions of the new law and then lectured his black audience. He warned that they "would be told that the Northern people emancipated them, and that they should be grateful to them, and should vote with the Radicals." This was a lie, for "it was not the purpose of the Northern people to emancipate them—for three years after the war commenced the intention was not to do so, but the natural drifting of the war brought it about whether they desired it or not."

No matter how it came, freedom had arrived, and now, remarkably, the vote. Echols spoke as if he were "a colored man and advise you as such. Don't mingle up with any party as a body, for that will be no profit to you. Don't go as a class with the radicals for that makes a gulf deep and wide between you and your own people, and don't let it be said that you, as a class, are arrayed against the whites as a class." If the black men built up a radical party against the white majority of Virginia, they must acknowledge that the whites would have "every advantage in the contest." Echols told the black men sitting before him to "let each one think and act for himself as a freeman should. Every tub should stand on its own bottom. Don't act like a flock of sheep."

Echols, like other white Southerners talking to black people, abruptly pivoted to sentimentality when he thought it might be helpful. "Have you no love for those with whom you have been raised?" he asked. Echols professed his own "warmest affection for his servant boy and for the old colored woman who nursed him." The editor transcribing the speech thought the general "beautifully alluded to the ties which should bind the whites and blacks of the South together, in words that brought tears to many eyes."

General Echols ended on a sterner note, warning against confiscation of property, "which would be a ruin to all, white and black." Asked whether "any honest colored man" would want the forty acres of which some had spoken, the audience heard "a very weak 'yes' from a back corner, whereupon a respectable colored man informed the house he was happy to say that man didn't belong to his community." The general, after counseling "honesty, sobriety, and purity of life," encouraged education, work, and saving. He ended with a strange amalgam of encouragement and apocalyptic warning: "Take the course I have pointed out and you have it in your power to give an illustration of the regeneration of a race, such as the world never saw, and prosperity, and the highest position may be yours. Follow any other, allow yourselves to be led astray; give way to feelings of bitterness and hatred and I can see but one fate for you—DESTRUCTION."

Following General Echols, loud calls echoed in the court house for a number of black speakers. Each of the four men called upon to speak had been enslaved and had gone before the Freedmen's Bureau the year before to declare their marriages under slavery. Benjamin Downey was married to Frances Ware and they had nine children; he had been born in Augusta, she in Washington, D.C. Henry Davenport was married to Lucynda Lett. He was a gardener, born in Augusta, and she was from nearby Rockingham; they had no children listed. James Scott was married to Esther Crawford, both from Augusta County, and they had two children. Philip Roselle was married to Fanny Jones. He was a butcher, born in Augusta; she was also a native and they had four children. All four men lived in Staunton. Unlike many other counties in Virginia and in the South, previously enslaved men rather than men who had been free before led the campaign for political rights in Augusta.

Henry Davenport, for his part, "was happy to say the day had come for the first time for the colored and white man to meet together upon equal terms. God help us to live together as brethren! My brethren, my fellow-citizens, my fellow-travelers to the bar of God, with a warm heart and a welcome hand I greet you." Davenport could barely believe that "the day is come, when the white man and the black can meet at the County seat, on such conditions, when we are called up to the mountain top."

The Reverend James Scott, identified as a "colored local preacher," politely dissented from General Echols. The former Confederate had "related pretty fables," which brought to mind one of Scott's own, that of the boys and the frogs. That fable told of boys who threw rocks into a pond, trying to make them skim on the surface, their fun thoughtlessly killing innocent frogs. One of the oldest and bravest frogs lifted his head out of the water and cried out—"please, boys, stop—what is sport to you is death to us." Black people's very lives, Scott conveyed in the allegory, depended on the political games played by white men. His analogy was met with "Loud Applause."

Scott offered another metaphor as well: he "had always heard it was right to 'praise the bridge that carried you over safely,'" and that bridge was the Republican party. Scott pronounced himself completely "for the party that made him free." Everyone knew that "actions speak louder than words" and the "Republicans had acted as our friends." People knew who their friends were—"even his dog knew his friends." Scott had "no hard feelings against the whites—he had been raised up kindly and treated as one of the family, but he was for his rights—his friends politically." Scott's bold endorsement of the Republicans and his clever turns of phrase were met with "Great Applause and Laughter."

Benjamin Downey, also a minister, appreciated General Echols's words, given in the "most beautiful figures. Nevertheless, we are men, as he says, and we must look at which is best." Downey said that "he knew the black man well, but not the white man, though he had lived with him 61 years." Those white men did not seem to want to know Downey, for they "never talked politics before him or tried to teach him, more than enough for their own profit." Downey had "no prejudice against our white people. Some are kind, some not," but he asked a pointed question that must have occurred to many of the African-American men present: "Why did the Southern people wait so long before becoming such good friends?" Downey wished he had understood the subtleties of General Echols's argument more clearly, but the "white folks, South, never taught them A. B. C.—the Yankees did." The Reverend Downey reminded his listeners, black and white, that "the Radical party has made great sacrifices for us, to give us knowledge of the Living God; by coming from comfortable homes North, to teach us."

The Reverend Downey thought the local white people, who claimed to know black people so well, were "not as thankful as they ought to have been to the nigger for taking care of their families whilst they were in the war." If it had been the duty of black people to care for whites during the war, a duty they fulfilled, Downey asked, "was it not the duty, of the whites when they came back to do something for this faithful race; to at least help to educate them? But they didn't. They said the nigger didn't know anything—let him go—the Yankees freed him, let them feed him &c." Downey admitted that "there had been enough said, more than he could take in at once, and he didn't believe many white men could either. Let all think over what they had heard and pray God to give them consciences to act right, in friendship and love to all."

Philip Roselle, the chairman of the meeting, "being loudly called for," pronounced that "he did not care who set him free," for "he believed it was accidentally done anyway, didn't think either party intended it, and he was for making the best of it." The question was who was going to help him now. Roselle, in slavery, had "belonged to people who knew he would not let him be imposed on, by white or black, and that made him feel himself." Now, white "men who never owned a 'nigger,' who would not have owned one had slavery lasted 100 years, cursed them on the streets—gentlemen never did." White men had threatened "to knock him on the head for going to the Richmond Convention" of freedpeople, but Roselle "reckons they were only fooling, as nobody had hit him yet." As for confiscation of Confederate property, Roselle claimed that he did not believe in general confiscation, but slyly offered to take a slice of the land of

Mr. Michael Harman, "as he belonged to and worked for him a number of years." Roselle was selected as a delegate to a gathering in Richmond to prepare for the constitutional convention, along with the Reverend N. C. Brackett, the Northern-born white superintendent of the freedmen's schools in the Valley, who rented a house in Staunton.[5]

The Staunton meeting adjourned "amid cheers and much laughter, but a general appearance of good feeling," the genial reporter of the *Valley Virginian* concluded. A reporter from the *Spectator* admitted that "the drift of the feelings of the freedmen was clearly exhibited, as every Radical sentiment expressed by any of their speakers was applauded to the echo," but reported that "the meeting was highly enjoyed by all present. The happy hits made by the colored speakers were greatly enjoyed by the whites." The editor noted that "the tone of all the speakers was friendly with the exception of James Scott. The tone of his voice, which cannot be disguised, betrayed embittered feelings towards the Southern people." Another paper praised the "conservative" tone of the remarks of the black people at the meeting, ignoring what the reporters themselves witnessed and transcribed.[6]

None of the white editors commented on the resolutions passed by the meeting. Those resolutions told anything but a conservative story. The African-American men in attendance resolved their "grateful thanks" to the "gallant armies of the United States," and held in "reverent remembrance the memories of those who fell in the cause of freedom, and especially, of Abraham Lincoln." The black men of Augusta expressed their "profound gratitude" to the Congress that had forged Reconstruction and declared their desire to "seek affiliation" with the party. They demanded that all elections employ a secret ballot, "that no man shall be ineligible to office by reason of sect or color," that they be admitted to jury lists, that whipping and maiming be prohibited, and that taxes be fairly assigned. The convention called for "extraordinary State provision for the free education of the young of all classes."[7]

To promote and protect these purposes, the black men in Staunton voted to "unite as one man in support of those candidates whose nominations are ratified at mass meetings." They deprecated "the attempt, wherever or however made, to deter us from the free and untrammeled exercise of the franchise." They would "look with contempt upon any who are willing to sell this dear bought right for 'a mess of pottage.'" They would ignore the pleas and threats of their former masters and maintain their solidarity with one another.[8]

The *Spectator* printed the demands and resolutions, and warned black men against acting on them. If, as the white editor doubted, his black neighbors understood and agreed with these pronouncements, they were embarking upon "folly approximating madness." The threat was direct: "The whites have the advantages of numbers, of capital and property, of intelligence and education. The whites constitute the employing, and the blacks the employed class." If the blacks insisted on a unified opposition to the whites, as the resolutions declared, "the whites will unite against them. Then the weaker party would be pushed to the wall, and the blacks would repent of their mad folly when too late to repair it."[9]

The Staunton paper, even as it issued warnings to black men, told white readers that they should not judge too harshly the black men who attended the meeting. "Great allowances should be made for them. They are ignorant and credulous." Surely, the editor thought, Augusta's black people "have no ill will to those who have shown them only kindness throughout their lives." The white people of the county should have sincere conversations with the black people they knew, explaining that Southern whites had nothing to do with bringing black people into slavery "from the wilds of Africa"; the transatlantic slave trade had been the work of New England. The black people of Augusta had become free only through "the exigencies" of war, not through the intention of the Yankees. The freedpeople should know that the Republicans held "no desire to see them awarded justice," but simply that "the power and spoils might remain in the hands of the Radical leaders," no crumb of which will go "to those who wear dusky skins." Out of such arguments did white men expect to persuade black people whom they had owned.[10]

Soon after the March meeting in the Augusta Court House, men of both races were required to register to vote for delegates to the constitutional convention to be held in Richmond that fall. White men debated whether to register or vote at all; they might demonstrate their contempt by refusing to participate. Though Virginia held a large white majority, everyone knew that "every colored man will register," in part because the head of the Freedmen's Bureau in Virginia issued a circular letter instructing the officers of the Bureau to do all in their power to assure that black men did so. In response, the newspapers urged white men to register as well, "for results transcendently important depend upon it." The *Spectator* warned that "if the Anglo-Saxon element is to retain its fair share of political power, it must display that energy and courage which have heretofore marked that race from the days of Hastings down to Appomattox Court House."[11]

The freedpeople and their white allies met at the court house again in July. About two hundred black men and fifty white men gathered in Staunton, with the black men dominating. After introductory comments by two white attendees, offering the usual counsel of caution, Philip Roselle was "loudly called." Roselle, as in his remarks in March, conveyed a great sense of self-confidence and great skepticism of white people, North and South. He denounced those, including the editors of the newspapers of Staunton, who referred to black people as "niggers." He also said, with dangerous allusions to interracial sex, that though "some white folks despise the colored people," the "greatest fault he found was that they loved them too well. If you didn't believe it go to the colored schools and look at the complexion."

Thomas Jackson, the current Freedmen's Bureau agent for Staunton, told the group that only one question should determine who they supported in the coming election: loyalty or disloyalty. Could a white man who had supported the Confederacy be expected to support the interests of the people freed by the war? True loyalty could easily be determined: "go back a few years, trace a man up, and know who was loyal and who was not."

The Freedmen's Bureau agent apparently miscalculated. While Jackson said he did not want to lecture his black audience, he did tell them that it was not a good idea for the freedmen to have "so many meetings," for "every meeting meant the loss of a day's work." The white editor of the *Valley Virginian* thought that Jackson's speech did not go down well with the freedmen. "They seemed to think he talked to them like a man who owned them and whom they were bound to obey, if we could judge by the remarks around us. One or two said, 'Its no man's business how many meetings the Freedmen hold.'" The meeting expressed its enthusiastic support for Reconstruction and named three white men and two black to attend the Republican convention in August.[12]

As the election for delegates to Virginia's constitutional convention drew closer, anxious whites tried to steady their own nerves. They warned their black neighbors not to vote. With black men pulled between the Radicals and local white conservatives, "we tell you, honestly, there is but one course to pursue. It is the same you pursued during the war. Work and let white people settle this question—don't vote at all." If black people did not want to be exterminated by the whites as the American Indians had been—"once upon a time, the Indians, over a thousand to one, made war upon the whites, and where are they?", an editor rhetorically asked—black people's "only escape" was to make themselves "the best body of laborers in the world." They should hold on to their registration but not vote. "The fruit is very tempting, but you had better throw yourself on the generosity of the whites, and wait until it is fully ripe." [13]

In the meantime, Southerners looked to the North, where many states were holding their own elections, to gauge the momentum behind or against Reconstruction there.

☆

THE DEMOCRATS OF PENNSYLVANIA proclaimed their opposition to Reconstruction for what it was doing to both the South and the North. The Democratic platform for the upcoming state elections of the fall of 1867 charged that the "Radical majority in Congress" had "dismembered the Federal Union and subverted republican government by a long series of usurpations." The *Valley Spirit* connected the self-interest of Pennsylvania voters with sympathy for the white people of the South. "With a debt of three thousand millions hanging over the country and an exhausted treasury unable to pay the interest as it falls due, Congress continues to rob the people of their hard earnings by recklessly appropriating large sums of money to keep up an expensive military establishment in the South, in order to perpetuate the Radical party in power." Reconstruction was constitutionally wrong, racially dangerous, and irresponsibly expensive. "All this enormous drain upon the treasury could be saved if the Southern people were permitted to govern themselves and defray the expenses of their own government, as they are willing and anxious to do, but this would not answer the selfish and ambitious ends of these Radical traitors."[14]

The Republicans agreed that the upcoming state and congressional elections would turn around Reconstruction. "The issue, as we understand it, is whether this Union of ours, shattered and broken by a wicked rebellion, is in its reconstruction to be fashioned into a perfect Republic wherein all men shall be free," the Republicans proclaimed, a union where "all men shall be entitled to the same right and privileges of citizenship." The alternative, offered by the Democrats, was a Union that would be merely "a re-cast of the old, in which all its flaws and imperfections" would be even more unsightly.[15]

The elections of 1867 for congressional and state seats across the North and West tested the support of voters for Reconstruction. The Democrats of Pennsylvania claimed a strong victory six months after the Republicans passed the Reconstruction act. In Franklin County, the Democrats bragged, we "have substituted a Democratic majority of 189 for last year's Radical majority of 19. We have elected our whole county ticket." For many years, "Franklin county has been under the thralldom of Republicanism. It is refreshing therefore to hear her speak, and speak in such emphatic tones, in favor of conservatism." Indeed, the entire state "has thundered her denunciations of the Radical Congress." The voters of Pennsylvania determined "to quench the unnatural thirst for vengeance, and to proffer the hand of friendship to submissive and penitent rebels." They had declared that "the sooner we leave behind us the bloody scenes of the late war, the better for us as a nation." The Democrats won power from coast to coast, with major victories in New York, Ohio, and California. In Ohio, Kansas, and Minnesota, voters rejected black suffrage in their states even as it was being forced upon the South.[16]

The Republicans were disheartened to see how quickly support for the rights of black Americans in the South lost elections in the North. The urgency of the looming elections for the Southern conventions became even clearer, for if change did not come now it was not likely to come at all. If the Republicans could not establish a base of support in the South they would lose twice, alienating Northerners without gaining black Southerners. That fact drove both sides in the battles over constitutional conventions in Virginia and other Southern states.

☆

ALL THREE PAPERS in Augusta County—like their counterparts across Virginia—called for their readers to vote against holding a convention, denying the legitimacy of constitutional revision made under "bayonets." In the meantime, largely out of the sight of white people, the black men of Augusta prepared to vote. Hundreds of conversations in churches, homes, and fields steeled black men to vote and to vote together. Thomas Jackson of the Freedmen's Bureau in Staunton described the awkward relations between the races as the election approached. "The whites say little except occasional individual threats, being at last satisfied that it is useless to continue the endeavor to make the Freedmen believe they are their 'best friends.'" The large majority of white voters registered in Augusta—3,484 white versus 1,206 black in July—made the whites "more indifferent, as they think they can easily out-vote them at the Polls."[17]

Despite their advantages of numbers, Jackson thought, "the senseless fears of 'social equality' make the prejudiced whites unable to see any steps made in advance by Freedmen, in any other light than an encroachment upon their own rights and safety." Anything the black people did for themselves seemed to come at the expense of white people, for "the idea of political independence seems to them little less than a heinous crime." In the face of such attitudes, the "demeanor of the Freedmen is however peaceable." Some black men, accurately gauging the hostility of the white men among whom they lived, had waited until close to the election before registering. The Freedmen's Bureau agent had "been working day or night to 9 or 10 at night on Registration & election."[18]

As the November election approached, white editors continued to "counsel" black voters. They warned that the Yankees were hypocrites. "Have you ever thought of the reason why Northern people were so anxious to get rid of slavery?" the *Spectator* asked its imagined black readers. "Was it from affection to you? Quite the reverse. There are thousands of poor white people in the North, who want to come here. They want the places you now hold, and the profits of the employment you now have." There was no evidence of such movement, but it was true that black voters who supported the Republicans risked a great deal. In the coded language of the time, whites warned, you could "lose your old friends, and gain no new ones."[19]

The newspapers of Augusta called for "every Conservative to cast his vote for the same candidate" as a delegate to the convention or to risk "the disgrace of having as our representative, a radical, a republican or renegade or negro!" The three conservative candidates included Joseph A. Waddell, the former editor of the *Spectator* who had spent the war years caring for his large family, serving in the quartermaster's office, and keeping a detailed and candid diary in which he had privately expressed doubts about the justice of slavery and about the leadership of the Confederacy. He must have been gratified by the description in the paper announcing his nomination, which read simply: "JOSEPH A. WADDELL is too well and favorably known to require any introduction to the voters of Augusta County."[20]

Waddell and another white delegate won by about four hundred votes, but their victory was much narrower than it should have been given the white majority in Augusta County. The *Vindicator* worried about what the surprisingly close election foretold. "The colored people turned out and polled very nearly their registered strength, while the whites failed here, as well as at other points in the county, to poll any thing like their strength." The reason for the "apathy" was mysterious but troubling. Augusta "could and should have given a majority of 1600 against a Convention and for the Conservative ticket." As it was, 1,257 men—1,024 of them black—voted for the convention while 1,655 men—9 of them black—voted against the convention. Most white men—1,788 of them—chose not to vote, "indisposed to wage what they felt was a useless contest with the Congress of the United States, supported by the military power of the government." Over three-fourths of the black men over 21 in Augusta County voted in the first election for which they were eligible; only about a third of white men did.[21]

Shocked that the black men who depended on them for employment would vote for their own self-interest, white landowners and business owners fought back by withholding work. "Since the election there has been a most outrageous attempt to deter freedmen from voting again except they vote as ordered by their masters," Thomas Jackson of the Freedmen's Bureau reported.

"Owing in a great measure to this," Jackson thought, "contracts have not been so frequent the last half of this month." On Jackson's advice, the freedmen "refrain almost entirely from discussion."[22]

The lesson of the election was clear, Jackson thought: "Politically the whites have compelled the freedmen to take sides against them. The Conservative candidates openly proclaimed their opposition to education, franchise or elevation for the Colored men and of course they naturally voted for the Republicans who were willing they should enjoy these privileges." Although white men in Augusta repeatedly lectured black men about where their self-interest lay, black men offered a different calculation. They were willing to take their chances on being able to get another job, but they knew they might never have another chance to win the things they most wanted: public schools, fair laws, and the right to vote for their own destiny.[23]

In the state as a whole, voters approved a constitutional convention by a count of 107,342 to 61,887. The vote split strictly on racial lines. Only 12 percent of registered white voters cast ballots for Republicans. The convention prevailed because black voters turned out and white voters stayed home: 88 percent of black voters went to the polls while only about two-thirds of eligible whites voted. Of the 105 convention members, 68 would be Republicans, 24 of them black.

Most of the Republican votes came from districts with large black majorities. The concentration of enslaved people in counties east of the Blue Ridge and the wartime and postwar migration of black people to the cities and Union-occupied areas of eastern Virginia gave them concentrated political power in those districts. Augusta County was separated from counties, such as Albemarle and Nelson, that voted heavily Republican only by the Blue Ridge that defined the eastern border of the Valley. Though its new African-American citizens were mobilized and eager to vote, Augusta's predominantly white population kept it in the conservative column along with the rest of the Valley.[24]

White Virginians reacted with disgust to their defeat and the prospect of a convention. "The large majority of the white and negro Radical representatives in the Convention will know about as much about framing a Constitution as a pig does about astronomy," sneered the *Spectator*. The only hope was that at least half the voters in the state had to ratify any constitution produced by the convention. If that ratification failed, "the whole fabric of Radical reconstruction falls to the ground." The task, then, was to ensure that whites won the next vote, the one that would sanction any constitution the convention drafted. "The negroes (with some few honorable exceptions, never to be forgotten) have raised their hands against the whites and threaten us with ruin, simply because we are white," the *Valley Virginian* wrote with surprise, incomprehension, and no apparent sense of irony.[25]

As soon as the vote for the convention and its delegates had passed, people began preparing for the vote on the Constitution the convention would produce. "The overshadowing topic is the political aspect of affairs," the Freedmen's Bureau agent in Staunton reported. "The whole energy of Rebellion is thrown into the attempt to array White against Black and every lie which will serve the purpose of agitation is eagerly copied by the press and circulated among the people." The agent had seen committees "organized for each magisterial district ostensibly to canvass on behalf of the conservative interests and bring out every voter against the Constitution, but from the talk in the County, really to terrorize over loyal men white and black."

Violence quickly followed. "Four attempted attacks with pistols have been made during this month by white men upon Freedpeople," Jackson wrote his central office, "and if the present systematic agitation continues there must be general disorder and freedmen will not vote at the coming election." The Bureau agent regretfully reported "that the feeling of the colored toward the whites is becoming daily more unfriendly."[26]

The conservatives of Virginia decided to hold a convention of their own to organize themselves for what lay ahead. They would form a new Conservative Party that would unify former Whigs and Democrats, former unionists and secessionists. The white people of Augusta met in the Court House in December 1867 to elect delegates to the first meeting of the new party in Richmond. "This noble old State is on the verge of the abyss of ruin," cried the *Spectator*. "Our mother is threatened with a fate more to be dreaded than death. Can any of her sons refuse to fly to her relief?" The goal was to rouse every white voter to register and vote against whatever constitution the convention meeting in Richmond produced. A large crowd gathered at the Augusta Court House and turned to the men who had long led the white people of the county: Alexander H. H. Stuart and John Brown Baldwin. Stuart spoke at length, hitting all the points that had been so well rehearsed in preceding months by conservatives— the hypocrisy of abolitionism and Republicanism, the ignorance and gullibility of the new black voters, the necessity of united action by white voters.[27]

Baldwin agreed with all that his law partner, in-law, and good friend said, striking the same notes he had sounded in his testimony before the congressional Joint Committee on Reconstruction nearly two years earlier. A reporter summarized Baldwin's argument: "He had the kindest feelings for the negro. He spoke as a friend of 'Cuffee'—he liked him in his place, and he wished it distinctly understood that he looked forward to a war of races with no pleasure." In a particularly startling juxtaposition, Baldwin "urged, as a friend of the negro, that we should vote down the Constitution to be framed, keep the negro in his proper place and save his throat from being cut. In a struggle between the races, this is the inevitable result." A white man who would not register and vote in such a situation, Baldwin concluded, was worse than a deserter during the late war.[28]

Not surprisingly, Virginia's white press hailed the Conservative gathering of eight hundred delegates a "sublime spectacle," "great in numbers, intelligence, character and patriotism." Augusta, the very embodiment of a reasoned and principled conservative county, shaped the convention to a remarkable extent: Stuart presided and Baldwin wrote the plan of organization that resulted. The Convention voted to "sincerely cooperate with all men throughout the Union, of whatever name or party" to restore the Constitution "under the control of the white race."[29]

With the vote on ratification of the new constitution pending in April 1868, white men of Augusta County organized themselves into groups of ten, with one man responsible for seeing that nine other men got to the polls, for "no white man of common intelligence, with the proper instincts of his race, can fail to appreciate the fearful magnitude of the impending crisis." The agent of the Freedmen's Bureau thought this strategy was also meant to disguise vigilance against black voters, for the freedpeople of Augusta were "fully alive to the vital importance to them of the issues now at stake." They would turn out to vote at the ratification for the new constitution "unless the conservative organization 'by tens' is allowed to control the voters at the polls."[30]

☆

UNDERSTAFFED AND OFF-BALANCE since its arrival in Staunton soon after Appomattox, the Freedmen's Bureau office grew weaker over time. Federal troops were removed in January 1866 and the office was reduced from a staff of several men to a single agent working on his own. Six agents came and went during the three and a half years the Bureau operated in Augusta, none staying as long as a year and some only a few months. Those agents tried to bring stability and justice to an inherently unstable and unjust situation. Judged by their own standards and words, they struggled while politics in Washington, Richmond, and Augusta shifted beneath their feet.[31]

As each agent arrived in Staunton, he evaluated conditions by responding to questions on forms from the central office. The agents spoke from the perspective of moderate Republicans, sympathetic to the freedpeople and skeptical of the white people around them. Each agent rediscovered what his predecessor had learned. The reports were cyclical, seasonal, with the same problems recurring each year, hope reviving despite overwhelming challenges.

The freedpeople had no recourse other than the Freedmen's Bureau. "About fifty complaints have been made at this Office during the present month by Freedmen, the most of which have been claims against Citizens for labor," an agent reported in January 1867. "The White Citizens seem to think that the Black Man has no right to complain of his wrongs, no matter how grievous they may be he must bear them all in silence, and if he ventures to make them known it is a heinous offence for which he must be brutally knocked down and beaten with the first thing that can be gotten hold of."[32]

Even those freedmen who avoided violence complained that "they cannot collect their wages when due which of course is a great disadvantage to them," an agent noted. And all the Freedmen's Bureau could do after the troops had been withdrawn and the Freedmen's Bureau courts dissolved in early 1866 was to turn to the civil courts, putting the laborers' bills "in the hands of an Officer for collection." Those officers were white magistrates in local districts, and their inaction often meant that the freedmen's cases were "defered from one Court to another until their patience becomes exhausted, and perhaps their families suffer for bread." As a result, a report from Augusta in the spring of 1867 discovered, "very few contracts have been made." The freedpeople had "lost confidence in the Whites' intentions to perform the conditions, and are therefore negligent in having any made, and the Whites are only too well pleased to avoid having anything to do with the Bureau in making such contracts."[33]

Deeper problems persisted. Workers frequently moved from one employer to another, "incurring heavy expense in shifting their families and goods," but found no better situation after they moved. Laboring families without money bought food on credit at high rates. When the agent asked the freedmen why they did so, "the common answer is 'I could not get money and my family had to eat and be clothed.'" Petty fraud aside, the bottom line was that "the white man expects to receive the labor of the colored man for about two-thirds of what he is willing to pay the white laborers for the same service." Black people were paid less simply because they were black and could be exploited without consequence.[34]

Taking everything into account, the Freedmen's Bureau agent thought the freedpeople "deserve a vast deal of credit for accomplishing what they have, toward becoming a thrifty and self supporting people especially when we consider the disadvantages under which they labor." Whenever the "honorable ambitious industrious effort" of the freedpeople was met with "full and impartial justice and protection under existing laws" they would seize "every opportunity within their reach and so advance as to convince their old masters even that they are capable of higher things in the scale of civilization than that of being mere hewers of wood and drawers of water." Yet the day when justice might arrive seemed far distant in 1867.[35]

☆

THE ENTIRE NATION WATCHED with wonder as constitutional conventions met in ten states of the former Confederacy. All the politics of the North, Franklin's *Repository* admitted, "are but the surface ripples" of the political sea, "while the great ground-swell is to be found in that steady and resistless flood-tide of public sentiment at the South which flows on to reconstruction."[36]

Virginia offered a clear example to nearby Pennsylvania of what was at stake. "In Virginia the negroes voted almost to a man in favor of a constitutional convention," Franklin's *Repository* noted. "There was nothing surprising in this, at least to any one who had credited the Negro with sufficient judgment to discriminate between friend and foe. That he should want to exercise the rights of citizenship, since he is compelled to bear its burdens, it is natural, just as natural as it was for him when a slave to covet his freedom." But even though the black Virginian had acted just as he should in the American political system, the former rebels "turn upon him with a ferocity that would disgrace even the negroes were the situation of the parties reversed. They propose to drive him from employment, to deny him the common right of all God's creatures, that of toil, and to bring upon him all the horrors of absolute and hopeless want. Such madness and stupidity combined, have seldom been equalled in the same people."

Alexander McClure, leader of the Republican party and editor of the Franklin *Repository*, had watched the recent elections from a distance, as he and his wife took a railroad excursion to the Far West. Summarizing the state of affairs as 1867 drew to a close, writing from Montana, McClure likened the current state of Reconstruction to the Civil War itself. After each military defeat, McClure reminded his fellow Republicans, the Democrats clamored that "Congress must recede!" The Democrats made the same call now, demanding the Congress recede from reconstructing the South. Fortunately, "the enfranchisement of a race is an achievement that cannot be undone by any temporary political revulsion." Resistance would naturally confront that progress, for men often "most hate those they have most wronged." The political defeats of Reconstruction would be like the military defeats of the Civil War, temporary and avenged with later victories. The political losses of the Republicans "will be the Bull Run, the Fredericksburg, the Chancellorsville and the Chickamauga of the struggle, and the Gettysburg, the Vicksburg, the Nashville and the Appomattox will as surely follow in the fullness of time."[37]

The Democrats laughed at McClure's elaborate analogies, for the true issue was simple. Would white men rule the United States?: "Get ready for the plain issue. It is before you," they challenged their fellow Democrats. "You must meet it. Meet it like men.—Meet it like white men."[38]

☆

THE VIRGINIA CONSTITUTIONAL CONVENTION met in December 1867. The thirty-six Conservatives were generally young and relatively prosperous, often college-educated. Joseph Waddell would have stood out among them for his age and lack of means. The twenty-three white Radicals ("carpetbaggers"), like their counterparts across the South, had often settled in Virginia before or soon after the war, when no prospect of black voting could have beckoned. They were men of middling property, several of them college-educated. The twenty-one native white Republicans ("scalawags") were generally quiet men from Unionist backgrounds without much political experience.

Of the twenty-four African-American delegates, at least nineteen were literate. About half of them were of mixed racial background, three times the proportion in Virginia. More than half of them had been free before the war or had escaped slavery in Virginia and lived in the North until after slavery's demise. They represented districts, either urban or in the east, with heavy black majorities.[39]

A letter to the *Spectator* provided the typical white perspective, mixing disdain, disgust, and harsh racist humor. The twenty-four colored men varied "in complexion from the bright mulatto to the blackest African," and the correspondent admitted "that most of this class conduct themselves in a manner which shows they were well brought up—that is, they are polite and unobtrusive. Of course they are uneducated and ignorant." Five or six of the black delegates "aspire to statesmanship and oratory, and discuss the most difficult questions with all the self-complacency that Daniel Webster could exhibit." Another delegate, though, gave a speech "entirely without meaning, a mere string of words having no connection or sense."

The white Radicals, the paper judged, "have apparently little more intelligence than the negroes, and have doubtless come from the lowest ranks of the people." The correspondent merely invented backgrounds for these men, imagining them as undistinguished Union army veterans who "were probably employees of the Freedmen's Bureau, and when that institution dispensed with their services were left here stranded like frogs in a dried-up mill pond." Now, they were "jubilant" with eight dollars a day and the "anticipation of the fat offices they are to get by means of the same voters who sent them to the Convention."[40]

By April 15, 1868, the body produced a progressive document. It created Virginia's first system of public education. In the political sphere, the constitution established universal manhood suffrage and shortened residency requirements for voting. In the judicial sphere, it prohibited discrimination in jury selection and shielded debtors from unjust treatment. After months of attack, some white Virginians sheepishly admitted that most of the constitution was a reasonable document. Joseph Waddell acknowledged "that the Constitution proposed was, in some respects, better than could have been anticipated."[41]

But Conservatives protested that the proposed constitution would disenfranchise all men who had held any civil or military office in the Confederacy by requiring an "Ironclad Oath" that the taker had never supported secession or the Confederacy. Advocates of the rigorous oath knew that in a majority-white state the Republicans could only retain power by keeping established white leaders out of contention for office.[42]

The Conservative members of the convention published a long denunciation of the document as soon as it emerged. They pointedly specified the Northern origins of many white Republicans and predicted a grim future in which every officeholder in the state—including the governor—would be black. "The only part in the administration of the government which has been almost exclusively assigned to the whites is the payment of the taxes," read one sarcastic remark. Another declared that "the negroes will also make ample provision for houses of refuge, and other charitable institutions, which they can enjoy without any of the anxieties which will trouble those who have to pay for them." Free public schools were only a way for blacks to send their children to school with white children, conservatives charged, though that provision had already been removed.[43]

Virginia, which had long prided itself on its statesmanship and moderation, watched as most other Southern states in 1868 successfully completed and ratified their new constitutions. Those states elected new state officers, adopted the Fourteenth Amendment, won the approval of Congress to rejoin the Union as full and equal states, and looked forward to participating in the upcoming presidential election. Virginia, by contrast, stood on the sidelines. The appointed governor said there was not enough money to hold a vote on the new constitution so it would be up to Congress to allocate those funds. But Congress, consumed with the impeachment hearing of Andrew Johnson, took no action. In the meantime, Virginia watched, adrift, while others shaped the future of the nation.

☆

NORTHERN DEMOCRATS EXPRESSED SYMPATHY with the "white men of 'District Number One,' formerly known as Virginia." Closer to home, the Democrats worried about the Republicans taking the White House as well as Congress in the election of 1868. The Republicans had persuaded Ulysses Grant to run for office. Grant was the most admired man across the North and West. The Republicans did not hesitate to frame the election in military terms, as their "boys in blue" marshaled "for a conflict with the same enemies they were compelled to meet and overthrow before. The hosts that fought under Lee, and shouted for Davis in 1864, are again banded together as one man, to accomplish by the ballot the same purposes they sought to effect by arms," they boasted. "Their object is the same, their inspiration the same, their leaders the same, their allies the same." Fortunately, Grant, the hero who won "Liberty and Union, now undertakes to accomplish for us Fraternity and Peace."[44]

The *Repository* offered a brutally direct, and quite long, list titled "Who Are Democrats?" Some samples:

Every person who recognized the rebellion as 'legitimate, legal and just,' was a Democrat.

Every man who insulted the loyal armies of the Union by declaring 'the war a failure,' was a Democrat.

Every man in the North who sympathized with traitors and treason in the South during the late civil war, was a Democrat.

Every draft rioter, sneak and bounty jumper was a Democrat.

Every person in the North who opposed conferring suffrage upon Union soldiers in the field was a Democrat.

Every man who, during the war, asserted that the Republic was Dying! Dying!! DYING!!! was a Democrat.

Every person who engaged in shooting down negroes in the streets, or burning negro school houses, was a Democrat.

In short, the Democratic party had become "a common sewer" for "every element of treason North and South."[45]

The Republican message worked. In October elections for state offices, the Republicans won Pennsylvania in the largest vote ever cast in the state. Two weeks later, Grant carried Pennsylvania and twenty-three of the other thirty-four states in the Union, winning 53 percent of the total vote and a more impressive victory in the Electoral College—214 votes to 80. While he did well across the country, the high turnout of votes of African-American men casting their first ballots in the reconstructed states secured those states for the Republicans.[46]

The Northern Democrats dreaded the grim future they imagined would result from Reconstruction. "The majority of the white population of the South will remain disfranchised. Those governments will be placed entirely in the hands of the negroes. The negroes, puffed up with an aura of their importance, will become arrogant, overbearing, tyrannical." With their newly affirmed power, the black men of the South "will commit outrages of the most brutal kind. Riots will ensue and the continuation of military governments then become a necessity to keep the peace. And in four years more, the Radicals will justify the continuation of military rule on the ground that the Southern whites would not allow the negroes to ride rough shod over them."[47]

☆

AS MONTHS AND THEN YEARS passed without resolution, Americans wondered if things could have been different. If Lincoln had lived, some dreamed, had Johnson been a statesman, had more moderate Republicans taken the reins, Reconstruction could have mended rather than divided the nation, they argued. Some Radicals, for their part, believed that a firmer stand by the North at the moment of surrender, when the white South was malleable and quiescent, might have set the nation on a course of greater justice.

The fact was, though, that the white South had never, for a moment, proved willing to accept more than the end of slavery and the end of the Confederacy as the price of defeat. Former Confederates would have unleashed violence against black people whenever those black people posed an immediate threat.

Northern voters supported aggressive Republican actions only because they saw that white Southerners had not disavowed their purposes in the war. Without Southern intransigence, black codes, riots, reelected Confederate leaders, and broken contracts with freedmen, there may well have been no Fourteenth Amendment.

Reconstruction, it turned out, moved by counterpoint and reaction as well as by intention and fulfillment. Just as white Southerners' secession made emancipation possible, so did their resistance to basic civil rights for black people create the possibility for votes and office-holding for black people. Northern Democrats did their part, too, to move history in the direction opposite to what they sought, encouraging Andrew Johnson to believe that he could defy his own party and negate much of what the war had won. Black Southerners, as they had throughout the war and in war's aftermath, took advantage of any opportunity, whether opened by their friends or their enemies, to control their own fate.[48]

The rhythms of the American political order, some constitutionally ordained and others the product of tradition and habit, had helped ensure that Abraham Lincoln could not be removed during the worst months of military failure. Those same rhythms also defined the boundaries of Reconstruction. Sometimes, the system was susceptible to the whims of Andrew Johnson or the timing of state elections; at other times, legislation and law moved slowly even though conditions on the ground shifted rapidly.

The more than six months between the surrender and the reconvening of Congress gave Andrew Johnson a constitutionally mandated interval to do as he wished. State elections held across the North every year during Reconstruction kept voters agitated and legislators off-balance. The reliance on amendments to the United States Constitution to enact change in the South—the requirements for conventions to be called, delegates elected, and amendments ratified in the states—dragged out for years. Legal processes of disfranchisement of former Confederates and systematic registration of new black voters, signed oaths and lengthy testimony, demonstrated the democratic intent of Reconstruction even as it slowed progress toward those democratic goals.

☆

IN THE SPRING OF 1868 VIRGINIA, despite all the energy invested in elections and conventions, remained in limbo. Southern states that had seceded sooner and more eagerly than Virginia had regained admission to the Union, but the state that prided itself on its statesmanship had not. Such a condition slowed economic development as well as political and racial peace. Virginia would have to find its own way forward.

The United States Senate delayed funding for Virginia's vote on the new constitution until some time in 1869. In the interim, Alexander H. H. Stuart launched a bold campaign to enable former Confederates to help lead Virginia. He proposed supporting black suffrage in exchange for the reinfranchisement of men who had served the Confederacy. Stuart adopted a phrase from the Republicans—"universal suffrage and universal amnesty"—and wrote a public letter laying out his plan in early December 1868. He sent it to leading Richmond newspapers over a pseudonym, "Senex," a wise old man.

Other leading white men, including John Brown Baldwin, rallied around Stuart's idea. After meeting in Staunton and Richmond, they sent a Committee of Nine to Washington in January. That committee, with no official power, offered to accept, on behalf of Virginia, black suffrage "as an offering on the altar of peace, and in the hope that union and harmony may be restored on the basis of universal suffrage and universal amnesty."

The self-appointed Virginians enjoyed remarkable access to the leaders of the United States. They met with President Johnson, Chief Justice Salmon P. Chase, President-elect Ulysses S. Grant, and the Senate Judiciary Committee. The Senate committee, impressed with the arguments of the Virginians, suggested that they produce a written statement of their position. The visitors then met with the House Committee on Reconstruction. The appointed Republican governor of Virginia, Henry Wells, warned that committee that loyal white men in Virginia would suffer "wrong and outrage" if the former Confederates were allowed back in power, but powerful Republicans continued to listen to the Committee of Nine.

"We have to live together under one government," John Brown Baldwin argued in Washington, and the only way to do that was "to remove out of the way, North and South, all the remaining causes of bitterness and strife." A proposed Fifteenth Amendment, prohibiting discrimination in voting on the basis of race, seemed a "fearful and dangerous experiment" to them, but the Committee of Nine "have made up our minds that we will not stand in the way of the establishment of that policy, but will give it a fair, an honest and unequivocal support." [49]

The Committee of Nine's audacious assumption of speaking for all white Virginians met with scathing attacks by newspapers across Virginia, especially Conservative papers. Baldwin and Stuart went before their neighbors in a public meeting in Staunton to explain their motivations. Stuart assured them, an editor in the audience recorded, that he had always opposed "allowing the power of the State to pass into the hands of an alien and inferior race. He was now as then for making this a white man's government. He had not changed in his purpose—he had only changed in regard to the means of accomplishing that purpose, and that change had been rendered necessary by the altered condition of the country." Stuart, accustomed to support and praise, declared himself "at a loss to account for the violent opposition" his committee had unleashed. "The constitution was to be submitted in some form or other," he argued, "and the only question was shall it be submitted with all its defects embodied in it, or shall it be submitted with four of the worst of them stricken out?"[50]

The editor of the Staunton *Vindicator,* unimpressed with Stuart's speech, quoted in contrast an eloquent spokesman who had addressed a "large and enthusiastic meeting" in Staunton in June 1866: "We have been overwhelmed, but we have not yet been degraded. That can be inflicted only with our own consent, and that consent never will be given. Our rights may be ravished from us by violence but we will never agree that Virginia shall be placed in the position of a political prostitute by giving consent to her own degradation and dishonor." That speaker had been Alexander H. H. Stuart himself, two and a half years before.[51]

☆

WHILE LEADING WHITE VIRGINIANS jostled over the new constitution, a remarkable scene played out in Staunton in the early winter of 1869. A "Radical" meeting in the Town Hall, attended mainly by black men, nominated Major John Harman as the president of the session. Harman had been a large slaveholder in Augusta County, owning eight men and seven women in 1860. His landholdings and other property placed him among the county's elite. He had been a newspaper editor, cattle farmer, and stage line operator. In his late thirties and father of five children, Harman might have avoided service for several years into the war. Instead, he served as a brigade quartermaster for Stonewall Jackson and Jubal Early and, on occasion, acted as quartermaster for the entire Army of Northern Virginia.

Why John Harman would align himself with the Radical

Republicans is a mystery. He was still a wealthy man in the 1860s and had earned enduring respect for his service for the Confederacy. In fact, his new would-be Republican allies were skeptical; at first, they voted down his nomination. The white postmaster who nominated Harman for the presidency then "assured the meeting that Maj. Harman was now thoroughly identified with the Radical party. Phil. Roselle (colored) then said that if that was the case he and his colored friends would vote for him." Harman, taking the chair, "said that he felt embarrassed—that he was in a novel position—but that he could assure the meeting that he cordially endorsed the reconstruction measures of Congress." The *Spectator*, recording these proceedings with a tone of disbelief, simply concluded its account by saying "comment is unnecessary."[52]

Another editor painted a more detailed picture. "This meeting was mixed—very much mixed, there being a huge preponderance of the colored element, with only a very few whites participating." When the reporter looked for a seat, one black attendee asked another to move over "and let the 'white folks' have their seats. 'No,' said he. 'We want a little mixin in this thing—the white folks have had sugar in thern and now by G—we are going to have sugar in ourn.'" Like the *Spectator*, the *Vindicator* disclaimed comment. "As to the whites who participated in the meeting here, or who affiliate with Southern Republicans elsewhere, we have nothing to say."[53]

Soon thereafter, the Republicans held another meeting, this one in the African Church. "The meeting, we learn, was of the character of a political love-feast," reported the *Vindicator*, listing all five of the white men there, beginning with John Harman, who "reiterated with increased emphasis and force, with the fervent zeal of a new convert, his previously expressed purpose to unite, heart and hand, soul, mind, and strength with his colored friends." Another newspaper reported that "Rev. Bowser (colored) grew eloquent in speaking of the conversion of Maj. Harman, likening him when opposed to the Republican party to Saul of Tarsus, but when converted, to Paul, whom, with open arms, the colored people welcomed, as the Rock of their salvation in this section." To the reporters, such scenes represented precisely why the proposed constitution could not pass.[54]

As white Virginians expressed their disdain for the Republicans, many also criticized the attempt at compromise by Stuart and his counterparts in other Southern states. Jubal Early wrote from Canadian exile to denounce the movement, as did wartime Virginia governor John Letcher. Throughout March 1869, charges and attacks flew in the press. In a series of arcane maneuvers, the Republicans split into factions competing for Virginia's governorship, a post to be decided in the July vote along with the fate of the proposed state constitution. One Republican faction was led by Gilbert Walker, a moderate Pennsylvanian who had moved to occupied Virginia in 1864, and the other by Henry Wells, a New Yorker and former Union general then serving as appointed governor. Wells's running mate for lieutenant governor, Joseph D. Harris, was African-American.

The Conservatives, like the Republicans, also vehemently disagreed with one another about the best strategy, some calling for digging in and others for compromising. Under a headline composed only of question marks, the *Spectator* admitted that no one seemed to know anything. Three long paragraphs of questions followed, including: "Which wing does Grant favor? Which does Congress favor? What good can we expect from either or both? What influence has Grant? Has he any or not? What indication

has he given of conservatism? What is his mode of effecting reconciliation and establishing peace? Has he any policy, and would
it make any difference whether he has or not?" And so on.[55]

The urgency and confusion in the situation increased when
President Grant announced in April 1869 that Congress would
finally establish a day for Virginians to vote on the proposed state
constitution. Congress, apparently having listened to the Committee of Nine from Virginia, gave Grant the authority to separate
provisions of the constitution as he deemed best, allowing Virginians to vote on black suffrage and white disenfranchisement
separately. The Virginia General Assembly selected at the same
election would then be required to ratify a Fifteenth Amendment
to the United States Constitution, an amendment that forbade the
denial of the vote to any citizen because of "race, color or previous
condition of servitude." The two elections, Grant determined,
would be held on July 6, 1869, only three months in the future.

With so much at stake in such a short period, with so much
uncertainty and conflict on so many levels and in so many places,
tempers became short. Governor Wells, the Radical Republican,
on a speaking tour around Virginia, arrived in Staunton in June.
Major Harman introduced Wells to an audience, the *Vindicator*
judged, of a "motley appearance, the gallery being occupied by
the ebony and topaz clan and the lower floor by all sorts of whites,
conservatives, democrats, moderate republicans and scalawags.
Many were drawn there for the purpose of seeing what kind of
animal Wells was."

When John Harman spoke, his "flattering allusion to the colored population elicited applause from the gallery, which was
met by faint hisses from the floor." Harman chastised the white
audience, saying that "geese and snakes can hiss and so can puppies." This remark, the paper mocked, "surprised the audience

much, they not being aware that puppies had a hissing propensity." ("Puppy" was a popular nineteenth-century insult for a man, a somewhat more polite version of "son of a bitch.") The *Spectator*, hearing Harman praise black voters, groaned that "how deeply must be grieved the sainted spirit of Gen. Stonewall Jackson!" The speeches that followed, by both white and black men, judged the white editor, did "the conservative cause much good," arousing "the people from their apathy, and every man has now become a working man" on behalf of the Conservative cause.[56]

"This election is as important as any which has ever been held in this State—its result will determine most momentous questions," announced the *Spectator*. "All should vote, of course, for striking out the test-oath and disfranchising clauses which will be submitted separately." Alexander Stuart wrote a public letter urging his fellow white citizens to accept black suffrage in return for restoring white suffrage. Not only would such a compromise lead "to the withdrawal of military supervision and control over us," but "within a year or two, after the excitement incident to these political struggles shall have passed away, we can call a new convention and form a new constitution adapted to our existing condition."[57]

Despite publicly announcing their intention to take black votes away as soon as they could, white Virginians still expected black men to vote with them. Black voters in Staunton invited several white men to address them as the election approached. Each of those men, including John Baldwin, assured their listeners that black men would keep their votes and could therefore afford for white men to have theirs. African-American voters could secure their own suffrage and win the good will of the men who employed them. If they did not support the compromise, if "they are so deaf to friendly counsel and unmoved by irrefutable arguments," then they "voluntarily and knowingly" opposed their white neighbors and would pay the consequence.[58]

The election, after so much turmoil, proved to be orderly. Black voters, as they had been implored, cast ballots to remove the white disenfranchising clause. "As we have none other than the kindest feeling for that class of our population, we heartily rejoice, for their sakes, that they have acted so wisely, and that the election resulted as it did," the *Spectator* quietly and yet ominously remarked. "We would counsel the whites to exercise charity towards the colored, and, remembering the circumstances in which they were placed and the influences brought to bear upon them by more guilty parties wearing white skins over black hearts, to make due and liberal allowances for them, and not to visit upon them the punishment due to those who deceived and misled them." Some black men had voted for the Radical Republican candidate for governor and his African-American running mate, but that could be forgiven.[59]

The moderate Republican coalition, supported by many Conservatives, won by 30,000 votes. They secured not only the constitution but also a majority in the Virginia General Assembly and in Congress. Augusta County led the entire state in its margin of support for the compromise on universal suffrage and universal amnesty. On January 26, 1870, President Grant signed the document that readmitted Virginia to representation in Congress.[60]

☆

BY 1870, WITH THE RATIFICATION of the Fifteenth Amendment and the readmission of all the Southern states, the fundamental changes of Reconstruction had been initiated, if not firmly established, across the South. Federal troops would remain in several former Confederate states for another seven years while Republican governments held on in the face of relentless violence and resistance. President Grant and the Republicans would launch investigations into the Ku Klux Klan, but neither Congress nor the president would try to extend the reforms of Reconstruction. Virginia, with a white majority, complicit national officials, and adroit leadership by Alexander H. H. Stuart and John Brown Baldwin, anticipated a process all the Southern states would eventually undergo, accepting—and then controlling and suppressing—black voting in exchange for local white autonomy. The bargain would hold for another thirty years, until even more confident white Southerners wrote new constitutions that disenfranchised black voters.

In retrospect, it appeared that Reconstruction began to end as soon as it began. The bold effort to remake the South confronted determined and often violent resistance from the great majority of Southern whites as well as fractures among moderate and radical Republicans, Northern and Southern Republicans, and black and white Republicans. At every step, Northern Democrats decried Reconstruction as an injustice and a boondoggle.

The struggle to establish black suffrage, following the struggle to defeat the Confederacy, end slavery, and establish black citizenship, exhausted the will of white Northern Republicans and the resources of Southern Republicans, black and white. Republicans began losing elections in the North as soon as they started winning in the South. Though a temporary bi-regional coalition elected Grant in 1868 and reelected him in 1872, by the latter year the Republicans had begun to count on Northern and Western white voters for future victories. Everyone could foresee the demise of black Southern voting.

Reconstruction truly was radical. The Republicans who drove the fight for black civil rights, voting, office holding, and legislative power pushed against the weight of all American history. For Reconstruction to work it had to reconstruct every part of the Southern social order. It had to create constitutional amendments, rewrite state constitutions, enfranchise black men, and disfranchise former Confederates. It had to build social power on the ground with the Freedmen's Bureau and it had to sustain justice with vigilance and force. To a remarkable extent, the Republicans built the comprehensive structures of Reconstruction in a short time and in a coherent way.

But the strength of the effort behind Reconstruction also proved to be its weakness. Its very comprehensiveness exposed many flanks. The necessity of keeping the Freedmen's Bureau going opened charges of rampant spending, the necessity of black voting opened charges of corruption, the need for constitutional change opened the possibility of that process being co-opted. It was not that Reconstruction failed from some internal flaw. Rather, each success consumed political energy, and so did each loss. The Republicans constructed a remarkable machine at every level of government and society, but they ran out of electoral fuel to run that machine.

The Past Is Not Dead

1868 through 1902

*R*elationships between black and white Southerners followed twisting
paths during and after Reconstruction. The United States Supreme
Court allowed the South to go its own way and every Southern state followed its own route to a common destination: complete legal segregation,
disenfranchisement, and subjugation of black Southerners. Lynching and
other forms of violence against black people went unchecked.

Even the memories of the people of the South followed divergent paths.
White Southerners remembered the Civil War and Reconstruction in
highly ritualized and public ways that suppressed memories of conflict,
resistance, and dissension. Black Southerners kept alive memories of slavery, war, emancipation, and Reconstruction that emphasized their determination to survive injustice and chaos. The accomplishments of formerly
enslaved people in the first years after emancipation established a foundation for continued black accomplishment and activism. When history
presented other opportunities, they would be ready.

☆

JOHN SCOTT, WORKING IN STAUNTON for the American Missionary Association, bragged about his school to the home office. "Numbers are coming from the country to take board in the city that they may attend school. Children are teasing their parents to let them come." One mother "told me her sick daughter a little girl of seven had not sat up for days but arose immediately on hearing of my arrival—and begged to go school." Scott claimed that he had "to keep out of sight as much as possible, for the sight of me in the street is a guarantee for a fresh crowd of children next day."[1]

When his assistant arrived—a white woman named "Mrs Daveson (or some such name which I have hardly learned)"—Scott worried that she was unqualified by experience. "There are so many petty schools here among the colored people that this must be made superior to be successful—Nor will it do to let a teacher teach the 'Alphabet' class," for "some of the more advanced ones will often call on her, and soon find out if she is not capable."[2]

Sarah Davison threw herself into the work and in January 1869 reported what she had discovered in Augusta County. "The people generally appear glad and willing to receive instruction—It is evidently a pleasure to them to have the teachers visit them as they always seem ready to see us and we are sure of a welcome. I am a stranger here but find no difficulty in making friends with them." Scott was teaching a Sabbath School and Davison was recruiting students and planned to offer a sewing class, for "many can neither buy nor make their own clothes."

Sarah Davison wrote touchingly of the children. "It seems to me it is very pleasant work to try and help those who are so willing to learn. I do not regret coming here and I like the work I am engaged in very much." The Northern teacher admitted that "I did not expect to find so many pretty and interesting children among colored people there are some pretty and smart children in our school—Some of them are quite small and yet are allmost the best and farthest advanced scholars we have—And look as bright as they are in reality—It is indeed a pleasure to see their pleasant and happy faces."[3]

Davison thought that "the prejudices which some of the more educated of the colored people have" against the white teachers "are gradually wearing away." Davison, at the request of one of her small students, visited the girl's Aunt Carrie, "an old colored woman who has been sick for some years. She told me she could not read but would like to have me read the Bible to her." Davison promised that she would visit the elderly woman each week, and "so every Sunday morning she looks for me and during the many conversations I have had with her she has proved herself a Christian." Davison had another class of students who lived a mile from Staunton. "They meet in the house of one of their neighbors two afternoons in a week. The distance provides me with a long walk. A good change after the day teaching in a crowded school room."[4]

"The people were much pleased to see us," Sarah Davison wrote evocatively of one trip. "One of my scholars, a little girl, was standing upon a hill near her house—We saw her before she saw us but as we drew near her she recognized us and we soon knew she did—She stood a minute looking at us—Then threw up her hands and shouted a welcome turned and ran off as fast as she could to tell her mother who were coming." When Davison and Scott reached the house, they found "one of the neatest we had seen among the colored people—The Mother a most interesting colored person both in manner, and appearance so much like white that if she were seen north her color and skin would never be suspected."

Another young girl had stopped coming to school and the teachers visited to find out why. "She explained she had to keep her house for her father while her mother who is hired out was from home—She told us almost in tears she could not come to day school and her father would not allow her to attend night school." Looking for a solution, Davison invited the girl to join a class of "five adult scholars which meet every afternoon at a neighbors house. I asked her if she would like to meet with these and recite her lessons—She was much pleased with the plan and has not missed coming one day yet." In another neighborhood, several mothers told the teachers they "could not afford to pay the ten cents per week for tuition" for their children, so Davison and Scott invited them "to send their children without pay— They thanked us—And the next week three of the children came."[5]

Notwithstanding such successes, John Scott and the other American Missionary Association teachers left in May 1869. A few months later, the Presbyterian Missionary Society sent Amelia Knapp, another white teacher from the North, to establish schools in Augusta, including an industrial school. Knapp taught up to a hundred students a day. The superintendent of schools wrote that "the schools have been the principal cause of the hopefulness and patience with which they (the freedmen) have endured the hunger, the nakedness and the unavenged wrongs of their transition state."[6]

But Knapp's school, too, would soon fade away. Despite devoted effort, the missionary schools in Augusta could not meet the needs they confronted. The best hope of African-American education lay in the free public schools called for in the new constitution.

☆

THE STORIES OF THE CIVIL WAR, emancipation, and Reconstruction began to be revised even before the events had ended. Northerners and Southerners, black people and white, Democrats and Republicans, fought over the plot, moral, and meaning of these stories. Borders and boundaries drawn in the flux of history came to seem inevitable and immutable.

The Democrats, eager to find some cause that would stir their voters in late 1868, called on Northerners to leave the "dead issues" of the past behind. Only three years after Appomattox, the Republicans replied, "Is it so very long since the nation was involved in a death-struggle with slavery"? Of course, the living should always look forward, but the fact remained that "the past is not dead nor its issues—but lives in us and for us."[7]

The political parties of the North and South had always known the importance of telling the right story. Their thousands of editorials, news reports, anecdotes, jokes, and admonitions were narrative devices, constantly sifting through conflicting evidence to tell stories compelling enough to get men to the polls, to view their rivals as enemies. Much of Abraham Lincoln's enduring genius lay in his ability to give shape and form to chaotic events through his words and his actions. Much of Andrew Johnson's failure lay in his inability to do more than insult, caricature, and attack.

White Southerners had effectively used words to shape the story of Reconstruction from the outset, the very names of characters assigning their roles. "Carpetbaggers" were, by definition, shiftless, unrooted, and opportunistic; "scalawags" were, by definition, weak and immoral; and, in the longest-lived and most insidious naming in all of American history, "niggers" were intrinsically worthless, ridiculous until threatening. White Southerners guarded the boundaries of the permissible with words and stories.

☆

AS RECONSTRUCTION BEGAN to collapse in the South, white men who had cast their lot with the Republicans tried to salvage something from their stance. William Dewes, who two years earlier had testified before the United States Congress about the injustice in Augusta, wrote to the head of the Freedmen's Bureau, Orlando Brown, in the summer of 1868. Because of his support for the Union, the Freedmen's Bureau, and the Republican Party, said Dewes, "I find it totally impossible to make a support for myself and child at my profession on account of the direct and indirect influences operating against the interests of loyal men." Accordingly, Dewes wrote to "seek employment in some branch" of the government. He asked for "a clerkship or any situation in your gift in your Dept where I could be useful and derive a support for myself and child." [8]

When Frederick Tukey, the Freedmen's Bureau agent in Augusta in 1867, returned to Staunton in 1869, the local newspapers, relatively generous during his term of office, savaged him. "Mr. Tukey, ex-Freedmen's Bureau agent, and carpet-bag landed in our town on Tuesday last." Tukey had lost his race for delegate to the constitutional convention in 1867. Considering it "morally impossible for a gentleman that had figured so long and successfully in the political world to be defeated in a fair election," the paper sarcastically remarked, Tukey attempted to contest the results of the election but failed. "Nothing daunted, he packed up his portable goods, took passage on the Chesapeake and O. R.R. and in due time reached the County of Caroline, where the negro majority was large, and, consequently, where he thought the attempt to enter, by means of the said negro majority, the House of Delegates, would be as easy as it would be for an adept in the art of

466

'lifting' to relieve you of a ten dollar bill, when you weren't 'looking.'" Tukey lost again, however, and "now he is perambulating
about the country, reviewing the scenes of past defeat, preparatory
to his final departure from a State that would not gratify his ambitious soul." Could not the gods "help poor Tukey to an office?"[9]

☆

MORE IMPORTANT STORIES CAME to an end in the years of
Reconstruction's culmination. Thaddeus Stevens died in 1868
and Chambersburg tolled its bells and closed all places of business.
While the Republican "Boys in Blue" lowered their flag to half
mast, "a general feeling of sadness and sorrow over the death of
this great patriot and statesman was everywhere manifested." The
Democrats' newspaper, which had attacked, vilified, ridiculed,
and fought against Stevens and all he stood for, remained silent,
merely reporting that members of the Franklin County bar had
passed resolutions of sympathy.[10]

When news of the death of Robert E. Lee spread in the fall of
1870, the newspapers of Staunton bordered their pages in heavy
black symbols of mourning. "Virginia, sorrow-laden, bends in
agony over the loss of her greatest, purest and best beloved son;
the Southland weeps; the Nation mourns him gone; the whole
world unites in sorrowing sympathy," the *Valley Virginian* intoned.
"Our beloved and noble old leader is dead, but his memory will
live forever in the hearts of his countrymen, and his name will
be honored through all time." Bells tolled across the hills of
Staunton and all businesses closed. A gathering at the courthouse
unanimously passed a resolution of respect and chose a delegation
to send to Lee's funeral in Lexington, where he would be buried
at Washington College.[11]

While many in the North admired Lee, Franklin's *Repository* could not forgive him. "Whilst other civil and military leaders failed and disappeared under the turbulent waves of the war, General Lee seemed to rise higher and higher, until during at least the last year of the struggle the only hope of the South was centered on him," the paper recalled. "The love and veneration which he excited among the people of the Southern States seems to have been real and permanent," not merely "the ephemeral growth of some brilliant and unexpected military achievement."

Lee's tortured delay in aligning himself with the Confederacy at the outset of the war ennobled him in some eyes, but the Republican paper thought the delay gave Lee the opportunity to learn of "the plans and secrets" of the United States. The *Repository* also criticized Lee for refusing to surrender in 1864 and 1865 when it had become clear that the Confederacy could no longer win, his stubbornness costing many lives. "Upon him, far more than upon any person does the responsibility of all the sacrifices of the last year of the war lie."

Lee's final failure came in the years of peace, the Republican paper judged, when he "entirely withdrew from public life, abstained from all intercourse with the public and gave no public expression to his opinions." Widely praised for his reticence and decorum, Lee also "scrupulously abstained from the expression of anything tending to heal up the wounds." Rather than living up to the terms of Appomattox, Lee "played the part of a defeated, but likewise a discontented, dissatisfied old man." Though he could have done "more for the permanent good and material prosperity of Virginia and the whole South than any other man in the country, he refused to open his mouth." The Republican paper could not bring itself to offer the customary absolution of the dead, suggesting that Americans should simply "let his deeds be buried in the grave with his body."[12]

☆

STORIES EXERTED GREAT PRACTICAL power in the aftermath of the war. The United States government, in an attempt to compensate the true Union people of the Confederacy for their losses and sacrifices in the war, launched the Southern Claims Commission in 1871. The Republicans hoped not only to serve justice but also to cement the loyalty of white Southerners to the party. Union people felt abandoned by both their white Confederate neighbors and by the federal government for which they had sacrificed. Initially intended to operate for two years, the Commission instead worked for eight. Southerners filed over 22,000 cases, claiming more than $60 million in damages. Commissioners traveled throughout the former Confederate states, taking testimony as people responded to a list of dozens of questions, listening to witnesses for and against the claims. The claimants had to prove that they had been loyal throughout the war and had to show that Federal troops had taken their property for official purposes. With such burdens of evidence—and with considerable skepticism on the part of the commissioners—only a third of the claims were judged worthy.

The Southern Claims Commission came to Augusta County in 1871 and returned in 1874, 1875, 1876, and 1879. The commissioners heard 137 cases and allowed 36 awards. The testimony showed that dissent and resistance had been more common in the county than the Confederates and their newspapers had acknowledged.

The Mennonites, Dunkers, and other faith communities that saw war as sinful did what they could to avoid supporting the Confederacy and aid those of their faith who sought to escape. George Hollar, for example, came before the Commission in 1876 to testify that twelve years earlier, during General David

Hunter's raid in the Valley, Federal troops took a mare worth $175 from him. Hollar's staccato testimony told a powerful story. "I have harbored and fed refugees and deserters and have helped them to escape," he acknowledged. "I have given them money to go with. I have gone with them in the night to show the way." He harbored two deserted Confederate soldiers for weeks and "then persuaded them to go north and gave them money to go with." Hollar "collected about 30 refugees at one time who met at my house by appointment for supper and started the same night for the mountains with a Pilot." He testified of "various depots among the farmers about the country where these refugees were harbored and kept. I suppose I knew of as many as 300 who were run through by this route."

Hollar had voted for Union delegates to the convention that decided Virginia's secession and on the day of the election for secession he fled his Augusta County home. He "knew that if I voted I should vote for the Union, and I was afraid of my life if I did." Hollar had heard the "terrible threats against Union men if they voted against Secession or if they refused to vote for Secession" and two men who cast ballots for the Union at his precinct "were near being killed. I heard men talk of hanging them" and Hollar knew those who "offered to furnish the rope and stand between the law and any man who would hang them."

Hollar presented witnesses of his loyalty and of his loss. A preacher in the Dunker Church testified that he had talked with Hollar often during the war. "He was a very decided union man, he always opposed secession and supported the cause of the Union." On the evening that news of Virginia's secession had arrived in their community, the minister testified, Hollar said 'To night the sun goes down on our liberties.'" In the spring of 1862,

Hollar had helped lead a group of refugees into the mountains but they were captured by the Rebels. Hollar himself was imprisoned for five weeks before the Confederacy changed its policy and allowed people of his faith to pay a fine rather than serve the Confederacy more directly.

Hollar lost the horse for which he was claiming compensation— "a young bay Morgan Mare of good size and style, in fine order and well broke"—when "a large body of cavalry" stopped nearby and went through the stables of the nearby farmers. The minister recognized Hollar's horse, for a Federal soldier took the minister's saddle for it. The soldier "told me his own was near giving out and he must have another. No receipt was given, nor asked for." The Claims Commission, persuaded, awarded George Hollar $125 for his long-departed horse.[13]

George Hollar's claim was the sort the commissioners were looking for: brave defiance, start to finish, against secession and the war it unleashed. The commissioners found other kinds of loyalty, however, for which they were less prepared. Mary Blackburn, in 1875, presented a claim for a large amount for particularly damaging losses. She testified that in 1864 the Federal army had taken two horses, two cattle, bacon, flour, a saddle, and two bridles. Such losses would have been devastating for any average farmer in Augusta County, but they were especially painful because Mary Blackburn had been enslaved, purchased by her husband not long before the war. In 1864, General William Averell had come through Augusta County. Pausing for a short time about a half mile away, soldiers came to the Blackburn farm and rode away with the stock and carried the bacon and flour on their shoulders. Her husband was sick and could offer no complaint. Blackburn "told one of them I thought he might leave me a little flour."

Like Hollar, Blackburn had been a brave ally of the United States. Michael Carwell, a white neighbor, testified that he had known Blackburn during the war and "always found her willing and ready to do all she could for the Union cause. She would receive and conceal provisions &c for persons who were making their escape from the rebel army through the lines. She could be depended on." Blackburn's husband, now dead, had been "a faithful co-worker." The couple "were past common for their industry and economy." Carwell was "a Union man myself, and always felt safe in confiding in them, and trust my secrets and plan with them." Both Blackburn and Carwell had been threatened by rebels "because of their intimacy with Union men and because they were suspected for harboring Union men and provisions." After Blackburn's husband died she married Samuel Blackburn, who had been a slave. He, too, had aided the Union army. "I have no doubt of his loyalty," Carwell testified, for "his reputation is that of an honest man."

Another witness, William Poindexter, made a straightforward argument: Mary Blackburn, "being colored, regarded the cause of the Union, as her friend." Blackburn told her own story briefly. "My husband bought me the year the War commenced, I think it was. I lived with my husband who rented land and farmed, he had been a free man for about ten years before he purchased me. He paid over a thousand dollars for me." They ran their own farm. Most importantly, Mary Blackburn testified, "I am the mother of three children all by my first husband, and all of them sold to traders whilst I was in slavery. I have never heard from them since, and know not where they are or whether dead or living." Her motivation for helping the Union Army was obvious: "I felt a willingness to help the cause of the Union at all times, because of the manner in which my children were torn from me." The commissioners, persuaded by the testimony, awarded Mary Blackburn $355 dollars.[14]

Thomas and Mary Jefferson, also African-American, offered claims in 1872 and then again in 1877. They asked for compensation for nursing a senior Union officer wounded near Waynesboro in 1865 as well as for three barrels of flour and a hog. "Our Loyalty is indisputable, as we are colored persons," they testified. They allowed their house to be used as a hospital, "and furnished sustainance and the attendance upon the sick soldier, because he was wounded at our door, and the Confederates would have striped and murdered him after he was wounded he was shot down, had he not been cared for by us. It would only be an act of Justice to pay us." The commissioners agreed they deserved reward for the food, worth $42, but regretted that the other claim lay beyond their jurisdiction.[15]

The commissioners were not persuaded by most of the other claimants and expressed their disbelief with some candor. Another black person, Isaac Ware, testified that the Union troops had taken a horse from him. The commissioners quoted Ware when he said that "the horse was led off by officers & soldiers." "That is an absurd statement," the report read. "If led off at all only one would lead him off." They denied his claim.[16]

More common was the comment on the case of Adams Lushbaugh, a white man, the evidence of whose loyalty was "weak and utterly devoid of important & significant facts." Lushbaugh's case was undermined because the Confederates paid him for two wagons they took from him and "men with Union sentiments were generally well known in the Shenadoah valley & the Confederates did not pay Union men for their property." Lushbaugh, like other white claimants, introduced the testimony of his own former slave. Henry Carter painted a remarkable scene when he described how he and his owner "often talked about the War." Though Carter never heard his master "talk in the presence of others," he "was always free in talking to me. He used to set for hours and talk to me about it and always was against it. I of course was in favor of the Union." The commissioners often discounted such testimony, assuming that freedpeople might be induced to testify by fear or financial inducement. In this case, they judged that "while there is nothing in the evidence showing affirma-tively that the claimant was a secessionist, there is not enough in it to remove all doubt." The commissioners studied the records of votes cast for secession and found Lushbaugh's name there. His large claim of $931 was disallowed.[17]

In general, the Southern Claims Commission, like the Repub-licans who called for the Ironclad Oath, held Southern Unionists to high standards. Successful claimants had demonstrated their loyalty at every juncture and at every opportunity. They had voted against secession and then had helped deserters reach Union lines or hide in the mountains, purchased substitutes, suffered violence and threats, been arrested by the Confederate authorities, sent their sons away, fled the Confederacy, or enlisted in the Union Army. Mere doubt, reluctance, or passive resistance to the Con-federacy was not enough to prove loyalty to the Union—even if those actions had been enough to subject people to charges of disloyalty by the Confederates.

☆

FRANKLIN COUNTY HAD ITS own struggles with claims against the federal government. Its "border war claims" dragged on for years after the war. The Pennsylvania legislature had paid $900,000 between 1865 and 1868 to compensate the people of the county for property burned by John McCausland in 1864. This amount met only half the total that residents claimed. The state asked the federal government to meet the rest, but it never did so. Franklin put forward 1,500 claims, while Adams County and Gettysburg made about 1,000; other nearby counties entered from a handful to several hundred applications. The claims in Franklin accounted for about $800,000 out of $1.2 million all Pennsylvanians put forward.[18]

The citizens of the county had to endure charges that the invasions and losses they suffered were their own fault. As Alexander McClure diplomatically recalled decades later, "distant portions of the State, which were at no time imperiled by the Civil War, were inflamed to a considerable degree against our relief bill by the united efforts of demagogues and lobbyists." The half a million dollars ultimately requested to rebuild Chambersburg "was a startling proposition, and candidates for the Legislature in very many of the districts openly pledged themselves against what they called the border raid bill." McClure noted that "the entire northern tier of counties, then almost wholly agricultural, and where extreme frugality was the rule of the every-day lives of the people, were appalled by the proposition to take half a million dollars from the treasury of the State." Elaborate party machinations behind the scenes eventually led a vice-president of the Pennsylvania Railroad—a native of Franklin County—to support Chambersburg's claims by mobilizing his immense power with the legislature. Despite the hard-fought victory, "a number of the heaviest losers did not receive one dollar."[19]

Chambersburg struggled as well with its monument to the Franklin County men who fell in the Civil War. As early as 1868, both the *Repository* and the *Valley Spirit*—in a rare moment of agreement—called for aid to the memorial association. The effort was led by the "town ladies" and began with a strawberry festival and an ice cream social, followed by open-air concerts. "There is not a man or woman in Franklin county who cannot do something to encourage and assist this worthy object," urged the Republican paper. "To work for this noble enterprise should be a pleasure; it is a duty we owe to our hundreds of widows and orphans, to our heart-broken sisters and mothers, to our fathers and brothers, to the patriotic comrades of those who died, to the dead themselves." The message of the memorial would be clear: "those who die for their country and their country's flag shall ever be remembered by a grateful people."[20]

Unfortunately, the campaign failed, with only about a third of the needed money raised. The effort languished until 1876, when another attempt began to erect a monument in time for the nation's centennial. A local resident cautioned against a "gloomy monument" and proposed soldiers from each side "holding a canteen between them." That effort also failed, but it was resurrected in 1878, only to divide over the proper kind of memorial. Women thought a fountain would be best, but a soldiers' committee preferred a statue of a male figure. Finally, both sides won when a life-sized soldier, facing south, standing before a six-tiered fountain, won approval. The memorial went up later that year.[21]

Augusta County followed a different path to a similar destination. After the reinterment of 1,700 soldiers in Thornrose Cemetery, gathered from battlefields from McDowell, Cross Keys, Port Republic, and Piedmont, the cemetery became the site of remembrance. A memorial association was created in 1870—led by men, despite the pioneering role of women in memorialization—which worked to fund and erect a fitting tribute. It took eighteen years to raise the money for a statue of a Confederate infantryman, rising 22 feet above the graves of the men lying beneath him.[22]

☆

ACTUAL VETERANS DID NOT always get the attention bestowed on their marble counterparts. Some parlayed their wartime reputations into politics, with Union veterans dominating the presidency through the rest of the century and Confederate veterans dominating the Southern Democratic party for just as long. Thousands of other veterans struggled with injuries, visible and invisible, they bore from the war.

In 1890 the federal government conducted a census of Union veterans. Pensions for veterans and their widows constituted the largest part of the United States budget after Reconstruction and soldiers needed to be able to find former comrades to testify on their behalf. About 75,000 men were registered in the census.

In Franklin County, the veterans' census captured the enduring effects of the war that had ended a quarter of a century before. The census listed 2,016 men, their regiment, company, and rank as well as when they enlisted and were discharged. About 1,500 of the men had been privates; another 85 sergeants. Most important in 1890 was the information on their health, which helped determine the size of the pension they or their widows received. It is disheartening to read the list of injuries and infirmities, a chronicling of disabilities men carried from their twenties for the rest of their lives. Many men had lost all or part of their hearing, and many suffered from partial blindness. Many could not work because they had lost limbs or suffered unending pain since they had survived prison camps or disease-filled hospital tents.

John Christy, the oldest and most eloquent of the brothers who had enlisted in the United States Colored Troops at the first opportunity in 1863, like so many of the veterans, suffered from rheumatism. His younger brother Samuel "had malarial fever while in service leaving weakened constitution. The fever returns spring and fall." David Demus, married during the war to Mary Jane Christy, did not appear in the census, for he had died not long after returning home from the war, never recovering from the head wound he received at Fort Wagner in 1863. He and Mary Jane were not able to buy the home they had dreamed of.

☆

MANY OF THE MEN who had enlisted in Franklin County no longer lived there in 1890. Samuel Cormany, whose remarkable diary portrayed an appealing young man and soldier, led a harder life after the war than his talents, character, and wartime accomplishment anticipated. Rachel Cormany, whose equally remarkable diary conveyed deep love and admiration for her husband as well as great character and faith, suffered disappointment of her own.

The disappointment began while Samuel remained stationed in Lynchburg, Virginia, after Appomattox. Like other Union soldiers, Samuel longed to come home but was kept in the South to patrol the first months of freedom. Bored and restless, Samuel found himself acting in ways that contradicted his own high standards for himself. He apparently drank and gambled, while also engaging in some unspecified behavior with local women he himself considered shameful.

Rachel's last entries in her diary convey her sadness. On August 27, 1865, Samuel finally returned home, five months after the peace. "Joy to the world—My little world at least. I am no more a war widdow—My Precious is home safe from the war," she exulted. Not worrying about Samuel every day, Rachel was "happy all the time now. I do not feel now as if I were alone in the world." She could not wait to get their own home. "We are certainly a happy little family—God grant that we may be a good family too."

That evening, though, after Rachel had written these words and put her diary away for the evening, Samuel wrote in his own diary that he had confessed to Rachel "the very worst features of my shortcomings and lapses—during my army life." He felt that God had forgiven him, and they "so earnestly prayed together, and sought divine help to let the dead past hide its gloomy spots." After the prayer, "Oh! the peace, the joy, the rest that came to and possessed us, and how sweetly we fell asleep in each others arms."

Though Samuel felt relief from his confessions and Rachel's forgiveness, her next entry, four days later, described "the saddest week of my life. My heart is almost broken." She had prayed to God and took comfort in the prayer, but "it takes all the powers of my mind & soul to bear up under this my greatest of sorrows so as to hide the anguish of my heart." Rachel felt that she had forgiven Samuel "with all my heart." For his part, Samuel "seems almost heartbroken over his missteps & I feel that it needs an effort to save him from despair." Rachel worried that "May be I should not have put this on paper—but my mind seemed so over-burdened & the smothered feeling must escape or—"[23]

Rachel and Samuel left Chambersburg a few weeks later for a new home in Missouri. They were accompanied by an African-American man named George, who had been Samuel's servant during the war and who wore a new suit the Cormanys had purchased for him. George worked on the Cormany farm and then built a new life for himself in the West. The farm Samuel and Rachel had abandoned in Missouri to move to Chambersburg had deteriorated over the years they were gone. Rachel became ill in her new home and the Ku Klux Klan harassed the former Union soldier. They moved to Kansas and then to a series of other places as Samuel tried to recover his health and to establish himself as a minister and in business. Rachel died of cancer in 1899 at the age of 62. Samuel, disabled, lived on the federal pension he received in 1890. Suffering from multiple diseases and living with his daughter Cora, Samuel lived until 1921. He was buried beside Rachel.[24]

☆

THERE WAS NO NATIONAL CENSUS for Confederate veterans and no federal pensions. Many of those soldiers lost more than any of their neighbors in the war, for those who had fallen victim to wounds, amputation, disease, or imprisonment remained poorer than their neighbors decades later. Many were forced to live with relatives or in other extended families. Their widows and orphans suffered as well, for the ratio of women to men in the white South would take decades to balance. [25]

Veterans and their families struggled largely on their own, for impoverished states only gradually mobilized themselves and their resources to create homes for the aging veterans. Organizations such as the Sons of Confederate Veterans and United Daughters of the Confederacy, as well as local churches and leaders, worked to care for them and celebrate their service, but many veterans suffered from disease, poverty, and neglect well into the twentieth century. Memorial Day events and the erection of statues continued, but day-to-day, and in the flesh, veterans had little to show for their service to the Confederacy.

Two Confederate veterans from Augusta County proved able to use their wartime experience to adapt to the new order of postwar America. John Imboden wrote stirring battle accounts and personality sketches, beginning with "Reminiscences of Lee and Jackson" in the national *Galaxy Magazine* in 1871. Imboden did not claim to write either biography or history, but—in manly language characteristic of his wartime correspondence and pronouncements in the Augusta press—"in the first person and under my own signature, both for convenience in narration and to assume the proper responsibility for my statements." That strategy also permitted Imboden to weave himself into the stories he told, giving himself a prominent role alongside the most famous men in the Confederacy.

In tune with the tradition of Civil War writing that would dominate for generations, Imboden focused entirely on the battlefield and headquarters. He wrote of Harpers Ferry and First Manassas, of Gettysburg and the 1862 Valley Campaign, of the retreat from Gettysburg and the battle at Piedmont, where he sought to shift blame for the loss to the fallen General Jones and away from himself. His pieces from the late 1870s became parts of the richly illustrated and enormously popular series, *Battles and Leaders of the Civil War*, first published in 1887. Imboden also became a popular speaker as he traveled throughout the country.[26]

In addition to his success in writing and speaking, Imboden spent the decades after the war pursuing more lucrative purposes. Fired with the same restless ambition he took into combat, Imboden dreamed of turning Virginia into a thriving industrial state. His major publication had nothing to do with his adventures in the Civil War but was instead the widely consulted compendium, *The Coal and Iron Resources of Virginia*, published in 1872. Serving as a promoter of those resources and of railroads, Imboden spoke at expositions across the nation.[27]

Despite the many words John Imboden had written about the Civil War, in 1881 he claimed to be sick of the subject. "I don't care a damn about the truth or falsehood of history so far as that war is concerned—I know it ruined me financially—and nobody thanks me for my efforts in a common cause then, and never will unless I get rich," he confided to his best friend. Imboden admired "matter of fact *business* men in Pittsburgh, who see money in *Coal & Iron* in the late Confederate states, but none in the mysty vaults of a defunct, starved out, naked & ragged pseudo nationality." Thaddeus Stevens could not have described the Confederacy more harshly.

Imboden told his friend that "a man is making a damn fool of himself who gives his time to other people's affairs. It don't pay in money & nothing else is worth working for. I have given some of the best years of my life to the public & you know, for you have told me so over and over again, that I have not ½ doz. friends left in the Vally of Va. I worked so hard for." The years of glory and sacrifice in the Civil War seemed to count for little in the prosaic years that followed.[28]

Imboden did his best to emulate the business men he so admired, patenting a series of inventions that he hoped would make him rich but did not. Finally, he poured himself into a vast speculative enterprise in the mountains of the far southwest corner of Virginia. He founded the town of Damascus—named, he claimed, after the oldest continuously occupied city in the world—which he imagined as a great industrial center. Instead, John Imboden died there of cholera in 1895, seventy-two years old, broke, alone, far from his fourth wife, freezing in a mountain cabin. Later, his body was taken to Hollywood Cemetery in Richmond to be buried alongside other generals of the Confederacy.[29]

Jedediah Hotchkiss, like John Imboden, aggressively sought opportunities in the New South even as he told stories of the Confederacy. The multitalented and hardworking Hotchkiss struggled financially for decades after the war, trying everything from textbook sales to coal land promotion. Like Imboden, Hotchkiss seemed perpetually on the verge of becoming rich and his impressive and idiosyncratic home in Staunton—"The Oaks"—suggested that he was rich. But he was almost always in debt.

Like Imboden, Hotchkiss found a market for relating his wartime experiences in speaking and writing. Taking advantage of his remarkable graphic skill, Hotchkiss developed a popular talk on the Valley Campaign of 1862 that he illustrated with colored crayons on a blackboard as he described the unfolding action that he had helped orchestrate. Hotchkiss delivered that presentation at the American Historical Association meeting and was praised by the prominent historian George Bancroft.[30]

After the war, Hotchkiss produced new maps based on the wartime sketches, drafts, and maps he had produced for Stonewall Jackson and Jubal Early. These beautiful maps became an important part of the *War of the Rebellion*, the publication by the United States government of the extant records of the war. Hotchkiss contributed more maps than any other cartographer to the striking atlas that accompanied the vast set of volumes. Despite the efforts of the federal government to acquire them, Hotchkiss and his family held on to his maps, which decayed without proper care at his home until they were given to the Library of Congress in 1948, along with his Civil War journal and letters to his wife Sara. He died in 1899 and was buried alongside Sara in Thornrose Cemetery in Staunton.[31]

Joseph Waddell, who could not serve the Confederacy because of his eyesight, age, and home responsibilities, never became famous and never flirted with wealth. In many ways, however, Waddell enjoyed a more satisfying life after the war than his friends John Imboden and Jedediah Hotchkiss. After his service at the constitutional convention of 1867 Waddell represented Augusta County in the state senate and rose to president pro tem. He also became president of the boards of the Institution for the Deaf, Dumb, and Blind and the Western Lunatic Asylum in Staunton. Waddell published expurgated versions of his diary in his *Annals of Augusta County*, first in 1886 and in a second edition in 1902. He defiantly observed in the latter that "I have been somewhat criticized on the score that I have devoted more space to persons comparatively obscure than to prominent men. I have done this purposely, my object being to give an account of *the people*. Distinguished or prominent men have other historians or biographers."[32]

☆

ALEXANDER K. MCCLURE, the most prominent and articulate person from Civil War–era Franklin County, left Chambersburg soon after the conflict. Selling the *Repository*, McClure set off on a great adventure, described in *Three Thousand Miles Through the Rocky Mountains*, published in 1869, and like John Imboden and Jedediah Hotchkiss, became excited by the prospects of mining. On his return to Pennsylvania, McClure immediately settled in Philadelphia and campaigned for Ulysses Grant. He became dissatisfied with the corruption of the Republicans, however, and shifted his loyalties to the new Liberal Republican Party, a reform party. He was elected to the Pennsylvania Senate, narrowly lost the mayoral election of Philadelphia in 1874, and founded a newspaper, the *Philadelphia Times*, which he edited until 1901.

McClure's *Recollections of Half A Century*, published in 1902, recounted the remarkable things he had witnessed in the Civil War era, including his intimate conversations with Abraham Lincoln. McClure's fiery, brave, and persuasive editorials of the Reconstruction years in the Franklin *Repository*, celebrating emancipation, Thaddeus Stevens, and the Fourteenth Amendment, seemed

Alexander K. McClure in later life

far in the past by the turn of the new century. In his *Recollections*, McClure described Reconstruction in the terms common among white people at the time, North and South. "For nearly a decade," McClure wrote with his characteristic verve, "this rule ran riot in profligacy, theft, and the most violent prostitution of authority." The South, "after having suffered all the fearful desolation of four years of war, utterly impoverished, with its wasted fields and its silent shops, was compelled to suffer for eight years or more a political mastery that was worse than war save the sacrifice of life." The *Valley Spirit* could hardly have described Reconstruction in words more sympathetic to the former Confederates.[33]

Alexander McClure's counterpart in Staunton, Alexander H. H. Stuart, left his own final reflections on Reconstruction. Stuart, like McClure, moved easily between words and action. His contemporaries respected him for being reasonable, generous, and efficacious. Invited by the Virginia Historical Society in 1888, when he was eighty-one years old, to reflect on his role in ending

Virginia's brief Reconstruction, Stuart gathered his notes and his energies to tell the story.

Stuart reprinted the text of speeches he had given at the Augusta County courthouse before one of the many "mass meetings of the people" that marked that time and place. Characterizing in 1888 the constitution produced by the convention of 1867–68 as a document "at war with every principle of civil liberty, bristling with test oaths and disfranchisements and other enormities," Stuart shuddered at the memory of "provisions artfully and insidiously worded," so as "to throw the whole political power of the State into the hands of the most ignorant classes of her people." Under that constitution's rule, "no man who could not take the Congressional test oath could be allowed *to vote* at any public election, or *be eligible to any public office*, or to be allowed *to serve on any jury!*" Not surprisingly, "the publication of this monstrous document filled the public mind with horror and dismay."[34]

Stuart told of the remarkable twists and turns in negotiations over the readmission of Virginia in Richmond and Washington, praising his friend, kinsman, and ally John Brown Baldwin, who had died at the age of fifty-three in Staunton in 1873. Stuart concluded his detailed, stirring narrative with the outcome everyone knew: the Conservatives won, the test oaths and disfranchisements were abolished, and a legislature was elected "which reflected the sentiment of the people. Virginia was thus practically restored to her place in the Union and her citizens invested with all the rights of freemen!" Stuart gave credit to President Grant for the triumph of white democracy. "He was the head and front of a great party flushed with victory and still laboring under the excitement of the recent fierce conflicts of the war. But he was more. He was a patriot."[35]

By the late nineteenth century, Alexander McClure and Alexander H. H. Stuart, powerful voices of emancipation and Reconstruction on one side and of moderation and peace on the other, agreed that Reconstruction had been a great error. Both counted themselves lucky to have lived to see the error corrected and the United States glorying in reunion and prosperity. Neither mentioned black Americans and what they lost in the reconciliation.

☆

WILLIS M. CARTER of Staunton wrote a brief "sketch of my life and family record" sometime in the 1890s, setting down his experiences for his children. He told of the remarkable course of a life forever shaped by the events of war and Reconstruction.[36]

Carter was born in 1852, "the first of eleven children of Rhoda Carter the wife of Samuel Carter. My lot being that of a slave. It was an age of ignominy," Carter wrote with clear-eyed bitterness, when "the tyrannical and iron hand of slavery accompanied by some of the greatest inhumanities that have ever stained with cold blood the pages of the history of any nation." Carter considered himself fortunate to belong to a "philanthropic family" and to be the child of "a woman who was highly respected by both the white and sable races for her honest impartial and Christian character."

During "one of the most cruel wars ever known in the history of the world" enslaved people suffered when "impressment began upon the poor bondsmen in the South for the purpose of getting men to throw up breastworks." Those slaves were "dragged brutally to different places, and forced under the scourge to build fortifications" against those "in whose hands were held the proclamation of their emancipation." Carter's father "fell a victim to this terrible command." Impressed by the Confederates, the young father "was taken below Richmond Virginia to help fortify it where soon afterward, he had an attack of pneumonia which proved fatal" in 1863.

When "the atrocious war" ended, and slavery along with it, Carter "was then in my thirteenth year and was seized with a greater desire to improve my mind, which spirit had shown itself from early childhood." During the war, the boy had listened as white students recited their lessons; Carter acquired a spelling book so that "when emancipation came I was very good at spelling and reading." With freedom, Carter was "like one who had wandered in a wilderness of darkness" and then escaped into light. On the other hand, as the oldest son of a widowed mother with six other children, Carter knew he would have to contribute to the family.

Starting in 1868, Carter worked at a sawmill owned by his former master, who had "taken notice of my very good knowledge of figures." The boy was promoted to fireman, tending the voracious flames that drove the mill while continuing his studies. Carter "attended Sunday school which was begun at Craigsville by a white gentleman sent out to do educational work among the colored people of that section." (It is possible that that gentleman was John Scott, the New England teacher who traveled through Augusta County teaching in these years.) Soon, Carter's mother, having lost another husband to illness, bought a small farm near Waynesboro. Carter got a job on the railroad as a flagman, "a position of considerable trust." Like other freedpeople of Augusta, Carter traveled to work as a waiter in the mountain resorts west of the county, opened by the railroads.

Emboldened by his success in the resorts, Carter left Augusta in 1874 for Washington to serve as a head waiter in a well-known dining saloon and to gain more education. From there, the young man

Willis M. Carter

traveled to New York, Newport, and Philadelphia, where in 1876 he saw the Centennial Exposition celebrating American ingenuity. Over the next few years, Carter continued to travel, work, and further his education at Wayland Seminary in Washington. Just as he finished, in 1878, Carter received a telegram telling him his mother had died. He decided to settle in Augusta County, where he stood for his certificate to teach in the new public schools established by the constitutional convention of 1867. He was awarded the certificate from Superintendent Grattan in Staunton and opened a school on "Smokey Row" in 1881. Two years later, Carter became the principal of the West End school in Staunton, "holding said position for ten consecutive years, and still there at this writing."

In 1888, Willis Carter married Miss Serena B. Johnson of Augusta, "tall, graceful and of a comely figure, possessing a wealth of dark hair, of very light complexion with sparking blue eyes." Serena's parents had declared their own marriage in the register maintained by the Freedmen's Bureau in 1866 and she had been educated in the new public schools of Staunton. Serena Johnson Carter was 19 when she married the thirty-five-year-old Willis Carter. Their first child was born in 1889.

Carter's sketch of his life ended there, at a happy moment, and his remarkable life continued. In the 1890s, Carter addressed obstacles that he and other African-Americans continued to confront, building on enduring legacies of emancipation and Reconstruction: public education, religion, self-help organizations, and politics.

Education, gained piecemeal and with sacrifice, had created all the opportunities in Carter's own life, so he devoted himself to creating those opportunities for other African-Americans. He served as both teacher and administrator, overseeing the education of hundreds of students in crowded rooms. Carter benefited from and promoted teachers' institutes that helped advance black teachers' professional expertise, and he led organizations of teachers who advocated for their professional needs. Staunton welcomed a convention of black teachers in 1896 and opened Gypsy Hall Park to them for the one day of the year African-Americans were permitted to use the public retreat. The teachers met in several of the black churches their congregations had built in Staunton. Carter belonged to Mt. Zion Baptist Church.

In their meeting, reported the *Richmond Planet*, the leading African-American paper in Virginia, the teachers engaged in a "red hot debate" that resolved in the conclusion that "women make the best teachers." While the number of black male teachers was growing in these decades, the number and proportion of black female teachers was growing even faster. By 1900, two-thirds of the African-American teachers in the state were women. The men who remained often held leadership and administrative positions.

Serena and Willis made a striking couple, active and visible within the black community of Staunton, both of them working to advance the opportunities for African-Americans. The young mother started her own school in 1890, for which her husband offered classes in vocal music. Serena also served as corresponding secretary of the Women's Christian Temperance Union in Staunton, an active ally in the lives of children and women. She played a leading role in the True Reformers, a black economic self-help organization based in Richmond that fostered leadership opportunities for women and men.

Unfortunately, Serena Carter died in 1898, at the age of twenty-nine, in their home on North Augusta Street, "after several months painful illness." A Staunton newspaper gave her obituary under the title "Useful Colored Woman Dead." Carter, on his own with a young son, continued to teach in the Staunton public schools. Despite his record of success, he was earning barely more than he made when he had started nearly two decades earlier.

The 1890s, years of several of Carter's successes, saw a systematic attack by whites on black Southerners. Segregation and disfranchisement strangled ever more of the possibilities not only for remarkable individuals such as Willis and Serena Carter but for all black people. Carter fought back on every front.

After Reconstruction's abrupt end in Virginia in 1870, a biracial political movement called the Readjusters arose on the foundations of black aspiration and white political opportunism. The coalition sought to "readjust" the state's antebellum debt so as to create new state investment and opportunity for poor and working people. As in Reconstruction, Conservative whites mobilized in every way to stop a party that challenged them, a party they portrayed as the resurrection of Reconstruction's corruption, irresponsibility, and "negro rule." White newspapers fed the flames, arguing that the expansion of black schools came at the expense of good white citizens. The Staunton *Vindicator* reprinted an inflammatory circular from white men in Danville, telling of the "awful state of *humiliation* and *wretchedness*" they suffered. In November 1883 a "riot" there pitched armed white men against black, resulting in the deaths of several African-Americans. In the elections that soon followed, the Readjusters, afraid for their lives, stayed away from the polls and the Conservatives exerted even greater control.

Black Virginians protested, with Staunton leading the way. Fifteen hundred people, many of them white, gathered at the Augusta Street Methodist Episcopal Church in November to hear a black minister denounce the rioters and the writers of the circular as "murderers in the sight of God and man." Two days later, five African-American men from Staunton were appointed to "confer with similar committees in other parts of the state for the purpose of taking into consideration the feasibility of emigrating from this state to other sections of the country." Carter, only thirty-one years old at the time, was one of the five. The group staged a memorial to those lost in the Danville massacre.

Carter became involved in other demonstrations of black pride and assertion. In Staunton, African-Americans staged Decoration Day ceremonies, celebrating the end of slavery and the triumph of Federal troops in Virginia as a counter to the "Lost Cause" celebrations that had flourished since the war. Hundreds of black people marched through the streets to the National Cemetery for United States soldiers on the outskirts of Staunton. Willis Carter helped lead these annual events, where American flags were placed on the graves of the men whose struggles had helped end slavery. Carter also worked in efforts across the state to commemorate the Emancipation Proclamation by creating a "National Thanksgiving Day for Freedom, to be annually observed by the Negro Race."

Carter decided to start a newspaper in Staunton in the early 1890s, working alongside the *Richmond Planet* and other black papers that advocated for the race. Only one issue of the paper survives, bearing the motto "JUSTICE TO ALL" on its masthead. Though the paper did not succeed, Carter became ever more visible in Virginia and beyond. He served as a "commissioner for Staunton" to attend the exposition in Atlanta where Booker T. Washington delivered a famous speech in 1895.

Carter became important in the Republican Party of Virginia, which had survived not only the Reconstruction era but also the Readjuster struggle. The party continued to elect black men to state and local offices, especially in the eastern counties where African-Americans predominated. The party, and black political leadership in general, had come under relentless assault across the South as white Democrats sought to remove any challenge to their political dominion. The Virginia Republicans met in Staunton in 1896, protesting the Democrats' campaign to destroy black voting and undermine the public school system.

These efforts to promote democracy failed. The threat they posed, in fact, helped prompt Virginia's Democrats in 1901 to write a new constitution for the state to replace the one adopted in 1868. Willis M. Carter was one of nine black men who sent an address to the Constitutional Convention. The document reflected the struggles and accomplishments of people such as Carter, who had seized the narrowest of opportunities in Staunton to create a remarkable record in the three decades since the end of Reconstruction: "We have striven to add a higher and more intelligent class of people to the body politic, in the education of ourselves and our children," they wrote with quiet pride and determination, and "we have, in the acquisition and improvement of property, striven to add to our comforts of home life and increase the taxable values of the Commonwealth." Their accomplishments demonstrated that "we act just as other people do who aspire to a high civilization, and that our hopes and fears, our desires and aspirations, are the same as are found in the best people of the world."

The petitioners, seven of them ministers, appealed for an "adequate public school system for all citizens, regardless of color, holding that this is the spirit of a Christian civilization, and the chief requisite to good and intelligent citizenship, which must in the end decide the State's destiny; into which every individual, regardless of race or color, must enter in making up its aggregate intelligence and wealth." The black petitioners argued that "Virginia needs intelligence and thrift, and the cultivation of our brains, whether in black or white heads, will bring even greater returns than the cultivation of the other resources of the State." Black people knew "when the principles laid down in the Declaration of Independence are being violated; we know when the national Constitution is being abrogated in letter, as well as spirit; we can distinguish prejudice from justice."

The letter was tabled and never publicly acknowledged. The convention, like those in every other Southern state in the years around the turn of the new century, suppressed black voting. For decades to follow, Virginia would witness one of the lowest rates of political participation, for whites and for blacks, in the entire nation. The new constitution also put into place an unequal system of funding for black education that hobbled the state for generations.

Willis M. Carter died in 1902, at the age of forty-nine, of tuberculosis. "His death is a great loss to the colored people," a white Staunton newspaper briefly noted.

☆

THE DECADES AFTER THE END of Reconstruction witnessed a quiet, often invisible, struggle over the memory of the war and its consequences. While men such as John Imboden and Alexander McClure polished and revised their memories in print, other people inscribed their names and deeds in less visible places, in neglected reports and dusty records in the courthouse. People such as Willis Carter, building lives amid the wreckage of slavery and Reconstruction, would not see themselves memorialized in public. Yet they, too, touched the history in which they lived.

Epilogue

Augusta and Franklin followed the paths of many places in the United States in the decades after Reconstruction. Both kept up to date with telephones and electric lights, with automobiles and radios. Both contributed their sons and daughters to the wars of the twentieth century.

Black people slowly left both Augusta and Franklin, finding greater opportunities in larger cities or in new farming lands to the west and southwest. Although the sharecropping that devastated the cotton South did not take hold in Augusta, neither did the black landholding that emerged in other parts of Virginia and the upper South. African-Americans left each decade, especially in the 1940s. By 1950 black people—once nearly a quarter of Augusta's population—accounted for only 5 percent.

Chambersburg, like other areas near the border, followed a path of race relations much like that of the South, with segregation in fact if not in name. Many black people decided they could do better in Philadelphia or Pittsburgh, so the black population of Franklin County declined to only 3 percent after World War II.[1]

The Civil War maintains a living presence in both Staunton and Chambersburg. Dedicated historical and genealogical societies work in both communities to broaden and deepen the stories of their pasts.

In Staunton, Thornrose Cemetery is carefully maintained on one end of town and the Federal Cemetery for fallen Civil War soldiers at the other. Tours visit African-American homes, cemeteries, parks, and businesses preserved from the past. Joseph Waddell's small house, unmarked, stands on a hill overlooking the town.

In Chambersburg, the statue of the vigilant soldier still faces south, defining the center of town in the Diamond. A large stone monument nearby records the toll of the fire of 1864 and a brass plaque set into the sidewalk marks the place where Robert E. Lee stood before he departed for Gettysburg.

In Mercersburg, in southern Franklin County, a marker erected in 2009 at the Zion Union Cemetery celebrates the memory of the thirty-eight African-American veterans of the United States Colored Troops buried there. In the cemetery lie four Christy brothers and their sister, Mary Jane Christy Demus.

The marker records that Pennsylvania supplied one in five men for the 54th Massachusetts, that Mercersburg was second only to Philadelphia in providing men from the state, and that "the valor shown by the regiment improved regard for Black soldiers."

The shadows of war and the thin light of freedom still fall across the Valley.

ACKNOWLEDGMENTS

This book has a long history. Its origins lie in 1991, when I conceived of the Valley of the Shadow digital archive at the University of Virginia. The idea was to tell the story of the Civil War era from the viewpoint of both a Northern and Southern community, including all the people in those places and welcoming visitors to explore that history for themselves in an archive on the then-new World Wide Web.

I published the first volume of the story from that archive in 2003, by which time I had become Dean of the College and Graduate School of Arts and Sciences at Virginia. Those duties prevented me from starting this second volume for several years. I then became president of the University of Richmond, a job I was honored to hold for eight years. That position, too, was all-consuming and so it was not until I completed that task in 2015 that I was able to turn to this book.

Any story that takes that long to unfold necessarily crosses the paths of many people. My colleagues on the Valley Project, then graduate students and now professors, made the rest of the story possible. The project, funded in part by the National Endowment for the Humanities, ended up being larger and more complex than I could have imagined, involving many allies and friends along the way. William G. Thomas, Anne Sarah Rubin, Amy Murrell Taylor, Susanna Lee, Scott Nesbit, and Andrew Torget led the project through various stages of development. Dozens of other students and friends, their contributions named on the Valley site, made important contributions to the project. I will always be grateful to them and to the University of Virginia, especially Bradley Daigle, for maintaining the Valley of the Shadow all these years. I hope readers of this book will explore that endlessly fascinating archive for themselves.

My colleagues at the University of Richmond helped keep the embers of this book alive while I served as president. Lori Schuyler, Carolyn Martin, Ann Lloyd Breeden, Carrie Caumont, and Martha Pittaway managed my work as president, allowing me to stay active in history. The board of trustees, led by rectors George Wellde, Charles Ledsinger, and Patricia Rowland, encouraged my teaching, writing, and public engagement as a historian. Other friends on the board, especially Ann Carol Marchant and Allison Weinstein, offered their warm support, as did my wonderful colleagues in the cabinet. I loved my time as president at Richmond and am pleased to be a professor there now.

Brian Balogh, Gary Gallagher, and Alan Taylor read the manuscript with the deep insight and generous spirit characteristic of such gifted scholars and good friends. Steve Forman of W. W. Norton has been a loyal ally over all these years, patiently waiting for this volume and then moving quickly to help it come to fruition when I had time to write. Steve's skill as an editor has made every page better.

Our family is larger now than it has appeared in the acknowledgement pages of earlier books, and we are delighted that Lance, Rachael, and Avery have joined us. Nathaniel designed the beautiful maps in this book, and Hannah and Lance offered remarkably thoughtful comments. Abby has been with me through every adventure. I could not be more fortunate, or more grateful.

A NOTE ON THE
DOCUMENTATION

Unless otherwise specified, all primary sources quoted in the book are in the Valley of the Shadow archive, transcribed, annotated, and searchable at http://valley.lib.virginia.edu. The listing below indicates the original archival location of each manuscript collection. In some cases, as when private individuals loaned papers and images to include in the digital archive, those sources are available only in the Valley archive. Some generalizations in the text are based on statistical patterns from the databases on the Valley of the Shadow website.

MANUSCRIPT COLLECTIONS CONSULTED

Albert and Shirley Small Special Collections Library, University of Virginia, Charlottesville, Virginia
    Augusta
        Blackford Family Letters
        Nancy Emerson Diary
        Malcolm Fleming Letter
        Francis McFarland Diary

McGuffin Family Papers

Joseph Addison Waddell Diary

American Missionary Association Archives Collection

    Augusta

        C. E. Dewey Letters

        Sarah H. Davison Letters

Fredericksburg and Spotsylvania National Battlefield Park,
Fredericksburg, Virginia

    Augusta

        A. W. Kersh Letters

Kittochtinny Historical Society, Chambersburg, Pennsylvania

    Franklin

        Abraham Essick Diary

        William Heyser Diary

        Franklin Rosenberry Letters

        Benjamin S. Schneck Papers

        George C. Traxler Papers

Library of Congress, Manuscripts Division, Washington, D.C.

    Abraham Lincoln Papers

    Augusta

        Jedediah Hotchkiss Papers

    Franklin

        Alexander K. McClure Papers

National Archives and Records Administration, Washington, D.C.

    Franklin

        Compiled Military Service Records for the Civil War, RG 94

        Pension Files, RG 15

Pennsylvania Historical and Museum Commission, Harrisburg,
Pennsylvania

    Franklin

        Bloss Family Collection

Personal Papers Collection, Library of Virginia, Richmond, Virginia

    Augusta

        Evans-Sibert Family Papers

Southern Historical Collection, Wilson Library, University of North
Carolina at Chapel Hill
    Augusta
        Achilles J. Tynes Papers
        Marguerite E. Williams Papers
    Franklin
        J. Kelly Bennette Diary
        Franklin Gaillard Papers
        Abram David Pollock Papers
        H. C. Kendrick Papers
        Iowa Michigan Royster Papers
        James Peter Williams Papers
Special Collections Department, William R. Perkins Library, Duke
University, Durham, North Carolina
    Augusta
        Eli Long Papers
        Houser Family Letters
        James M. Schreckhise Papers
Special Collections, James G. Leyburn Library, Washington and Lee
University, Lexington, Virginia
    Augusta
        John P. Dull Letters
Stuart Hall Alumnae Association, Staunton, Virginia
    Augusta
        Sarah Cordelia Wright Diary
U.S. Army Military History Institute, Carlisle Barracks, Pennsylvania
    Franklin
        Sylvester McElheney Papers
Virginia Historical Society
    Augusta
        William Clark Corson Papers
        Benjamin Lyons Farinholt Papers

York County Heritage Trust, York, Pennsylvania
 Franklin
  Miller Family Papers
Private Collections
 Augusta
  D. C. Snyder Collection
 Franklin
  Stouffer Family Papers
  Nellie Harris Collection

PUBLISHED DOCUMENTS

 Augusta
  Hildebrand, Jacob R., ed., *A Mennonite Journal, 1862–1865: A Father's Account of the Civil War in the Shenandoah Valley* (Shippensburg, PA: Burd Street Press, 1996)
  Miller, Joyce DeBolt, ed., *"Until Seperated by Death": Lives and Civil War Letters of Jesse Rolston, Jr., and Mary Catharine Cromer* (Bridgewater, VA: Good Printers, Inc., 1994)
 Franklin
  Mohr, James C., ed., *The Cormany Diaries: A Northern Family in the Civil War* (Pittsburgh, PA: University of Pittsburgh Press, 1982)

NOTES

MAPS

The most useful sources for the maps include:

Ted Alexander, *Southern Revenge! Civil War History of Chambersburg, Pennsylvania* (Shippensberg, PA: White Mane Publishing, 2013)

Raymond K. Bluhm, Jr., *The Shenandoah Valley Campaign, March–November 1864* (Washington, D.C.: Center of Military History, United States Army, 2014)

Kent Masterson Brown, *Retreat from Gettysburg: Lee, Logistics, and the Pennsylvania Campaign* (Chapel Hill: University of North Carolina Press, 2005)

John L. Heatwole, *The Burning: Sheridan's Devastation of the Shenandoah Valley* (Charlottesville: Rockbridge Publishing, 1998)

David W. Hogan, Jr., *The Overland Campaign, 4 May–15 June 1864* (Washington, D.C.: Center of Military History, United States Army, 2014)

Scott C. Patchan, *The Battle of Piedmont and Hunter's Raid on Staunton: The 1864 Shenandoah Campaign* (Charleston, S.C.: The History Press, 2011)

James A. Ramage, *Gray Ghost: The Life of Col. John Singleton Mosby* (Lexington: University Press of Kentucky, 1999)

Shenandoah at War: Visitor's Guide to the Shenandoah Valley's Civil War Story (Shenandoah Valley Battlefields National Historic District, 2008)

PREFACE

1. You may visit the project at http://valley.lib.virginia.edu and read about its evolution in my book, *What Caused the Civil War? Reflections on the South and Southern History* (New York: W. W. Norton and Company, 2006).

2. *In the Presence of Mine Enemies: Civil War in the Heart of America, 1859–1863* (New York: W. W. Norton and Company, 2003).

PROLOGUE

1. The military situation in 1863 is recently and expertly analyzed in Brooks D. Simpson, *The Civil War in the East* (New York: Praeger, 2011); Donald Stoker, *The Grand Design: Strategy and the U.S. Civil War* (New York: Oxford University Press, 2010); and Ethan S. Rafuse, *Robert E. Lee and the Fall of the Confederacy, 1863–1865* (Lanham, MD: Rowman and Littlefield, 2008). The classic synthesis is James M. McPherson, *Battle Cry of Freedom: The Civil War Era* (New York: Oxford University Press, 1988).

2. See Yael Sternhell, *Routes of War: The World of Movement in the Confederate South* (Cambridge, MA: Harvard University Press, 2012), for a perspective that emphasizes the constant moving of soldiers, enslaved people, refugees, and deserters during the war.

3. See Peter W. Roper, *Jedediah Hotchkiss: Rebel Mapmaker and Virginia Businessman* (Shippensburg, PA: White Mane Publishing Company, 1992); Archie P. McDonald, ed., *Make Me a Map of the Valley: The Civil War Journal of Stonewall Jackson's Topographer* (Dallas: Southern Methodist University Press, 1973); and William J. Miller, *Mapping*

for Stonewall: The Civil War Service of Jed Hotchkiss (Washington, D.C.: Elliott and Clark, 1993).

This book uses Hotchkiss's letters to his wife Sara rather than his journal; those letters, in addition to being more affecting, are more revealing of Hotchkiss's opinions and emotions. Those letters are transcribed for the first time in the Valley of the Shadow archive.

4. *Valley Spirit,* May 6, 1862.

5. Edward L. Ayers, *In the Presence of Mine Enemies: Civil War in the Heart of America* (New York: W. W. Norton and Company, 2003), pp. 367–9.

6. Waynesboro *Village Record,* May 8, 1863.

7. Jacob Christy to Mary Jane Demus, May 1863, no day specified.

8. Ayers, *Presence of Mine Enemies*, pp. 18–24, and William G. Thomas III and Edward L. Ayers, "The Differences Slavery Made: A Close Analysis of Two American Communities," *American Historical Review* (December 2003) and the digital version at www2.vcdh.virginia.edu/AHR/.

9. *Staunton Spectator,* October 13, 1863.

10. Robert Heinrich and Deborah Harding, *From Slave to Statesman: The Life of Educator, Editor, and Civil Rights Activist Willis M. Carter of Virginia* (Baton Rouge, LA: LSU Press, 2016), pp. 104–5.

11. *Staunton Spectator,* October 27, 1863. On the impressment of slaves, see Jaime Amanda Martinez, *Confederate Slave Impressment in the Upper South* (Chapel Hill: University of North Carolina Press, 2013).

12. Rachel Cormany diary, June 20 through June 23, 1863, in James C. Mohr, ed., *The Cormany Diaries: A Northern Family in the Civil War* (Pittsburgh: University of Pittsburgh Press, 1982), pp. 333–36.

13. Borders and communities have become prominent themes in Civil War scholarship. Recent examples include Diane Multi Burke, *On Slavery's Border: Missouri's Small Slaveholding Households, 1815–1865* (Athens: University of Georgia Press, 2010); Nicole Etcheson, *A Generation at War: The Civil War Era in a Northern Community* (Lawrence: University Press of Kansas, 2011); Christopher Phillips, *The Rivers*

Ran Backward: The Civil War and the Remaking of the American Middle Border (New York: Oxford University Press, 2016); Stephen I. Rockenbach, *War Upon Our Border: Two Ohio Valley Communities Navigate the Civil War* (Charlottesville: University of Virginia Press, 2016); and Matthew E. Stanley, *The Loyal West: Civil War and Reunion in Middle America* (Urbana: University of Illinois Press, 2017).

CHAPTER 1: THE GREAT INVASION

1. The literature on the Battle of Gettysburg is, of course, enormous. The books I have found most useful include Stephen W. Sears, *Gettysburg* (Boston: Houghton Mifflin, 2003); Steven E. Woodworth, *Beneath a Northern Sky: A Short History of the Gettysburg Campaign* (Lanham, MD: Rowman and Littlefield, 2008); and Allen C. Guelzo, *Gettysburg: The Last Invasion* (New York: Alfred A. Knopf, 2013). Lee is quoted in Sears, *Gettysburg,* p. 15. Donald Stoker, in *The Grand Design: Strategy and the U.S. Civil War* (New York: Oxford University Press, 2010), p. 279, agrees that Lee's target was Northern public opinion.

2. The following account is drawn from a remarkable study by Kent Masterson Brown, *Retreat from Gettysburg: Lee, Logistics, and the Pennsylvania Campaign* (Chapel Hill: University of North Carolina Press, 2005), pp. 10–12.

   New perspectives from environmental history are represented in Lisa M. Brady, *War Upon the Land: Military Strategy and the Transformation of Southern Landscapes during the American Civil War* (Athens: University of Georgia Press, 2012); Megan Kate Nelson, *Ruin Nation: Destruction and the American Civil War* (Athens: University of Georgia Press, 2012); Kathryn Shively Meier, *Nature's Civil War: Common Soldiers and the Environment in 1862 Virginia* (Chapel Hill: University of North Carolina Press, 2013); R. Douglas Hurt, *Agriculture and the Confederacy: Policy, Productivity, and Power in the Civil War South* (Chapel Hill: University of North Carolina Press, 2015); and Brian Allen Drake, ed., *The Blue, the Gray, and the Green: Toward an*

Environmental History of the Civil War (Athens: University of Georgia Press, 2015).

3. Spencer C. Tucker, *Brigadier General John D. Imboden: Confederate Commander in the Shenandoah* (Lexington: University of Kentucky Press, 2002), pp. 73, 139–72, and *passim*; Harold R. Woodward, Jr., *Defender of the Valley: Brigadier General John Daniel Imboden, C.S.A* (Berryville, VA: Rockbridge Publishing Company, 1996), pp. 70–7.

4. Nancy Emerson diary, March 6, 1863.

5. Joseph Waddell diary, June 19, 1863.

6. Joseph Waddell diary, June 16 and 17, 1863.

7. Joseph Waddell diary, June 19, 1863.

8. Jedediah Hotchkiss to Sara Hotchkiss, June 24, 1863.

9. L. M. Blackford to his father, June 28, 1863.

10. Sears, *Gettysburg*, pp. 28–30, 90–1.

11. *The War of the Rebellion: A Compilation of the Official Records of the Union and Confederate Armies* (Washington: Government Printing Office, 1880-1901), hereafter abbreviated, *OR*, Edwin M. Stanton, June 16, 1863.

12. William Heyser diary, June 14, 1863.

13. Philip Schaff diary, June 19, 22, and 23, 1863, in *Old Mercersburg*, Woman's Club of Mercersburg, Pa. (Williamsport, PA: Grit Publishing, 1949), pp. 167–71.

14. *Village Record*, January 9, 1863.

15. *Village Record*, April 17, 1863

16. *Valley Spirit*, January 7, 1863.

17. *Valley Spirit*, February 14, 1863.

18. *Valley Spirit*, March 4, 1863.

19. For helpful overviews of the political situation in the North, see Joel H. Silbey, *A Respectable Minority: The Democratic Party in the Civil War Era, 1860–1868* (New York: W. W. Norton and Company, 1977); Jean H. Baker, *Affairs of Party: The Political Culture of Northern Democrats in the Mid-Nineteenth Century* (Ithaca, NY: Cornell University Press, 1983); Mark E. Neely, *The Union Divided: Party Conflict in the Civil War North* (Cambridge, MA: Harvard University Press, 2000); Adam

I. P. Smith, *No Party Now: Politics in the Civil War North* (New York: Oxford University Press, 2006); and James Oakes, *Freedom National: The Destruction of Slavery in the United States, 1861–1865* (New York: W. W. Norton and Company, 2012).

20. *Staunton Spectator,* June 6, 1863.

21. *Staunton Spectator,* June 23, 1863.

22. Sears, *Gettysburg,* pp. 114–6

23. *OR,* Robert E. Lee, June 27, 1863.

24. H. C. Kendrick to his mother, June 6, 1863.

25. See Peter W. Roper, *Jedediah Hotchkiss: Rebel Mapmaker and Virginia Businessman* (Shippensburg, PA: White Mane Publishing Company, 1992) and Archie P. McDonald, ed., *Make Me a Map of the Valley: The Civil War Journal of Stonewall Jackson's Topographer* (Dallas, TX: Southern Methodist University Press, 1973).

26. Benjamin Farinholt to Leila Farinholt, July 1, 1863.

27. James Williams to his father, June 28, 1863.

28. Thomas Gordon Pollock to his father, June 30, 1863.

29. Franklin Gaillard to "Sonny" Gaillard, June 28, 1863.

30. *Richmond Dispatch,* June 26, 1863.

31. *Franklin Repository,* July 8, 1863.

32. William Heyser diary, June 14, 1863.

33. *Franklin Repository,* July 8, 1863.

34. Thomas Creigh diary, June 26, 1863. For an excellent account of the African-Americans who lived on the border, see David G. Smith, *On the Edge of Freedom: The Fugitive Slave Issue in South Central Pennsylvania, 1820–1870* (New York: Fordham University Press, 2013). Smith writes: "Confederate prison records are ambiguous, but would seem to indicate between ten and forty African-Americans from Pennsylvania wound up in Confederate prisons in Richmond—mainly African-Americans who could claim that they were free. Hundreds more were sent to depots at Winchester, Staunton, and elsewhere to be reclaimed as fugitive slaves; others were sold to slave traders near the front, and some may have been detailed on Richmond's fortifications." Smith, *Edge,* p. 190.

35. William Heyser diary, June 19, 1863.

36. *Valley Spirit,* July 8, 1863.

37. Rachel Cormany diary, June 23 through July 2, 1863, in James C. Mohr, ed., *The Cormany Diaries: A Northern Family in the Civil War* (Pittsburgh, PA: University of Pittsburgh Press, 1982), pp. 333–39. See Edward L. Ayers, *In the Presence of Mine Enemies: The Civil War in the Heart of America* (New York: W. W. Norton and Company, 2003), pp. 405–7, and Sears, *Gettysburg,* pp. 110–12, for accounts of the capture of black people in Lee's invasion.

38. *Valley Spirit,* July 8, 1863.

39. *Franklin Repository,* July 15, 1863.

40. *Franklin Repository,* July 15, 1863.

41. Brown, *Retreat,* pp. 28–35, quote on p. 35.

42. Sears, *Gettysburg,* pp. 124–138.

43. Sears, *Gettysburg,* p. 164.

44. Alexander McClure, *Old Time Notes of Pennsylvania* (Philadelphia: John C. Winston, 1905), Vol. II, pp. 100–2.

45. McClure, *Notes,* pp. 100–2; Brown, *Retreat,* pp. 16–7.

46. *OR,* Jonathan Buford, June 30, 1863.

47. *OR,* George G. Meade, June 30, 1863.

48. Rachel Cormany diary, June 23 through July 2, 1863, *Cormany Diaries,* p. 582.

CHAPTER 2: A GIGANTIC FORLORN HOPE

1. A recent book by a leading military historian of the war emphasizes the centrality of the fighting on this scale. See Earl J. Hess, *Civil War Infantry Tactics: Training, Combat, and Small-Unit Effectiveness* (Baton Rouge: Louisana State University Press, 2015).

2. Joseph Waddell diary, July 2, 1863.

3. Joseph Waddell diary, July 3–11, 1863.

4. *Franklin Repository,* July 8, 1863.

5. *Franklin Repository,* July 15, 1863.

6. *The War of the Rebellion: A Compilation of the Official Records of the*

Union and Confederate Armies (Washington: Government Printing Office, 1880–1901), hereafter abbreviated, *OR*, Robert E. Lee to John D. Imboden, July 1, 1863.

7. Kent Masterson Brown, *Retreat from Gettysburg: Lee, Logistics, and the Pennsylvania Campaign* (Chapel Hill: University of North Carolina Press, 2005), pp. 28–34; Eric. J. Wittenberg, J. David Petruzzi, and Michael F. Nugent, *One Continuous Fight: The Retreat from Gettysburg and the Pursuit of Lee's Army of Northern Virginia, July 4–14, 1863* (New York: Savas Beatie, 2008).

8. Brown, *Retreat*, p. 83.

9. John D. Imboden, "Lee at Gettysburg," *The Galaxy* 1871, pp. 507–14.

10. Rachel Cormany Diary, July 3, 4, 1863, in James C. Mohr, ed., *The Cormany Diaries: A Northern Family in the Civil War* (Pittsburgh, PA: University of Pittsburgh Press, 1982), pp. 339–41.

11. Samuel Cormany Diary, June 30–July 6, 1863, in Mohr, *Cormany Diaries*, pp. 322–27; Rachel Cormany, July 6, 1863, pp. 341–2.

12. Brown, *Retreat*, pp. 34–8.

13. See Margaret Humphreys, *Marrow of Tragedy: The Health Crisis of the American Civil War* (Baltimore, MD: Johns Hopkins University Press, 2013); Brian Craig Miller, *Empty Sleeves: Amputation in the Civil War South* (Athens: University of Georgia Press, 2015).

14. Brown, *Retreat*, p. 78.

15. Imboden, "Lee at Gettysburg," pp. 507–14.

16. Rachel Cormany, July 6, 1863, pp. 341–2.

17. William Heyser diary, July 7, 1863.

18. Jacob Hoke, *Reminiscences of the War* (Chambersburg: M. A. Foltz, 1884), pp. 493–4.

19. Brown, *Retreat*, pp. 151–2, 159–60.

20. John L. Collins, "A Prisoner's March from Gettysburg to Staunton," *Battles and Leaders of the Civil War*, Vol. III (New York: The Century Company, 1884, 1888), pp. 429–33.

21. Brown, *Retreat*, p. 287.

22. Imboden, "Lee at Gettysburg," pp. 507–14.

23. Abraham Essick diary, July 1863.

24. *Franklin Repository*, July 22, 1863.

25. Jedediah Hotchkiss to Sara Hotchkiss, July 7, 1863.

26. Jedediah Hotchkiss to Sara Hotchkiss, July 14, 1863.

27. Brown, *Retreat*, pp. 377–80.

28. Joseph Waddell diary, July 11, 1863.

29. Joseph Waddell diary, July 17, August 15, 1863.

30. Joseph Waddell diary, July 17, 22, 1863.

31. *OR,* J. H. S. Funk, August 18, 1863.

32. Sears, *Gettysburg*, pp. 498–9.

33. Sears, *Gettysburg,* p. 496.

34. Alexander McClure, *Old Time Notes of Pennsylvania* (Philadelphia: John C. Winston, 1905), Vol. II, pp. 96–107.

35. William Heyser diary, July 7, 1863.

36. Jacob Hoke, *Reminiscences of the War* (Chambersburg: M. A. Foltz, 1884), pp. 171–3; Teresa Barnett, *Sacred Relics: Pieces of the Past in Nineteenth-Century America* (University of Chicago, 2013), pp. 102–5.

37. For helpful overviews of Gettysburg's place in the larger war, see Brooks D. Simpson, *The Civil War in the East* (New York: Praeger, 2011), pp. 88–96, and Donald Stoker, *The Grand Design: Strategy and the U.S. Civil War* (New York: Oxford University Press, 2010), pp. 279–304.

38. *Staunton Spectator*, July 21, 1863.

39. Jedediah Hotchkiss to Sara Hotchkiss, July 17, 20, 1863.

40. *Staunton Spectator,* July 28, 1863.

41. See Edward L. Ayers, *In the Presence of Mine Enemies: Civil War in the Heart of America* (New York: W. W. Norton and Company, 2003), p. 366.

42. *Franklin Repository,* June 29, July 29, 1863, PDF.

43. The preceding account is drawn from William A. Dobak, *Freedom by the Sword: The U.S. Colored Troops, 1862–1867* (Washington, DC: Center of Military History, US Army, 2011), pp. 47–53, including quote on p. 52, and Joseph T. Glatthaar, *Forged in Battle: The Civil War Alliance of Black Soldiers and White Officers* (New York: The Free Press, 1989), pp. 135–42.

44. David Demus to Mary Jane Demus, July 26, 1863; William Christy to Mary Jane Demus, August 2, 1863.

45. William Christy to Mary Jane Demus, August 2, 1863; David Demus to Mary Jane Demus, November 19, 1863.

46. David Demus to Mary Jane Demus, October 7, 1863.

47. Jacob Christy to Mary Jane Demus, November 24, 1863.

48. *Franklin Repository*, July 29, 1863.

CHAPTER 3: THE GREAT TASK REMAINING BEFORE US

1. This account draws from the excellent book by Martin P. Johnson, *Writing the Gettysburg Address* (Lawrence: University of Kansas Press, 2013).

2. See Evan C. Jones and Wiley Sword, eds., *Gateway to the Confederacy: New Perspectives on the Chickamauga and Chattanooga Campaigns, 1862–1863* (Baton Rouge: Louisiana State University Press, 2014).

3. Jacob Hoke, *Reminiscences of the War* (Chambersburg: M. A. Foltz, 1884), p. 174.

4. *Franklin Repository*, November 25, 1863.

5. Hoke, *Reminiscences*, p. 174.

6. Johnson, *Writing the Gettysburg Address, passim.*

7. Abraham Lincoln to James C. Conkling, August 26, 1863, in *Abraham Lincoln: Speeches and Writing* (New York: Library of America, 1989), pp. 495–9.

8. On "nation," see Eric Foner, *The Fiery Trial: Abraham Lincoln and American Slavery* (New York: W. W. Norton, 2011), pp. 266–8.

9. Historians disagree about the impact of the Gettysburg Address. The strongest argument for its importance is Garry Wills, in *Lincoln at Gettysburg: The Words that Remade America* (New York: Simon and Schuster, 1992); the strongest rebuttal is Gary Gallagher, *The Union War* (Cambridge, MA: Harvard University Press, 2011), pp. 81–86.

10. *Franklin Repository,* December 2, 1863.

11. See Brooks D. Simpson, *The Civil War in the East* (New York: Praeger, 2011), pp. 95–101; Jones and Sword, eds. *Gateway to the Confederacy.*
12. Joseph Waddell diary, December 5, 1863.
13. Joseph Waddell diary, December 31, 1863.
14. A long historical literature has debated the sources of Confederate cohesion and dissension. The strongest argument in favor of cohesion appears in Gary Gallagher, *The Confederate War* (Cambridge, MA: Harvard University Press, 1999) and examples that emphasize dissent are Victoria E. Bynum, *The Long Shadow of the Civil War: Southern Dissent and its Legacies* (Chapel Hill: University of North Carolina Press, 2010) and Barton A. Myers, *Rebels Against the Confederacy: North Carolina's Unionists* (Cambridge: Cambridge University Press, 2014). For an insightful local analysis that includes Augusta County, see William Blair, *Virginia's Private War: Feeding Body and Soul in the Confederacy, 1861–1865* (New York: Oxford University Press, 1998).
15. Compare Blair, *Virginia's Private War*, and Myers, *Rebels Against the Confederacy*, to see the difference geography made.
16. See George C. Rable, *The Confederate Republic: A Revolution against Politics* (Chapel Hill: University of North Carolina Press, 2007).
17. *Staunton Vindicator*, January 22, 1864; *Republican Vindicator*, January 8, 1864.
18. *Staunton Vindicator*, January 29, 1864.
19. *Staunton Spectator*, March 15, 29, 1864. See William G. Thomas, "Nothing Ought to Astonish Us: Confederate Civilians in the 1864 Shenandoah Valley Campaign," in Gary W. Gallagher, ed., *The Shenandoah Valley Campaign of 1864* (Chapel Hill: University of North Carolina Press, 2006), pp. 222–56.
20. *Staunton Spectator*, December 22, 1863.
21. *Staunton Spectator*, January 12, 19, 1864.
22. *Staunton Spectator*, January 19, 1864.
23. The roles and attitudes of white women in the Civil War South have been much debated. For insightful examples, see Drew Gilpin Faust, *Mother of Invention: Women of the Slaveholding South in the American Civil*

War (Chapel Hill: University of North Carolina Press, 2004); Catherine Clinton and Nina Silber, eds., *Battle Scars: Gender and Sexuality in the American Civil War* (New York: Oxford University Press, 2006); and Stephanie McCurry, *Confederate Reckoning: Power and Politics in the Civil War South* (Cambridge, MA: Harvard University Press, 2010).

24. *Staunton Spectator*, August 11, 1863.
25. *Staunton Spectator*, September 29, 1863.
26. *Staunton Spectator,* February 2, 1864; *Staunton Vindicator,* March 4, October 2, 1864.
27. *Staunton Spectator,* March 8, 1864.
28. Joseph Waddell diary, November 29, 1863.
29. Jesse Rolston, Jr. to Mary Rolston, December 6, 13, 1863; January 19, 1864.
30. Jesse Rolston, Jr. to Mary Rolston, February 3, 28, 1864.
31. *Staunton Spectator*, February 9, 1864. A long compilation of such quotes from across the South appeared in the *Franklin Repository*, January 27, 1864.
32. *Staunton Spectator*, March 29, 1864.
33. James Long to Cynthia Long, April 10, 1864.
34. James McCutchan to Rachael McCutchan, March 21, 1864; John Pearce to Lizzie Brown, December 21, 1863.
35. Mollie Houser to James Houser, November 2, 1863, February 28, 1864.
36. Mollie Houser to James Houser, April 5, 28, 1864.
37. *Staunton Spectator,* February 9, 1864; Blair, *Virginia's Private War,* p. 103, which emphasizes steps the Confederate Congress took to make support for the war more equitable.
38. *Staunton Spectator*, February 9, 1864.
39. Jesse Rolston, Jr. to Mary Rolston, March 11, 1864. (Their name is spelled "Ralston" in the census and in the newspaper.)
40. *Staunton Spectator,* February 9, 1864. Desertion in the Army of Northern Virginia was 8 percent between July and September, 10 percent between October and December, and only 5 percent between January and March; the fall numbers were the highest in the war until the same season the following year: Joseph T. Glatthaar, *Soldiering in the Army of*

Northern Virginia: A Statistical Portrait of the Troops Who Served Under Robert E. Lee (Chapel Hill: University of North Carolina Press, 2011), p. 15.

41. *Staunton Spectator,* February 9, 1864.
42. *Staunton Spectator,* March 1, 1864.
43. *Staunton Spectator,* March 8, 1864.
44. *Staunton Spectator,* March 29, 1864.
45. *Staunton Spectator,* March 29, 1864.
46. See Jean H. Baker, *Affairs of Party: The Political Culture of Northern Democrats in the Mid-Nineteenth Century* (Ithaca, NY: Cornell University Press, 1983); Mark E. Neely, *The Union Divided: Party Conflict in the Civil War North* (Cambridge, MA: Harvard University Press, 2000); Jennifer L. Weber, *Copperheads: The Rise and Fall of Lincoln's Opponents in the North* (New York: Oxford University Press, 2006); Andrew L. Slap and Michael Thomas Smith, eds., *This Distracted and Anarchical People: New Answers for Old Questions about the Civil War–Era North* (New York: Fordham University Press, 2013).
47. Timothy S. Huebner, *Liberty and Union: The Civil War Era and American Constitutionalism* (Lawrence: University of Kansas Press, 2016).
48. Joel H. Silbey, *A Respectable Minority: The Democratic Party in the Civil War Era, 1860–1868* (New York: W. W. Norton and Company, 1977); Adam I. P. Smith, *No Party Now: Politics in the Civil War North* (New York: Oxford University Press, 2006).
49. *Valley Spirit,* February 10, 1864.
50. *Franklin Repository,* February 1, 1864. See Weber, *Copperheads.*
51. *Franklin Repository,* March 2, 1864.
52. Jim Downs, *Sick from Freedom: African American Illness and Suffering during the Civil War and Reconstruction* (New York: Oxford University Press, 2012).
53. *Valley Spirit,* January 27, 1864.
54. *Franklin Repository,* February 24, 1864.
55. For overviews, see William H. Nulty, *Confederate Florida: The Road to Olustee* (Tuscaloosa: University of Alabama Press, 1994), and Douglas R. Egerton, *Thunder at the Gates: The Black Civil War Regiments That Redeemed America* (New York: Basic Books, 2016), pp. 213–50.

56. David Demus to Mary Jane Demus, February 4, 24, 1864.

57. Jacob Christy to Mary Jane Demus, March 22, 1864; David Demus to Mary Jane Demus, March 4, 1864.

58. William A. Dobak, *Freedom by the Sword: The U.S. Colored Troops, 1862–1867* (Washington, DC: Center of Military History, US Army, 2011), p. 68.

59. *Franklin Repository*, March 30, 1864.

60. Jacob Christy to Mary Jane Demus, May 13, 1864.

61. David Demus to Mary Jane Demus, May 20, 1864.

62. Jacob Christy to Mary Jane Demus, May 13, 1864.

CHAPTER 4: THE EARTH WILL TREMBLE

1. Alfred C. Young III, *Lee's Army during the Overland Campaign: A Numerical Study* (Baton Rouge: Louisiana State University Press, 2013), p. 218; Robert E. L. Krick, "Repairing an Army: A Look at the New Troops in the Army of Northern Virginia in May and June 1864," in Gary Gallagher and Caroline E. Janney, eds., *From Cold Harbor to the Crater: The End of the Overland Campaign* (Chapel Hill: University of North Carolina Press, 2015), pp. 32–72.

2. Joseph T. Glatthaar, "U. S. Grant and the Union High Command during the 1864 Valley Campaign," in Gary Gallagher, ed., *The Shenandoah Valley Campaign of 1864* (Chapel Hill: University of North Carolina Press, 2006), pp. 34–55.

3. For concise overviews, see Brooks D. Simpson, *The Civil War in the East* (New York: Praeger, 2011); David W. Hogan, Jr., *The Overland Campaign, 4 May–15 June 1864* (Washington, DC: Center of Military History, 2014); and James M. McPherson, *Battle Cry of Freedom: The Civil War Era* (New York: Oxford University Press, 1988), pp. 718–50.

4. *Franklin Repository*, April 6, 1864.

5. *Staunton Spectator*, April 15, 1864.

6. Barton A. Myers, *Rebels Against the Confederacy: North Carolina's Unionists* (Cambridge: Cambridge University Press, 2014); Noel C. Fisher,

War at Every Door: Partisan Politics and Guerrilla Violence in East Tennessee,
1860–1869 (Chapel Hill: University of North Carolina Press, 2001).

7. Spencer C. Tucker, *Brigadier General John D. Imboden: Confederate*
Commander in the Shenandoah (Lexington: University of Kentucky
Press, 2002), p. 199, and *passim.*

8. Tucker, *Imboden*, pp. 134–9, 199.

9. Young, *Lee's Army during the Overland Campaign*, p. 218; Mark Grims-
ley, *And Keep Moving On: The Virginia Campaign, May–June 1864*
(Lincoln: University of Nebraska Press, 2002), pp. 94, 138–9, 148,
161–2.

10. *Valley Spirit*, May 18, 1864.

11. *Staunton Spectator*, May 17, 1864.

12. *Staunton Vindicator*, May 13, 1864.

13. *Staunton Spectator*, May 17, 1864.

14. Francis McFarland diary, May 15, June 4, 23, 1864. For thoughtful
studies of the meaning of death for Civil War–era families, see Drew
Faust, *This Republic of Suffering: Death and the American Civil War* (New
York: Alfred A. Knopf, 2008), and Mark S. Schatz, *Awaiting the Heav-
enly Country: The Civil War and America's Culture of Death* (Ithaca, NY:
Cornell University Press, 2008).

15. Tucker, *Imboden,* pp. 208-9.

16. See Charles Knight, *Valley Thunder: The Battle of New Market and the*
Opening of the Shenandoah Campaign, May 1864 (El Dorado Hills, CA:
Savas Beatie, 2010).

17. *Staunton Spectator*, May 17, 1864.

18. See Richard R. Duncan, *Lee's Endangered Left: The Civil War in West-
ern Virginia, Spring of 1864* (Baton Rouge: Louisiana State University
Press, 1999); Scott C. Patchan, *Shenandoah Summer: The 1864 Valley
Campaign* (Lincoln: University of Nebraska Press, 2007); Raymond
K. Bluhm, Jr., *The Shenandoah Valley Campaign, March–November 1864*
(Washington, DC: Center of Military History, 2014).

19. Cecil D. Eby, ed., *A Virginia Yankee in the Civil War: The Diaries of
David Hunter Strother* (Chapel Hill: University of North Carolina
Press, 1961), p. 222, entry for May 15, 1864.

20. Edward A. Miller, *Lincoln's Abolitionist General: The Biography of David Hunter* (Columbia: University of South Carolina Press, 1997).

21. Eby, *Virginia Yankee*, p. 237, entry for May 22.

22. Scott Patchan, *The Battle of Piedmont and Hunter's Raid on Staunton: The 1864 Shenandoah Campaign* (Charleston, SC: The History Press, 2011), p. 49.

23. Aaron Sheehan-Dean, "Success Is So Blended with Defeat: Virginia Soldiers in the Shenandoah Valley," in Gary W. Gallagher, ed., *The Shenandoah Valley Campaign of 1864* (Chapel Hill: University of North Carolina Press, 2006), pp. 257–98.

24. Eby, *Virginia Yankee*, p. 243, entry for June 3, 1864.

25. The following account is drawn from the excellent book by Scott Patchan, *The Battle of Piedmont*.

26. Tucker, *Imboden*, p. 228.

27. Eby, *Virginia Yankee*, p. 245, entry for June 5, 1864.

28. Eby, *Virginia Yankee,* p. 245, entry for June 5, 1864.

29. Patchan, *Piedmont,* p. 127.

30. Patchan, *Piedmont*, pp. 128–9.

31. Patchan, *Piedmont*, p. 129; Eby, *Virginia Yankee,* p. 246, entry for June 5, 1864.

32. Eby, *Virginia Yankee,* p. 247, entry for June 5, 1864.

33. Mark A. Snell, *West Virginia and the Civil War: Mountaineers Are Always Free* (Charleston, SC: The History Press, 2011), p. 143.

34. Eby, *Virginia Yankee,* p. 247, entry for June 5, 1864.

35. Eby, *Virginia Yankee,* p. 248, entry for June 5, 1864; Patchan, *Piedmont,* p. 132.

36. Eby, *Virginia Yankee,* p. 251, entry for June 7, 1864.

37. The following account is from Margaret Briscoe Stuart Robertson, "My Childhood Recollections of the War: Life in the Confederate Stronghold of Staunton, Virginia." Written in 1915, "Printed Christmas, 1925."

38. *The War of the Rebellion: A Compilation of the Official Records of the Union and Confederate Armies* (Washington: Government Printing

Office, 1880–1901), hereafter abbreviated, *OR,* Ulysses Grant to David Hunter, June 6, 1864.

39. Eby, *Virginia Yankee,* pp. 250–1, entry for June 9, 1864.

40. Samuel Cormany diary, June 12, 1864, in James C. Mohr, ed., *The Cormany Diaries: A Northern Family in the Civil War* (Pittsburgh: University of Pittsburgh Press, 1982), pp. 434–5.

41. On the critical role of railroads in the war in Virginia, see Aungus James Johnston II, *Virginia Railroads in the Civil War* (Chapel Hill: University of North Carolina Press, 1961); Kenneth W. Noe, *Southwest Virginia's Railroad: Modernization and the Sectional Crisis* (Urbana: University of Illinois Press, 1994); Scott Reynolds Nelson, *Iron Confederacies: Southern Railways, Klan Violence, and Reconstruction* (Chapel Hill: University of North Carolina Press, 1999); John Majewski, *A House Dividing: Economic Development in Pennsylvania and Virginia Before the Civil War* (Cambridge: Cambridge University Press, 2000); John E. Clark, Jr., *Railroads in the Civil War: The Impact of Management on Victory and Defeat* (Baton Rouge: Louisiana State University Press, 2001); William G. Thomas, *The Iron Way: Railroads, the Civil War, and the Making of Modern America* (New Haven, CT: Yale University Press, 2011); and Thomas F. Army, Jr., *Engineering Victory: How Technology Won the Civil War* (Baltimore, MD: Johns Hopkins University Press, 2016). This rich literature demonstrates both the importance and the limitations of the railroads of Virginia and the relative strength of the northern system. Virginia's railroads served the state well enough in peacetime, developing the communities through which they passed and connecting them with the coast and the cities on the coast. Many of the roads had been built with slave labor, which was convenient and inexpensive for the railroads. In wartime, however, the rivalries among competing railroads, lack of connections in cities where more than one line converged, varying width of rails, quickly laid rails without roadbeds, and lack of manufacturing capacity for rails and for rolling stock meant that the Confederacy struggled with every facet of railroad transportation.

Ironically, the disconnected system of Virginia's railroads emphasized the centrality of the railroads the state did have. While Lee's army would have benefited enormously from greater rail supply, that army depended entirely on the few lines still crossing the southern half of Virginia in 1863.

42. Eby, *Virginia Yankee,* p. 252, entry for June 9, 1864.

43. Eby, *Virginia Yankee,* p. 263, entry for June 11, 1864.

44. Joseph Waddell diary, June 5, 10, 11, 1864.

45. *Staunton Vindicator,* July 8, 1864.

46. Nancy Emerson diary, July 9, 13, 15, 16, 19, 21, 1864. These kinds of episodes between Union soldiers and Confederate women recurred throughout the South. See Lisa Tendrich Frank, *The Civilian War: Confederate Women and Union Soldiers during Sherman's March* (Baton Rouge: Louisiana State University Press, 2015).

47. Eby, *Virginia Yankee,* pp. 265–6, entry for June 18, 1864.

48. Eby, *Virginia Yankee,* p. 269, entry for June 11, 1864.

49. Journal by William B. Stark, published as "The Great Skedaddle," *Atlantic Monthly,* July/August 1939, pp. 86–7.

50. Eby, *Virginia Yankee,* pp. 273–4, June 27, 1864.

51. Quoted in Snell, *Mountains,* pp. 146–7.

52. William G. Watson, "A Union soldier in the Shenandoah Valley, 1864." Virginia Military Institute Archives, Manuscript 0037.

53. Charles F. Wisewell to his brother, June 21, 1864, printed in an undated Seneca County, New York, newspaper and reprinted at http://www.bluegrayreview.com/2014/06/21/bushwacker-aversion/

54. Joseph Waddell diary, June 16, 1864.

55. On Jessie Scouts, see Daniel Sutherland, *A Savage Conflict: The Decisive Role of Guerrillas in the American Civil War* (Chapel Hill: University of North Carolina Press, 2009), p. 96.

56. Joseph Waddell diary, June 19, 1864.

57. Joseph Waddell diary, June 26, 1864.

58. The classic account of these first moments of contact between enslaved people and the United States Army is Leon Litwack, *Been in the Storm So Long: The Aftermath of Slavery* (New York: Alfred A. Knopf, 1979).

59. Patchan, *Piedmont,* p. 130.

60. Eby, *Virginia Yankee,* p. 254, entry for June 11, 1864.

61. Virginia Waddell to Joseph Waddell, June 6, 1864, enclosed in his diary.

62. Joseph Waddell diary, June 16, 1864.

63. Nancy Emerson diary, July 13, 1864.

64. Quoted in Edward A. Miller, *Lincoln's Abolitionist General: The Biography of David Hunter* (Columbia: University of South Carolina Press, 1997), p. 209.

65. Stark, "Great Skedaddle," p. 87.

66. Eby, *Virginia Yankee,* p. 275, entry for June 29, 1864.

67. See Paul F. Paskoff, "Measures of War: A Quantitative Examination of the Civil War's Destructiveness in the Confederacy," *Civil War History* (2008): 35–62; Stephen V. Ash, *When the Yankees Came: Conflict and Chaos in the Occupied South, 1861–1865* (Chapel Hill: University of North Carolina Press, 1995).

CHAPTER 5: TO BURN SOMETHING IN THE ENEMY'S COUNTRY

1. Michael Vorenberg, *Final Freedom: The Civil War, the Abolition of Slavery, and the Thirteenth Amendment* (New York: Cambridge University Press, 2001), pp. 38–40.

2. Adam I. P. Smith, *No Party Now: Politics in the Civil War North* (New York: Oxford University Press, 2006), pp. 7–8, 111, 123.

3. Joel H. Silbey, *A Respectable Minority: The Democratic Party in the Civil War Era, 1860–1868* (New York: W. W. Norton and Company, 1977), pp. 149–57.

4. Alexander McClure, *Old Time Notes of Pennsylvania* (Philadelphia: John C. Winston, 1905), Vol. II, pp. 147–9.

5. Douglass quoted in Vorenberg, *Final Freedom,* p. 157.

6. Vorenberg, *Final Freedom,* pp. 141–3, 160–7.

7. Vorenberg, *Final Freedom,* pp. 160–7.

8. *Valley Spirit,* April 27, 1864.

9. *Valley Spirit,* June 29, July 26, 1864.

10. *Valley Spirit*, June 15, 1864.

11. *Valley Spirit*, June 15, July 6, October 12, 1864.

12. Louis P. Masur, *Lincoln's Last Speech: Wartime Reconstruction and the Crisis of Reunion* (New York: Oxford University Press, 2015), pp. 117, 118.

13. Quoted in Donald Stoker, *The Grand Design: Strategy and the U.S. Civil War* (New York: Oxford University Press, 2010), p. 375.

14. For the Democrats' platform, see http://www.presidency.ucsb.edu/ws/?pid=29578

15. Stephen W. Sears, *George B. McClellan: The Young Napoleon* (New York: DeCapo Press, 1999), p. 376.

16. *Valley Spirit,* July 6, 1864.

17. *Franklin Repository*, July 20, 1864.

18. Joseph Waddell diary, June 28, 1864.

19. Jedediah Hotchkiss to Sara Hotchkiss, June 22, 28, 1864.

20. Edward A. Miller, *Lincoln's Abolitionist General: The Biography of David Hunter* (Columbia: University of South Carolina Press, 1997), p. 229; Ted Alexander, *Southern Revenge: The Confederate Burning of Chambersburg* (Shippensburg, PA; White Mane Publishing, 1989), pp. 94–105. For other interpretations of the burning of Chambersburg and its larger significance, see Everard H. Smith, "Chambersburg: Anatomy of a Confederate Reprisal," *American Historical Review* 96 (April 1991): 432–455, and Megan Kate Nelson, *Ruin Nation: Destruction and the American Civil War* (Athens: University of Georgia Press, 2012), pp. 29–44.

21. David L. Phillips, *Tiger John: The Rebel Who Burned Chambersburg* (Leesburg, VA: Gauley Mount Press, 1993), pp. 302–4.

22. Phillips, *Tiger John*, p. 311.

23. Phillips, *Tiger John,* pp. 293–320.

24. Diary of J. Kelly Bennette, July 30, 1864.

25. Diary of Achilles Tynes, July 29, 1864.

26. Malcolm Fleming to his mother, August 10, 1864, University of Virginia Special Collections, MSS 38–651.

27. Alexander, *Southern Revenge,* p. 128.

28. Benjamin S. Schneck to Margaretta S. Keller, August 3, 1864.

29. Emma V. Stouffer to Amos Stouffer, August 1, 1864.

30. Eliza R. Stouffer to Her "Sister in Faith," August 17, 1864.

31. Reverend Joseph Clark, *Presbyterian*, August 6, 1864, reprinted in Jacob Hoke, *Reminiscences of the War* (Chambersburg: M. A. Foltz, 1884), p. 118.

32. Hoke, *Reminiscences*, p. 115.

33. *Franklin Repository*, August 31, 1864.

34. *Valley Spirit*, August 31, 1864.

35. Fielder C. Slingluff quoted in Phillips, *Tiger John*, pp. 320–5; on the legal ambiguity of the burning in Chambersburg and guerilla fighting in the Civil War, see John Fabian Witt, *Lincoln's Code: The Laws of War in American History* (New York: Free Press, 2012), pp. 274–5.

36. *Staunton Vindicator,* August 12, 26, 1864.

37. *Franklin Repository*, September 7, 1864.

38. *Franklin Repository,* August 31, 1864.

39. *Valley Spirit*, August 31, 1864.

40. *Valley Spirit*, August 31, 1864.

41. *Franklin Repository*, August 24, 1864.

42. *Valley Spirit*, August 31, 1864.

43. *Valley Spirit*, August 31, 1864.

44. *Harper's Weekly,* Vol VIII, No. 399 (August 20, 1864), p. 541.

45. *Harper's Weekly,* Vol VIII, No. 399 (August 20, 1864), p. 530.

46. Alexander, *Southern Revenge*, p. 112.

47. Joseph T. Glatthaar, "U. S. Grant and the Union High Command during the 1864 Valley Campaign," in Gary Gallagher, ed., *The Shenandoah Valley Campaign of 1864* (Chapel Hill: University of North Carolina Press, 2006), pp. 12–3.

48. Joseph Waddell diary, August 4, 6, 1864.

49. Joseph Waddell diary, August 9, 1864.

50. Joseph Waddell diary, September 14, 16, 1864.

51. Joseph Waddell diary, August 18, 24, 1864.

52. Jeffry D. Wert, *From Winchester to Cedar Creek: The Shenandoah Cam-*

paign of 1864 (Shoal Lake, MB [Canada]: South Mountain Press, 1987), pp. 126–39, quote on p. 127.

53. David Alan Johnson, *Decided on the Battlefield: Grant, Sherman, Lincoln, and the Election of 1864* (Amherst, NY: Prometheus Books, 2012), Chapter 5.

54. Jedediah Hotchkiss to Sara Hotchkiss, September 23, 1864.

55. William C. Davis, *Breckinridge: Statesman, Soldier, Symbol* (Baton Rouge: Louisiana State University press, 1974), pp. 451–2.

56. *Franklin Repository*, September 21, 1864; *Valley Spirit*, September 28, 1864.

57. *Franklin Repository*, September 28, 1864.

58. R. Douglas Hurt, *Agriculture and the Confederacy: Policy, Productivity, and Power in the Civil War South* (Chapel Hill: University of North Carolina Press, 2015), pp. 206–7.

59. Joseph Waddell diary, September 21, 23, 1864.

60. Joseph Waddell diary, September 24, 1864.

61. James A. Garfield quoted in Wert, *From Winchester to Cedar Creek*, p. 141.

62. Clay Mountcastle, *Punitive War: Confederate Guerrillas and Union Reprisals* (Lawrence: University of Kansas Press, 2009), pp. 126–8; Wert, *From Winchester to Cedar Creek*, pp. 147–56.

63. Wert, *From Winchester to Cedar Creek*, pp. 142–3; Michael G. Mahon, *Shenandoah Valley, 1861–65: The Destruction of the Granary of the Confederacy* (Mechanicsburg, PA: Stackpole Books, 1999).

64. Wert, *From Winchester to Cedar Creek*, p. 159. For a helpful overview of Federal policy regarding Sheridan's burning and the "hard but humane" war waged by the Union more generally, see D. H. Dilbeck, *A More Civil War: How The Union Waged a Just War* (Chapel Hill: University of North Carolina Press, 2016), especially pp. 131–40 on the Valley in 1864.

65. Joseph Waddell diary, October 8, 10, 12, 1864.

66. Daniel K. Schreckhise to James M. Schreckhise, October 17, 1864.

67. John L. Heatwole, *The Burning: The Devastation of the Shenandoah Valley* (Berryville, VA: Rockbridge Publishing Company, 1998), p. 41.

68. Heatwole, *Burning,* pp. 42, 41, 39.

69. *Staunton Vindicator,* October 21, 1864.

70. Thomas D. Mays, "The Battle of Saltville," in John David Smith, ed., *Black Soldiers in Blue: African American Troops in the Civil War Era* (Chapel Hill: University of North Carolina Press, 2002), pp. 200–26.

71. Andrew R. Barber to Dear Cousin Mary, October 23, 1864.

CHAPTER 6: A CAMPAIGN OF TERRIBLE MOMENT

1. *New York Times,* September 3, 1864.

2. For an excellent military history of the war that characterizes the campaign in the East as "as terrible a bloodletting as the American people have ever experienced" and argues that "the result was a casualty bill that threatened the political basis on which the North was fighting the war," see Williamson Murray and Wayne Wei-Siang Hsieh, *A Savage War: A Military History of the Civil War* (Princeton, NJ: Princeton University Press, 2016), pp. 412–3; Josiah Bloss to "Dear Sister," October 20, 1864.

3. *Franklin Repository,* October 19, 1864.

4. *Valley Spirit,* October 26, 1864.

5. *Franklin Repository,* November 2, 1864.

6. Jedediah Hotchkiss to Sara Hotchkiss, October 11, 1864.

7. Keith Bohanan, "'The Fatal Halt' versus 'Bad Conduct': John B. Gordon, Jubal A. Early, and the Battle of Cedar Creek," in Gary Gallagher, ed., *The Shenandoah Valley Campaign of 1864* (Chapel Hill: University of North Carolina Press, 2006), pp. 56–84, quote on p. 71.

8. Gary Gallagher, "Two Generals and a Valley: Philip H. Sheridan and Jubal A. Early in the Shenandoah" in Gallagher, ed., *Shenandoah Valley Campaign,* pp. 22–3.

9. Hotchkiss quoted in Robert E. L. Krick, "Repairing an Army: A Look at the New Troops in the Army of Northern Virginia in May and June 1864," in Gary Gallagher and Caroline E. Janney, eds., *From Cold Harbor to the Crater: The End of the Overland Campaign* (Chapel Hill: University of North Carolina Press, 2015), p. 78.

10. William G. Thomas, "Nothing Ought to Astonish Us: Confederate Civilians in the 1864 Shenandoah Valley Campaign," in Gallagher, ed., *Shenandoah Valley Campaign,* pp. 222–56.

11. Joseph T. Glatthaar, *General Lee's Army: From Victory to Collapse* (New York: Free Press, 2008), pp. 383–4.

12. *Official Records of the War of the Rebellion,* Series I, v. 43, pt. 1, 37.

13. Smith, *No Party Now,* pp. 91–2.

14. Alexander McClure, *Old Time Notes of Pennsylvania* (Philadelphia: John C. Winston, 1905), Vol. II, pp. 158–69.

15. McClure, *Old Time Notes,* pp. 149–50.

16. *Franklin Repository,* July 20, 1864.

17. Jonathan W. White, *Emancipation, the Union Army, and the Reelection of Abraham Lincoln* (Baton Rouge: Louisiana State University Press, 2014).

18. *Valley Spirit,* September 28, 1864; *Franklin Repository,* September 28, 1864.

19. McClure, *Old Time Notes,* pp. 149–50.

20. *Franklin Repository,* September 21, 1864.

21. *Valley Spirit,* October 19, 1864.

22. *Valley Spirit,* October 19, 1864.

23. *Franklin Repository,* October 26, 1864 (PDF).

24. *Franklin Repository,* October 19, 1864.

25. McClure, *Old Time Notes,* pp. 150–5.

26. John C. Waugh, *Reelecting Lincoln: The Battle for the 1864 Presidency* (New York: Crown Publishers, 1997), pp. 339, 353; David Alan Johnson, *Decided on the Battlefield: Grant, Sherman, Lincoln, and the Election of 1864* (Amherst, NY: Prometheus Books, 2012), Chapter 7; *Valley Spirit,* November 2, 1864.

27. McClure, *Old Time Notes,* pp. 150–5.

28. Steven J. Ramold, *Across the Divide: Union Soldiers View the Northern Home Front* (New York: New York University Press, 2013), pp. 156–62.

29. Franklin Rosenberry to John Rosenberry, October 16, 1864; Henry Metzger to his father, October 29, 1864.

30. Daniel Helker to Dear Cousin, November 2, 1864.

31. Samuel Cormany diary, November 8, 1864, in James C. Mohr, ed., *The Cormany Diaries: A Northern Family in the Civil War* (Pittsburgh, PA: University of Pittsburgh Press, 1982), p. 490.

32. Quoted in White, *Emancipation,* p. 128; for discussion of turnout, see pp. 112–17.

33. *Franklin Repository,* November 9, 1864; November 19, 1864; *Valley Spirit,* November 23, 1864.

34. Sean Nalty, "'Come Weal, Come Woe, I Am with the Anti-Slavery Party': Federalism and the Formation of the Pennsylvania Union Party, 1860–1864" in Gary W. Gallagher and Rachel A. Shelden, *A Political Nation: New Directions in Mid-Nineteenth-Century American Political History* (Charlottesville: University of Virginia Press, 2012), pp. 143–66.

35. Nine districts in Franklin supported the Republican leader in both elections, eight voted against Lincoln in both elections, four voted for him in 1860 but not in 1864, and no districts shifted from the Democrats to the Republicans. As in 1860, the more prosperous southernmost districts in Franklin County voted for the Republicans in 1864 while the poorer and more rural northern districts voted for the Democrats. In almost every district both parties made a respectable showing; the largest margin was in Quincy township, where 309 men voted for McClellan and 181 voted for Lincoln. Chambersburg's northwest district registered the largest margin for Lincoln—278 to 143—but the southwest district in the same town showed only a 30-vote margin for the Republican. The soldier vote gave Lincoln a 248-to-137 advantage, but there, too, the numbers varied widely among different units.

36. *Franklin Repository,* November 9, 1864.

37. McClure, *Old Time Notes,* p. 157.

38. See Mark E. Neely, *The Union Divided: Party Conflict in the Civil War North* (Cambridge MA: Harvard University Press, 2000).

39. Silbey, *Respectable Minority,* pp. 154–56.

40. Silbey, *Respectable Minority,* p. 149.

41. See, for example, Phillip Shaw Paludan, *"A People's Contest": The Union and the Civil War, 1861–1865* (New York: Harper and Row,

1988), pp. 89, 378, who argues for the help parties offered, and Neely, *Union Divided,* pp. 178–201, who argues against that position.

42. Neely, *Union Divided,* pp. 167–78.

43. *Franklin Repository,* November 18, 1864.

44. *Franklin Repository,* December 28, 1864.

45. *Pottsville Standard,* quoted in *Valley Spirit,* December 28, 1864.

46. Joseph Waddell diary, November 7, 12, 15, 1864.

47. *Staunton Vindicator,* November 18, 1864.

48. Jedediah Hotchkiss to Sara Hotchkiss, dates missing.

49. Joseph Waddell diary, November 15, 1864. (He found another notebook later, helpfully for the historian.)

50. See George C. Rable, *The Confederate Republic: A Revolution against Politics* (Chapel Hill: University of North Carolina Press, 1994), for an insightful analysis. As Rable puts it, "If the president and his administration often seemed adrift and unable to exert strong leadership in military, political, or financial affairs, the opposition (including but not limited to the ardent libertarians) also lacked organization, direction, and energy." In summary, "what remains most remarkable about the Confederacy was not its internal weaknesses—political, social, or economic—but its staying power and especially the ability of so many men and women to endure and make sacrifices. . . . If anything, the political culture of national unity, with its patriotic appeals and symbols, was a source of strength." Rable, *Confederate Republic,* pp. 254, 300.

On the centrality of the Confederate army in Confederate identity, see Gary Gallagher, *The Confederate War: How Popular Will, Nationalism, and Military Strategy Could Not Stave Off Defeat* (Cambridge, MA: Harvard University Press, 1999).

CHAPTER 7: THE COLOSSAL SUICIDE OF WORLD HISTORY

1. Those resources were indeed remarkable. As one scholar has calculated, between 1861 and 1865 "the national government in the North spent roughly $1.8 billion in 1860 dollars, more than the combined

total of all previous United States government expenditures." The Union army was supplied "with roughly 1 billion rounds of small arms ammunition, 1 million horses and mules, 1.5 million barrels of pork and 100 million pounds of coffee, 6 million woolen blankets, and 10 million pairs of trousers." Mark R. Wilson, *The Business of the Civil War: Military Mobilization and the State, 1861–1865* (Baltimore, MD: Johns Hopkins University Press, 2006), p. 1.

2. *Franklin Repository*, December 14, 1864.

3. *Franklin Repository*, November 30, 1864; William C. Harris, *With Charity for All: Lincoln and the Restoration of the Union* (Lexington: University of Kentucky Press, 1997); Michael F. Holt, *Political Parties and American Political Development from the Age of Jackson to the Age of Lincoln* (Baton Rouge: Louisiana State University Press, 1992), pp. 323–53; Eric Foner, *The Fiery Trial: Abraham Lincoln and American Slavery* (New York: W. W. Norton and Company, 2010).

4. James Oakes, *Freedom National: The Destruction of Slavery in the United States, 1861–1865* (New York: W. W. Norton and Company, 2012); Michael Vorenberg, *Final Freedom: The Civil War, the Abolition of Slavery, and the Thirteenth Amendment* (Cambridge: Cambridge University Press, 2004), pp. 192–3.

5. Vorenberg, *Final Freedom*, pp. 176–8; Leonard Richards, *Who Freed the Slaves? The Fight over the Thirteenth Amendment* (Chicago: University of Chicago Press, 2015); Jean H. Baker, *Affairs of Party: The Political Culture of Northern Democrats in the Mid-Nineteenth Century* (Ithaca, NY: Cornell University Press, 1983).

6. Vorenberg, *Final Freedom*, pp. 71–9, 142, 163–5.

7. Richards, *Who Freed the Slaves?*, p. 185.

8. *Franklin Repository*, February 8, 1865.

9. *Valley Spirit*, February 8, 1865.

10. *Franklin Repository*, March 8, 1865.

11. *Valley Spirit*, February 15, 1865.

12. *Franklin Repository*, February 22, 1865.

13. Ira Berlin, *The Long Emancipation: The Demise of Slavery in the United States* (Cambridge, MA: Harvard University Press, 2015); Patrick

Rael, *Eighty-Eight Years: The Long Death of Slavery in the United States, 1777–1865* (Athens: University of Georgia Press, 2015).

14. *Franklin Repository*, February 8, 1865.

15. *Valley Spirit*, February 2, 1865.

16. *Franklin Repository*, February 1, 1865.

17. *Staunton Vindicator*, December 16, 1864.

18. Joseph Waddell diary, December 20, 22, 23, 1864.

19. *Staunton Vindicator*, December 23, 1864.

20. *Staunton Vindicator*, December 23, 1864.

21. *Staunton Vindicator*, January 20, 1865.

22. Joseph Waddell diary, December 31, 1864.

23. Joseph Waddell diary, January 12, 1865.

24. *Staunton Vindicator*, December 2, 1864.

25. William Blair, *Virginia's Private War: Feeding Body and Soul in the Confederacy, 1861–1865* (New York: Oxford University Press, 1998), pp. 117–20; Joseph T. Glatthaar, *General Lee's Army: From Victory to Collapse* (New York: Free Press, 2008), p. 467; J. Tracy Power, *Lee's Miserables: Life in the Army of Northern Virginia from the Wilderness to Appomattox* (Chapel Hill: University of North Carolina Press, 1998).

26. Glatthaar, *General Lee's Army*, p. 464; Grant quoted in David Alan Johnson, *Decided on the Battlefield: Grant, Sherman, Lincoln, and the Election of 1864* (Amherst, NY: Prometheus Books, 2012), Chapter 4; Perry Jamieson, *Spring 1865: The Closing Campaigns of the Civil War* (Lincoln: University of Nebraska Press, 2015).

27. Glatthaar, *General Lee's Army*, pp. 438–40, 468–9.

28. John Dull to Genny Dull, December 22, 1864.

29. John Dull to Genny Dull, January 11, 1865.

30. John Dull to Genny Dull, January 11, 1865.

31. John Dull to Genny Dull, January 14, February 20, 1865.

32. Nancy Emerson diary, November 19, 1864.

33. D. C. Snyder to Rachel Snyder, January 12, 1865.

34. D. C. Snyder to Rachel Snyder, January 21, 1865.

35. William Clark Corson to Jennie, January 17, 1865.

36. Peter W. Roper, *Jedediah Hotchkiss: Rebel Mapmaker and Virginia*

Businessman (Shippensburg, PA: White Mane Publishing, 1992), pp. 79–81; Peter Cozzens, "Custer's First Stand," *New York Times*, March 2, 1865: http://opinionator.blogs.nytimes.com/2015/03/02/custers-first-stand

37. Samuel Cormany diary, November 29, 1864, in James C. Mohr, ed., *The Cormany Diaries: A Northern Family in the Civil War* (Pittsburgh, PA: University of Pittsburgh Press, 1982), p. 495.

38. Samuel Cormany diary, December 6, 1864, in Mohr, *Cormany Diaries,* pp. 496–7; for a portrayal of men with similar identity and pride in their service, see Kanisorn Wongsrichanalai, *Northern Character: College-Educated New Englanders, Honor, Nationalism, and Leadership in the Civil War Era* (New York: Fordham University Press, 2016). For the way that other soldiers and civilians dealt with such conflicts, see J. Matthew Gallman, *Defining Duty in the Civil War: Personal Choice, Popular Culture, and the Union Home Front* (Chapel Hill: University of North Carolina Press, 2015).

39. Samuel Cormany diary, January 9, 1865, in Mohr, *Cormany Diaries,* pp. 510–1.

40. Samuel McElheney to Harriet McElheney, October 6, November 29, 1864.

41. Samuel McElheney to Harriet McElheny, December 14, 1864.

42. Jacob Shearer to Harriet McElheney, March 26, 1865.

43. Francis Pleasants to Harriet McElheney, May 10, 1865.

44. Joseph Waddell diary, January 12, 1865.

45. Bruce Levine, *Confederate Emancipation: Southern Plans to Free and Arm Slaves During the Civil War* (New York: Oxford University Press, 2006). A copy of Cleburne's memo was not to surface until 1890: Stephanie McCurry, *Confederate Reckoning: Power and Politics in the Civil War South* (Cambridge, MA: Harvard University Press, 2010), pp. 315–22.

46. Jedediah Hotchkiss to Sara Hotchkiss, November 8, 1864.

47. *Staunton Vindicator*, December 16, 1864.

48. McCurry, *Confederate Reckoning,* pp. 340–57.

49. *Staunton Vindicator*, December 2, 1864.

50. *Staunton Vindicator*, December 2, 1864; February 10, 24, 1865.

51. Jedediah Hotchkiss to Nelson Hotchkiss, December 30, 1864, January 3, 1865.

52. Frances McFarland diary, December 20, 21, 1864.

53. *Valley Spirit*, November 23, 1864.

54. Jacob Christy to Mary Jane Demus, August 10, 1864.

55. David Demus to Mary Jane Demus, August 24, 1864.

56. John M. Christy to Mary Jane Demus, October 10, 1864.

57. David Demus to Mary Jane Demus, January 24, 1865.

58. Mary Jane Demus to David Demus, March 15, 1865.

59. *Staunton Vindicator*, March 24, 1865.

60. *Staunton Vindicator*, March 24, 1865.

61. *Staunton Vindicator*, March 31, 1865.

62. *Staunton Vindicator*, March 24, 1865.

CHAPTER 8: THE PERILS OF PEACE

1. *Franklin Repository*, March 8, 1865 (PDF).

2. *Franklin Repository*, March 8, 1865 (PDF).

3. *Valley Spirit*, March 8, 1865.

4. *Valley Spirit*, March 15, 1865, quoting the Albany *Argus*.

5. *Valley Spirit*, April 5, 1865 (PDF).

6. Samuel Cormany diary, April 3, 1865, in James C. Mohr, ed., *The Cormany Diaries: A Northern Family in the Civil War* (Pittsburgh, PA: University of Pittsburgh Press, 1982), p. 531.

7. Samuel Cormany diary, April 5–7, 1865, in Mohr, *Cormany Diaries*, pp. 531–5.

8. Samuel Cormany diary, April 7, 1865, in Mohr, *Cormany Diaries*, pp. 535–6.

9. Samuel Cormany diary, April 9, 1865, in Mohr, *Cormany Diaries*, p. 540.

10. For an eloquent portrayal, see Elizabeth R. Varon, *Appomattox: Victory, Defeat, and Freedom at the End of the Civil War* (New York: Oxford University Press, 2014).

11. Joseph Waddell diary, April 15, 1865.

12. Joseph Waddell diary, April 14, 1865.

13. Joseph Waddell diary, April 17, 1865.

14. *Franklin Repository*, April 5, 1865; *Valley Spirit*, April 5, 1865.

15. *Franklin Repository*, April 5, 1865.

16. *Valley Spirit*, April 12, 1865.

17. Joseph Christy to Mary Jane Demus, April 27, 1865.

18. David Demus to Mary Jane Demus, May 8, 1865.

19. Jacob Christy to Mary Jane Demus, May 29, 1865.

20. *Franklin Repository*, June 14, 1865. See Brian Matthew Jordan, *Marching Home: Union Veterans and Their Unending Civil War* (New York: Liveright, 2014), and M. Keith Harris, *Across the Bloody Chasm: The Culture of Commemoration among Civil War Veterans* (Baton Rouge: Louisiana State University Press, 2014).

21. James O. Lehman and Steven M. Nolt, *Mennonites, Amish, and the American Civil War* (Baltimore, MD: Johns Hopkins University Press, 2007), pp. 212–4.

22. *Valley Spirit*, April 19, 1865; *Franklin Repository*, April 18, 1865.

23. Seymour Drescher, *Abolition: A History of Slavery and Antislavery* (Cambridge: Cambridge University Press, 2009), pp. 329–32.

24. Joseph Waddell diary, April 19, 1865.

25. Joseph Waddell diary, April 26, 1865. On Lincoln's assassination and aftermath, see Martha Hodes, *Mourning Lincoln* (New Haven, CT: Yale University Press, 2015), and Richard Wightman Fox, *Lincoln's Body: A Cultural History* (New York: W. W. Norton and Company, 2015).

26. On Andrew Johnson, see Annette Gordon-Reed, *Andrew Johnson* (New York: Times Books, 2011).

27. *Valley Spirit,* April 26, 1865.

28. *Franklin Repository,* May 17, 1865.

29. John C. Rodrigue, *Lincoln and Reconstruction* (Carbondale: Southern Illinois University Press, 2013); Louis P. Masur, *Lincoln's Last Speech: Wartime Reconstruction and the Crisis of Reunion* (New York: Oxford University Press, 2015).

30. The two most thorough surveys of Reconstruction are Eric Foner,

Reconstruction: America's Unfinished Revolution (New York: Harper and Row, 1988), and Mark W. Summers, *The Ordeal of the Reunion: A New History of Reconstruction* (Chapel Hill: University of North Carolina Press, 2014). For helpful overviews of historians' recent thinking on the issue, see Aaron Sheehan-Dean, "The Long Civil War: A Historiography of the Consequences of the Civil War," *Virginia Magazine of History and Biography* 119 (2011): 106–53; Brooks D. Simpson, "Consider the Alternatives: Reassessing Republican Reconstruction," in Gary W. Gallagher and Rachel A. Shelden, eds., *Political Nation: New Directions in Mid-Nineteenth-Century American Political History* (Charlottesville: University of Virginia Press, 2012); Gregory P. Downs and Kate Masur, *The World the Civil War Made* (Chapel Hill: University of North Carolina Press, 2015); William A. Blair, "Finding the Ending of America's Civil War," *American Historical Review* (December 2015): 1753–66; John David Smith, ed., *Reconstruction* (Kent, OH: Kent State University Press, 2016).

In a generous retrospective essay on the study of Reconstruction since his magisterial work, Foner identifies several areas of focus embodied in the present book: examination of the local level, providing "a far richer sense of the texture of life"; the "expansion of Reconstruction's cast of characters," including women; the expansion of politics beyond the "electoral arena to the many locations where struggles for power occur"; and an expansion of "chronological boundaries" before and after formal Reconstruction. Eric Foner, "Afterword," in Bruce E. Baker and Brian Kelly, *After Slavery: Race, Labor, and Citizenship in the Reconstruction South* (Gainesville: University Press of Florida, 2013), pp. 221–30.

31. The patterns of Federal occupation are described in Stephen V. Ash, *When the Yankees Came: Conflict and Chaos in the Occupied South, 1861–1865* (Chapel Hill: University of North Carolina Press, 1995). For a useful mapping of the Union military presence, see http://mappingoccupation.org/, produced by Gregory Downs and Scott Nesbit, as well as Gregory P. Downs, *After Appomattox: Military Occu-*

pation and the Ends of War (Cambridge, MA: Harvard University Press, 2015).

32. Joseph Waddell diary, April 30, 1865.
33. Joseph Waddell diary, May 1, 1865.
34. Joseph Waddell diary, May 2, 1865.
35. Joseph Waddell diary, May 14, 1865.
36. Joseph Waddell diary, May 30, June 7, 1865. Such feelings of confusion and betrayal marked many of the white people of the South. See James L. Roark, *Masters Without Slaves: Southern Planters in the Civil War and Reconstruction* (New York: W. W. Norton and Company, 1977).
37. Joseph Waddell diary, May 10, 12, 15, June 20, 1865.
38. Joseph Waddell diary, May 29, 1865.
39. Joseph Waddell diary, July 5, 1865.
40. For an insightful analysis of the role of gender in these transitions, see Anne Sarah Rubin, *A Shattered Nation: The Rise and Fall of the Confederacy, 1861–1868* (Chapel Hill: University of North Carolina Press, 2005).
41. *Franklin Repository*, June 21, 1865. See Michael Green, "Reconstructing the Nation, Reconstructing the Party: Postwar Republicans and the Evolution of a Party," in Paul A. Cimbala and Randall M. Miller, eds., *The Great Task Remaining Before Us: Reconstruction as America's Continuing Civil War* (New York: Fordham University Press, 2010), pp. 183–204.
42. *Valley Spirit*, June 28, 1865.
43. *Franklin Repository*, June 28, 1865.
44. *Franklin Repository*, July 26, 1865.
45. *Franklin Repository*, July 26, 1865.
46. *Valley Spirit*, September 20, 1865.
47. Alexander Keyssar, *The Right to Vote: The Contested History of Democracy in the United States* (New York: Basic Books, 2000; 2009), pp. 74–82; David Donald, *The Politics of Reconstruction, 1863–1867* (Baton Rouge: Louisiana State University Press, 1965).
48. Paul A. Cimbala, *Under the Guardianship of the Nation: The Freedmen's*

Bureau and the Reconstruction of Georgia, 1865–1870 (Athens: University of Georgia, Press, 1997); Paul A. Cimbala, *The Freedmen's Bureau: Reconstructing the American South after the Civil War* (Malabar, FL: Krieger, 2005); Mary Farmer-Kaiser, *Freedwomen and the Freedmen's Bureau: Race, Gender, and Public Policy in the Age of Emancipation* (New York: Fordham University Press, 2010).

49. T. A. Torbert to Oliver O. Howard, July 13, 18, 1865.

50. Angus James Johnston II, *Virginia Railroads in the Civil War* (Chapel Hill: University of North Carolina Press, 1961), p. 253.

51. W. Storer How to Orlando Brown, July 28, 1865; How to J. H. McKenzie, August 7, 1865.

52. W. Storer How to J. H. McKenzie, August 7, 1865.

53. Quoted in Alfonso John Mooney IV, "Shadows of Dominion: White Men and Power in Slavery, War, and the New South" (PhD dissertation, University of Virginia, 2007), pp. 84–6.

54. L. P. Dangerfield to [unknown], July 15, 1865; W. Storer How to L. P. Dangerfield, August 7, 1865.

55. W. Storer How to Orlando Brown, August 8, 1865.

56. W. Storer How to Orlando Brown, September 1, 1865.

57. A. J. Gilkeson to Gilkeson's brother (probably Hugh Gilkeson), January 21, 1866.

58. On loyalty, see Amy Murrell Taylor, *The Divided Family in Civil War America* (Chapel Hill: University of North Carolina Press, 2005); Rubin, *Shattered Nation*; William A. Blair, *With Malice Toward Some: Treason and Loyalty in the Civil War Era* (Chapel Hill: University of North Carolina Press, 2014); Aaron Sheehan-Dean, *Why Confederates Fought: Family and Nation in Civil War Virginia* (Chapel Hill: University of North Carolina Press, 2007); Amy E. Murell, "'Of Necessity and Public Benefit': Southern Families and Their Appeals For Protection," in Catherine Clinton, ed., *Southern Families at War: Loyalty and Conflict in the Civil War South* (New York: Oxford University Press, 2000); Wayne Wei-Sang Hsieh, "'I Owe Virginia Little, My Country Much': Robert E. Lee, the United States Regular Army, and Unconditional Unionism," in Edward L. Ayers, Gary W. Gallagher, and Andrew J. Torget, eds., *Crucible of the Civil War: Virginia from*

Secession to Commemoration (Charlottesville: University of Virginia Press, 2006), pp. 35–57.

59. George H. Reese, ed., *Proceedings of the Virginia State Convention* (Richmond: Virginia State Library, 1965), IV, pp. 69–71, 184–5; John R. Hildebrand, *The Life and Times of John Brown Baldwin, 1820–1873: A Chronicle of Virginia's Struggle with Slavery, Secession, Civil War, and Reconstruction* (Staunton, VA: Augusta County Historical Society, 2008), p. 139; *Staunton Spectator*, May 14, 1861.

60. *Staunton Vindicator*, March 24, 1865.

61. See Michael Perman, *Reunion Without Compromise: The South and Reconstruction, 1865–1868* (Cambridge: Cambridge University Press, 1973), pp. 25–30.

62. Hildebrand, *Baldwin,* pp. 183–5.

63. Hildebrand, *Baldwin,* pp. 183–5.

64. *Staunton Spectator*, September 14, 1865.

65. Joseph Waddell diary, September 18, 27, October 18, 1865.

66. Joseph Waddell diary, October 18, 1865.

67. *Valley Spirit*, October 18, 25, 1865.

68. *Franklin Repository*, October 18, 1865; see Hans L. Trefousse, *Thaddeus Stevens: Nineteenth-Century Egalitarian* (Chapel Hill: University of North Carolina Press, 1997); on the origins of the radicals in antebellum antislavery, see Summers, *Ordeal of the Reunion*, pp. 82–3.

69. *Franklin Repository*, November 8, 1865.

CHAPTER 9: REBELISM

1. W. Storer How to Orlando Brown, January 8, 1866.

2. W. Storer How to Orlando Brown, January 9, 11, 22, 1866; Frederick S. Tukey to W. Storer How, January 31, 1866.

3. For helpful overviews of women and the Freedmen's Bureau, see Mary Farmer-Kaiser, *Freedwomen and the Freedmen's Bureau: Race, Gender, and Public Policy in the Age of Emancipation* (New York: Fordham University Press, 2010); Laura F. Edwards, *Gendered Strife and Confusion: The Political Culture of Reconstruction* (Urbana: University of Illinois Press, 1997); Thavolia Glymph, *Out of the House of Bondage:*

The Transformation of the Plantation Household (Cambridge: Cambridge University Press, 2008).

4. Augusta Jordan to O. O. Howard, April 14, 1866. See Heather Andrea Williams, *Help Me to Find My People: The African American Search for Family Lost in Slavery* (Chapel Hill: University of North Carolina Press, 2012); Ira Berlin and Leslie Rowland, eds., *Families and Freedom: A Documentary History of African-American Kinship in the Civil War Era* (New York: New Press, 1997); Peter W. Bardaglio, *Reconstructing the Household: Families, Sex, and the Law in the Nineteenth-Century South* (Chapel Hill: University of North Carolina Press, 1995); Catherine A. Jones, *Intimate Reconstructions: Children in Postemancipation Virginia* (Charlottesville: University of Virginia Press, 2015); Amy Feely Morsman, *The Big House after Slavery: Virginia Plantation Families and Their Postbellum Domestic Experiment* (Charlottesville: University of Virginia Press, 2010).

5. Thomas P. Jackson to John A. McDonnell, July 3, 1867.

6. Thomas P. Jackson to Hein Rell Porterfield, August 23, 1867.

7. Thomas P. Jackson to John A. McDonnell, October 3, 1867; *In Search of . . . : Selections from Freedmen's Bureau Records for Augusta County and Staunton, Virginia* (compiled and published by Augusta County Genealogical Society, Fishersville, VA, 2012), p. 10.

8. Thomas P. Jackson to John Selby, November 23, 1867.

9. Statement of Isabella Burton, January 17, 1868.

10. April 21, 1866; *In Search Of*, p. 19.

11. W. Storer How to R. S. Lacey, November 10, 1865; Max Woodhull to Orlando Brown, December 18, 1865.

12. Priscilla Marshall to Orlando Brown, April 4, 1866.

13. Anthony Marston to Thomas P. Jackson, December 2, 1867.

14. *In Search of*, pp. 7–8; G. L. Peyton to David Fultz, June 25, 1867.

15. *In Search Of*, p. 13.

16. *In Search Of*, p. 15.

17. For a skeptical view of the Freedmen's Bureau's oversight of these marriages, see Elizabeth Regosin, *Freedom's Promise: Ex-Slave Families*

and Citizenship in the Age of Emancipation (Charlottesville: University Press of Virginia, 2002).

18. Thomas P. Jackson to Orlando Brown, August 31, 1867.

19. *Valley Spirit,* February 14, 1866.

20. *Franklin Repository,* February 28, 1866.

21. *Reports of Generals Steedman and Fullerton on the Condition of the Freedmen's Bureau in the Southern States, May 3, 1866;* Gregory P. Downs, *After Appomattox: Military Occupation and the Ends of War* (Cambridge, MA: Harvard University Press, 2015), pp. 130–3.

22. *Report of the Joint Committee on Reconstruction, Report No. 30,* pp. viii, x.

23. *Report of the Joint Committee,* p. xvi.

24. Donald G. Nieman, *To Set the Law in Motion: The Freedmen's Bureau and the Legal Rights of Blacks, 1865–1868* (Millwood, NJ: KTO Press, 1979).

25. *Report of the Joint Committee,* testimony of John Brown Baldwin, February 10, 1866, pp. 102–9, 110–13.

26. *Report of the Joint Committee,* testimony of William J. Dewes, February 14, 1866, pp. 110–13; *Staunton Spectator,* January 30, 1866.

27. *Staunton Spectator,* January 30, 1866.

28. *Report of the Joint Committee,* testimony of William J. Dewes, February 14, 1866, pp. 110–13.

29. *Valley Spirit,* May 9, 1866; *Franklin Repository,* May 16, 1866.

30. *Staunton Vindicator,* May 4, 1866.

31. Quoted in John R. Hildebrand, *The Life and Times of John Brown Baldwin, 1820–1873: A Chronicle of Virginia's Struggle with Slavery, Secession, Civil War, and Reconstruction* (Staunton, VA: Augusta County Historical Society, 2008), pp. 202–3.

32. *Staunton Spectator,* February 20, *Valley Virginian,* March 21, 1866; *Staunton Spectator,* April 3, 1866.

33. For thoughtful interpretations of these dynamics, see William Blair, *Contesting the Memory of the Civil War in the South, 1865–1914* (Chapel Hill: University of North Carolina Press, 2004); Anne Sarah Rubin,

A Shattered Nation: The Rise and Fall of the Confederacy, 1861–1868 (Chapel Hill: University of North Carolina Press, 2005); and Caroline E. Janney, *Burying the Dead but Not the Past: Ladies' Memorial Associations and the Lost Cause* (Chapel Hill: University of North Carolina Press, 2012).

34. *Valley Virginian*, April 4, April 11, 1866.

35. *Staunton Vindicator*, May 4, 1866.

36. *Valley Virginian*, May 9, 1866.

37. *Staunton Vindicator*, May 18, 1866; *Staunton Spectator*, May 22, 1866.

38. *Staunton Spectator*, June 26, 1866; *Valley Virginian*, June 27, 1866.

39. *Valley Virginian*, June 27, 1866.

40. *Franklin Repository*, May 16, 1866.

41. *Staunton Vindicator*, May 18, 1866.

42. See Stephen V. Ash, *A Massacre in Memphis: The Race Riot that Shook the Nation One Year After the Civil War* (New York: Hill and Wang, 2013).

43. *Franklin Repository*, August 8, 1866.

44. *Staunton Spectator*, July 3, 1866.

45. *Valley Virginian*, September 26, 1866.

46. *Valley Virginian*, October 3, 1866.

47. *Valley Spirit*, November 14, 1866.

48. *Franklin Repository*, November 14, 1866.

49. *Franklin Repository*, November 21, 28, 1866.

50. *Valley Spirit*, December 12, 1866; *Valley Virginian*, November 14, 1866.

51. F. S. Tukey to Samuel Hunt, October 16, 1865; F. S. Tukey to Unknown, November 4, 1865.

52. Included in F. S. Tukey to Unknown, November 4, 1865.

53. C. E. Dewey to Samuel Hunt, December 2, 1865.

54. William L. Coan to Samuel Hunt, December 4, 1865; John Scott to Samuel Hunt, December 20, 1865.

55. John Scott to Samuel Hunt, December 20, 1865.

56. John Scott to Samuel Hunt, December 20, January 11, 1865.

57. C. E. Dewey to Samuel Hunt, January 31, 1866.

58. John Scott to Samuel Hunt, February 28, 1866.

59. *Valley Virginian*, April 4, 1866.

60. *Staunton Vindicator*, April 6, 1866.

61. *Valley Virginian*, April 11, 1866.

62. *Staunton Vindicator*, April 20, 1866.

63. Nelson Irwin to John M. Schofield, October 8, 1866.

64. George T. Cook to R. S. Lacey, October 26, 1866.

CHAPTER 10: WE MUST BE ONE PEOPLE

1. *Franklin Repository*, January 30, 1867.

2. *Staunton Vindicator,* February 2, 1867.

3. *Valley Virginian*, February 27, 1867.

4. *Staunton Vindicator*, March 15, 1867.

5. *Staunton Vindicator*, May 3, 1867; *Valley Virginian*, May 1, 1867, with some quotes worked in from April 17, 1867. There was remarkable agreement among the accounts.

6. *Staunton Spectator*, April 30, 1867; *Valley Virginian*, April 17, 1867. The African-American men who led in Augusta were, like those elsewhere in Virginia, a bit wealthier and more literate than their followers. See Richard Lowe, "Local Black Leaders during Reconstruction in Virginia," *Virginia Magazine of History and Biography* 103 (April 1995): 181-206.

7. Michael W. Fitzgerald, *The Union League Movement in the Deep South: Politics and Agricultural Change During Reconstruction* (Baton Rouge: Louisiana State University Press, 2000).

8. *Staunton Spectator*, March 23, 1867.

9. *Staunton Spectator*, March 23, 1867.

10. *Staunton Vindicator*, March 26, 1867.

11. *Staunton Vindicator*, June 6, 1867; *Staunton Spectator*, June 4, 1867.

12. *Valley Virginian*, July 31, 1867.

13. *Valley Virginian*, August 21, 1867. For a portrayal of the deep roots and "remarkable speed" of such political mobilization by new black voters, see Steven Hahn, *A Nation Under Our Feet: Black Political Struggles in the Rural South from Slavery to the Great Migration* (Cambridge, MA: Harvard University Press, 2003), pp. 163–215.

14. *Valley Spirit*, June 19, July 10, 1867.

15. *Franklin Repository*, September 11, 1867.

16. *Valley Spirit*, October 16, 1867; Michael Les Benedict, *Preserving the Constitution: Essays on Politics and the Constitution in the Era of Reconstruction* (New York: Fordham University Press, 2006), p. 31, argues that "the elections of 1867 marked a turning point in the history of the Republican Party. They set the limits on reform in Reconstruction. They confirmed leadership of the party in conservatives and centrists. They convinced Republicans that radicalism was not a viable political creed."

17. Thomas P. Jackson to Orlando Brown, July 31, 1867.

18. Thomas P. Jackson to Orlando Brown, August 31, 1867; Thomas P. Jackson to R. M. Manly, October 18, 1867.

19. *Staunton Spectator*, October 15, 1867.

20. *Staunton Spectator*, October 15, 1867.

21. *Staunton Vindicator*, October 25, 1867; *Staunton Spectator*, October 29, 1867; Joseph Waddell, *Annals of Augusta County, from 1726 to 1871* (Staunton, VA: C. R. Caldwell, 1902), p. 348.

22. For the perpetual threat and reality of violence, see Douglas R. Egerton, *The Wars of Reconstruction: The Brief, Violent History of America's Most Progressive Era* (New York: Bloomsbury Press, 2014); Carole Emberton, *Beyond Redemption: Race, Violence, and the American South after the Civil War* (Chicago: University of Chicago Press, 2013); Stephen Budiansky, *The Bloody Shirt: Terror After Appomattox* (New York: Viking, 2008).

23. Thomas P. Jackson to Orlando Brown, October 31, 1867.

24. Richard G. Lowe, *Republicans and Reconstruction in Virginia, 1856–70* (Charlottesville: University Press of Virginia, 1991), pp. 125–6.

25. *Staunton Spectator*, October 29, 1867; *Valley Virginian*, November 11, 1867.

26. Thomas P. Jackson to Orlando Brown, November 30, 1867.

27. *Staunton Spectator*, November 19, 1867. See Jack P. Maddex, Jr., *The Virginia Conservatives, 1867–1879: A Study in Reconstruction Politics* (Chapel Hill: University of North Carolina Press, 1970).

28. *Valley Virginian,* November 27, 1867.

29. *Staunton Spectator,* December 17, 1867; *Staunton Vindicator,* December 20, 1867.

30. *Staunton Spectator,* December 3, 1867; Thomas P. Jackson to Orlando Brown, December 31, 1867.

31. See Paul A. Cimbala, *The Freedmen's Bureau: Reconstructing the American South after the Civil War* (Malabar, FL: Krieger, 2005).

32. Frederick S. Tukey to John A. McDonnell, January 25, 1867.

33. Frederick S. Tukey to Orlando Brown, February 28, 1867; John A. McDonnell to Orlando Brown, April 30, 1867.

34. Thomas P. Jackson to Orlando Brown, August 31, 1867; Thomas P. Jackson to Orlando Brown, September 30, 1867; John W. Jordan to John A. McDonnell, April 30, 1868.

35. John W. Jordan to Orlando Brown, June 30, 1868.

36. *Franklin Repository,* November 6, 1867.

37. *Franklin Repository,* December 4, 1867.

38. *Valley Spirit,* December 4, 1867.

39. Lowe, *Republicans,* pp. 131–3.

40. Quoted in Waddell, *Annals,* pp. 349–52.

41. Waddell, *Annals,* p. 353.

42. Lowe, *Republicans,* pp. 144–5.

43. *Staunton Spectator,* April 28, 1868.

44. *Franklin Repository,* August 12, 1868.

45. *Franklin Repository,* October 21, 1868.

46. Mark W. Summers, *The Ordeal of the Reunion: A New History of Reconstruction* (Chapel Hill: University of North Carolina Press, 2014), pp. 151–2.

47. *Valley Spirit,* November 11, 1868. See Erik B. Alexander, "The Fate of Northern Democrats after the Civil War: Another Look at the Presidential Election of 1868," in Gary W. Gallagher and Rachel A. Shelden, eds., *Political Nation: New Directions in Mid-Nineteenth-Century American Political History* (Charlottesville: University of Virginia Press, 2012), pp. 188–213.

48. The people of Augusta County, like their counterparts throughout

the South, had already worked through critical issues of citizenship. Legal scholars emphasize how much change took place in the law and legal rights even before the Fourteenth Amendment. Timothy S. Huebner, in *Liberty and Union: The Civil War Era and American Constitutionalism* (Lawrence: University of Kansas Press, 2016), pp. 418–19, emphasizes that many "manifestations of black freedom—mobility, family life, religious expression, educational pursuits, economic gains, contractual rights—took hold by 1868, and none relied explicitly on the Fourteenth or Fifteenth amendments for its existence or protection. These fundamental yet far-reaching rights had issued from the simple reality of emancipation, supported by the presence of federal troops, Freedmen's Bureau officials, Northern missionaries—and, on some level, a widespread, grudging acknowledgement among white Southerners that they had lost the war and that those whom they had previously held as slaves had attained the status of free people in a new federal Union."

Laura F. Edwards stresses that in the nineteenth century "governance took place through an array of institutions: those that were relatively private, such as households, churches, and communities as well as those that were formally public, such as local, state, and federal governments in their judicial, legislative, and administrative forms. . . . To the extent that national legal principles emerged during Reconstruction, they owed as much to the various efforts of diverse groups of people working in localized contexts as they did to federal policy." *A Legal History of the Civil War and Reconstruction: A Nation of Rights* (Cambridge: Cambridge University Press, 2015), p. 175.

49. John R. Hildebrand, *The Life and Times of John Brown Baldwin, 1820–1873: A Chronicle of Virginia's Struggle with Slavery, Secession, Civil War, and Reconstruction* (Staunton, VA: Augusta County Historical Society, 2008), pp. 236–42.

50. *Valley Virginian,* January 28, 1869.

51. *Staunton Vindicator,* January 29, 1869.

52. *Staunton Spectator*, February 23, 1869.

53. *Staunton Vindicator*, February 26, 1869.

54. *Staunton Spectator,* March 2, 1869; *Staunton Vindicator,* March 5, 1869.

55. *Staunton Spectator,* March 23, 1869.

56. *Staunton Vindicator,* June 17, 1869; *Staunton Spectator,* June 15, 1869.

57. *Staunton Spectator,* May 25, June 1, 1869.

58. *Staunton Spectator,* June 29, 1869.

59. *Staunton Spectator,* July 20, 1869.

60. See Louis Moore, "The Elusive Center: Virginia Politics and the General Assembly, 1869–1871," *Virginia Magazine of History and Biography* 103 (April 1995): 207–36; Michael Perman, *The Road to Redemption: Southern Politics, 1869–1879* (Chapel Hill: University of North Carolina Press, 1984), pp. 13–21. Perman describes similar efforts in Mississippi and Texas, though they were defeated there.

CHAPTER 11: THE PAST IS NOT DEAD

1. Thomas P. Jackson to R. M. Manly, November 4, 1867; John Scott to E. P. Smith, November 30, 1868.

2. John Scott to E. P. Smith, December 12, 1868. On the eagerness of black students and teachers, see Heather Andrea Williams, *Self-Taught: African American Education in Slavery and Freedom* (Chapel Hill: University of North Carolina Press, 2005). For a helpful overview of these missionary efforts and civic nationalism, see Edward J. Blum, *Reforging the White Republic: Race, Religion, and American Nationalism, 1865–1898* (Baton Rouge: Louisiana State University, 2005). As Blum points out, "The drive to provide humanitarian relief and education to southern freedpeople was an interdenominational and interracial crusade that brought thousands of northerners into a common cause and generated massive amounts of concern for African-Americans' rights and privileges." More than eight thousand men and women, black and white, came to the South to help and northern organizations raised $20 million for their work. Pp. 54–60.

3. Sarah H. Davison to E. P. Smith, January 1, 1869.

4. Sarah H. Davison to E. P. Smith, February 3, 1869.

5. Sarah H. Davison to E. P. Smith, March 1, 1869.

6. Laten Ervin Bechtel with Susie Brent King, *"That's Just the Way It Was": A Chronological and Documentary History of African-American Schools in Staunton and Augusta County* (Staunton, VA: Lot's Wife Publishing Company, 2010), pp. 39–41.

7. *Franklin Repository,* September 9, 1868.

8. William J. Dews to Orlando Brown, July 8, 1868.

9. *Valley Virginian,* September 16, 1869.

10. *Franklin Repository,* August 19, 1868; *Valley Spirit,* August 19, 1868.

11. *Valley Virginian,* October 14, 1870; *Staunton Spectator,* October 18, 1870.

12. *Franklin Repository,* October 19, 1870.

13. Southern Claims Commission: Claim of George W. Hollar, 1876, Claim No. 21,827. For an eloquent and original study of this body, see Susanna Michele Lee, *Claiming the Union: Citizenship in the Post–Civil War South* (New York: Cambridge University Press, 2014).

14. Southern Claims Commission: Claim of Mary Blackburn, 1875, Claim No. 1378.

15. Southern Claims Commission: Claim of Thomas and Nancy Jefferson, 1877, Claim No. 15,385.

16. Southern Claims Commission: Claim of Isaac Ware, August 21, 1871, Claim No. 12,671.

17. Southern Claims Commission: Claim of Adams Lushbaugh, March 7, 1873, Claim No. 19,932.

18. Gordon Boyer Lawrence, "The Burning and Reconstruction of Chambersburg, Pennsylvania, 1864–1870" (MA thesis, University of Richmond, 2008), p. 12.

19. Alexander H. McClure, *Old Time Notes of Pennsylvania* (Philadelphia: John C. Winston, 1905), Vol. II, pp. 170–80.

20. *Valley Spirit,* June 17, 1868; *Franklin Repository,* December 2, 1868.

21. http://valley.lib.virginia.edu/VoS/memory/franklinmemory_p3b.html

22. http://www.thornrose.org/history.html

23. Samuel Cormany diary, August 27, 1865; Rachel Cormany diary, September 1, 1865, in James C. Mohr, ed., *The Cormany Diaries: A*

Northern Family in the Civil War (Pittsburgh, PA: University of Pittsburgh Press, 1982), pp. 581, 582.

24. Mohr, ed., *Cormany Diaries*, pp. 583–6.

25. See the eloquent portrayal in Jeffrey W. McClurken, *Take Care of the Living: Reconstructing Confederate Veteran Families in Virginia* (Charlottesville: University of Virginia Press, 2009).

26. See, for example, Imboden, "Stonewall Jackson in the Shenandoah," *The Century* 30:2 (June 1885), pp. 280–293.

27. John D. Imboden, *The Coal and Iron Resources of Virginia: Their Extent, Commercial Value, and Early Development Considered. A Paper Read Before a Meeting of Members of the Legislature and Prominent Citizens in the Capitol at Richmond, February 19th, 1872* (Richmond, VA: Clemmitt & Jones, printers, 1872).

28. Imboden to John Marshall McCue, February 1, 1881, quoted in Alfonso John Mooney IV, "Shadows of Dominion: White Men and Power in Slavery, War, and the New South" (PhD dissertation, University of Virginia, 2007), pp. 175–6.

29. Mooney, "Shadows of Dominion," and Spencer C. Tucker, *Brigadier General John D. Imboden: Confederate Commander in the Shenandoah* (Lexington: University of Kentucky Press, 2003).

30. Peter W. Roper, *Jedediah Hotchkiss: Rebel Mapmaker and Virginia Businessman* (Shippensburg, PA: White Mane Publishing Company, 1992), pp. 154–5.

31. Roper, *Hotchkiss,* p. 203.

32. Joseph A. Waddell, *Annals of Augusta County, Virginia, from 1726 to 1871* (second edition) (Staunton, VA: C. R. Caldwell, 1902), p. v.

33. *Colonel Alexander K. McClure's Recollections of Half a Century* (Salem, MA: The Salem Company, 1902), p. 303. For a useful survey of the large literature on such sentiments, see Nina Silber, "Reunion and Reconciliation, Reviewed and Reconsidered," *Journal of American History* (June 2016): 59–83.

34. Alexander H. H. Stuart, *A Narrative of the Leading Incidents of the Organization of the First Popular Movement in Virginia in 1865* (Richmond, VA: Wm. Ellis Jones, 1888), p. 17.

35. Stuart, *Narrative*, p. 68. Jack P. Maddex points out that "the Committee of Nine was only one of several Virginia groups pursuing the same task at the same time. The moderate Republicans probably changed more minds than did the nine, who did, nevertheless, win the confidence of a few very influential individuals, including apparently the president-elect." Some complained that Stuart "exaggerated his own importance." See Jack P. Maddex, Jr., *The Virginia Conservatives, 1867–1879: A Study in Reconstruction Politics* (Chapel Hill: University of North Carolina Press, 1970), pp. 67, 71.

36. The following account of Carter's life is drawn from an impressive work of historical detection: Robert Heinrich and Deborah Harding, *From Slave to Statesman: The Life of Educator, Editor, and Civil Rights Activist Willis M. Carter of Virginia* (Baton Rouge: Louisiana State University Press, 2016).

EPILOGUE

1. Richard K. MacMaster, *Augusta County History, 1865–1950* (Staunton, VA: Augusta County Historical Society, 1987); David G. Smith, *On the Edge of Freedom: The Fugitive Slave Issue in South Central Pennsylvania, 1820–1870* (New York: Fordham University Press, 2013), p. 211.

INDEX

Page numbers in *italics* refer to illustrations.

abolitionists, xxi
  aiding fugitive slaves in Franklin County, 11–12
  criticism of Republicans, 290–91
  on linking end of slavery to Union cause, 36
African Americans
  in Augusta County
    after Reconstruction, 497
    children in, as subjects of contention, 378–79
    lack of opportunity to speak for themselves, 415–17
    leaders, 545n6
  Baldwin on equality for, 388–91

formerly enslaved people, *see* freedmen
  in Franklin County, 11–12, 376
  after Reconstruction, 497
  capture into slavery by Confederate soldiers, 45–46, 49, 512n34
  in Massachusetts Infantry Regiments, *see* 54th Massachusetts Infantry Regiment; 55th Massachusetts Infantry Regiment
massacre of
  in Memphis, 401–3
  in New Orleans, 403

African Americans (*continued*)
schools for, 35, 406–14, 462–64, 492
in United States Colored Troops, 12, 91, 94–95, 134–37, 315–18, 329, 334–35, 376, 401–2, 477–78, 498
at Virginia Constitutional Convention, 445
voting rights for, 354, 459
election of 1864 and, 194
election of 1867 and, 431–32, 434–38
election of 1868 and, 448–49
Staunton meetings on, 421–30, 453–55, 457–58
violence following, 438–39
see also enslaved people; slavery
Alesouth, Eliza, 376
American Missionary Association of Albany, 406–7, 408–9, 462, 464, 504
American Party, 127
Appomattox, surrender at, 329–31, 418
Arkansas, 10
Army of Northern Virginia, 123–24, 140, 299–300, 322
desertion in, 300, 518n40
hunger of, 26–27, 318
retreat from Gettysburg, 68–74, 71, 76–81

retreat from Petersburg, 326
victory at Chancellorsville, 1–2, 25
wounded soldiers at Gettysburg, 64, 69, 72–74, 75–76, 77, 86, 87
wounded soldiers at Staunton, 72, 83
Army of the Potomac, 32, 54, 142, 145–46
Army of the Shenandoah, 227
Atlanta, Ga., 141, 190–91, 231–32
Augusta County, Va., xxi, 4–6, 6
African Americans in
children as subjects of contention, 378–79
leaders, 545n6
after Reconstruction, 497, 498
Civil War as straining slavery in, 15–16
deaths during Civil War in, 14, 38, 84, 146, 339
enslaved people in, 380–81
in 1860, 15
in 1863, 111–12
after the war, 344
Hotchkiss's mapping of, 4–6, 5
memorial association created in, 476
men enlisted in Confederate army in, demographics on, 338–40

military recruiters in, 111

newspapers in, *see Staunton Spectator*; *Vindicator*

path from Unionism to Confederate loyalty in, 38–40

prisoners of war from, number of, 339

Sheridan's raid on, 239–41, 250

struggle with food shortages, 295–97

see also Staunton, Va.

Averell, William Woods, 144, 149, 156, 157, 173, 175, 184, 185, 206–8, 210, 471

Baldwin, John Brown, *361*, 404, 439–40, 451–52, 457–59, 486

efforts to save Union while protecting slavery, 360–62

in election of 1865, 364, 365

loyalty to Confederacy, 362

on race, 388–91, 439–40, 457–58

reunification proposal of, 363–64

support for "universal suffrage and universal amnesty," 451–53, 459

testimony before committee on Confederate States, 387–91, 394

Bancroft, George, 483

Barber, Andrew R., 243

Baritz, William, 35

Bennette, J. Kelly, 208–9, 505

Bethell, Jane, 374

Blackburn, Mary, 471–73

Blackburn, Samuel, 472

black codes, 388–89, 395

Blow, Henry T., 387

Booth, John Wilkes, 338, 341

Breckinridge, John C., 120, 127, 151–52, *151*, 174, 180, 231, 233, 242–43

Brown, John, xxi, 11–12

Brown, Lizzie, 120

Brown, Orlando, 466

Bucker, Horace, 375

Buford, John, 53–54

Burnside, Ambrose, 36

Burton, Benjamin, 375

Burton, Horace, 375

Burton, Isabella, 375

Carson, James E., 374

Carter, Henry, 473–74

Carter, Rhoda, 487, 488

Carter, Samuel, 487–88

Carter, Serena B. Johnson, 489–90, 491

Carter, Willis M., 16, 487–91, *489*, 492–95

Carwell, Michael, 472

Cedar Creek, Battle of, 249–50

Cemetery Committee, 398, 400–401

Cemetery Ridge, 58, 62, 65–66, 87, 134

Chambersburg, Pa., 7–8, *8*

after Reconstruction, 497–98

burning of, 204–12, *205, 211,* 214–19, *222, 224*

criticism for lack of defense in, 223–24

Harper's Weekly coverage of, 225–26

local economy after, 222–23

state compensation for, 225, 475

Confederate soldiers' occupation of

African Americans' rush into, before invasion, 45–46, 47–48

amount of livestock and food seized by, 51

arrival of, 40–41, 48–49

desire for retaliation, 41–42, 45

envy of enemy, 43

Lee's orders regarding, 41, 217

reactions to Pennsylvanians, 41–44

historical and genealogical societies in, 498

monument to men who died in the war, 475–76, 498

newspapers of, 8–9, 34–35

see also Franklin Repository; Valley Spirit

reaction to Lee's surrender, 333–34

residents' fears of invasion after Milroy's defeat, 33

see also Franklin County, Pa.

Chancellorsville, Battle of, 61, 100

Army of Northern Virginia's victory at, 1–2, 25

Franklin soldiers wounded and killed in, 14

Charleston, S.C., 91–93

Charlottesville, Va., 166, 167

Chase, Salmon P., 451

Chattanooga, Tenn., 100, 106, 107, 125, 133, 140

Chickamauga, Battle of, 100, 101, 133, 309, 444

Christy, Jacob, 12, 91, 93, 94–95, 135, 136, 137, 315–16, 335, 498

Christy, John, 315, 316–17, 477

Christy, Joseph, 91, 318, 334, 498

Christy, Mary Jane, 12, 91, 134–35, 136, 315, 316–18, 334–35, 478, 498

Christy, Samuel, 91, 477–78

Christy, William, 91, 93–94, 134–35, 317–18, 498

Civil Rights Bill (1866), 384, 395

Cleburne, Patrick, 309–10

Coal and Iron Resources of Virginia, The (Imboden), 481, 482

Coffroth, Alexander Hamilton, 259, 287–89

Cold Harbor, Battle of, 198

Committee of Nine, 451–53, 456, 552n35

Confederate Congress, 118–19, 311

Confederate States of America
    Congressional hearings on status of, 385–88
        Baldwin's testimony in, 387–91, 394
        Dewes' testimony in, 391–94
        reactions to report from, 394–95
    consideration of enlisting enslaved people as soldiers, 310–11, 320, 322
    Constitution of, 110
    defeat of, 329–31
    dependency on enslaved people during war, 111–12
    diminished goals for war, 138
    enslaved population of, 10
    Federal military presence in, after war, 343–48, 458–59
    hunger/food shortages in, 26–27, 112, 119, 295–97, 298–99, 308–9, 318
    identity of, 108
    impressing of enslaved people

    to build fortifications, 15–16, 109, 487–88
    incorporation of guerrilla-style fighting, 19–20, 28, 153, 156, 177–78, 184–86, 236–37, 243, 253
    inequities in, 121–22
    internal dissatisfaction within, 293–94
    lack of party system in, 13, 110, 128
    need for more soldiers, 309
    peace talks in Hampton Roads, Va., 292–93
    role of white women in, 114–16, 517n23
    states' ceding of power to, 109–10
    treatment of wounded African-American soldiers, 135, 242–43

Conkling, Roscoe, 387

Conscription Act in 1863, 89–90

contraband camps, 20, 35, 132

"contrabands," 20, 35, 39, 45–47, 49, 59, 177

Cormany, Cora, *18*

Cormany, Rachel, 17, *18*, 65–67, 305
    on Confederate soldiers in Chambersburg, 19, 48–49, 55, 65
    death of, 479

Cormany, Rachel (*continued*)
  fears for husband, 56
  frustration with life with in-
    laws, 17
  on Samuel's behavior after
    finally returning home,
    478–79
  on Samuel's visit home after
    Gettysburg, 67
  on wounded Confederate left
    to suffer after Gettysburg,
    74
Cormany, Samuel, *18*
  on Battle of Gettysburg, 65–66
  behavior after the war, 478–79
  death of, 480
  on election of 1864, 264–65
  on escape from rebel infantry,
    327–28
  furlough home, 305–6
  Ku Klux Klan's harassment of,
    479–80
  on Lee's surrender, 329
  in Petersburg, 326–27
  on tearing up railroad, 167–68
  on visit home after Gettysburg,
    66–67
Couch, Darius, 32, 52, 207, 213,
    226
Crater, Battle of the, 213, 226
Crawford, Esther, 425
Crawford, Sam, 371
Crawford, Sydney, 344

Creigh, Thomas, 46–47
Crook, George, 144, 149, 153,
    156, 157, 166–67, 173, 184
Cuff, Findlay, 47
Cumberland Valley Railroad, 8
Curtin, Andrew, 34, 98–99,
    100–101, 129, 212–13
Custer, George Armstrong,
    304–5

Damascus, 482
Daughters of Confederate Veter-
    ans, 480
Davenport, Henry, 425
Davis, Jefferson, 26, 115, 226,
    277, 309–11, 320, 330, 368
Davis, William H., 84
Davison, Sarah, 462–64
Democrats and Democratic
    Party, 127
  Chambersburg newspaper of,
    see Valley Spirit
  conflicts in the North between
    Republicans and, 10–11,
    36–37, 106–7, 128–29,
    137–38, 418
  election of 1864 and, 129–33,
    189–92, 194–97, 254–71,
    267, 277, 531n35
  election of 1865 and, 366–69
  election of 1866 and, 405
  election of 1867 and, 431–32,
    433–34

on failure of Hampton Roads
  peace talks, 292–93
Johnson and, 450
race and, 192–94, 273–74, 287,
  314–15, 349–53
resistance to enslaved people as
  Union soldiers, 314–15
on Sheridan's burning of grain,
  246–48
Thirteenth Amendment and,
  286–90
Demus, David, 91, 93, 94,
  134–37, 315, 316, 317–18,
  334–35, 478
Demus, George, 91
desertion, 84, 113, 114, 118, 138,
  140, 144, 162, 184, 264,
  332, 440, 470, 474, 518n40
Dewes, William J., 391–94, 466
Dewey, Miss C. E., 408, 410–11,
  504
disease during Civil War from,
  14, 26–27, 300, 339
Doke, Abraham, 374
Doke, Estaline, 374–75
Douglass, Frederick, 11–12, 91,
  191
Douglass, Lewis, 91, 92
Downey, Benjamin, 425, 426–27
draft
  in Pennsylvania, 129
  riots over, 89, 352
Dull, Genny, 300, 301

Dull, John, 300–302
Dunkers, 469
Dunn, Mrs. (teacher), 407

Early, Jubal, 168, 175, 201, 227–28,
  231, 254, 265, 294, 303–4
background of, 201–2
defeat at Cedar Creek, 249
defeat at Winchester, 233, 235
escape from Waynesboro, 304
in Lynchburg, 174–75, 177
orders to burn Chambersburg,
  204, 205, 206, 207, 215–16,
  218–20, 221, 238
retreat to Waynesboro, 238
in Staunton, 200–201
on Stuart's compromise, 455
Echols, John, 423–25, 426
Edwards, Laura F., 548n48
elections
  of 1860, 9, 12, 127, 266, 285,
    354
  of 1861, 285
  of 1862, 34, 285
  of 1863, 100–101, 285
  of 1864, 101, 128–33, 188–92,
    194–97, 244, 254–71, 267,
    274–76, 277, 284–85, 287,
    531n35
  of 1865, 364–69
  of 1866, 404, 405
  of 1867, 432, 433–38, 546n16
  of 1868, 447–49, 459

Eliza (formerly enslaved person), 344–45

Emancipation Proclamation, 192, 285–86
  authorization of African-American soldiers in, 12
  criticism of, 36–37, 104, 131–32
  issuing of, 34
  Valley Spirit on, 35–36, 37
  Village Record on, 34–35
  white South's judgment of, 39, 392

Emerson, Catherine, 171

Emerson, Nancy, 29–30, 170–73, 182–83, 302

enslaved people
  in Augusta County, 380–81
    in 1860, 15
    in 1863, 111–12
    after the war, 344
    in Staunton during Hunter's occupation, 180–83
  Confederate government's impressing of, to build fortifications, 15–16, 109, 487–88
  cost of, average, 15
  as flexible forms of property, 15, 182
  former, *see* freedmen
  freedmen sold by Confederate soldiers as, 45–46, 49, 512n34

fugitive, 11–12, 376
  population of, under Confederate States of America, 10
  runaway, rewards for, 311–12
  as soldiers for Confederate army, 309–11
  Union soldiers and, 181–83, 185
  violence against masters, 313–14

Essick, Abraham, 79, 504

Everett, Edward, 99, 102, 104, 106

Ewell, Richard S., 42, 70

Farinholt, Benjamin Lyons, 42–43, 45, 505

Fifteenth Amendment, 452, 456, 458

5th Virginia Infantry Regiment, 59, 83, 119, 146, 147, 148

52nd Virginia Infantry Regiment, 59, 83, 146, 148, 362

54th Massachusetts Infantry Regiment, 12, 91–93, 134–36, 334–35, 498
  see also United States Colored Troops

55th Massachusetts Infantry Regiment, 91, 134, 315
  see also United States Colored Troops

Fillmore, Millard, 162

Fisher's Hill, Battle of, 233, 234, 235–36, 242

Fleming, Malcolm, 210, 503

Florida, 134–36, 375, 380

Fort Wagner, 91–93

Fourteenth Amendment, 395, 397, 403–6, 420, 447, 450

Franklin, Battle of, 310

Franklin County, Pa., xxi
  abolitionists in, 11–12
  African Americans in, 11–12, 376
    after Reconstruction, 497
    in Massachusetts Infantry Regiments, see 54th Massachusetts Infantry Regiment; 55th Massachusetts Infantry Regiment
    victimization by Confederates, 376–77
  after Reconstruction, 497–98
  claims against federal government, 474–75
  deaths during Civil War in, 14, 33–34, 92, 339
  as haven for fugitive slaves, 376
  Hotchkiss's mapping of, 7, 8
  men enlisted in U.S. Army in, demographics on, 338–40
  newspapers in, see Franklin Repository; Valley Spirit; Village Record
  prisoners of war from, number of, 339
  see also Chambersburg, Pa.

Franklin Repository, 8–9, 50, 106, 198–99, 418, 484
  account of Battle of Gettysburg, 60–62
  aid to memorial association, 476
  on constitutional conventions, 443
  criticism of Lee, 79–80, 468
  on Early, 218, 220
  on election of 1864, 130, 131, 256, 258, 259, 260–61, 266
  failure to cover riots, 89
  on fall of Richmond, 333
  on Fourteenth Amendment, 405–6
  on future of freedmen, 291–92, 350
  on internal differences within Confederacy, 293–94
  on Joint Committee on Reconstruction's report, 394–95
  on Lincoln's murder, 338
  on Lincoln's second inauguration, 323
  reprinting of Gettysburg speeches, 103, 106
  on "riots" in Memphis, 401–2, 403
  on Thirteenth Amendment, 285, 288, 289
  on welcoming soldiers returning from battle, 335–36
  on wounded from Battle of Gettysburg, 96–97

Fredericksburg, Battle of, 61
  Franklin soldiers wounded and
    killed in, 14, 36
  victory of Army of Northern
    Virginia in, 1–2
freedmen
  assistance for, *see* Freedmen's
    Bureau
  camps for, 20, 35, 132
  common last names used by,
    382
  former owners' contracts with,
    357–58, 360
  former owners' treatment of,
    356–59, 373, 442
  marriage and, 381–83, 425
  U.S. soldiers and, 344–46
  violence against, 371–72
Freedmen's Bureau, xxii, 354,
    364, 391, 394, 396
  agents' reports, 358–59, 371–
    72, 441
  assistance in locating/trans-
    porting family members,
    373–77
  creation of, 355
  as enabling/enforcing mar-
    riage and gender relations,
    381–82
  investigation of Irwin's case,
    416
  register compiled by, 379–82,
    489

report assessing progress of,
    384–85
  schools and, 406–7
  settling of disputes, 356–57,
    373, 415
  in Staunton, 355–56, 358,
    372–75, 379–81, 431, 434–
    35, 438–39, 440–42
Freedmen's Bureau Act, 383–
    84
Free Soil Party, 127
Fremont, John C., 179
Fugitive Slave Act of 1850,
    108–9
fugitive slaves, 11–12, 108–9

Gaillard, Franklin, 44, 505
Gallaher, Mrs. H. L., 116
gender roles, *see* women
Georgia, 109, 141, 190–91,
    231–32
Gettysburg, Battle of, xxi, 51–54,
    58, 59, 67, 68, 81–82
  Cemetery Ridge in, 58, 62,
    65–66, 87, 134
  deaths in, 66, 67, *76, 77,* 79,
    84, 88, 96
  Imboden and, 62–65
  newspapers' accounts of,
    60–62, 84
  Pickett's Charge at, 58, 60,
    61
  reactions to, 60, 90

souvenir seekers after, 85,
86–87
as a turning point in Civil
War, debates about, 87
wounded soldiers in, 64, 69,
72–74, 75–76, 77, 84, 86,
87, 97
Gettysburg Address, 97, 99–100,
101, 102–4, 105, 516n9
Gilgarnett, Jeremiah, 375
Gilgarnett, Johnny, 375
Gilkeson, A. J., 359–60
Gish, Jacob, 84
Gordon, Mary, 378
Grant, Ulysses S., 141, 186, 190,
195, 221, 227, 254, 299,
308, 326, 451, 484
in election of 1868, 447–49,
459
investigations into Ku Klux
Klan, 459
Lee's surrender to, 329–30
Sheridan and, 227, 234–35,
236, 249, 253, 304
at Vicksburg, 106
Virginia campaign of, 145–46,
149–50, 152, 186, 198
on Virginians voting on pro-
posed state constitution,
456
Great Valley, see Augusta
County, Va.; Franklin
County, Pa.

Halleck, Henry, 363
Hanger, Kit, 121
Harman, John Alexander, 70–72,
453–55, 456–57
Harpers Ferry raid, 12
Harper's Weekly, 225–26, 255
Harriet (runaway slave), 312
Harris, Mary, 378–79
Hess, Joseph, 312
Heyser, William, 33, 46, 47–48,
74–75, 85, 504
Hildebrand, Catherine, 336, 337
Hildebrand, Gideon Peter,
336–37
Hildebrand, Jacob R., 336–37,
506
Hoke, Jacob, 85–87, 101, 102–3,
214–15
Hoke, Margaret, 101, 102
Hollar, George, 469–72
Hooker, Joseph, 25, 27, 32, 41,
47, 53
Horn, Jacob, 84
horses and mules, hunger and
starvation among, 27
Hotchkiss, Jedediah, 275, 399
career after the war, 483
creation of Great Valley maps
for Confederate army, 3–6
Augusta County, Va., 4–6, 5
Franklin County, Pa., 7, 8
escape from Waynesboro raid,
304–5

Hotchkiss, Jedediah (*continued*)
on fight between Early and
Sheridan, 231, 233
letters to wife, 42, 248–49
on Early's army, 203–4
on election of 1864, 276
on enslaved people as soldiers, 310
on Pennsylvanians' impression of Southerners, 42
on retreat from Gettysburg,
80–81
on riots in North, 90
photograph of, 3
purchase of enslaved person,
312–13
Hotchkiss, Nelson, 312
Hotchkiss, Sara, 2, 42
Houser, Mollie, 120–21
How, W. Storer, 356–57, 358–
60, 371–72, 376–77, 379
Howard, Jacob M., 387
Howard, O. O., 355
Hughes, John, 84
hunger, Confederate soldiers
and, 26–27, 112, 308–9,
318
Hunter, David, *154*, 185, 236
inability to coordinate components of command, 169
at Piedmont, 158–60
retreat from Lynchburg, 174–
75, *176,* 177–78

in Shenandoah Valley, 153–62,
235, 470
in Staunton, 160–62, 165, 166,
173, 183, 184–85
Virginia Central Railroad and,
166, 168, 177

Imboden, John D., *63*, 144, 155,
157, 184
background of, 28–29
career after the war, 480–82
contracts with formerly
enslaved people, 357–58
death of, 482
disruption of Sigel's troops,
151–52
health of, 231
letter to Augusta asking for
contributions, 124
occupation of Williamsport,
Md., 77–78
at Piedmont, 159, 160
recruitment of partisan rangers, 28–29, 111, 156
return from Gettysburg, 68–70,
71, 71–74, 76–78, 83
role in Gettysburg campaign,
62–64
at Waynesboro, 168
immigrants, riots by, 89
Inquirer (Philadelphia), 60–61
In the Presence of Mine Enemies
(Ayers), xxi

Ironclad Oath, 446, 474

Irwin, Nelson, 415–16

Jackson, Andrew, 127, 256

Jackson, Mary Ann, 372

Jackson, Thomas Jonathan
"Stonewall"
death of, 55, 70
Imboden and, 29
orders to Hotchkiss, 3
rebuffing of Federal army in
Virginia, 1

Jackson, Thomas, 431, 434–35,
436–37, 438–39

James (boy raised by Peyton),
378

Jefferson, Mary, 473

Jefferson, Thomas, 473

Jesse Scouts, 179–80

Jim (formerly enslaved person),
346

Johnson, Andrew, 353, 368, 450
in election of 1864, 188
position on Reconstruction,
366–69, 403
as president, 341–42, 349
Republicans' clashes with, 370,
383–84, 386
slavery and, 343
vetoing of bill extending
Freedmen's Bureau, 383–84

Johnson, Serena B., 489–90, 491

Johnston, Joseph E., 60, 141, 326

Jones, Fanny, 425

Jones, William, 155–57, 158–60,
168, 169, 184, 481

Julia (enslaved person), 313–14

Kiner, Benjamin, 375–76

Kiner, Frances, 375–76

Knapp, Amelia, 464

Know-Nothing Party, 127

Ku Klux Klan, 459, 479

Larke & Wright, 375

Leary, Madison, 376

Lee, George, 312

Lee, Robert E., xxi, 56, 97, 140–
41, 157, 167, 186, 190, 202,
254, 299–300, 308, 318, 322
at Chambersburg, 40–41, 59
death of, 467
on enlisting enslaved people
as Confederate soldiers,
310–11, 320
Franklin Repository's criticism
of, 80–81, 468
at Gettysburg, 51–52, 58, 61,
66, 67, 87
Grant's Virginia campaign
against, 145, 146
at Hagerstown, 78–79, 88
on Imboden's predictions of "a
big raid," 144–45
Lynchburg and, 168, 177
near Richmond, 146, 155

Lee, Robert E. (*continued*)
  orders regarding soldiers'
    behavior, 41, 217
  orders to Imboden to return to
    Virginia, 68–69
  physical description of, 50
  political calculations in move
    to Great Valley, 25–28, 29,
    30–31
  reactions to failed invasion in
    Pennsylvania, 82, 83
  reaction to Gettysburg loss,
    64–65
  request for citizens to pledge
    rations to soldiers, 318
  retreat from Petersburg, 326
  surrender of, 329–30, 331,
    333–34
  victories in Chancellorsville
    and Fredericksburg, 1–2
  Winchester and, 29, 30
Letcher, John, 168, 455
Lett, Lucynda, 425
Lincoln, Abraham, 88, 254, 292,
  428
  appointment of Meade as com-
    mander of Army of the
    Potomac, 54
  assassination of, 337–38, 341
  death of son, 99
  depression of, 191
  in election of 1860, 9, 12, 266,
    354
  in election of 1864, 101, 129,
    130, 188–89, 194–96, 197,
    244, 255, 261–63, 264–65,
    266–67, 268–69, 271, 274–
    75, 277, 531n35
  Gettysburg Address of, 97,
    99–100, 101, 102–4, 105,
    516n9
  Hooker and, 32
  issuing of Emancipation Proc-
    lamation, 34, 285–86
  peace talks in Hampton Roads
    and, 292–93
  on Reconstruction, 284
  second inauguration of, 323–
    24
  Sheridan and, 232, 249
  on slavery, 104–5, 324
  Thirteenth Amendment and,
    284–85, 387
  use of pardons and amnesty,
    284
  Valley Spirit's criticism of,
    35–37, 247, 325
Lincoln, Mary Todd, 99
Lincoln, Tad, 99
Liz (enslaved person), 313
Long, James, 119–20
Loyal Political Society, 421
Lushbaugh, Adams, 473–74
Lynchburg, Va., 166–67, 168,
  174, 177–78, 373
Lynn, W. H., 422–23

MacRichardson, 376–77

Maddex, Jack P., 552n35

Manassas, First Battle of, 38, 111,
    202, 481

marriage, freedmen and, 381–83,
    425

Marshall, Elizabeth, 312

Marshall, Priscilla, 377

Martson, Anthony, 377

Martson, Mary Ann, 377

Mason, C. R., 182

Mason-Dixon Line, 7, 33, 376

massacres of African Americans
    in Memphis, 401–3
    in New Orleans, 403
    in Saltville, 241–43

McCausland, John, 206, 227
    burning of Chambersburg,
        204–8, 205, 210, 215, 475
    in Staunton, 156, 168

McClellan, George
    in election of 1864, 196, 197–
        98, 261–62, 263, 264, 265,
        266, 268, 269, 270, 531n35
    Lincoln's removal from com-
        mand, 36, 47, 196

McClure, Alexander K., 34,
    52–53, 130, 485
    on compensation for rebuild-
        ing Chambersburg, 475
    discussion with Johnson about
        reconstruction, 367–69
    election of 1864 and, 191, 255,

256, 258–59, 260–63, 266,
    268

election of 1865 and, 367–68

farm of, Confederates burning
    of, 256

on freedmen, 291–92

influence on elections, 129–
    30

on Lee's defeat and capture of
    Vicksburg, 85

on Reconstruction, 444, 485–
    87

on responsibilities of Lincoln's
    new administration, 323–24

on slavery, 272, 290

speech after Lee's surrender,
    334

urging of Lincoln to reinstate
    McClellan's command, 47

McCue, J. M., 119

McCutchan, James, 120

McElheney, Harriet, 306–7, 308

McElheney, Sylvester, 306–8,
    505

McFarland, Francis, 148–49,
    313–14, 503

McFarland, Robert, 148–49

McLeune, Mrs. (teacher), 407

Meade, George, 72, 82, 87, 97
    challenges after Gettysburg, 76
    as commander of Army of the
        Potomac, appointment of,
        54

Meade, George (*continued*)
  congratulatory order to men
    after Gettysburg, 62
  at Williamsport, 78
Memphis massacre in 1866, 401–3
Mennonites, 469
Mercury, 50–51
Military Reconstruction Acts,
    420, 421, 422
Miller, George, 264
Milliken's Bend, 93
Milroy, Robert, 29, 30, 33
miscegenation, 193, 287, 412–14
Monocacy, Battle of, 204
Monroe, Richard, 378
Moore, Reuben, 378–79
Morris Island, 92–93
Mosby, John Singleton, 150
mules, hunger and starvation
    among, 27

Nashville, Battle of, 140, 444
National Union Party, 188–92,
    194, 261, 263, *267,* 268
Newcomer, C. M., 211–12
New Market, Battle at, 152, 153,
    159, 186
New Orleans massacre in 1866, 403
newspapers
  in Chambersburg, Pa., 8–9,
    34–35
  see also Franklin Repository;
    Valley Spirit

in Staunton, Va., 13, 17, 121–
    23
  see also Staunton Spectator;
    Vindicator
North Carolina, 10, 109

Olustee, Battle of, 134–36
Overland Campaign, 145, 186

partisan rangers, 28–29, 45–46, 49
Pearce, John, 120
Pence, William, 239
Pennsylvania
  Battle of Gettysburg, *see* Get-
    tysburg, Battle of
  Confederate soldiers' occu-
    pation of, 40–51, 68–69,
    88–89, 91
  draft in, 129
  election of 1864 and, 128–30,
    255–67, 270, 287, 531n35
  election of 1865 and, 364–65,
    366
  election of 1866 and, 405
  election of 1867 and, 432,
    433–38
  election of 1868 and, 447–49
  see also Franklin County, Pa.
Peyton, G. L, 378
Philadelphia Times, 484
Philkill, John, 47
Pickett's Charge, 58, 60, 61
Piedmont, Battle of, *158,* 158–
    60, 186

Pierpoint, Francis H., 363

Pitman (runaway slave), 312

Pleasants, Francis, 307

Poindexter, William, 472

Pollock, Thomas, 43–44

Pomeroy, Stephen, 53

Port Hudson, 93

Presbyterian Missionary Society, 464

race

    Baldwin on, 388–91, 439–40, 457–58

    Democrats and, 192–94, 273–74, 287, 314–15, 349–53

    discussions about, at Staunton meetings on voting, 420–27

    violence following election of 1867, 438–39

racism, "miscegenation" as, 193, 287, 412–14

railroads of Virginia, 523n41

    see also Virginia Central Railroad

Readjusters, 491–92

rebelism, 387, 398

Recollections of Half A Century (McClure), 484–85

Reconstruction, xix–xx, xxi–xxii, 450, 459–60

    collapse of, 465–66, 491

    Fifteenth Amendment and, 452, 456, 458

    Joint Committee on, 385–88

        Baldwin's testimony to, 387–91, 394

        Dewes' testimony to, 391–94

        reactions to report of, 394–95

    Lincoln on, 284

    Military Reconstruction Acts and, 420, 421, 422

    opposition of Democrats of Pennsylvania to, 432–33

    Stuart's support for, 363

religion

    missionary schools for African Americans, 406–11, 413, 462, 464

    as solace during war, 301–2

Republicans and Republican Party, xxii, 127

    attempt to stop the spread of slavery in the 1850s, xxi–xxii, 9

    Chambersburg newspaper of, see Franklin Repository

    conflicts in the North between Democrats and, 10–11, 36–37, 106–7, 128–29, 137–38, 418

    election of 1864 and, 128–31, 188, 189–92, 196, 254–72, 277, 284–85, 531n35

    election of 1865 and, 366–69

Republicans and Republican
    Party (*continued*)
  election of 1866 and, 404, 405
  election of 1867 and, 433–35,
      437, 546n16
  election of 1868 and, 447–49,
      459
  Johnson's clashes with, 370,
      383–84, 386
  Reconstruction and, 433
  on Sheridan's burning of grain,
      246–48
  Thirteenth Amendment and,
      286–87, 288, 289–90
retaliation, 174, 199
  burning of Chambersburg as,
      208–9, 216, 217–18, 228–
      29
  against civilians, celebration
      and fear of, 20
  Richmond Dispatch urging of,
      44–45
  Whig's call for, along Lee's
      march, 50
Rhoda (enslaved person), 313
Richmond, Va.
  fall of, 326, 330, 333
  Overland Campaign against,
      145
  wounded from battles outside,
      146–48
Richmond Dispatch, 44–45, 219
Richmond Enquirer, 219

riots in New York City, 89, 352
Rolston, Jesse, Jr., 117–18, 122–
    24, 506
Rolston, Mary, 117, 118, 122
Roselle, Philip, 423, 425, 427–
    28, 430–31, 454

Saltville massacres, 241–43
Schaff, Philip, 33
Schneck, Benjamin, 212–13,
    504
Schofield, John M., 415, 421
schools for African Americans,
    35, 406–14, 462–64, 492
Schreskhise, Daniel, 239
Scott, James, 425–26, 428
Scott, John, 407–8, 409–10, 411–
    14, 462, 463–64, 488
scurvy, 26
secession of Southern states from
    Union, 9–10
Seddon, James, 26
Selena (formerly enslaved per-
    son), 347
77th Pennsylvania Regiment,
    133–34
Shaw, Robert Gould, 91, 92
Sheffey, Hugh, 312
Shenandoah Valley, 142, 143–45,
    185, 190
  Campaign of 1862, 125
  Grant's orders to Sheridan in,
      234–35, 253

Sheridan's destruction of, 237–41, *238*, 250–53, *253*

Sheridan, Philip H., *288*, 247–54, 257, 263, 271, 304, 326

Battle of Trevilian Station and, 166, 167

burning of grain, 237–38, *238*, 245–47, 253, *253*, 297

at Cedar Creek, 249–50

as commander of Army of the Shenandoah, 227, 231

Custer and, 304

Grant's orders to, in Shenandoah Valley, 234–35, 236

raid on Augusta County, 239–241

victory at Winchester, 233–34

Sherman, William T, 106, 195, 199, 220, 255, 257, 304, 326, 330, 343

at Atlanta, 141, 190–91, 232, 271

March to the Sea, 200, 245, 300

Shueman, William, 84

Sigel, Franz, 149, 150–54, 178, 185

slavery, xix, xxi–xxii, 1, 98

abolishment of, 277, 286–90, 318, 365, 392

Civil War's strain on, 15–16, 109, 180–82, 311–14, 487–88

conflicts in the North between

Democrats and Republicans over, 10–11, 36–37, 137–38

Fugitive Slave Act of 1850 and, 108–9

in Gettysburg speeches, 104

as issue in election of 1864, 131–33, 189, 191–92

Johnson and, 343

Lincoln on, 104–5, 283, 324

United States Colored Troops' liberation of, 334

Smith, David G., 512n34

Smith, J. C, 75–76

Snyder, D. C., 302–3, 506

Snyder, Jacob, 75

Soldiers' Aid Society of Zion Church, 116

Soldiers' Cemeteries, 398

Sons of Confederate Veterans, 480

South Carolina, 9

Southern Claims Commission, 469–74

speculation, 112–13

Spencer, Patience, 373–74

Spotsylvania Courthouse, Battle of, 145, 198

St. James Island, 93

Stanton, Edwin M., 32, 234

Staunton, Va., 4

after Lee's surrender, chaos in, 331

Cemetery Committee in, 398, 400–401

Staunton, Va. (*continued*)
  Early's army in, 200–201
  on enlisting enslaved people as
    Confederate soldiers, 320
  enslaved people in, 311
    during Hunter's occupation,
      180–83
    runaway, 311–12
    from 1860 to 1863, 112
  Federal soldiers in, after war,
    344–48
  founding of, 4
  Freedmen's Bureau in, 355–
    56, 358, 372–75, 379–81,
    431, 434–35, 438–39,
    440–42
  Freedmen's School in, 406–14,
    462–64
  historical and genealogical
    societies in, 498
  Hotchkiss's mapping of, 4, *5*
  newspapers in, 13, 121–23
    see also Staunton Spectator;
      Vindicator
  railroad in, 157, 162, 163, 165
  Union soldiers' occupation
    of, 160–66, 170–73, 178,
    180–83, 185
  voting rights meetings with
    freedmen in, 421–30, 453–
    55, 457–58
  wounded soldiers at, 72, 83,
    147–49
Staunton Spectator, 13, 143
  on clash at New Market, 152
  on compromise on univer-
    sal suffrage and universal
    amnesty, 458
  criticism of impressing
    enslaved people to build
    fortifications, 17
  on Harman, 457
  on petition for protection of
    Union men of Augusta, 393
  reprinting of attack on "Lin-
    coln's war," 126
  on riots in North, 60, 89
  on speculation, 112
  on Staunton meeting on
    Reconstruction, 454
  on Staunton meeting on vot-
    ing rights for freedmen,
    428–30
  on unburied from war, 397
  Union soldiers' destruction of
    press of, 170
  on U.S. strategies to subjugate
    the Confederacy, 38–40
  on Virginia Constitutional
    Convention, 445–46
Stephen (Legh Waddell's
  enslaved person), 230
Stevens, Thaddeus, 34, 367, 377,
  385, 406, 418–19, 467, 482,
  484–85
Stonewall Brigade, 38, 48, 84,
  116, 119, 146, 147, 186, 399
Stouffer, Eliza, 213–14, 506

Stouffer, Emma, 213, 506

Strother, David Hunter, 152–55, 158, 159, 161–63, 166, 169, 174–75, 177, 181, 183

Stuart, Alexander H. H., 162, 164, 346, 348, *361*, 396, 439–40, 459, 485–87
defense of Irwin, 416
efforts to save Union while protecting slavery, 361
in election of 1865, 364
proposal for "universal suffrage and universal amnesty," 451–53, 455, 457, 459
Reconstruction and, 363
from Unionism to Confederate loyalty, 320–21, 362

Stuart, J. E. B., 52, 70, 78

Stuart, James, 373

Stuart, Margaret, 164–65

suffrage, *see* voting rights

Tate, Jimmy, 331

tax assessments on land, 360

Tennessee, 10, 420

Thirteenth Amendment, 277, 286–90, 293, 318, 322, 324, 365, 387

Thornrose Cemetery, 400, 476, 498

Three Thousand Miles Through the Rocky Mountains (McClure), 484

Torbert, A. J. A., 355–56

Trevilian Station, Battle of, 167

Tukey, Frederick, 372, 379, 407, 409, 414, 416, 466–67

Tynes, Achilles, 210, 505

United States Colored Troops, 12, 91, 94–95, 134–37, 315–18, 329, 334–35, 376, 401–2, 477–78, 498
see also 54th Massachusetts Infantry Regiment; 55th Massachusetts Infantry Regiment

Valley of the Shadow archive, xx–xxi, 503

Valley Spirit, 198
aid to memorial association, 476
on arrival of Confederate soldiers, 48
on burning of Chambersburg, 220–21
on camps for formerly enslaved people, 132
on Chambersburg economy after burning, 222–23
on Coffroth, 288–89
criticism of Lincoln administration, 10, 35–37, 325
on election of 1864, 130, 132, 257–58, 259–60, 262
on failed peace talks in Hampton Roads, 293
failure to cover riots, 89

Valley Spirit (*continued*)
   on fall of Richmond, 333
   on Johnson as president, 342
   on Joint Committee on Recon-
      struction's report, 394
   on Lee's surrender, 333–34
   on Lincoln's murder, 337–38
   on Lincoln's second inaugura-
      tion, 323–24
   on Reconstruction, 432–33
   resistance to enslaved people as
      Union soldiers, 314
   on Sheridan, 234, 246, 247–48
   on Union army in Virginia, 146
   on the word "miscegenation,"
      193
Valley Turnpike, 4, 27–28, 33,
   59, 154
Valley Virginian, 397–98, 401,
   404–5, 412, 421, 428, 431,
   467
Vaughn, John, 159, 160
vengeance, *see* retaliation
Vicksburg, Miss., 100
   capture of, reactions of Penn-
      sylvanians to, 85, 90
   Grant at, 106, 140
   Waddell on fall of, 59–60,
      82–83
Village Record, 34–35
Vindicator, 13
   on burial of dead, 398–401
   on burning of Chambersburg,
      218–19
   on election of 1867, 436
   on enslaved people as Confed-
      erate soldiers, 310
   on expansion of black schools,
      492
   on food shortage, 298–99
   on Fourteenth Amendment,
      395–96
   on Harman, 455
   on Lee's request for rations,
      318–19
   on Lincoln's annual message, 294
   on long delays in reconcilia-
      tion, 419
   on miscegenation, 413, 414
   on responsibilities of the local
      population, 295–96
   on Sheridan's raid, 240
   on Stuart's speech about new
      constitution, 453
   Union soldiers' destruction of
      press of, 170
   on wounded from battles out-
      side Richmond, 147
Virginia
   Committee of Nine and, 451–
      53, 456, 552n35
   Constitutional Convention
      in 1867, *422,* 428, 430–32,
         434, 437, 443–47, 466,
         489
      in 1901, 493–94
   election of 1867 and, 431–32,
      438

Grant's campaign in, 145–46,
149–50, 152, 186, 198
on loyalty issue in 1865, 360–
61
names and marriage law in,
381
secession from Union, 9, 360–
62
see also Augusta County, Va.
Virginia Central Railroad, 4–5,
27–28, 147, 355–56
Richmond civilians' reliance
on, 300
Sheridan's orders to destroy,
166, 236, 253
Union soldiers' destruction
of, 163–64, 166, 167–68,
177
Virginia General Assembly, 388–
89, 456, 458
Virginia Military Institute, 168,
177
voting rights
for African Americans, 354,
459
election of 1864 and, 194
election of 1867 and, 431–32,
434–38
election of 1868 and, 448–49
Staunton meetings on, 421–30,
453–55, 457–58
violence following, 438–39
won in the late 1860s, undermining of, xxiii

Waddell, Joseph, *31*, 58–59, 106,
107, 180, 276, 294, 498
on adjusting to demands of
wartime, 117
on burning of Chambersburg,
228–29
on captured Union soldiers,
30
on Confederacy, 332
on Confederate soldiers beating enslaved person, 230
at Constitutional Convention,
444, 446
on departure of Early's army,
202–3
in election of 1865, 364–65
in election of 1867, 435–36
on election of 1864, 274–75
on fall of Vicksburg, 59–60
on Fisher's Hill, 236
on fleeing from Sheridan, 238–
39
on food shortage, 296, 297–98
on formerly enslaved people,
344–47
on Lee's surrender, 331
life after the war, 484–85
on Lincoln's death, 341
on national identity, 347–48
on need for more soldiers, 309
reaction to Jones's death, 169–70
on slavery, 181–82
on Staunton after Hunter's
raid, 179

Waddell, Legh, 169, 179–80, 236, 345, 346

Wade and Davis Manifesto, 226

Walker, Gilbert, 455

Walker, Jane, 372

Wallace, Ann, 375

Wallace, Hester, 375

Wallace, Isaac, 375

Wampler, Willie, 67

Ware, Frances, 425

Ware, Isaac, 473

Washington, Booker T., 493

Watson, William G., 178

Waynesboro, Pa.
  Custer's raid on, 305
  Soldiers' Aid Society of Zion Church in, 116
  Union meeting in, 11
  Village Record of, 34–35

Webster, Daniel, 445

Wells, Henry, 452, 455, 456

Whig, 50

Whigs, 13, 127, 361, 391, 420, 439

white disenfranchising clause, removal of, 451–55, 457–58

Wilderness, Battle of the, 145, 198

William (Hotchkiss's enslaved person), 2, 313

Williams, James, 43

Williamsport, Md., 69, 77–78, 80

Wills, David, 98–99, 101

Winchester, Va., 4, 29–30, 233–34, 235, 236, 359, 512n34

Wise, Henry, 321

Wisewell, Charles, 178

women
  marriage and gender relations for, Freedmen's Bureau's enabling and enforcing of, 381–82
  roles of, during the war, 19, 114–16, 184, 517n23
  soldiers' treatment of, 172, 173, 240, 348

Zion Union Cemetery, 498